# THE
# LIFTING
# OF THE VEIL

## ACTS 15:20-21

AVRAM YEHOSHUA

Order this book online at www.trafford.com
or email orders@trafford.com

Most Trafford titles are also available at major online book retailers.

Print information available on the last page.

ISBN: 978-1-4907-6255-5 (sc)
ISBN: 978-1-4907-6257-9 (hc)
ISBN: 978-1-4907-6256-2 (e)

Library of Congress Control Number: 2015911426

*Trafford rev. 07/30/2015*

 Trafford PUBLISHING www.trafford.com

North America & international
toll-free: 1 888 232 4444 (USA & Canada)
fax: 812 355 4082

This book is dedicated to Messiah Yeshua, whose Spirit and Word have shown me the Way of Life. May its words glorify You,

my Lord.

This book is also dedicated to my wife Ruti, whose love for Yeshua has been a *Beacon Light* for me in this world of darkness.

Thank you, my love.

A veil has been placed over the eyes of my Jewish people concerning Messiah Yeshua (2nd Cor. 3:14-16).

A similar veil has been over the eyes of the Bride of Christ concerning the Law of Moses (Daniel 7:25).

In these last days the Father is lifting both veils, to the eternal Glory of His Son, Messiah Yeshua!

# THE LIFTING OF THE VEIL

## ACTS 15:20-21

## Table of Contents

# Abbreviations

ALGNT ...Analytical Lexicon of the Greek New Testament

AHCL ......The Analytical Hebrew and Chaldee Lexicon

ARA.........A Rabbinic Anthology

ASV .........American Standard Version (Bible)

CED .........Collins English Dictionary

DBI .........Dictionary of Biblical Imagery

GELNT ...A Greek-English Lexicon of the New Testament

GELNTS ...Greek-English Lexicon of the New Testament: Semitic Domains

HALOT ...The Hebrew and Aramaic Lexicon of the Old Testament

IBD .........The Illustrated Bible Dictionary

ISBE.........The International Standard Bible Encyclopedia

JNTC ......Jewish New Testament Commentary

KJV .........King James Version (Bible)

NAGL ......The New Analytical Greek Lexicon

NASB ......New American Standard Bible

NBDBG ...The New Brown, Driver, Briggs, Gesenius Hebrew and English Lexicon

NGEINT ...The New Greek-English Interlinear New Testament

NIV .........New International Version (Bible)

NKJV ......New King James Version (Bible)

NRSV ......New Revised Standard Version (Bible)

NU .........Nestle–Aland Greek New Testament–United Bible Societies third corrected edition

TALGNT ...The Analytical Lexicon to the Greek New Testament

TGELNT ...Thayer's Greek-English Lexicon of the New Testament

TDNT ......Theological Dictionary of the New Testament

TDOT ......Theological Dictionary of the Old Testament

TLOT ......Theological Lexicon of the Old Testament

TWOT ......Theological Wordbook of the Old Testament

UBD.........Unger's Bible Dictionary

WBC ......The Wycliffe Bible Commentary

WNCD ......Webster's New Collegiate Dictionary

## Acknowledgements to the First Edition

I am indebted to Hannah Cooperman and Ruti Yehoshua for their tireless efforts in proofreading the manuscript as well as for their keen insights. Many mistakes were corrected because of their diligence.

## Acknowledgements to the Second Edition

I want to thank Yakov Snyder for bringing a number of my typographical errors in the first edition to my attention. I'm also grateful to Katie Hoogerheide for proofreading the revised manuscript, making numerous corrections and offering many fine suggestions. All mistakes remain the responsibility of the author.

## Notes to the Third and Fourth Edition

The third and fourth editions have allowed me to further edit, revise and refine the concepts presented in this book, as well as to correct a number of my typographical errors. The fourth edition has also afforded me the opportunity of expanding two chapters: *Acts 15:10—The Yoke* and *Acts 15:21—The Preachers of Moses*.

May the Lord Yeshua bless you as you read,

*The Lifting of the Veil*,

*Avram Yehoshua*

San Diego, California USA
28 July 2015

# INTRODUCTION

The Book of Acts forms a divine bridge between the Gospels and the letters of Peter and Paul, etc. Without Acts we'd be at a tremendous loss, not knowing what happened in Jerusalem after the resurrection with the subsequent giving of the Holy Spirit on Pentecost. We also wouldn't know of the many thousands of Jewish people who came to believe in Yeshua[1] (the Hebrew name for Jesus) and we wouldn't realize what Peter, Stephen or Philip did, nor what happened to Paul on the road to Damascus. We also wouldn't know anything about how the question of 'Gentile salvation and the Law of Moses' was settled in Acts 15, which is vital for us today.

Salvation is based on biblical faith in Jesus plus nothing else. There's no law or good deed that anyone can do that will transform his nature into the nature of Yeshua. That's why the keeping of the Law can never give anyone eternal life. Justification by faith is the gracious work of the Father through His Son for forgiveness, transformation and eternal glorification.

The Church (collectively consisting of all organized churches) teaches that the Law of Moses was nullified by the sacrificial death of Jesus Christ. The Feasts of Israel, the dietary laws and the 7th day Sabbath are 'only for the Jews who rejected Jesus' and who are still 'under the Law.' Christians are 'under Grace' and free from the Law, or as F. F. Bruce wrote, Christianity is a 'law-free gospel.'[2] Acts 15 is a major place in Scripture that the Church points to in order to prove its position. The chapter deals with the issue of whether Gentile believers needed to be circumcised and keep the Law, along with their faith in Yeshua, in order to be *saved* (Acts 15:1, 5).

The Church supports its teaching of a 'law free Gospel' by misinterpreting the four rules of James (Acts 15:20). Theologians teach that the rules apply to table fellowship and that these are the *only* rules or laws for Christians other than the moral laws. Their anti-Law theology[3] supports their false perception. This in turn sets up their inability to correctly understand the meaning of the next verse (v. 21), where James speaks of the Law of Moses being taught in the synagogues every Sabbath day.

---

[1] Some places in Acts where Jews believe in Yeshua are Acts 2:41, 47; 4:14; 5:14; 6:1, 7; 9:31, 35, 42; 13:43; 14:1; 17:1-4, 10-12; 18:4, 8, 19-21; 21:20.

[2] F. F. Bruce, Author; Gordon D. Fee, General Editor, *The New International Commentary on the New Testament: The Book of the Acts* (Grand Rapids, MI: William B. Eerdmans Publishing Company, 1988), p. 285.

[3] Church theology on the Law has been challenged in the last 35 years by E. P. Sanders (*Paul and Palestinian Judaism*; 1977), James Dunn (*The Theology of Paul the Apostle*; 1998) and N. T. Wright (*Paul: In Fresh Perspective*; 2005). Equating the Law of Moses with legalism is finally being seen as a perversion and caricature of God's holy Law (Rom. 3:31; 7:7, 12, 14).

F. F. Bruce spoke of the Council of Acts 15 as 'epoch-making.'[4] Howard
Marshall agreed and believes it was theologically important because,

> 'Luke's account of the discussion regarding the relation
> of the Gentiles to the law (*sic*) of Moses forms the center
> of Acts both structurally and *theologically*.'[5]

Marshall and Bruce are right about the importance of Acts 15, but they
fail to understand its meaning and implications. The words of James are
nothing less than the fulcrum point where the Law of Moses is declared
valid for all believers, but it's at this crucial point that the Church falters
by creating a theological veil so thick that it has kept Christians from seeing their ancient Hebraic heritage—how the Father wants them to walk
out their faith in His Son. This failure in turn has led the Church into anti-
Semitism and pagan celebrations 'in the Name of Jesus,' neither of which
Jesus, James or Paul ever intended.

Almost two thousand years ago, in 48 AD, all the believing Jewish Apostles and Elders of Jerusalem assembled to discuss the matter of Gentile belief in the Jewish Messiah (Acts 15:6). They needed to know exactly what
constituted salvation for the Gentile. Paul, Barnabas and others from the
congregation of Antioch were also there that day. The Jewish leadership
in faraway Antioch had requested a ruling.[6] Acts 15:1-2 states,

> "Some men came down from Judah and began teaching
> the brethren, 'Unless you are circumcised according to the
> custom of Moses, you cannot be *saved*.' And when Paul
> and Barnabas had great dissension and debate with them,
> the brethren determined that Paul and Barnabas and some
> others of them should go up to Jerusalem to the Apostles
> and Elders concerning this issue."[7]

---

[4]   Bruce, *The Book of the Acts*, p. 282.

[5]   I. Howard Marshall, M.A., B.D., Ph.D., Author; Professor R.V.G. Tasker,
      M.A., B.D., General Editor, *Tyndale New Testament Commentaries: Acts*
      (Leicester, England: Inter-Varsity Press, 2000), p. 242.

[6]   Antioch was 300 miles (482 kilometers) from Jerusalem. It had a population
      of 500,000, 70,000 of which were Jews. 'Josephus ranked it as the third great-
      est city of the Roman Empire, behind Rome and Alexandria' (Josephus, *Jew-
      ish Wars* 3.29); http://www.biblegateway.com/resources/commentaries/IVP-
      NT/Acts/Gentile-Mission-Antioch.

[7]   Most Scripture quotes are taken from the New American Standard Bible or
      the New King James Version. Also, changes have been made to texts where
      *The Hebraic Perspective* (translation) seems more suitable. Unless otherwise
      stated, *italics* are my way of emphasizing a word or a phrase, while proper
      nouns are capitalized (e.g. Aaron the High Priest, the Law, the Temple, etc.)
      and the Name of the God of Israel (Yahveh) is written as such, instead of the

Those men from Judah wanted the Gentiles to be circumcised, which was seen at that time as a way of becoming part of Israel (to become a Jew),[8] but more to the point, it meant keeping the Law for eternal life (symbolized in physical covenantal circumcision; Gen. 17:10-14). The Gentile would then be part of the people that God was redeeming (Israel). God's intent, though, was that both Gentile and Jew would enter the Kingdom and be justified in the same way—by faith in Yeshua, which is *God's* gracious action towards man (Acts 2:37-40; 15:11; Rom. 4:1f.). In the aftermath of the decision by James, in which he struck down the false notion that eternal life hinged upon Law keeping, four rules were issued (v. 20). Proper interpretation of them is vital in understanding what James ruled, and what the Council ratified, and therefore, what God through them intended for the Gentile believers *after* they had entered into the Kingdom of Jesus by faith.

What the Holy Spirit issued through James for the Gentile was conceptually no different from what God had done for Israel through Moses when He brought Israel out of Egyptian slavery. The Hebrews were not saved by circumcision or the Law, but by the blood of the lamb and their faith in Moses (Ex. 12).[9] It follows, then, that the Gentile wouldn't be saved by circumcision or the Law, either. After Hebrew deliverance (salvation) from Egypt, Yahveh brought Israel to Mt. Sinai to *learn* of His ways: *Who* was this God who had just brought Egypt, the mightiest nation in the

---

ubiquitous term 'the LORD.' The name *Yahveh* is found about 6,800 times in the *Tanach* (Old Testament).

[8] Becoming a proselyte meant that the Gentile was 'now a Jew.' This is how it was seen in the days of Peter and Paul, and how it's seen today, but it's an unbiblical and false concept of Rabbinic Judaism. Nowhere does God ever say that a Gentile becomes a Jew. The Gentile who 'came alongside' Israel was certainly part of Israel, so much so that God speaks of there being 'one law for the stranger' (whose heart is to be with Israel), 'and the native born' (the Israeli). This 'stranger' is specifically called a *ger* רֵּג in Scripture and is different from other 'strangers' (non-Israelis) in Scripture. I bring out the differences in the section, *The Stranger and the Native-Born,* on p. 268f.

[9] Alfred Edersheim, *The Temple: Its Ministry and Services* (Peabody, MA: Hendrickson Publishers, 1994), pp. 183-184. Edersheim writes that the sacrifice of the Passover lamb in Egypt was a picture of the sacrifice of Yeshua. No other sacrifice 'could so suitably commemorate His death, nor yet the great *deliverance* connected with it, and the great union and fellowship from it.' It 'had been instituted and observed before Levitical sacrifices existed; *before the Law was given;* nay, before the Covenant was ratified by blood (Ex. 24). In a sense, it may be said to have been the cause of all the later sacrifices of the law (*sic*) and of the Covenant itself.' The Jew was not saved from Egyptian slavery by either circumcision or the Law, but by the blood of the lamb, which was the grace of Yahveh to Israel, the prototype of *the* Lamb.

world at that time, to its knees? What did He consider sin? What was pleasing and right in His eyes?

God didn't set Israel free to do her own thing, willing to accept whatever any Hebrew thought was 'right in his own heart.' He gave Israel His holy Law (Dt. 4:5-8; Rom. 7:12, 14) so that she would know right from wrong. Why would it be different 'in Christ'? Why would God's holy ways be invalid for the Gentile believer in the Jewish Messiah? Some might say, 'The only thing we need to do is to love God and our neighbor.' This *is* the *heart* of the Law (Dt. 6:4-5; Lev. 19:18) and this is how Yeshua spoke of *summing up* the Law, but He didn't do away with all the *other* commandments and statutes that *define God's love* (Mt. 22:35-40).

Others might say, 'we have the Spirit to guide us in God's will,' yet it's the *express* purpose of the Spirit to write the Law of God upon the heart of every believer (Jer. 31:33; Ezk. 36:26-27; Heb. 8:10). How is it, then, that many who have this Spirit balk at the very Law that the Spirit desires to place upon their heart? If the Law is truly written on the heart, wouldn't believers want to keep Passover and God's 7th day Sabbath holy, etc.?

In the days of the Apostles, the Gentile who was saved by faith in Yeshua learned God's Law and became part of Israel by his faith in Messiah, not by being physically circumcised (Jn. 10:16; Rom. 11:24; 1st Cor. 7:17-19; Eph. 2:13). He learned the Law by going to the synagogue (unbelieving or believing; Jam. 2:2) on the Sabbath day (Acts 15:21). The Law taught him *Who* the God of Israel was and his new Family Rules and History, so that he might walk in those rules in the power and love of the Spirit, just as all the Apostles and Jewish believers did after the resurrection (Acts 21:20).

It's not without a compelling truth that the Lord uses the expression *Born Again* (or *Born from Above*, Jn. 3:3, 7) to indicate one's birth or entry into His Kingdom *by His Spirit*. An infant is born into a family, without keeping any of the family rules, 'by the grace of the parents.' Does this mean that the child will not be required to keep the family rules when it comes of age? Does it matter if the child obeys the father and does the will of his father? Or should the will of the child overrule the father's will? Would the father be pleased if the child walked in rules that contradicted his own values? Knowing *the will of the Father* and doing it is central to being a son or daughter of God. Yeshua said in Matthew 7:21,

> 'Not everyone who says to Me, 'Lord, Lord' will enter
> the Kingdom of Heaven, but he who does the *will* of My
> Father who is in Heaven will enter.' (See also Mt. 12:50)

What is the will of God in relation to the Law? Many in the Church say, 'The Law has been done away with,' yet Marshall, before he theologizes the Law away, says that the Law of Moses is the *will* of God our Father:

> What 'evidence was there that the law (*sic*), which *repre-sented the will of God* for his covenant people, had been repealed?'[10]

God gave those rules to Israel *after* they had been *saved* from Egyptian slavery. The same concept holds true for the believer today. Once saved, once 'in' the Kingdom of Yeshua, the Law is our divine guideline of how we're to walk out our faith in Christ. It's the will of God, showing us what is sin and what is right *in His eyes*. Messiah Yeshua said that love was the basis for all the laws of Moses (Mt. 22:40), so Christians keep the *essence* of the will of God. Unfortunately, the organized churches teach against everything in the Law except for what they perceive to be the moral laws. Therefore, Christians are ignorant of the specifics of God's Law and are horrified to even consider them. The mere mention of 'the Law' as part of God's will brings puzzled looks, fear or contempt to the faces of many, who in their pride and ignorance think they rightly understand the full implications of God's Grace. Those same facial expressions were also seen on the Pharisees, who boasted of their own righteousness and interpretations of God's Word (Lk. 18:9-14; Mt. 15:1-20) while rejecting the understanding of God the Son, who stood right before them.

On the other hand, some extremists in the Law Camp say that Christians who don't keep the 7th day Sabbath and Passover, etc., are going to Hell. This, too, is wrong. Anyone who loves Jesus and his neighbor is keeping the heart of the Law (Dt. 6:4-5; Lev. 19:18; Lk. 10:25-28). Those extremists fail to realize that even if someone is keeping Sunday and eating ham, if he has a living relationship with Jesus he will be forgiven of those sins (1st Pet. 4:8). Yeshua's sacrifice is that great (Acts 13:38-39), but a believer walking in those sins is not what the Holy Spirit wants. Committing those sins has its negative effect upon the Christian, as well as on others. Striving to reflect Yeshua's pure and undefiled Truth and be an example to others is a divine goal for all of us.

Of course, there are Christians who hear that eating pig won't send them to Hell, so they're not concerned about the Law, but sinning against God is no light matter. Building a theological house on sand is much more disastrous than building a real house on it (Mt. 7:24-27). Reading into Acts 15, and other passages of the New Testament, that the Law has been done away with is a false interpretation of the texts, and false theology leads to perverse and sinful lifestyles. This distorts the picture of the true Jesus that godly believers want to emulate and present to others. This false picture also offends many Jews, who understand, and correctly so, that their

---

[10]  Marshall, *Acts*, p. 242.

Messiah wouldn't do away with the Law of Moses. Jews know that the only true God is the God of Israel and that He gave the Law to Moses. Yahveh Himself warns them in the Law that if anyone entices them to follow something else, they're to be stoned to death (Dt. 13:1-5; 17:2-13). At this point, a 'Jesus (or Paul) who has done away with the Law' becomes a salvation issue for the entire Jewish community. Placing this stumbling block in the way of the Jewish people is nothing less than satanic.

Most Israelis are taught in grade school that Jesus started another religion: Christianity. It *hates* the Jewish people and the Law of Moses. Is that really what Jesus did? It certainly can't be found in the words of Jesus, nor the Book of Acts, nor Paul, but the last 1,900 years of Church theology and history toward the Jewish people confirm this sinister attitude toward both God's Law and His Chosen People Israel (Rom. 11:11-36).

In the New Covenant, whenever salvation is pitted against the Law (or circumcision, which implied that the Gentile was to become a Jew[11] and keep the Law for salvation along with his faith in Christ), the Law is rightly rejected as a means of obtaining and maintaining the new birth and the new life. Paul's emphasis of non-circumcision for the Gentile (1st Cor. 7:17-19; Gal. 2:3) was always against the keeping of the Law *for salvation*, which circumcision implied (Gal. 2:16, 19, 21; 5:4). One cannot add anything to the finished Work of Messiah Yeshua's sacrifice, but once that is established, the Law rightfully comes to the forefront in the New Testament for how one should live out their new life of faith in Messiah. Christian scholar David Williams, not a Law keeper himself, nevertheless writes that Paul understood this: 'for Paul, the law (sic) remained *the authoritative guide to Christian living.*'[12]

All the Jewish believers kept the Law (Acts 21:20), including Paul (Acts 21:23-24, 26; 23:1-5; 25:8), who also *commanded his followers to keep it* (Rom. 3:31; 7:7, 12, 14; 1st Cor. 7:19). If Paul, then, wrote to Gentile be-

---

[11]   E. P. Sanders, *Wikipedia: The Free Encyclopedia* at http://en.wikipedia.org/wiki/E._P._Sanders). Sanders first raised Christian awareness that circumcision meant the Gentile was to become part of the (supposedly eternally saved) Chosen People, a Jew who stayed 'in Covenant' by keeping the Law. (See Scot McKnight, *Jesus Creed* at http://blog.beliefnet.com/jesuscreed/2007/08/new-perspective-1.html).

David Stern, *Jewish New Testament Commentary* (Clarksville, MD: Jewish New Testament Publications, 1992), p. 273: Circumcision for the Gentile meant the circumcision party (Acts 15:1) was requiring the Gentile to become a proselyte (i.e. 'in every sense' a Jew).

[12]   David J. Williams, Author; W. Ward Gasque, New Testament Editor, *New International Biblical Commentary: Acts* (Peabody, MA: Hendrickson Publishers, 1999), p. 261.

6

lievers 'to follow him as he followed Christ,'[13] shouldn't the Gentiles be keeping the laws of Moses (that pertain to them)[14] from just this perspective? How can it be that the ancient Apostolic faith community loved the Law and adhered to it, while the modern faith community teaches against it? Are there two different faith communities in the one Flock of Jesus Christ (Jn. 10:16)?

The Church is adamant, though, that the Law doesn't pertain to Christians. Even the so-called Messianic Jewish community doesn't keep the Law of Moses (Torah), although they give lip service to it. They don't think that they, nor the Gentiles, need to keep Torah, even though they assemble on the 7th day Sabbath and have their Passover demonstrations, etc., because their theology on Law and Grace is similar to that of the Church.[15] The keeping of the Sabbath, etc., is only a facade, 'window dressing,' meant to impress the *unbelieving* Jewish community that Messianic Jews are 'still Jewish.' They're more concerned with 'looking Jewish' before the Jews who aren't saved than with looking biblical before their Jewish Savior.

Messianic Jews meet on the 7th day Sabbath, but they desecrate it by buying, selling and working on it. This is not what God meant when He said to keep His Sabbath day holy.[16] They also teach, by word and example, that the eating of unclean meats is acceptable to God. They are no different from their predecessors, the Jewish Christians, except for the wearing of their *tallits* and *kipas,* and the eating of bagels and cream cheese at their Sabbath assemblies. They don't understand that Torah is holy and valid for every believer—Jewish and Gentile. Instead, they teach that they are 'under Grace, not Law.' The 7th day Sabbath and the Feasts, etc., are just Jewish traditions for them to use in evangelizing unsaved Jews. Their false theology also allows them to maintain their relationship with the 'Law-free' Church, but this is extremely confusing to many Gentiles who come to them desiring to learn about the Law. Why would a Gentile, raised and nurtured in the anti-Law Church, want to keep the Law of

---

[13]  1st Cor. 4:14-17; 11:1; Phil. 3:15-17; 4:9; 1st Thess. 1:6-7; 2nd Thess. 3:7, 9.

[14]  Not all the commandments of Moses apply to everyone and many aren't able to be done today. Some apply only to the High Priest and the Levitical priests, and these, of course, aren't done today because there is no Temple. Other commandments only apply to women or to farmers, etc., but we must know the commandments in order to observe those that do apply to us. The major commandments that apply to everyone today are the 7th day Sabbath, the Feasts of Israel and the dietary laws.

[15]  See *Law and Grace* at http://SeedofAbraham.net/Law_and_Grace.html. Also, see *Goodbye Messianic Judaism!* at http://SeedofAbraham.net/gmesjud.html for why Messianic Judaism has failed to live up to its name.

[16]  Gen. 2:1-3; Ex. 16:23; 20:8; 31:12-17; 35:1-3; Dt. 5:11-15; Is. 56:2, 6; 58:13.

Moses?! Why, indeed!

While the Church and the Messianic community avoid the Law like a plague, the Spirit of Jesus is leading many Gentile and Jewish believers into observing the Law of Moses, from their heart. In these last days, the Holy Spirit is using the Law as a filter to see who will walk where Jesus is leading him, even if it goes against 1,900 years of staunch Church opposition. In this, it's not unlike the controversy that surrounded Yeshua as He confronted some of the synagogue teachers and teachings of His day (e.g. Mt. 15:1-20), or the religious opposition that has met with every fresh move of the Spirit of God since the days of Moses. Resisting the Work of the Holy Spirit is an all too common phenomenon among God's people (Psalm 95:6-11; 2nd Cor. 1:23; 12:21; 13:2, 10), but those who realize that the oasis that they're at is not the final one, are open to the leading of the Holy Spirit to the next oasis, even if the path appears dangerous.

With the writings of E. P. Sanders, James Dunn and N. T. Wright, the way is also being cleared at the scholarship level. Even though none of these men are advocating observance of the Law of Moses, within a generation, because of this new position concerning the Law (that it isn't legalism, but *God's will* on how to live a righteous life),[17] many believers, led of the Spirit of Yeshua, will read past the teachings of these men and walk into Torah, to the glory of Messiah Yeshua!

Millions of believers love Jesus with all their heart, but are enslaved, without even realizing it, to Church theology and traditions that *nullify* the God's Word. Great is the power of Satan to deceive, even and especially, the Bride of Christ (Dan. 7:25; Rev. 12:17). In the days of the Apostles, Gentiles were Born Again by the grace of God and learned all the commandments of Moses that applied to them (Acts 15:21). *The Lifting of the Veil* will establish this, and consequently, that it is God's will today that every believer walk out their faith in His Son through Torah, as interpreted by Yeshua, not the Rabbis (who pervert and twist God's Word). Once this is seen the veil will be removed from the eyes of Messiah's Bride so that she will be able to see her Bridegroom clearer than ever before, to the Glory of God the Father and God the Son!

---

[17] McKnight, Aug. 8th, 2007, at http://blog.beliefnet.com/jesuscreed/2007/08/new-perspective-3.html. McKnight sums up the position of Sanders, Dunn and Wright as agreeing on a number of things, one of which is that 'God gave Torah' to the Jews to show them 'how to live before God in righteousness.'

# THE FOUR RULES OF ACTS 15:20

The Church correctly understands Acts 15 to be a place where God declared that the Gentile didn't have to be circumcised and keep the Law of Moses, but they don't realize that it only pertained to salvation. Theologians then point to the four rules of v. 20 and erroneously say that these are the *only* rules for the Gentile[18] (other than loving God and neighbor).[19]

Church interpretation explains the four rules as 'an expression of Christian charity' toward 'the weaker brother'[20] (the Jewish believer).[21] The Jewish believer hadn't yet realized that he had been set free from the Law, but could *all* the Jewish Apostles have been blind to this? Didn't Jesus speak of the Law's demise in His 40 days with the Apostles *after* the resurrection, when He specifically taught them about His Kingdom (Acts 1:1-3)?

Interestingly enough, scholars recognize that all the Jewish believers, including Peter and Paul, continued to 'live by the Jewish law.'[22] Were *all* the Jewish believers wrong? According to the Church they were, and so, as not to offend Jewish sensibilities, the Gentiles were asked to walk in these four rules.[23] This way, theologians say, there could be 'a basis for fellowship' with the Jews, since the Jews were 'in every city' (15:21).[24]

F. F. Bruce, thinking that three of the four rules fall under the category of

---

[18] Marshall, *Acts*, p. 242: The Gentile was saved 'without accepting the obligations of the Jewish law.' Page 243: 'no more than these minimum requirements' (the four rules) 'should be imposed upon the Gentiles.'

[19] This contradicts the New Testament. If, as the Church teaches, only the 'moral laws' (e.g. stealing and murder) have passed into the New Testament, what makes something like homosexuality wrong (Lev. 18:22; 20:13; Rom. 1:27)? In other words, if a Greek man said that homosexuality for him was 'loving his neighbor as himself,' how could Paul say he was wrong? The Apostle could only turn to the Law. This is a clear indication that the four rules cannot be the only rules for the Gentile.

[20] Marshall, *Acts*, p. 242.

[21] Charles F. Pfeiffer, Old Testament, Everett F. Harrison, New Testament, *The Wycliffe Bible Commentary* (Chicago: Moody Press, 1977), p. 1152.

[22] Marshall, *Acts*, p. 243. *WBC*, p. 1152 states, 'the Jewish Christians' continued '*the practice of the Old Testament Law*;' p. 1150, 'It is apparent that *no Jewish believers gave up their Jewish practices* when they became Christians.' Williams, *Acts*, p. 256; the 'law *remained determinative for their lives*. They had no clear teaching from the Lord to the contrary.'

[23] Marshall, *Acts*, p. 253: 'Gentiles should abstain from certain things which were repulsive to Jews.'

[24] Pfeiffer, *The Wycliffe Bible Commentary*, p. 1152: 'The decree was issued... as a basis for fellowship' so as not to 'offend the weaker brother.'

dietary regulations (all but rule two), explains that the rules centered around *table fellowship* between Jew and Gentile.[25] In other words, they were given by James so that the Gentile believer would be able to eat and fellowship with the Jewish believer (who still kept the dietary laws; Lev. 11, etc.). The four rules of Acts 15:20 direct the Gentile to abstain from,

- 'the pollution of idols and of
- sexual immorality and of
- things strangled and of
- blood.'

Scholarship is unanimous that the first rule, 'pollution of idols,' deals with eating meat sacrificed to an idol. Also, the leftover meat from the sacrifice would be sold at the marketplace.[26]

'Things strangled' is interpreted to mean the Gentile shouldn't eat meat from a strangled animal—it should be properly slaughtered with the blood drained. The fourth rule, 'blood,' was said to refer to blood which might be found in meat that wasn't properly drained or adequately cooked (the Law prohibits the eating of blood; Lev. 3:17). The Church, *interpreting* these rules, says that out of consideration for Jewish sensibilities the Gentile believers wouldn't break them.[27]

The second rule, 'sexual immorality,' which the ASV, KJV, NASB and the NRSV call 'fornication,' is generally seen as any kind of illicit sex, such as adultery, homosexuality, pre-marital sex or incest, etc. Howard Marshall translates it as unchastity, 'variously understood as illicit sexual intercourse or as breaches of the Jewish marriage law (which forbade marriage between close relatives, Lev. 18:6-18).'[28]

---

[25] Bruce, *The Book of the Acts*, p. 285. Bruce states that after the decision that Gentiles needn't be circumcised, the Apostles and Elders 'turned to consider terms on which table fellowship between Jewish and Gentile Christians might become acceptable.' Marshall, *Acts*, p. 243, states that this is 'the question of how Jewish Christians, *who continued to live by the Jewish law* could have fellowship at table with Gentiles who did not observe the law.'

[26] Marshall, *Acts*, p. 253. Also, *WBC*, p. 1152: 'Often meat purchased in the market places had been sacrificed in pagan temples to heathen deities. The eating of such meat was offensive to sensitive Jewish consciences, for it smacked of taking part in the worship of the pagan deity.'

[27] Marshall, *Acts*, p. 253. 'The third element was meat which had been killed by strangling, a method of slaughter which meant that the blood remained in the meat, and the fourth item was blood itself...Nevertheless, some kind of compromise was necessary in order not to offend the consciences of the strict Jewish Christians, and he proposed that the Gentiles be asked to refrain from food dedicated to idols, from unchastity, and from meat containing blood' (p. 243).

*The Wycliffe Bible Commentary* is not certain as to what James, the half brother of Jesus, meant by 'fornication.' It follows Marshall as to illicit intercourse, but adds that it could point to cult prostitution:

> 'fornication may refer either to immorality in general or to *religious prostitution* in pagan temples. *Such immorality was so common among Gentiles* that it merited special attention.'[29]

Without realizing it, *Wycliffe* has hit upon the key to unlocking the proper interpretation of Acts 15:20—*religious prostitution*. The first rule, meat sacrificed to idols, falls under sacrificial idolatry. The second rule, 'fornication,' should also have been seen as part of sacrificial idolatry, simply from its word usage in the Bible, and also, from it being 'so common among Gentiles.' The second rule speaks of cult prostitution. These two rules are the major parts of a pagan ceremony—sacrificial-sexual idolatry.

The fourth rule of *blood* is easily incorporated into this concept and *things strangled* follows suit. Sadly, it wouldn't be until this book was published that all four rules were seen to pertain to sacrificial-sexual idolatry, and this only. As to where James got these four rules from and what they meant to the Gentile, R. J. Knowling writes that some thought the rules came from the seven laws of Noah. On the other hand, he comments;

> 'there are points of contact' yet 'it would seem that there are certainly four of the Precepts' (of Noah) 'to which *there is nothing corresponding* to the Decree.'[30]

In other words, why didn't James give the Gentiles all seven rules of Noah? Knowling goes on to write that some say that the rules were part of what was given to the 'stranger' (the *ger*) dwelling in Israel. He rightly dismisses this idea saying that this 'would be far from satisfactory' because the Jewish Christians, who kept all the Law (Acts 21:20), would be seen as superior, while only when the Gentile would keep the whole Law would he have the 'full privilege of the Christian Church and name.'[31]

Knowling also states that others consider the rules as coming from Lev. 17–18, but this too is awkward for him as it makes the 'written law...the source of the Jewish prohibitions.'[32] He says that attempts have been made to present the rules as 'binding upon proselytes in the wider sense, i.e.

---

[28] Ibid.

[29] Pfeiffer, *The Wycliffe Bible Commentary*, p. 1152.

[30] R. J. Knowling, D.D; W. Robertson Nicoll, M.A., LL.D., Editor, *The Expositor's Greek Testament*, vol. two: *The Acts of the Apostles* (Peabody, MA: Hendrickson Publishers, 2002), p. 335.

[31] Ibid.

upon the uncircumcised' that existed in the days of the Apostles, but 'of direct evidence...there is none.'[33] He further states that,

> 'the difficulty is so great in supposing Paul and Barnabas could have submitted to the distinction drawn between the Jewish Christians and the Gentile Christians that it led to doubts as to the historical character of the decree.'

Doubting the event, some state the decree was 'formulated after Paul's departure...But this view cannot be maintained' in light of Acts 16:4-5, 'where Paul is distinctly said to have given the decrees to the Churches to keep.'[34] Knowling adds that W. M. Ramsay, following John Lightfoot,

> thought 'it impossible to suppose that St. Paul would have endorsed a decree, which thus made mere points of ritual compulsory.'[35]

In the mostly Gentile churches of Paul, as Knowling puts it, the Apostle may not have enforced the Decree, with its 'blood and strangled,'

> because it would 'have been a cause of perplexity, a burden too heavy to bear, the source of a Christianity maimed by Jewish particularism.'[36]

All these views, from table fellowship to Noahide Law to thinking that Paul would never have accepted it, etc., rest upon the assumption that the Law of Moses 'was done away with.' Yet, David Williams writes that,

> 'those who argue that Paul could not have endorsed the decrees as they appear in the accepted text' don't 'show any appreciation of the situation in the church of the first century or of Paul's own attitude toward the law. There is considerable evidence that the decrees, as we have them, were not only issued, but observed in the Gentile churches for many years after their promulgation.'[37]

The Church teaches that the Law of Moses isn't for Christians. When the four rules are properly interpreted, though, that teaching will be seen as

---

[32]  Ibid.

[33]  Ibid., p. 336.

[34]  Ibid.

[35]  Ibid.

[36]  Ibid., p. 337.

[37]  Williams, *Acts*, p. 268. He cites as further evidence for the observance of the Decree, "Rev. 2:14, 22; Justin Martyr, *Dialogue* 34:8; Minucius Felix, *Octavius* 30:6; Eusebius, *Ecclesiastical History* 5.1.26; Tertullian, *Apology* 9:13; Pseudo-Clementine *Homilies* 7.4.2; 8:1, and 19."

false and the 'problem' with Paul accepting the Decree will be cleared up.

The four rules are the *filter*, the *first* rules the Gentile convert *needed* to address after salvation. The rest of the 'rules of Moses' would follow as he grew in Christ and went to the assembly on the Sabbath day to learn of 'Moses' (Acts 15:21). Why these four rules first? Because of Gentile propensity to add gods (Jesus) to the gods he already had and to continue to honor those gods and goddesses through *sacrificial-sexual idolatry*.

The four rules weren't made so that the Gentile believer could fellowship with the Jewish believer, as important as that is, but so that the Gentile could *retain* his salvation. The Gentile needed to know the boundaries of the Covenant into which he had entered. He had to realize what was permissible for him and what would cost him his eternal life.

The four rules of James are an inherent 'whole.' They are a 'package deal' or a *unit* on sacrificial-sexual idolatry. This pagan practice had to stop immediately if Gentile faith in Jesus was to be recognized as genuine.

The second rule is usually translated as 'sexual immorality' or 'fornication,' but there's overwhelming biblical evidence to support the understanding that *cult prostitution* is specifically what James meant. Translating the rule as 'sexual immorality' is totally unacceptable because it not only hides the true meaning of the second rule, it also *distorts the proper interpretation* of the entire Decree.

The first rule forbids the Gentile from eating the meat of a pagan sacrifice *at the sacrifice*. The second rule prohibits *cult prostitution* after the eating of the sacrifice. The third rule, *strangled*, speaks of a pagan sacrifice in which the neck was strangled and the fourth rule forbids the *drinking* of fresh, raw *blood* from the pagan sacrifice, which is the satanic counterpart of drinking Messiah's blood from the Third Cup of Passover.[38] The four rules specifically deal with sacrificial-sexual idolatry, something every Gentile in the ancient world fully understood and many practiced.

The four rules had nothing to do with table fellowship. They were designed to filter out gross idolatry. *That* would be very offensive to the God of Israel and cost the Gentile his life—his eternal life. One might think, in terms of Christianity today, that anyone coming to Jesus wouldn't imagine that they could worship Jesus and Zeus, too, but Gentiles in the days of the Apostles believed they could have as many gods as they wanted. As we'll see, their culture and souls were permeated with that view. 'Adding Jesus' to their pantheon wouldn't be seen as blasphemous by them. Of course, this would be an abomination in God's eyes. *This* is why James

---

[38] See *Passover* at http://SeedofAbraham.net/feasts2.html for the meaning of the Third Cup and why Yeshua chose this one to represent His blood.

gave the four rules *first*. He wanted the Gentiles to know that there were red lines that could not be crossed—even 'under Grace.'

Once it's understood that the four rules dealt with cultic idolatry and weren't rules chosen for 'table fellowship' to appease the 'weaker' Jewish believer, the *theological door* opens that leads to the authorized observance of the Law for the Gentile (Acts 15:21). The four rules were the filter that the Gentile had to pass through in order for his salvation to be seen as authentic, not some rules that he voluntarily observed in condescension to Jewish believers.[39] It will become apparent that these four rules weren't the 'only ones' for the Gentile, but the first of many that God gave to His people Israel, both Jewish and Gentile believers.

The Church has taken the mighty Wind of the Holy Spirit out of the sails of Acts 15:20 in presenting its interpretation of *table fellowship*. Even if 'sexual immorality' (KJV 'fornication') is addressed as cult prostitution, unless all four rules are seen as a unit on cultic idolatry, one is able to assume that the four rules are just random selections on the part of James toward 'Jewish sensibilities' that have little relevance for us today.[40]

The Church hasn't been able to understand this 'unit of cultic idolatry' because of its perception and vilification of the Law of Moses. The Church sees anyone that keeps the Law as being in bondage, but teaching that the Law is a bondage makes the God who gave it to Israel a malicious ogre.

---

[39]  It is the height of pride and ignorance to present the new Gentile believers as stronger in faith than the Jewish believers. All the Apostles had been walking for many years with the Holy Spirit, and as is attested, would keep the Law all their lives (Acts 21:20-24, 26; 22:12; 24:14; 25:8). The Church says the Apostles were wrong. Could it be that the Church is wrong?

[40]  Stern, *JNTC*, p. 278. In commenting on a possible interpretation of the four rules, Stern says that if 'these *food laws* were given only as practical guides to avoid disruption of *fellowship* between believing Jews and Gentiles in the social context of the first century' then 'the issue is irrelevant, and there is no need for Gentile Christians to obey a command never intended as eternal.' He adds, 'Messianic Jews today are a small minority in the Body of Messiah and few, if any, of them, take umbrage' at Gentile eating habits. Stern's logic is flawed and not only because the rules have nothing to do with food laws. Contrary to what he writes, there are many believing Jews today who are offended by Gentile eating habits (i.e. unclean meats). The only condition that has changed since James gave the ruling is that now there are more Gentile believers than Jewish believers, but as Paul said, 'if food causes my brother to stumble, I will never eat meat again, so that I will not cause my brother to stumble' (1st Cor. 8:13). Stern's position also doesn't speak of the example that Gentile Christians are supposed to be toward Jews that don't yet believe (Rom. 11:13-14). What kind of an example is it to a Jew who doesn't know the Jewish Messiah, for a Gentile Christian to tell him that he can eat pork, when the Jew *knows* that *God forbids such things* (Lev. 11:7; Dt. 12:8)?

Did Yahveh set the Hebrews free from Egyptian slavery only to shackle them 'to the accursed Law'? No wonder many Christians think that 'the God of the Old Testament' is very cruel and so very different from 'the loving Jesus.'

The Law, far from being a curse, is the basis for understanding not only Who the God of Israel is and what He has done and will do for Israel, but also what He thinks is sin and what is pleasing to Him.[41] The one who is cursed is the one not observing it.[42] What that means today, for many Christians who don't observe the Sabbath and who eat pig, etc., is that at these specific points they are breaking God's Law and sinning. They're not following God's will for their lives in these areas. Whether they understand it or not, they are suffering the consequences of these sins.

One doesn't have to understand (or even acknowledge) the laws of proper nutrition in order to be adversely affected by poor eating habits. Lack of knowledge or ignorance of a law is never a proper defense, whether in a court of law or before the heavenly Tribunal.[43]

Believers have Bibles today and the Holy Spirit to teach them the Way. The problem is that most have been *blinded* by the *tradition* of the Church, which nullifies the Law of Moses. In this the Church is Pharisaic. The Church says their doctrine is from God, but in reality, it nullifies and makes void God's teaching in this vital area (Mt. 15:3, 7, 9; Rom. 3:31).

All God's commandments are for our blessing and wisdom and reveal to us how much He loves us (Dt. 4:5-8; Mt. 22:35-40). When we fail to walk in any of them that pertain to us, whether intentionally or out of ignorance, we are the ones to suffer. That's why it's so important to properly understand what God is saying about the Law in the New Testament.

Being 'free in Christ' is not a license to sin. True freedom is walking in

---

[41]  Leland Ryken, James Wilhoit and Tremper Longman III, General Editors, *Dictionary of Biblical Imagery* (Leicester, England: InterVarsity Press, 1998), p. 489. Under 'Law' it states, 'The law expresses God's expectations for the moral and spiritual conduct of Israel, the guidelines God has given to Israel to enable them *to live life as he created it to be lived*....there is general agreement that it bears the connotations of guidance, teaching and instruction.' See also Ex. 31:12-17; Lev. 23; Dt. 4:5-8; Rom. 3:20; 7:7, 12, 14; 1st Jn. 5:2-3, etc.

[42]  Dt. 27:26: '"Cursed is he who does not confirm the words of this Law by doing them!' And all the people shall say, 'Amen!'"

[43]  Hosea 4:6: 'My people are destroyed for lack of knowledge. Because you have rejected knowledge, I will also reject you from being My priest. Since you've forgotten the Law of your God, I will also forget your sons.' (See Lev. 4:2; 5:17-19, the sacrifice for the sin of ignorance and Lk. 12:47-48. If someone breaks the Law in ignorance it's still a sin and has its consequences.)

15

His will. By understanding that all four rules center around sacrificial-sexual idolatry, Yakov (James in English, but more properly Jacob) was giving the Gentiles what Yahveh had given Israel when Israel was about to enter into the Promised Land. Yahveh sternly warned Israel about worshiping Him—and Him only! In Dt. 4–9 and 12–13, Yahveh admonished Israel concerning idolatry and its consequences. In the Ten Commandments Yahveh says,

> 'You must have *no other gods except Me*. You must not
> make for yourself an idol or any likeness of what is in the
> Heavens above or on the Earth beneath or in the waters
> under the Earth. You must not worship them or serve
> them, for I, Yahveh your God, am a jealous God, visiting
> the iniquity of the fathers on the sons to the third and the
> fourth generations of those who hate Me.' (Dt. 5:7-9)

There were to be no other gods for the Sons of Israel. They weren't to serve (sacrifice to or worship) them. The Gentiles, entering into the *Promised One* (Messiah Yeshua) were being warned in the very same way by the Holy Spirit through the head of the Assembly, Yakov. Just as God didn't expect Israel to learn all the Law in one day, so too, with the Gentiles, but the Gentiles were to be *immediately* aware of the most important thing—not to practice cultic idolatry.[44] After that they would learn the rest of the Law as they went to the synagogues where Moses was taught every Sabbath in all the cities of the world (Acts 15:21). Just as a child, adopted into a family, gradually learns all the family rules and values, so too, the Gentile would come to know all the laws of Moses that applied to him, as understood through the eyes of Jesus—not the Rabbis, nor the Sadducees, nor the Pharisees. This understanding of Acts 15:20, that Yakov gave the Gentiles 'a package deal' on sacrificial-sexual idolatry, hinges on the definition of the second rule. With this rule the concept either stands or falls. The Greek word for the second rule is πορνεια (*pornay'ah*).[45] It's usually translated in Acts 15:20 as 'sexual immorality' or 'fornication,' but if it means 'cult prostitution,' and not the vague term 'sexual immorality' or related concepts such as illicit sex, adultery, or even common prostitution,

---

[44]  Idolatry is not isolated to pagan altars. Astrology, Horoscopes and Tarot cards, etc., are also idolatrous and exclude believers from the Kingdom (Gal. 5:19-21), but James is specifically addressing pagan *sacrificial* rites.

[45]  Unless otherwise stated, Greek words used will be identical for both the Textus Receptus and the Nestle–Aland Greek New Testament–United Bible Societies third corrected edition. The latter is the Greek text used to translate the New Testament for the NRSV, NASB and other Bibles, while the former is the basis for the KJV and the NKJV. This means that the KJV and the NRSV, etc., have the same Greek word for Acts 15:20 (*pornay'ah*). When there's a difference it will be noted.

the traditional Church teaching of 'table fellowship' disintegrates, and with it, the Church's theological position on the Law of Moses—Acts 15:20 is that important and foundational. Once the four rules are seen as a conceptual unit on sacrificial-sexual idolatry, the idea that 'the Law has been done away with' collapses. The rules can't be seen, then, as the 'only ones,' but the first of many from the Law for the Gentile believer. The Law's proper place in the life of every Christian will then be re-established (Rom. 3:31) and Yeshua will be glorified.

Acts 15:20 is the filter through which the Gentile had to leave all his other gods and goddesses behind him. It's not the magic wand that makes the Law disappear, but quite the contrary, it precedes the verse that further establishes the Law in the life of every believer (Acts 15:21).

Acts 15:20 was the anointed admonition of Yakov to the Gentiles to break with pagan sacrificial rites. These four rules were the litmus test given to the Gentiles to determine their faith in Jesus. Yakov then adds verse 21, *knowing that for the last nine years* (from Acts 10), Gentile believers had been learning the Law at the synagogues, which is both a term for the traditional synagogue, and a place like the 'church' at Antioch and Ephesus. These Gentile believers were learning how to walk out their faith in Jesus through God's Law.

The understanding that the four rules pertain to sacrificial-sexual idolatry will shatter the Church's heretical teaching on the Law of Moses. The Church will no longer be able to use Acts 15 to place an unholy theological veil over the eyes of believers. Properly understood, the text reveals God's desire for His people to walk in the Law of Moses by the wisdom and the power of the Spirit of Yeshua, just as He did.

# THE FIRST RULE: SACRIFICIAL MEAT

In Acts 15:20, Yakov presents four rules to the Gentile believers. He says to keep away from,

1. 'the pollution of idols
2. and the sexual immorality
3. and the thing strangled[46]
4. and the blood.'[47]

The Greek phrase for the first rule (pollution of idols) is αλισγημάτων των ειδωλων (*alisgaymatone tone aydolone*). Wesley Perschbacher says the word for pollution (*alisgaymatone*) means, 'pollution, defilement, Acts 15:20.'[48] Bauer says it means to 'make ceremonially impure' and that the plural, *pollutions* (which is written in v. 20) 'denotes separate acts.'[49] Literally, it's 'the pollutions of idols.' Timothy Friberg agrees.[50] It's something that *defiles* and can be done *repeatedly*.

Perschbacher states that the word for idols ειδωλων (*aydolone*) means,

> 'a form, shape, figure; image or statue; hence, an idol, image of a god, Acts 7:41, et al.; meton.[51] a heathen god, 1st Cor. 8:4, 7.'[52]

Friberg states it's 'an object resembling a person or animal and worshiped

---

[46] The literal Greek rendering of this phrase is, 'and the strangled.' 'Thing' is not in the text, but it can be translated as 'the thing(s) strangled.'

[47] Robert K. Brown and Philip W. Comfort, Translators; J. D. Douglas, Editor; *The New Greek–English Interlinear New Testament* (Wheaton, IL: Tyndale House Publishers, 1990), p. 472. Taken from the English of the *Interlinear*. The definite article *the* is written in Greek before each of the rules.

[48] Wesley J. Perschbacher, Editor, *The New Analytical Greek Lexicon* (Peabody, MA: Hendrickson Publications, 1990), p. 15.

[49] Walter Bauer, augmented by William F. Arndt, F. W. Gingrich and Frederick Danker, *A Greek–English Lexicon of the New Testament and Other Early Christian Literature* (London: The University of Chicago Press, 1979), p. 37.

[50] Timothy and Barbara Friberg and Neva Miller, *Analytical Lexicon of the Greek New Testament* (Grand Rapids, MI: Baker Books, 2000), p. 43.

[51] J. M. Sinclair, General Consultant; Diana Treffry, Editorial Director, *Collins English Dictionary*, Fourth Edition (Glasgow, Scotland: HarperCollins Publishers, 1998), p. 980. The abbreviation 'meton.' means 'by metonymy.' It means 'the substitution of a word referring to an attribute for the thing that is meant.' An example of this is, 'the use of the crown to refer to a monarch.'

[52] Perschbacher, *The New Analytical Greek Lexicon*, pp. 118-119.

as a god idol, image.'[53] Bauer concurs, adding that it is a 'false god.'[54]

The four rules are mentioned twice more in Acts after Yakov initially declares them in 15:20 (15:29; 21:25) and this further clarifies what he meant for the first rule. Luke uses a very specific Greek word for idols in the latter two cites: ειδωλοθυτων (*aedolo'thutone*).[55]

Perschbacher says that it's an *animal* 'sacrificed to an idol...the remains of victims sacrificed to idols, reserved for eating; Acts 15:29; 21:25.'[56] Friberg writes almost the same thing, saying it was 'the remains of victims sacrificed to an idol and reserved for eating...Acts 21:25.'[57] David Williams also states it was an animal 'sacrificed to idols.'[58]

Bruce comments that the Gentiles were 'directed to avoid food which had idolatrous associations.'[59] This is vague as no time frame is indicated as to when the person was eating the sacrificial meat (at the sacrifice or somewhere else). This allows Bruce to think that the rules were part of the Noahide laws and given for table fellowship, even though he believes that the Gentiles didn't have to follow the four rules.[60]

David Stern is also vague on when the meat was eaten. He says the rule meant to stay away from 'food sacrificed to false gods.'[61] Howard Marshall says the 'pollutions of idols' referred,

> 'to meat offered in sacrifice to idols and then eaten in a temple feast or sold in a shop.'[62]

Bauer states that it's an animal sacrificed to an idol and eaten at the pagan temple in honor of the god, with the remains (if any) sold at the marketplace. He says,

> it's 'meat offered to an idol, an expression which...was possible only among Jews...and Christians.' (For what Gentile would call his god an idol?) 'It refers to sacrificial

---

[53] Friberg, *Analytical Lexicon of the Greek New Testament*, pp. 130-131.

[54] Bauer, *A Greek-English Lexicon of the New Testament*, p. 221.

[55] Brown, *The New Greek-English Interlinear New Testament*, p. 472.

[56] Perschbacher, *The New Analytical Greek Lexicon*, p. 118.

[57] Friberg, *Analytical Lexicon of the Greek New Testament*, p. 130.

[58] Williams, *Acts*, p. 267.

[59] Bruce, *The Book of the Acts*, p. 295.

[60] Ibid., p. 285. Bruce states, 'the last thing that would have occurred to him' (Paul) 'would be to quote a decision of the Jerusalem church as binding on Gentile Christians.'

[61] Stern, *Jewish New Testament Commentary*, p. 277.

[62] Marshall, *Acts*, p. 253.

> meat, part of which was burned on the altar, part was eat-
> en at a solemn meal in the' pagan 'temple and part was
> sold in the market...for home use,'[63] if there was anything
> left over.

Ben Witherington III, though, says it means 'something given, dedicated, even sacrificed to idols...*in a temple.*'[64] He rightly states that the theme of the four rules is only understood when the first rule of Acts 15:20, the 'pollutions of idols' is realized to be a sacrifice *'eaten in the presence of the idol.'*[65] Witherington says that it's extremely crucial, for a proper inter-pretation of what James ruled, to see that it's 'more than just a meat' or a food issue, but that it points directly to sacrificial meat eaten in a pagan temple *at the time of the sacrifice.*

Why is he correct? Why can't it also be the meat sold in the market? Be-cause the four rules center around *sacrificial*-sexual idolatry, not the possi-ble eating of the sacrificial meat 'leftovers' bought from the market. The Apostle Paul will address the issue of meat sold in the market. He will al-low pagan sacrificial meat to be consumed by believers *when taken from the market* (or eaten at another's dinner table) as long as it wasn't made known to the buyer (or guest) that it was meat sacrificed to an idol—but he will not allow believers to eat sacrificial meat *at the site of the sacrifice* (1st Cor. 10:21, 25, 27-28) as that would make them part of the worship of an idol (i.e. idolators). There wasn't any disagreement between Yakov and Paul. The Apostle to the Gentiles upheld Yakov's rules (Acts 16:4-5).

The meaning of Yakov's first rule centered around the eating of the sacri-ficial meat *at the time of the sacrifice*, not the eating of any excess meat that might later be sold to the marketplace for public consumption. The eating of the meat *at the temple* of the god or goddess would certainly *pol-lute* and defile the Gentile Christian however many times he would do it.

This brings 'pollutions of idols' into a much sharper focus. It wasn't meat that was somehow tainted with an idolatrous association, neither was it excessive sacrificial meat sold in the market. It was animal meat sacrificed to the god at the pagan temple and eaten there at the time of the sacrifice by the Gentile in honor of the god or goddess. The first rule falls squarely under sacrificial idolatry and sets up the theme for the other rules. Asser-tions that the rule was given because eating meat sacrificed to pagan gods would offend 'Jewish sensitivities,' begs the question of whether or not

---

[63]  Bauer, *A Greek-English Lexicon of the New Testament*, p. 221.

[64]  Ben Witherington III, *The Acts of the Apostles: A Socio–Rhetorical Commen-tary* (Grand Rapids, MI: William B. Eerdmans Publishing Company, 1998), p. 461.

[65]  Ibid., pp. 462-463.

*Jesus* would have been offended. What would He think if His Gentile followers sacrificed a bull to Zeus and ate the sacrificial meat in honor of Zeus?

Yakov's main concern in issuing the first rule was that the Gentile believer wouldn't eat the meat of an idolatrous sacrifice at the time of the sacrifice. He didn't go into an area that Paul would later address (sacrificial meat sold at the market), because he wasn't led to go down that trail.

No believer today would possibly think that it would be alright with Jesus if he participated in a pagan sacrifice to Artemis, Diana or Baal and ate the meat thereof, but in the book of Revelation this is exactly what some Gentile believers were doing in two of the seven assemblies! In Revelation 2:14, 20 the Lord speaks of the first two rules of James. Jesus rebuked them for eating meats sacrificed to idols (at the time of the sacrifice) *and* for participating in cult prostitution, thinking those two things were acceptable for Christians! Paul also had to warn many of his Gentile Christians about these idolatrous practices and their eternal consequences.

Yakov was not writing about meat that had been sacrificed to idols being sold in the marketplace. His first rule, to keep away from 'the pollutions of idols,'[66] is specifically directed against believing Gentiles participating in the eating of meat sacrificed to an idol at the time of the sacrifice. This sets up the conceptual theme of *sacrificial idolatry* for the four rules, not table fellowship.

---

[66] 'Pollutions' in the plural means that one was defiled by going to the pagan temples and eating of the sacrificial meat on every occasion that the Gentile would do it. The Gentile world was saturated with gods and goddesses, many of whom demanded animal (and human) sacrifice. Yakov was making reference to a Gentile believer going to the temple or shrine on more than one occasion, not to the different stages of the sacrificial meat (at the sacrificial site, at the marketplace and in the home).

As Bauer, *A Greek-English Lexicon of the New Testament*, p. 18, brought out, the plural 'denotes separate acts,' and as such, would entail the different times a Gentile would go 'to worship,' each time polluting himself (cf. Mt. 15:19).

# THE SECOND RULE:

# CULT PROSTITUTION

The second rule of Yakov (Acts 15:20) refers to cult prostitution. It was the 'high point' of the sacrificial event and what attracted many pagans: sexual idolatry. Satan knows how to lure man away from God—just equate worship with sex. The symbolic meaning of pagan animal sacrifice was union with the god or goddess, which found its 'fulfillment' through sex with the temple priestesses (cult harlots) or priests.

*The New Greek-English Interlinear New Testament* uses the term 'sexual immorality' to translate the Greek word πορνεια (*pornay'ah*), the second rule of Yakov. The New Revised Standard Version translates the word as 'fornication.'[67] This is nothing unusual, as different Bibles use various words to convey the meaning of a Greek or a Hebrew word, but what is sexual immorality? What is fornication? Are they interchangeable and do either of them represent what Yakov meant?

In the New Testament and the Old Testament (via the Septuagint) the Greek word *pornay'ah* has the basic meaning of 'prostitution,' either cultic or common. The concept of selling one's self (prostitution) is then figuratively expanded in a number of ways (e.g. to criticize Israel for making treaties with other nations while not relying upon Yahveh, or of one who practices magic, selling himself to it instead of Yahveh, etc.). It is also used as a derogatory epithet for an adulteress and for the nation of Israel as Yahveh's unfaithful wife when she deserts Him for another god.

Yakov was a Jew and spoke Hebrew, not Greek, at the Jerusalem Council in Acts 15,[68] therefore, his thoughts and words would have been rooted in

---

[67] Brown, *NGEINT,* p. 472, uses the New Revised Standard Version translation (on the outside of each page) as an aid to the reader. Some other Bibles that translate the Greek word as 'fornication' include the KJV and the NASB.

[68] David Bivin and Roy Blizzard, *Understanding the Difficult Words of Jesus* (Shippensburg, PA: Destiny Image Publishers, 2001). Biblical scholarship has had to take into account many recent (20th century) findings that have determined that Hebrew was the spoken language in Israel at the time of the Apostles. For centuries many thought that it was Aramaic, but even renowned Aramaic scholars like Matthew Black and Max Wilcox concede that 'Hebrew was' the 'living language' and the 'normal vehicle of expression' (ibid., pp. 12-13). This understanding rests on a number of findings in different fields. One is the discovery of the bar Kochba letters, dated at 134-135 AD, in which Hebrew is the language. Also, much of the literature of Qumran is in Hebrew, not Aramaic (ibid., pp. 14, 20-21). The ratio of Hebrew to Aramaic is 'nine to one' and it's most likely that the Aramaic found was written much earlier,

the Hebrew concepts of the word he used. The Greek word will affirm this. The Hebrew word Yakov spoke that day was זְנוּת (*zinute*).[69] After examining it and some associated words, along with places where it is used in the Bible, we'll turn to the Greek perspective on it. By examining the meaning of the word and surveying the practice of cult prostitution in Israel and in the ancient world, it will become very clear why Yakov gave

when Aramaic was a carryover from Babylonian captivity (ibid., p. 29). There's also the witness of the early Church Father Papias, Bishop of Hierapolis in Turkey (150-170 AD) who wrote, 'Matthew put down the words of the Lord in the *Hebrew* language' (ibid., pp. 23-24).

The three Synoptic Gospels, having been translated into Hebrew from the Greek text (for Israelis today) contain many places where the Greek words *form perfect Hebrew syntax and idiomatic expressions* (ibid., pp. 53-65). This confirms Papias. Also, of the 215 ancient coins at the Israel Museum covering a period of roughly 450 years, from the fourth century BC until 135 AD, '99 have Hebrew inscriptions' and 'only one has an Aramaic inscription' (ibid., p. 33; the other 115 coins are Roman).

Early Rabbinic literature was all written in Hebrew (ibid., p. 43), and the New Testament declares *Hebrew* to be the language of Yeshua and the Apostles. Unfortunately, scholars and translators have said that what the New Testament 'really meant' was Aramaic. That Aramaic was used is not to be denied, but just as an Englishman can say '*Bon appétit*' without anyone suggesting that all of Britain speaks French as its primary language, so too, could Yeshua use Aramaic words and phrases (Mk. 5:41; 7:34; Jn. 1:42).

The New Testament speaks of the inscription over the head of Yeshua being in *Hebrew*, Greek and Latin (Jn. 19:20), and of Mary addressing Him in Hebrew ('*Rabboni*,' Jn. 20:16). Paul says that Yeshua spoke to him in Hebrew (Acts 26:14) and Scripture records that Paul spoke to the crowd at the Temple in Hebrew (Acts 21:40; 22:2). There are also other references *specifically* to the Hebrew language (Jn. 5:2; 19:13, 17; Rev. 9:11; 16:16).

Geoffrey W. Bromiley, General Editor; Everett F. Harrison, Roland K. Harrison and William Sanford LaSor, Associate Editors, *The International Standard Bible Encyclopedia*, vol. one (Grand Rapids, MI: William B. Eerdmans Publishing Company, 1979), p. 233, IV *Aramaic and the NT:* With the finding of the Dead Sea Scrolls (1947f.), "*it became obvious* that Hebrew was indeed" the language of "the rank and file...In a compelling article on '*Hebrew in the Days of the Second Temple*' (*JBL*, 79 [1960], 32-47), J. M. Grintz has offered...evidence to show that Hebrew, rather than Aramaic, lay behind the Gospel of Matthew. A number of expressions in the Gospel can only be explained on the basis of Hebrew, like the use of 'Israel' (Aramaic regularly uses 'Jews') and 'gentiles' (Aramaic has no word like '*gôyîm*')."

The spoken language of Jesus and the Apostles was Hebrew, not Aramaic, and therefore, we know that Yakov spoke Hebrew at the Council of Acts 15.

69   תורה נביאים כתובים והברית החדשה (*Torah, Prophets, Writings and The New Covenant*...Jerusalem: The Bible Society of Israel, 1991), pp. 170-171, 180. The Greek *pornay'ah* of Acts 15:20 is translated into Hebrew as *zinute* זְנוּת (*prostitution*). It's the same for Acts 15:29; 21:25.

the four rules and why the second rule speaks specifically of cult harlotry.

## *The Hebrew Noun Zinute (Prostitution)*

It's important to understand what the lexicons (ancient Bible language dictionaries) say about Yakov's word, whether in Hebrew or in Greek. This way the primary meaning for the word in Acts 15:20 can be seen. Is it *cult prostitution, sexual immorality, adultery* or something else? In his classic Hebrew lexicon, Francis Brown states that *zinute* means 'fornication.' He lists three categories with Scripture cites concerning *fornication*:

1. 'sexual' Hosea 4:11,

2. 'international' Ezekiel 23:27 and

3. 'religious' Num. 14:33; Jer. 3:2, 9; 13:27; Ezk. 43:7, 9; Hos. 6:10.[70]

What does Brown mean by 'fornication'? As we'll see, all three categories deal first and foremost with *cult* prostitution. A secondary, figurative meaning comes when God denounces Judah for her whoring after Egypt, which entailed both figurative as well as literal cult prostitution, but all of Brown's cites speak of literal cult harlotry, except Numbers 14:33.

Brown's 'sexual' for Hosea 4:11 speaks of harlotry. The next verse (v. 12) defines this 'harlotry' as cult harlotry. Yahveh says, 'My people consult their *wooden idol.*' The 'consulting of wooden idols,' aligned with harlotry, can only mean cult harlotry, not common harlotry. In the verse after that (v. 13) Yahveh says, 'They offer *sacrifices,*' which again speaks of the harlotry as being cultic and not common. This is specifically confirmed in v. 14 where God states through Hosea that they 'offer *sacrifices* with *temple* prostitutes' (NASB, NRSV; NIV 'shrine prostitutes). In v. 17 the Lord also says, 'Ephraim is joined to *idols.* Let him alone!' 'Fornication' for Brown, that he describes as 'sexual,' is specifically cult harlotry.

The KJV and the NRSV translate the word in Hosea 4:11 as 'whoredom,' while the NASB and NKJV use 'harlotry.' Both the words 'whoredom' and 'harlotry' are synonyms for 'prostitution.' These Bibles would improve their translations considerably by using either 'cult whoredom' or 'cult harlotry' to distinguish it from common harlotry.

For 'international' Brown lists Ezk. 23:27. The KJV has 'your whoredom brought from the land of Egypt.' It's not hard to imagine what *kind* of

---

[70] Dr. Francis Brown, Dr. S. R. Driver and Dr. Charles A. Briggs, based on the lexicon of Professor Wilhelm Gesenius; Edward Robinson, Translator and E. Rodiger, Editor, *The New Brown, Driver, Briggs, Gesenius Hebrew and English Lexicon* (Lafayette, IN: Associated Publishers and Authors, Inc., 1978), p. 276.

'whoredom' they picked up in Egypt. Only three verses later God says,

> 'I will do these things unto thee because thou hast gone a
> whoring after the heathen and because thou art polluted
> with their *idols*.' (Ezk. 23:30 KJV)

With the use of 'idols' God can only be referring to cult harlotry. Hebrew parallelism is 'not a repetition of the same sound, but a repetition...of the same thought.'[71] It's 'the placing of two synonymous phrases or sentences side by side.'[72] The biblical phrase in Ezekiel, 'gone a whoring,' parallels 'their idols.' The 'harlot' must be a cult harlot. Brown's 'international fornication' also specifically refers to cult prostitution.

Brown then speaks of Israel's unfaithfulness to Yahveh (Num. 14:33) as 'religious' fornication. Israel refused to believe that God would bring them into the Promised Land. Instead, they chose to believe the lie of the ten spies (Numbers 13:25–14:4). There's no literal harlotry here, cultic or common. The idea is that Israel chose to rebel against Yahveh's word to them. This is a figurative meaning for *harlotry*, but Brown also cites Jer. 3:9 and 13:27, both of which specifically deal with the cult harlotry of Judah. Israel, as the wife of Yahveh, is metaphorically seen to be adulterous:

> 'Because of the lightness of her *harlotry*, she polluted the
> land and committed *adultery with stones and trees*.'

> 'As for your *adulteries* and your lustful neighings, the
> lewdness of your prostitution *on the hills* in the field, I
> have seen your abominations. Woe to you, Oh Jerusalem!
> How long will you remain unclean?!' (Jer. 3:9; 13:27)

Adultery 'with stones and trees' can't mean literal adultery, but the worship of pagan gods and the use of cult harlots. The phrase 'on the hills' is a reference to where men of Judah would go to engage in cult harlotry.

Judah was in covenant with Yahveh, figuratively married to Him and Him only (Is. 54:5; Jer. 3:14), therefore, when Judah worshiped *other* gods, she was committing *spiritual* adultery (Ezekiel 23:1-49). Judah copied the pagans, setting up stones and trees to their gods, and to their eternal shame, they would sacrifice and commit cult harlotry. Only in this *metaphorical* sense is 'adultery' ever used to describe Israel and Judah's *whoring* after other gods. Israel was in intimate covenant with God and the closest earthly parallel to that was the marriage covenant of a man to a woman.

In Brown's category on *religious*, 'figurative' is used (Num. 14:33) to describe Israel's unfaithfulness and disloyalty to Yahveh. Alongside those

---

[71]  Bivin, *Understanding the Difficult Words of Jesus*, p. 89.

[72]  Ibid.

terms is 'cult prostitution' (in Jeremiah). He lists two other passages in Ezekiel (43:7, 9), but these also relate to idolatrous harlotry, both the specifics of cult harlotry and the selling of one's soul to the idols of wood and stone. What Brown classifies as *religious* is Israel whoring after pagan gods, another case of cult prostitution (except for Num. 14:33).

Under Brown's cite of Hosea (6:10) the NASB reads:

> 'In the House of Israel I have seen a horrible thing;
> Ephraim's harlotry is there; Israel has defiled itself.'

One could try and make a case that this harlotry is common harlotry, as the verse doesn't give a specific form one way or the other, but Hosea's theme is not against common harlotry. It's against the northern kingdom of Israel *steeped* in sacrificial-*sexual* idolatry. The verse, therefore, reflects cult harlotry. This is noted in *TDOT* when it states that Israel,

> 'associated with the syncretistic cult at Gilgal and Beth-
> aven; this cult was harlotry in a double sense, since *actual
> sexual intercourse was part of the cult* (4:13f.) and its
> idolatry meant *faithlessness* toward Yahweh (4:15).'[73]

*TDOT*'s 'sexual intercourse' and 'idolatry' refers to cult prostitution. The cite of Hosea 4:15 was also a part of the passage connected to Hosea 4:11 that Brown listed above:

> "Though you, Israel, *play the harlot*, do not let Judah be-
> come guilty. Also, do not go to Gilgal or go up to Beth-
> aven and take the oath, 'As Yahveh lives!'" (Hosea 4:15;
> see also 1st Kings 12:25-33; 13:1-10.)

This verse speaks of the practice of cult harlotry 'in the Name of Yahveh' ('As Yahveh lives!' In Rev. 2:14 the same perverse sin happens 'in the Name of Jesus!'). *TDOT* states for Hosea 9:1 that 'Israel's harlotry...in forsaking Yahweh (*sic*) is associated with the *fertility cult*.'[74] These fertility cults and their 'sacred' harlots are *a major theme of the prophets*. They speak out against the faithlessness of the northern kingdom of Israel (2nd Kgs. 17:1-23) and the southern kingdom of Judah (Jer. 7:25; 35:15).

Commenting on Hosea 4:15, C. F. Keil writes that Yahveh was telling Judah not to become like her northern neighbor Israel or else she, too, would share in Israel's guilt. The reference to Gilgal here 'is not the Gilgal in the valley of the Jordan' (where Joshua first led Israel into the Promised Land;

---

[73]  G. Johannes Botterweck and Helmer Ringgren, Editors; John Willis, Translator, *Theological Dictionary of the Old Testament*, vol. IV (Grand Rapids, MI:
William B. Eerdmans Publishing Company, 1997), p. 102.

[74]  Ibid.

Josh. 4:20; 5:9-10), but 'northern Gilgal upon the mountains.'[75] This Gilgal had once been home to 'a school of the prophets' in the days of Elijah and Elisha (2nd Kgs. 2:1; 4:38), but it was now the 'seat of one form of idolatrous worship.'[76] Keil writes,

> 'Bethaven is not the place of that name mentioned in Josh. 7:2...but, as Amos 4:4 and 5:5 clearly show, a name which Hosea adopted from Amos 5:5 for Bethel...to show that Bethel, the house of God, had become Bethaven, a house of idols, through the setting up of the golden calf there' (1st Kgs. 12:29). 'Swearing in the name of Jehovah (*sic*) was commanded in the law,' Dt. 6:13; 10:20, 'but this oath was to have its roots in the fear of Jehovah...Going to Gilgal to worship idols, and swearing by Jehovah cannot go together. The confession of Jehovah in the mouth of an idolater is hypocrisy.'[77]

The northern kingdom of Israel was a land and a people defiled with cult prostitution, as Hosea spoke of in the verses just before 4:15. It's here we find the famous passage, 'My people are destroyed for lack of knowledge' (Hos. 4:6) because they had chosen to disregard Yahveh *and His Law*, which prohibited cult harlotry. Hosea 4:12 states that the 'people consult their wooden idol' and have a 'spirit of harlotry.' Keil writes that this,

> 'spirit of harlotry...includes both *carnal* and spiritual whoredom, since idolatry, especially the Asherah worship, was connected with *gross licentiousness*.'[78]

The category of 'religion' into which Brown puts Hosea 4:15 can only be speaking of Israel walking in cult harlotry when Scripture presents Israel as 'playing the harlot.' His three categories all dovetail into cult harlotry.

Benjamin Davidson says that *zinute* means 'whoredom.'[79] He doesn't list any cites, but says it can also apply to *idolatry*, which would mean cult harlotry. R. L. Harris, in the *Theological Wordbook of the Old Testament*, writes that *zinute* means 'fornication.'[80] Unfortunately, he doesn't list any

---

[75] C. F. Keil and F. Delitzsch, *Commentary on the Old Testament*, vol. 10: *Minor Prophets* (Peabody, MA: Hendrickson Publishers, 2001), p. 55.

[76] Ibid.

[77] Ibid., pp. 55-56.

[78] Ibid., p. 54.

[79] Davidson, *The Analytical Hebrew and Chaldee Lexicon* (Grand Rapids, MI: Zondervan Pub. House, 1979), p. 240.

[80] R. L. Harris, Editor; Gleason Archer, Jr. and Bruce Waltke, Associate Editors, *Theological Wordbook of the Old Testament*, vol. I (Chicago: Moody Press,

cites, either, but both men will flesh out their meaning of 'whoredom' and 'fornication' when they speak of the verb that *zinute* comes from.

The Hebrew term that James used in Acts 15:20 for the second rule, *zinute*, which Brown translates as 'fornication,' overwhelmingly refers to cult prostitution (from the cites that he lists). Only one time did he note a figurative sense (Israel's rebellion against Yahveh; Num. 14:33).

From its biblical context and usage in the lexicons, the word that Yakov used in Acts 15:20 conveys the idolatrous sin of cult harlotry. In Hosea the context revealed its idolatrous meaning. This principle of context also applies to the four rules of James. The placement of *zinute* (prostitution) immediately after the first rule on sacrificial idolatry points directly to cult prostitution and not common prostitution (nor adultery, incest or any other form of illicit sex). It's also the primary meaning of the word in Scripture.

The Hebrew verb will deepen this understanding that the word that James used that day spoke of cult harlotry. It would have been understood as such by all the Jewish believers there. This, despite the fact that other forms of unlawful sex can be associated with its secondary meaning.

## *The Hebrew Verb Zanah (to Prostitute)*

Hebrew nouns generally come from the verbs. *Zinute* is derived from the Hebrew verb זָנָה (*zanah*).[81] Francis Brown says that it means,

> to 'commit fornication, be a harlot...be or act as a harlot...Gen. 38:24...Dt. 22:21...improper intercourse with foreign nations...intercourse with other *deities*, considered as harlotry, sometimes involving *actual prostitution*...Ex. 34:15-16; Dt. 31:16; Lev. 17:7... especially of Israel, Judah and Jerusalem...*figuratively* of a lewd woman, Ezk. 16:15...moral defection, Is. 1:21.'[82]

Brown's primary meaning is 'harlotry' ('commit fornication...harlot') and cult harlotry ('actual prostitution...especially Israel, Judah and Jerusalem') and as we'll see, these primarily refer to cult harlotry.

Brown's reference for Gen. 38:24 is to harlotry in general. It can't be determined if it's cultic or common. Dt. 22:21 speaks of a new bride being accused of not being a virgin. She was classified as a harlot because she *acted* like a harlot (in having sex outside of marriage). Her punishment for

---

1980), p. 246.

[81]   Davidson, *The Analytical Hebrew and Chaldee Lexicon*, p. 240.

[82]   Brown, *The New Brown, Driver, Briggs, Gesenius Hebrew and English Lexicon*, p. 275.

not being a virgin was death by stoning. The Lord takes promiscuity very seriously.

Brown's cite of Ex. 34:15-16 shows Yahveh speaking of actual cult prostitution, as Brown states. God says,

> 'otherwise you might make a covenant with the inhabitants of the land and they would *play the harlot with their gods* and *sacrifice* to their gods and someone might *invite you to eat of his sacrifice* and you might take some of his daughters for your sons and his daughters might *play the harlot with their gods* and cause your sons also *to play the harlot* with their gods.'

Obviously, these harlots are cult harlots ('gods...eat of his sacrifice,' etc.). In the section on *Israel and Baal Peor* (p. 39f.) Israel engages in cult prostitution even before they reach the Promised Land. Brown's Deuteronomy passage (31:16; as well as his cite in Lev. 17:7) is similar in nature:

> "Yahveh said to Moses, 'Behold! You are about to lie down with your fathers and this people will arise and *play the harlot* with the *strange gods* of the land, into the midst of which they are going and will forsake Me and break My Covenant which I have made with them.'" (Dt. 31:16)

These cites all deal with cult prostitution, not only on physical and sexual levels, but also on spiritual and covenantal levels. Brown goes on to relate how Israel, Judah and Jerusalem could be called *harlots* in their going after other gods, which again refers to cult harlotry. He then speaks of the figurative (and derogatory) description of a *lewd woman*, but this woman is none other than Judah in her sin of sexual idolatry! Ezekiel 16:15 states,

> 'But you trusted in your beauty and *played the harlot* because of your fame and you poured out your *harlotries* on every passer-by who might be willing.'

As we'll see in a moment, the 'harlotry' of Judah that Ezekiel speaks of is cultic (Ezekiel 16). She was taken into captivity because she worshiped the gods of the fertility cults. Sacrifice and sexual harlotry figured prominently in the fertility cults and this is what made Judah a 'lewd woman.'

In Isaiah 1:21 the prophet uses the verb *zanah* (harlotry) to describe Jerusalem and her ungodly behavior—unfaithfulness, harlotry and murder. These fall under desertion of the Mosaic Covenant. Here, *zanah* is used in both a literal and figurative sense, Jerusalem having *sold herself* to things of unrighteousness, one of which was cult harlotry (as her history speaks of). Although other behavior can be spoken of as 'harlotry,' Brown's *pri-

*mary* meaning of 'to commit fornication' is cult harlotry.

Benjamin Davidson states that *zanah* means 'to commit whoredom, play the harlot; *frequently* also to commit *spiritual whoredom* or idolatry.'[83] In speaking of 'whoredom' and 'idolatry,' Davidson reveals the usage of the word as cult harlotry.

According to the *Theological Lexicon of the Old Testament* the basic meaning of *zanah* is,

> 'to whore, commit harlotry (of the woman; Num. 25:1 of the man).'[84]

It also states that originally it referred to 'unregulated, illicit sexual behavior between man and woman.'[85] This last phrase is a poor definition for *zanah* because it can speak of adultery. An adulteress can be called a harlot, but *only* in a derogatory sense. Adultery is not prostitution. When Scripture speaks of prostitution the context determines if it's common or cultic. As we've seen, the overwhelming majority of the references to *harlotry* are indeed idolatrous.

*TLOT* also says that a Hebrew who committed harlotry was 'an abomination in Israel' (Lev. 19:29) and that the word is used in a figurative sense 'to describe apostasy from Yahweh (*sic*) and *conversion* to other gods.'[86] It states, 'To whore away from Yahweh is synonymous with adultery.'[87] This is true on a spiritual level. Israel was Yahveh's unfaithful wife for most of eight centuries (1400–600 BC). Literally, though, as a people, they were practicing cult harlotry. That doesn't mean that common prostitution was unheard of, but idolatry mixed with sex was their gross sin. This is affirmed by what *TLOT* says concerning Jeremiah (and Hosea):

> 'The high hills, mountains, and green trees (2:20; 3:6) are *named as the sites of the harlotry* (as already *in Hosea* 4:13), apparently specific *Baalistic cultic* sites.'[88]

*TDOT* also states that Jeremiah was speaking of cult harlotry:

> "Jeremiah frequently uses the symbolism of *marriage*.

---

[83]   Davidson, *The Analytical Hebrew and Chaldee Lexicon*, p. 240.

[84]   Ernst Jenni and Claus Westermann, Authors; Mark E. Biddle, Translator, *Theological Lexicon of the Old Testament*, Volume 1 (Peabody, MA: Hendrickson Publishers, 1997), p. 389. The two cites that *TLOT* gives (Lev. 19:29; 21:9) specifically speak of harlotry, not adultery.

[85]   Ibid.

[86]   Ibid.

[87]   Ibid.

[88]   Ibid.

> Referring to Jer. 2:20 and Canaanite cultic practices he
> says, 'Upon every high hill and under every green tree
> you bowed down as a *harlot*' (Jer. 2:20)."[89]

*TDOT* states that Jeremiah compares this apostasy to adultery (Jer. 3), and says that Judah 'participates in the syncretistic *cult*.'[90] In Jer. 3 the adultery of Israel is linked with idols, which can only mean cult harlotry ('under every high hill,' Jer. 3:1-2; 6-9, 13, 20-21). Both *TLOT* and *TDOT* present the harlotry of Israel and Judah as Baal worship. Repeatedly, Israel and Judah are admonished and rebuked for sacrificial-sexual idolatry in their unfaithfulness as Yahveh's wife. Israel and Judah were heavily involved in cult prostitution. Their adultery was also seen as figurative because of their covenant-marriage to Yahveh (Jer. 3:1, 7-8, 20, etc.).

The *Theological Wordbook of the Old Testament* states that *zanah* means, to 'commit fornication, be a harlot, play the harlot.'[91] The linking of the English word 'fornication' with to 'play the harlot' reveals how 'fornication' is used by many academics. *In none of the lexicons, however,* has 'fornication' meant actual adultery between two human beings. Only in terms of its figurative use does it relate to Israel as an adulteress.

Translating *zinute* (harlotry) in Acts 15:20, as *sexual immorality*, one would be hard pressed to understand that its primarily use in Hebrew means cult harlotry. This is the problem with using 'sexual immorality' or 'illicit sex' to translate the second rule of Acts 15:20.

The *Theological Dictionary of the New Testament* states that the Hebrew word for harlotry can be used in figurative ways. People or nations can sell themselves to something other than God, yet Tyre and Nineveh were noted for their cult harlotry:

> 'In a few instances זנה' (*zanah*, to commit prostitution) 'is
> used figuratively in a different sense for the commerce
> which woos other peoples and the political devices which
> ensnare them. Thus Isaiah 23:15-18 refers to Tyre' as 'the
> forgotten harlot,' while Nahum 3:1-7 speaks of the whore
> Nineveh, who 'enmeshed the peoples with her harlotry
> and the nations with her magical arts, v. 4.'[92] It can also
> be used as a warning 'against surrender to the alien secu-

---

89 Botterweck, *TDOT*, vol. IV, pp. 102-103

90 Ibid., p. 103.

91 Harris, *Theological Wordbook of the Old Testament*, vol. I, p. 246.

92 Gerhard Kittel and Gerhard Friedrich, Editors; Geoffrey W. Bromiley, Translator and Editor, *Theological Dictionary of the New Testament*, vol. VI (Grand Rapids, MI: Wm. B. Eerdmans Publishing Company, 1999), p. 587.

lar wisdom of Greece.'[93]

William Wilson summarizes *zanah* and even though he doesn't specifically mention *cult* harlotry, we can see it in his use of *fornication*, etc:

> 'to commit fornication, to play the whore or harlot ...spoken of a female, *whether married or unmarried* ...Trop. of idolatry;[94] the relation existing between God and' Israel 'being...shadowed forth by the prophets under the emblem of...marriage...Hos. 1–2; Ezek. 16; 23, so that in *worshipping other gods*' they 'are compared to a harlot and adulteress. It is also said of superstitions connected with idolatry, Lev. 20:6, as to consult wizards, etc...to depart from the faith...due to God...whoredom, fornication' or 'any breach of fidelity towards God, e.g. of a murmuring and seditious people...metaph. for *idol worship*.'[95]

All the literal definitions of *zanah* speak of harlotry, a harlotry that is primarily cultic. This is how all the ancient peoples worshiped their gods and this is what enticed Israel. Scripturally, adultery is not harlotry. In Israel's case, however, because the harlotry of Israel involved other gods, this made her both a 'cult harlot' and a spiritual 'adulteress.' *TDOT* states,

> 'Because Jerusalem...committed *fornication* even though Yahweh (sic) made a covenant with her, her *fornication* is equivalent to adultery.'[96]

Jerusalem, in committing fornication, figuratively became an adulteress. The *Theological Dictionary of the Old Testament* further affirms that *zanah* primarily speaks of Israel's cult harlotry by stating that most 'of the occurrences of *zanah* and its derivatives' refer 'to Israel's faithlessness toward Yahweh *and worship of other gods*.'[97]

*TDOT*'s 'faithlessness' speaks of Israel worshipping 'other gods.' This can only be cult harlotry, which figuratively made Israel a spiritual adulteress. Biblically, the *primary* definition of *zanah* (prostitution) and its derivatives is a *prostitution* that is cultic. Ezekiel's rebuke of Judah vividly reveals this. It overflows with references to cult harlotry.

---

[93]  Ibid., p. 586.

[94]  Sinclair, *Collins English Dictionary*, p. 1637. 'Trop.' is an abbreviation for trope, which means 'a word or expression used in a figurative sense.'

[95]  William Wilson, *Wilson's Old Testament Word Studies* (Peabody, MA: Hendrickson Publishers, no publishing date given), p. 480.

[96]  Botterweck, *Theological Dictionary of the Old Testament*, vol. IV, p. 104.

[97]  Ibid., p. 99.

*TDOT* states that chapters '16 and 23 in particular use *sexual terminology* to depict the apostasy of the people.'[98] In these two chapters, *zanah* and its derivatives occur 42 times. In all the Old Testament the terms occur about 134 times.[99] In other words, more than 31% of the occurrences are in these two chapters where the prophet is denouncing Judah for her cult harlotry, not common harlotry, incest, homosexuality, adultery or premarital sex.

Cult harlotry was rampant in Judah before the Babylon destroyed Jerusalem, and *TDOT* confirms this by saying that Judah 'gave herself over to the worship of Canaanite gods' (Ezk. 16:16).[100] This 'worship' involved cult harlotry. *TDOT* also writes that the idolatry was 'adultery with disgraceful idols,'[101] another confirmation of Judah's lust for cult harlotry.

The lexicons reveal that *zanah* primarily refers to cult harlotry. God was in covenant with Israel and Judah and when they 'played the cult harlot' they were being unfaithful to Him, and so, the figurative meaning of an adulteress is also used to convey their sexual unfaithfulness and rebellion.

Both the Hebrew noun and verb reveal that Yakov's word primarily refers to cult harlotry, which, placed after Yakov's first rule on the prohibition of sacrificial meat at the pagan shrine, sets in motion the conceptual framework that the last two rules will also belong to the category of sacrificial-sexual idolatry. The Hebrew participle (*zonah*) will cement the meaning of the word in the English language as a harlot, and as we'll see, primarily a cult harlot. It will also reveal that adultery or illicit sex cannot possibly be what Yakov meant for his second rule in Acts 15:20.

---

[98] Ibid., p. 103.

[99] Jenni, *Theological Lexicon of the Old Testament*, Volume 1, p. 389.

[100] Botterweck, *Theological Dictionary of the Old Testament*, vol. IV, p. 103.

[101] Ibid., p. 104.

# *The Hebrew Participle Zonah (Prostitute)*

The Hebrew word used to describe the person who commits *zinute* (noun: prostitution; common or cultic) and who practices *zanah* (verb: to commit prostitution; common or cultic) is זוֹנָה (*zonah*). In English the meaning of *zonah* revolves around three synonymous words: *prostitute, whore* and *harlot,* and only these. Francis Brown[102] and Benjamin Davidson[103] describe such women as 'harlots.' *TDOT* states that the verb *zanah,*

> 'is the usual word for the activity of a harlot or prostitute; she is...called a *zonah*' (harlot) and that it's used 'of Tamar (Gen. 38), Rahab (Josh. 2:1; 6:17, 22, 25)' and 'the mother of Jephthah (Judges 11:1), etc.'[104]

There's no mention of an adulteress, only a harlot. Of the 138 times that the various terms for *harlotry* are used in the Old Testament, 110 times they specifically mean cult harlotry. Twenty-six times it can be either, but not once does it refer to *only* common harlotry. Here are the 11 terms and times of use in English from the King James Version Old Testament:

| Term | Occurs | Cultic | Either | Common | Neither |
|---|---|---|---|---|---|
| 1. Fornication | 4 | 4 | 0 | 0 | 0 |
| 2. Fornications | 1 | 1 | 0 | 0 | 0 |
| 3. Harlot | 37 | 30 | 7 | 0 | 0 |
| 4. Harlot's or harlots | 6 | 4 | 2 | 0 | 0 |
| 5. Prostitute | 1 | 0 | 1 | 0 | 0 |
| 6. Whore | 10 | 3 | 7 | 0 | 0 |
| 7. Whoredom | 22 | 20 | 2 | 0 | 0 |
| 8. Whoredoms | 32 | 31 | 0 | 0 | 1 |
| 9. Whore's or whores | 3 | 2 | 1 | 0 | 0 |
| 10. Whoring | 19 | 13 | 5 | 0 | 1 |
| 11. Whorish | 3 | 2 | 1 | 0 | 0 |
| **Totals** | **138** | **110** | **26** | **0** | **2** |

The five times that *fornication*[105] and its plural[106] are used speak of cult

---

[102] Brown, *NBDBG*, p. 275. From the Hebrew: *house of harlotry* (Jer. 5:7) and *women harlots* (1st Kings 3:16).

[103] Davidson, *The Analytical Hebrew and Chaldee Lexicon*, p. 240.

[104] Botterweck, *TDOT*, vol. IV, p. 99. Tamar posed as a cult harlot and Rahab was a cult harlot. Jephthah's mother may have been a cult or common harlot.

[105] *Accordance Bible Software*, version 9.2.1 (Altamonte Springs, FL: OakTree Software, 2010). *Fornication*: 2nd Chron. 21:11; Is. 23:17; Ezk. 16:26, 29.

harlotry. 30 of the 37 times that *harlot* appears specifically speak of Israel and Judah, etc., practicing cult harlotry.[107] The other seven times could be either a cult or a common harlot. *Harlots* and *harlot's* appear six times; four times it's a cult harlot, with one of those times being the specific term for cult harlotry (קְדֵשָׁה *kiday'sha*).[108] (More on that in the next chapter.)

*Prostitute* is mentioned once and includes cult harlotry.[109] Three of the ten times that *whore* is used speak of cult harlotry, while the rest could be either cult or common harlotry.[110] 20 of 22 times that *whoredom* is seen,[111] and 31 of the 32 times that *whoredoms* is written, specifically refer to cult harlotry.[112] Of the three times that *whores* or *whore's* are used, twice it refers to a cult harlot and once to either a cult or a common harlot.[113] 18 of the 19 times that *whoring* is seen include cult harlotry,[114] and two of three times that *whorish* is used specifically speak of cult prostitution.[115]

---

[106] Ibid., *Fornications:* Ezk. 16:15.

[107] Ibid., Three times the word for 'harlot' is *kiday'sha* (literally *cult* harlot; Gen. 38:21 (twice), 22. The rest are *zonah* (harlot), which in these cites speak of a cult harlot: Gen. 38:15, 24; Josh. 6:17, 25; Hos. 2:5; 3:3; 4:15.

These next cites speak of Israel, Judah or Jerusalem as a *zonah* (harlot), which means they practiced cult harlotry: Is. 1:21; 23:15-16; Jer. 2:20; 3:1, 6, 8; Ezk. 16:15-16, 28, 31, 35, 41; 23:5, 19, 44; Nahum 3:4; Micah 1:7 (3 times). These next seven cites of *zonah* refer to either a cult and/or a common harlot: Gen. 34:31; Lev. 21:14; Judges 11:1; 16:1; Prov. 7:10; Joel 3:3; Amos 7:17.

[108] Ibid., *Harlots*: 1st Kgs. 3:16; Prov. 29:3; (the first two cites aren't necessarily cult harlots, but can be); Jer. 5:7; Hos. 4:14. *Harlot's*: Josh. 2:1; 6:22.

[109] Ibid., *Prostitute* in Lev. 19:29 could be either cultic and/or common.

[110] Ibid., *Whore* as cult harlot: Dt. 23:17-18 (v. 17 *kiday'sha*); Ezk. 16:28.

*Whore* as either a cult or a common harlot: Lev. 19:29; 21:7, 9; Deut. 22:21; Judg. 19:2; Prov. 23:27; Is. 57:3.

[111] Ibid., *Whoredom* as cult prostitution: Lev. 20:5; Num. 25:1; Jer. 3:9; 13:27; Ezk. 16:17, 33; 20:30; 23:8, 17, 27; 43:7, 9; Hos. 1:2; 4:10-11, 13-14, 18; 5:3; 6:10. *Whoredom* as either: Gen. 38:24; Lev. 19:29.

[112] Ibid., *Whoredoms* as cult harlotry: 2nd Kgs. 9:22; 2nd Chr. 21:13; Jer. 3:2; Ezk. 16:20, 22, 25-26, 34 (twice), 36; 23:3 (twice), 7-8, 11 (twice); 14, 18-19, 29 (twice), 35, 43; Hos. 1:2 (twice); 2:2, 4; 4:12; 5:4; Nah. 3:4 (twice).

*Whoredoms* as unfaithfulness (Num. 14:33). This is figurative prostitution.

[113] Ibid., *Whores* as cult harlots: Ezk. 16:33; Hos. 4:14; as either: Jer. 3:3.

[114] Ibid., *Whoring* as cult harlotry: Ex. 34:15-16 (twice); Dt. 31:16; Judg. 2:17; 8:33; Ezk. 6:9; 23:30; Hos. 4:12; 9:1; 1st Chron. 5:25; 2nd Chron. 21:13; Ps. 106:39. *Whoring* as either cult and/or common prostitution: Num. 15:39; Ps. 73:27. *Whoring* as sacrificial idolatry, which includes cult harlotry: Lev. 17:7; 20:5. *Whoring* as idolatry, which is cult prostitution: Judges 8:27. *Whoring* as witchcraft, which doesn't speak of literal prostitution: Lev. 20:6.

Of the 138 words associated with harlotry, 112 times (81.2% of the time) they *specifically* speak of *cult* harlotry, while 24 times (17.4%) cult harlotry is included. This means that 136 out of 138 times (98.6%) these words refer to *cult* harlotry. The *harlotry* that God repeatedly came against in the Old Testament was overwhelmingly cultic, not common.

The Hebrew word that Yakov used that day (*zinute*–harlotry) spoke of cult harlotry, if only used by itself, but coming immediately after the first rule on sacrificial idolatry it emphatically cements the point that Yakov was speaking of *cult* harlotry, not common harlotry, and certainly not adultery, nor the vague term 'sexual immorality.' The next two rules, *blood* and *things strangled,* are also part of sacrificial idolatry. All four rules together form Yakov's conceptual unit on sacrificial-sexual idolatry.

This Hebrew word study has begun to take the foundation out from under those who translate Yakov's word as 'sexual immorality' or adultery, etc. Not even *common* harlotry can be what Yakov meant because it's certainly not the primary meaning of the word, nor does it fit into the first rule's context of sacrificial idolatry.

This also begins to show how unwarranted the teaching is that the four rules were given because the 'weaker Jewish brethren' clung to the 'outdated' Law and didn't know any better. The Council of Acts 15 was called to decide *what* constituted salvation *for the Gentile.* Acts 15:20, with its four rules, underscored that issue. The rules had nothing to do with table fellowship, but were a litmus test for genuine faith in Yeshua. This, in turn, will dismantle the false teaching that 'the Law is done away with.'

Is it really possible that all the Jewish Apostles living in Jerusalem somehow missed the Lord on *His* understanding of the Law in Acts 15, so many years *after* the resurrection (Mt. 13:10-11; Acts 1:1-3; 21:20)? Were they 'weaker' in their faith because they kept the Law of Moses—or is it possible that the Church is deceived with its paradigm of a 'Law-free Gospel'?

The next three sections will emphasize that *zonah* is a definition for a cult harlot, even when English Bibles only have *harlot,* and also bring out how thoroughly immersed ancient Israel was in cult harlotry. These chapters will round out Yakov's 'Family History' and why he gave these four prohibitions on sacrificial-sexual idolatry to the Gentile believers first.

---

[115] Ibid., Whorish as cult harlotry: Ezk. 6:9; 16:30; as either: Prov. 6:26.

# JUDAH AND TAMAR

The story of Judah and Tamar (Gen. 38) reveals that the term *zonah* (female prostitute) is synonymous for a cult prostitute and is conceptually the same as the specific Hebrew word for a cult prostitute קְדֵשָׁה (*kiday'sha*). Genesis 38 uses these two different Hebrew words for Tamar, but at first it's impossible to know if Judah thought that she was a common or a cult harlot because the text around the first times that *zonah* is used isn't descriptive enough to determine what kind of harlot Scripture is speaking of. Further on in the story, though, Judah's understanding about her is seen when his friend Hirah (Gen. 38:12, 20) uses קְדֵשָׁה (*kiday'sha*; cult harlot) to describe Tamar as the cult harlot that he couldn't find.

Tamar had veiled herself and had sat down by the road. She had made herself to look like a prostitute in order to deceive Judah. Not recognizing that it was his daughter-in-law, Judah speaks of her as a *zonah*, a harlot (לְזוֹנָה *lih'zonah*, to be a harlot, Gen. 38:15). What kind of a harlot (common or cultic) can't be determined from this verse.

After three months Tamar is found to be pregnant. She's charged by Judah with being a harlot and being with child by whoredom (*zanah*, KJV v. 24 twice). Did it mean that Judah now thought that Tamar was a cult harlot? From this verse, also, it can't be determined since the context neither reveals nor describes what Judah was thinking. There are two possibilities: Judah thought that Tamar had become pregnant by common or cultic harlotry.

The only way to tell what kind of harlot Judah thought he had encountered that day, who was sitting by the road, is from vv. 21-22. Three times the specific word for a female cult harlot is used. When Hirah tries to locate the harlot, to bring her wages to her, he specifically speaks of a *kiday'sha* (cult harlot). The men of the place told him that there hadn't been any *kiday'sha* there. Hirah returns and tells Judah that he couldn't find the *kiday'sha* (v. 21 twice, v. 22 once).

Davidson defines *kiday'sha* as a 'prostitute...devoted to prostitution *in honor of idols.*'[116] The NASB (vv. 21-22) calls her a '*temple* prostitute' and the NIV, a '*shrine* prostitute.' Unfortunately, the KJV and NKJV only use *harlot* for vv. 21-22, concealing the true meaning of the biblical word.

The use of the specific Hebrew word for a female cult harlot (*kiday'sha*), speaking of the same person who is also described as a harlot in Genesis 38:15 (and v. 24), reveals that *zonah* (harlot) is *interchangeable* with the specific Hebrew word for a female *cult* harlot. When *harlot* is mentioned

---

[116] Davidson, *The Analytical Hebrew and Chaldee Lexicon*, p. 654.

in vv. 15 and 24 we now realize that Judah thought she had been a cult harlot and not a common one. Davidson, the NASB and the NIV confirm this for vv. 21-22.

*The Illustrated Bible Dictionary* also confirms that *zanah* can specifically refer to cult prostitution and is identical with it. *IBD* writes,

> 'Tamar is described as both a harlot (Gen. 38:15) and a cult prostitute (Gen. 38:21, RSV mg.). The two Heb. words are used as parallels in Ho. 4:14.'[117]

The word for a prostitute (*zonah*) is conceptually the same as the specific term for a female cult harlot (*kiday'sha*). *TWOT* adds another confirmation when it writes of *temple* prostitutes, saying that 'the usage may be extended to refer to prostitution in general.'[118]

The use of *zonah* for a cult prostitute is almost 4,000 years old. In other words, it was already ancient in the days of James 2,000 years ago. He could speak of 'harlotry' (*zinute*) and *everyone* would have known that he meant cult harlotry. The use of the Greek word for a *harlot* will also equate her with cult harlotry, context determining if it's cultic or common.

The primary emphasis in both Scripture and in authoritative definitions of the Hebrew words for *prostitution* and *prostitute* reveal its overwhelming cultic use. With Tamar there's no question that what the KJV translates as 'harlot' means *cult harlot*.When a Jew like Yakov spoke of harlotry, having already begun with his first rule on *sacrificial* idolatry, there was certainly no need for him to elaborate about what kind of harlotry he meant. Everyone knew he meant cult harlotry. The theme of Acts 15 is Gentile salvation. As sinful as common harlotry is, it doesn't, unlike cult harlotry, involve union with another god, which would mean loss of salvation. The chapter on *Jesus and Divorce* (p. 87f.) will further reveal this.

The four rules of Acts 15:20 are a conceptual unit. Yakov was warning the new Gentile believers that sacrificial-sexual idolatry would endanger their salvation. To assign the second rule to something other than cult prostitution cannot be supported by the usage of the word in the Old Testament. The section on *Israel and Baal Peor* will further support this.

---

[117] J. D. Douglas, M.A., B.D., S.T.M., Ph.D., Organizing Editor, *The Illustrated Bible Dictionary*, part 3 (Leicester, England: Inter-Varsity Press, 1998), p. 1289.

[118] Harris, *Theological Wordbook of the Old Testament*, vol. II, p. 788.

# ISRAEL AND BAAL PEOR

Before the Sons of Israel ever entered the Land that Yahveh had promised to them, she disgraced herself in cult prostitution. *Webster's* assigns orgies to the Greeks or Romans,[119] but the Assyrians and Babylonians who preceded them[120] already had orgies as part of their idolatrous worship, as did the Moabites. The story of Israel at Baal Peor is a story of unchecked idolatrous lust:

> 'While Israel remained at Shittim the people began to *play the harlot* with the daughters of Moab, for they invited the people *to the sacrifices of their gods* and the people *ate* and bowed down to their gods. So Israel *joined themselves* to Baal of Peor and Yahveh was angry with Israel. Yahveh said to Moses,'

> 'Take all the leaders of the people and execute them in broad daylight before Yahveh, so that the fierce anger of Yahveh may turn away from Israel!'

> "So Moses said to the judges of Israel, 'Each of you slay his men who have joined themselves to Baal of Peor.' Then behold! One of the Sons of Israel came and brought to his relatives a Midianite woman in the sight of Moses and in the sight of all the Congregation of the Sons of Israel while they were weeping at the doorway of the Tent of Meeting."

> 'When Phineas, the son of Eleazar, the son of Aaron the High Priest saw it, he arose from the midst of the Congregation and took a spear in his hand and he went after the man of Israel into the tent and pierced both of them through—the man of Israel and the woman, through the body. So the plague on the Sons of Israel was checked. Those who died by the plague were 24,000. Then Yahveh spoke to Moses saying,'

> 'Phineas, the son of Eleazar, the son of Aaron the High Priest has turned away My wrath from the Sons of Israel in that he was jealous with My jealousy among them so that I did not destroy the Sons of Israel in My jealousy.

---

[119] Henry Bosley Woolf, Editor in Chief, *Webster's New Collegiate Dictionary* (Springfield, MA: G. & C. Merriam Co., 1980), p. 802.

[120] Alexander Hislop, *The Two Babylons*, 2nd American edition (Neptune, NJ: Loizeaux Brothers, 1959), pp. 22, 48-49, 71-80.

"Therefore say, 'Behold! I give him My Covenant of Peace and it shall be for him and his descendants after him a covenant of a perpetual priesthood because he was jealous for his God and made atonement for the Sons of Israel.'" (Num. 25:1-13)

In commenting on what *Pinhas* (Phineas) did, *The Chumash* states:

'*Pinhas*...saved them from calamity' and 'put an end to the devastating plague that had taken 24,000 lives in retribution for the *orgy*[121] *of immorality* with the Moabite and Midianite women.'[122] The Hebrews had fallen into 'debauchery[123] and *idolatry*.'[124]

The worship of Baal Peor entailed all this, as did the worship of other pagan gods. The sacrifices the Sons of Israel offered to Baal Peor *bonded* them to the god. They ate the sacrificial meat (and possibly drank the sacrificial blood, although no mention is made of this), bowed down and worshiped this god and engaged in sexual orgies with the women, thereby *joining* themselves to Baal Peor (Num. 25:3). Yahveh was so angry that He was ready to destroy the whole Congregation of Israel, so great was their offense (Num. 25:11). This is *biblical* fornication and expressly what Yakov didn't want believing Gentiles doing in their pagan temples.[125]

The name 'Baal Peor' means that it was the god Baal associated with the top of a mountain called Peor. The god, also known as Baal (Lord) or Molech (King), originally signified Nimrod deified, the first king of Babylon.[126] To the Greeks Baal was known as Bacchus. The Philistines knew Baal as Dagon. He had other names in different countries and different times, but his bloodthirsty and licentious worship rites basically remained the same:

---

[121] Woolf, *Webster's New Collegiate Dictionary*, p. 802. Orgy: '1: secret ceremonial rites held in honor of an ancient Greek or Roman deity and usually characterized by ecstatic singing and dancing 2a: drunken revelry b: an excessive, sexual indulgence (as a wild party).'

[122] Rabbi Nosson Scherman & Rabbi Meir Zlotowitz, General Editors, *The Chumash*, 2nd edition: 2nd impression (Brooklyn, NY: Mesorah Publications, Ltd., Feb. 1994), p. 876.

[123] Woolf, *WNCD*, p. 289. Debauchery: '1a: an extreme indulgence in sensuality, b: orgies, 2a: archaic: seduction from virtue or duty.'

[124] Scherman, *The Chumash*, p. 876.

[125] This kind of pagan 'worship' was going on all over the world in Yakov's day. *Biblical fornication* is sexual idolatry. Paul had to deal with this same issue in Corinth (1st Cor. 6:15-19; 10:21).

[126] Hislop, *The Two Babylons*, pp. 230-231.

'The sun, as the great source of light and heat, was worshiped under the name of Baal.'[127] (This is one of the reasons why the mountains and the high places were used for
worship; they were 'closer' to the heavens.) '*Infants* were
the most acceptable offerings at his altar...with the priest
of Baal *eating of the human sacrifice.*'[128]

It's not mentioned that Israel sacrificed their infants in Num. 25, but they
could have, for all too often the Bible confirms such monstrous events.[129]
If infant sacrifice happened at Baal Peor, it would only be an additional
reason for Yahveh's fierce anger against Israel.

In Num. 25:1 the Hebrew verb זָנָה (*zanah*) is used. It means 'to commit
whoredom, play the harlot; *frequently*' involving 'idolatry.'[130] Israel was
certainly playing the harlot. All idolatry is sin, but not all idolatry involves
cult prostitution. *Zanah,* in the context of idolatry, *always* speaks of sexual
*apostasy*, and not the vague term 'sexual immorality.' King David in his
adultery with Bathsheba didn't apostatize, as great as his sin was. He slept
with another man's wife. He committed adultery, not cult harlotry. The
biblical basis for a divorce between two believers is cult harlotry, not
adultery. I'll explain why in the section on *Jesus and Divorce* (p. 87f.).

One could say that cult prostitution falls under the general term 'sexual
immorality,' but how would anyone know that the term *cult harlotry* was
what James meant if the English translation of the second rule is *sexual
immorality*? It's not possible.

Unfortunately, even with translations that use 'fornication,' the problem
arises of it being defined by the popular misunderstanding instead of the
biblical definition. The difference amounts to placing what Israel did under a heading that is very general ('sexual immorality' as most define 'fornication' today) as opposed to the specific understanding of the spirit and
practice in which they engaged in—sexual idolatry. This revealed Israel's
faithless and perverse heart. This is apostasy and Israel was guilty of it
many times in her history.

In Num. 25:3 the Hebrew verb that states that Israel joined herself to Baal
Peor is צָמַד (*tzah'mahd*). It means 'to be bound to, joined to.'[131] The noun
means, a 'pair, couple, yoke (of oxen, mules, horsemen).'[132] The verb also

---

[127] Ibid., p. 226.

[128] Ibid., pp. 231-232.

[129] Dt. 12:31; 2nd Kings 16:3; 17:17; 21:6, 10; 2nd Chron. 28:1-4; 33:5-6; Ps.
106:34-39; Jer. 7:31; Ezk. 20:31; 23:37, etc.

[130] Davidson, *The Analytical Hebrew and Chaldee Lexicon*, p. 240.

[131] Ibid., p. 646.

means, 'specif. of (a) *girl with two lovers*' and to 'be attached, *attach one-self*, specif. be (religiously) devoted.'[133] The Sons of Israel, eating of the idolatrous sacrifice, solemnized a spiritual marriage to Baal Peor. The orgies consummated it. This wasn't common harlotry.

Here was Israel, Yahveh's Bride, with another lover, Baal Peor, while the Groom was still in the House! The Shekinah Glory Cloud, the visible manifestation of Yahveh, was continually over the Holy of Holies in the Wilderness (except when it led the way to another camp, Ex. 40:34-38; Num. 10:33-34). Keil says,

> 'the people began to commit whoredom with the daughters of Moab: they accepted the invitations of the latter to a sacrificial festival of their gods, took part in their sacrificial meals, and even worshipped the gods of the Moabites, and indulged in the licentious worship of *Baal-Peor*...זָנָה' (*zanah* harlotry) 'construed with אֶל' (*el*, as we find in Num. 25:1) 'as in Ezek. 16:28, signifies to incline to a person, to attach one's self to him, so as to commit fornication. The word applies to carnal and spiritual whoredom.'

> "The lust of the flesh induced the Israelites to approach the daughters of Moab and form acquaintances and friendships with them, in consequence of which they were invited by them 'to the slain-offerings of their gods,' i.e. to the sacrificial festivals and sacrificial meals, in connection with which they also 'adored their gods,' i.e. took part in the idolatrous worship connected with the sacrificial festival."

> 'These sacrificial meals were celebrated in honor of the Moabite god *Baal-Peor*, so that the Israelites joined themselves to him. צָמַד' (*tzah'mahd*) 'in the *Niphal*, to bind one's self to a person. *Baal-Peor* is the *Baal* of *Peor*, who was worshipped in the city of Beth-Peor (Deut. 3:29; 4:46; see' also Num. '23:28), a Moabite *Priapus*,[134] in honor of whom women and virgins prostituted themselves. As the god of war, he was called *Chemosh*.'[135]

---

[132]  Ibid.

[133]  Brown, *NBDBG*, p. 855.

[134]  Sinclair, *Collins English Dictionary*, p. 1226. *Priapus*: '(in classical antiquity) the god of the male procreative power and of gardens and vineyards.'

[135]  Keil, *The Pentateuch*, pp. 790-791.

42

Those 24,000 Israelis and Baal Peor were walking hand in hand. If you would have asked any one of them if they still believed in Yahveh, they would have said, 'Of course!,' but there can be no 'pairing up' of Yahveh's people with another god. In doing this those Israelis weren't worshiping the one true God and Him only (see Jer. 16:10f.). This was biblical fornication (cult harlotry) and was dealt with by Pinhas, who rescued the rest of Israel from certain destruction. Would God's attitude toward other gods and cult harlotry change when the Gentiles came to believe in His Son? Of course not (Ex. 22:20; 34:12-16; Mal. 3:6; Heb. 13:8; Rev. 18:4-5).

The Hebrew verb in Num. 25:11, that Yahveh used to describe what He was going to do to Israel if Pinhas had not intervened, is כָּלָה (*kahl'lah*) in the Piel (intensive) form. It means, 'to complete, finish, end...to waste, ruin, destroy' and 'to cause to vanish.'[136] Yahveh was very angry with those Hebrews because of their whoring hearts. Israel was God's wife and the Lord was ready to annihilate the whole Camp. Everyone was effected by their sin because Israel, like the Body of Messiah, is seen as one entity by God.

*Unger's Bible Dictionary* states,

> 'the worship of Baal-Peor was a *temporary apostasy* brought about by the temptations to licentious[137] indulgence offered by the rites of that deity.'[138]

It's not without dry wit that *Unger's* writes that is was a *temporary apostasy*, since all who took part in it were killed. Note well the seductiveness of pagan worship with its appeal to the lust of the flesh (the sexual orgies). The Moabites weren't unusual in their 'sexual indulgence,' but representative of pagan worship *all over the world*. (This will be brought out in the chapter on *Cult Prostitution in the Ancient World*, p. 56f.) Yahveh abhorred it for His people Israel and so would Yakov in Acts 15:20 for the new Gentile believers. Israel was only a tiny island in an ocean of cult harlotry, and sadly enough, Israel all too often drank from the same polluted waters as the rest of the nations.

A number of times in the Old Testament God calls Israel *adulterous* or *a prostitute* (harlot)[139] because Israel went after other gods. This related to

---

[136] Davidson, *The Analytical Hebrew and Chaldee Lexicon*, p. 379.

[137] Woolf, *Webster's New Collegiate Dictionary*, p. 657. Licentious: 'lacking legal or moral restraints; esp: disregarding sexual restraints.'

[138] Merrill F. Unger, *Unger's Bible Dictionary* (Chicago: Moody Press, 25th printing, 1976), p. 514.

[139] Jer. 2:20; 3:1; Ezk. 16:1-31, etc.

their idolatry, not their personal marriage relationships. Israel's *adultery* was literally cult prostitution—'adultery' wasn't used for an individual who practiced cult or even common harlotry.

The *Dictionary of Biblical Imagery* explains that there were times that the word 'harlot' or 'harlotry' could be used for a wicked person or people, but that *cult* harlot was *the chief meaning* for the terms:

> "Individuals and the Israelite nation as a whole are accused of harlotry when they seek security from mediums and spiritists (Lev. 20:6), military might (Nahum 3:1-4), political alliances (Ezek. 23:5-6) or commerce (Is. 23:17). *Because they value material gain too highly,*" Israelis "who accept bribes and abandon God's plan of social justice are also considered harlots (Is. 1:21-23). *Above all these however, idolatry* stands as the most common cause for the epithet 'prostitute.'"[140]

There are many times in the history of God's people, in the Land that He gave to them, where Yahveh rebuked Israel through His servants the Prophets. From just after Yehoshua's (Joshua's) death, until the captivity in Babylon, Scripture abounds with Yahveh grieving and being angry with His people because of their cult prostitution. He wasn't speaking of individuals committing adultery, but the nation committing apostasy through sacrificial, sexual and spiritual idolatry.[141] Sometimes it would include worship of Yahveh, while other times it wouldn't, but every time it was very offensive to God and to those in Israel who were righteous (1st Kgs. 19:18).

Many sons of Israel were involved in cult prostitution at Baal Peor. They had sexual orgies and bound themselves to another god, having eaten of the sacrifices (Num. 25:2). This directly attacked and severed the covenant marriage relationship they had with Yahveh. To eat the meat of the sacrifice was to be *one with the god* to whom it was sacrificed to. This is the first prohibition in Acts 15:20 ('to keep away from the pollutions of idols;' i.e. the eating of sacrificial meat offered to the idol at the time of the sacrifice). The eating of the sacrificial meat went hand in hand with the idolatrous ceremony of cult prostitution. That's what an orgy is, a feast of flesh, both animal and human. The sexual orgy crudely symbolized union with Baal Peor, another name for Satan.

In the Mosaic sacrificial system the eating of the sacrifice was only done

---

[140] Ryken, *Dictionary of Biblical Imagery*, p. 677.

[141] In Malachi 2:10-16 God remonstrates the men of Judah for cult harlotry, and also, for dealing treacherously with their wives. This doesn't mean they're one and the same, but that both were being committed by them.

by the common Israeli upon entry into the Covenant (Ex. 12:3-10); for the official ratification of the Covenant by the Elders (Ex. 24:4-11); and for the sacrifice of Shalom (peace, communion, union). It was at the Shalom sacrifice that the Israeli, along with his family and friends, sat down with the priest and ate some of the meat of the sacrifice (Lev. 3:1-17).[142] This spoke of peace and *oneness* with Yahveh and of God being pleased with them. In pagan rituals the symbolism was the same, just counterfeit.

In Acts 15:20 James was concerned with the Gentiles continuing to practice sacrificial-sexual idolatry. They, like Israel before them, could think that worship of Jesus and Diana was acceptable, but Yahveh wouldn't share that view with them. The danger that Yakov envisioned for the new Gentile believers was that they might not think it wrong to maintain their previous gods along with Jesus. With its appeal to the lust of the flesh, this practice would destroy the Gentile believer's covenant with the God of Israel just as surely as it had those Israelis at Baal Peor. This is why James gave the second rule—the prohibition of cult prostitution.

Those who translate the word as 'sexual immorality' or 'unchastity,' etc., do a grave injustice to the Word of God and a gross disservice to English readers of the Bible. Why use a word or a term that has no specific meaning (e.g. 'sexual immorality') when the Hebrew word has such a clear and powerful meaning?

By using the general term 'sexual immorality' instead of 'cult prostitution,' many classify this most abhorrent sin of sexual apostasy with other non-apostasy related sexual sins like premarital sex or adultery. This, of course, has tremendous theological ramifications for Acts 15:20, as well as other implications (i.e. the understanding of marriage and what constitutes a biblical divorce when Jesus says that a biblical divorce cannot take place 'except for fornication' [Mt. 5:32], which the Church has traditionally interpreted as adultery).

From the Hebrew word meanings, from Genesis 38, and now from Israel's apostasy at Baal Peor, the meaning of Yakov's word has consistently meant cult prostitution. With Yakov's first rule speaking against sacrificial idolatry, and his second rule prohibiting cult harlotry, two strong points are established toward the concept that Yakov's four rules are various aspects of sacrificial-sexual idolatry designed to keep the new Gentile believer 'in the right way.' The four rules have nothing to do with table fellowship.

---

[142] Unger, *Unger's Bible Dictionary*, pp. 948-949. 'The sacrificial feast' enjoyed by both priest and offerer alike symbolized God and man at table. In the Middle East, no stronger picture of fellowship, union, peace, security and of being in the 'Kingdom of God' on Earth could be displayed.

Israel's history is filled with the sacrificial-sexual worship of other gods. Cult prostitution was devastating to ancient Israel, and one more reason why Yakov gave his four rules to the Gentiles first.

# CULT PROSTITUTION

# IN ANCIENT ISRAEL

A brief survey of cult prostitution and how it affected Israel will reveal what Yakov, and every other Jew, knew about their own Family History. It will again confirm why Yakov's second rule should be understood the way the Hebrew Scriptures define *zanah* (and also the way the Greek will define *zanah's* counterpart *pornay'ah*) as '*cult* prostitution' and not as the vague term 'sexual immorality,' which totally distorts Yakov's ruling.

Throughout the *Tanach* (the Hebrew Bible/Old Testament) there are many references to cult prostitution and its sway upon Israel. Yahveh forbid His people from practicing it or becoming cult prostitutes. *TDNT* states:

> 'The Deuteronomic Law unconditionally forbids cultic prostitution. No girl is to be a temple devotee, no man a קָדֵשׁ' (*kadaysh*, the specific term for a *male* temple prostitute), '23:17. Profits derived' (from cult harlotry) 'are not to be used on behalf of'[143] God's Temple.

God wasn't interested in tithes, or anything else, given by a cult prostitute, male or female. The term 'dog' was a loathsome epithet for the male cult prostitute, but this didn't stop some in Israel from walking in this perversion. *The Illustrated Bible Dictionary* writes:

> 'In Dt. 23:17-18, the contemptuous phrase, 'dog' evidently refers to a male cult prostitute. In Rehoboam's time' (935-919 BC) 'the presence of such male prostitutes became widespread (1st Kings 14:24). Asa, Jehoshaphat and Josiah attempted to root out this abomination (1st Kings 15:12; 22:46; 2nd Kings 23:7).'[144]

The reason why these men were called 'dogs' is because of the way they performed their sexual idolatry on other men. Keil writes that the *kadaysh* 'received his name for the dog-like manner in which the male...debased himself.'[145]

Here is cult prostitution as homosexual idolatry. The term 'dogs,' used as late as the last chapter of Revelation (22:15), reveals the practice was still observed as 'worship' in the final days of the Apostle John (95 AD). Both

---

[143] Kittel, *Theological Dictionary of the New Testament*, vol. VI, p. 586.

[144] Douglas, *The Illustrated Bible Dictionary*, part 3, p. 1289.

[145] Keil, *The Pentateuch*, p. 949.

male and female cult prostitution were widespread in Canaan before the Hebrews got there. *UBD* states,

> "Israel was in covenant with Yahveh, married to God, pledging herself to Him and Him only (Ex. 19:3; 20:2, etc.). *Idolatry* was 'a political crime of the gravest nature, *high treason against the King.* It was a transgression of the covenant (Dt. 17:2-3), *the evil*' (emphasis theirs) 'pre-eminently in the eyes of Jehovah (1st Kings 21:25). Idolatry was a great wrong because of the licentious rites associated with it (Romans 1:26-32), thus debauching[146] the morals of its adherents.'"[147]

Male cult prostitutes were designated by the specific word קָדֵשׁ (*kadaysh*). The female cult prostitute was known as קְדֵשָׁה (*kiday'sha*, the feminine form of the word). This is what Tamar made herself out to be (Genesis 38:21-22). Some might ask,

> 'If Yakov's second rule spoke of cult prostitution, why didn't he use the specific words for cult prostitutes?'

Yakov used the generally accepted standard word for cult prostitution, which was more than sufficient since it covered both male and female cult prostitutes. Also, his four rules weren't a theological dissertation on cult harlotry, but four short rules concerning sacrificial-sexual idolatry. *Because* of their brevity, we know that everyone there knew what they meant. Witherington states that,

> 'all four items in the decree were *shorthand* for things that took place in pagan temples.'[148]

Tim Hegg also adds an insight when he says that the rules must have been very well known among both Gentiles and Jews. He cites the use of the Greek definite article ('the') 'before each item in the initial listing,' saying that 'they represented well-known entities' and both peoples would have been able to identify the meanings by the 'single terms.'[149] Everyone understood that Yakov meant cult harlotry.

The history of Israel is one sad commentary after another; the people and their leaders indulged in cult harlotry year after year, century after centu-

---

[146] Woolf, *Webster's New Collegiate Dictionary*, p. 289. Debauch: '1a: archaic: to make disloyal, b: to seduce from chastity, 2a: to lead away from virtue or excellence, b: to corrupt by intemperance or sensuality.'

[147] Unger, *Unger's Bible Dictionary*, p. 949.

[148] Witherington, *The Acts of the Apostles*, p. 463, note 420.

[149] Tim Hegg, *The Letter Writer: Paul's Background and Torah Perspective* (Littleton, Co: First Fruits of Zion, 2002), p. 272.

ry. There are those who see the God of the Old Testament as a wrathful angry God 'out to get you' as soon as you make a mistake, but the love and *long-suffering* God of the Old Testament is abundantly evident in the *eight centuries* that He didn't destroy the generations of Hebrews that committed cult harlotry. He pleaded with them through His Prophets, although most of the time Israel was deaf to the One who had created her, set her free and loved her (2nd Kgs. 17:1-23; Jer. 26:5; 35:15).

After the time of Joshua, the problem of cult prostitution manifested itself among the people of God and kept them in chains of darkness. Israel wouldn't be rid of this abomination until the northern kingdom of Israel was obliterated by Assyria in 721 BC. One hundred and thirty-five years later (586 BC) the southern kingdom of Judah was decimated and a small remnant was taken into captivity by the King of Babylon, Nebuchadnezzar. *ISBE* states:

> 'In the period of the Judges' (about 1350-1080 BC) '*religious prostitution* was one of the basic causes of the degradation of the people (Judges 2:17). They came to worship both the priestly ephod and certain Baals by means of *sacred prostitution* (8:27-35).'[150]

*ISBE* explains that the reason for the destruction of both kingdoms was because the people of God were infatuated with cult harlotry:

> 'The captivity of the half-tribe of Manasseh resulted from their participation in the *religious prostitution* connected with the Canaanite gods (1st Chron. 5:25). The same can be said of the fall of both the northern and southern kingdoms as the idolatrous practices they followed included such rites (Ezk. 16:16-58).'[151]

After the days of King Solomon his son Rehoboam assumed the Throne (935 BC), but foolishness was in his heart. He wouldn't relieve the heavy taxes that his father had placed upon the people. Instead, he told them they 'hadn't seen anything yet.' This caused the Israelis in the north to rebel, thus tearing David's Kingdom in two (1st Kings 12).

Rehoboam's propensity for idolatry was an indication of his wickedness. Son of an Ammonite (pagan) mother, he 'perpetuated the worst features of Solomon's idolatry (1st Kings 14:22-24).'[152] The 'worst features' of idolatry means that he indulged in cult harlotry, and most likely, sacrificed his infant sons. From the time of Rehoboam to the Babylonian captivity

---

[150] Bromiley, *The International Standard Bible Encyclopedia*, vol. one, p. 617.

[151] Ibid.

[152] Unger, *Unger's Bible Dictionary*, p. 514.

(935-586 BC, approximately 350 years), Judah would more often than not walk against the Law or Instruction of God.[153] Hezekiah, a righteous king (715-686 BC) would restore and purify the Temple,

> 'which was *dismantled and closed* during the latter part of his' father's reign (2nd Chron. 28:24; 29:3). 'But the reform extended little below the surface (Isaiah 29:13). *Idolatry* spread fearfully in the last times of the kingdom of Judah, until it brought down on the people the punishment of captivity in Babylon.'[154]

It's sad to realize that the Temple of Yahveh in Jerusalem was closed because the people were more interested in pagan gods and goddesses (i.e. cult prostitution) than Yahveh. The reform of Hezekiah didn't last because the hearts of the people were lustful. Cult prostitution was an immense problem for the people of Judah—and for Yahveh.

King Josiah, another righteous king, began his reign in 640 BC.[155] When he ascended the Throne, male cult homosexuality was socially acceptable in the kingdom and was even being practiced in the Temple of Yahveh! *TDNT* states:

> 'Josiah's sharp attack, under which the houses of the *kedeshim*' (male and female cult prostitutes) 'in the Temple were destroyed, shows that the evil had made its way even into the Temple cultus in Jerusalem, 2nd Kings 23:7.'[156]

Cult harlotry severed the covenant protection that Israel had with Yahveh and opened them up to their enemies. Sacrificial-sexual idolatry was brazen unfaithfulness on the part of Israel. It was apostasy, yet Yahveh didn't immediately act upon it as He had at Baal Peor. It didn't mean, though, that the people escaped unscathed. *ISBE* writes:

> 'The degradation of the human being through *religious prostitution* becomes a figure for the spiritual infidelity that Israel and Judah show to God. The Old Testament

---

[153] The word *Torah* means, to teach, instruct or direct, and therefore, is not 'law' *per se*, but *the Teachings/Instructions of Yahveh for Israel*. Davidson, *The Analytical Hebrew and Chaldee Lexicon*, p. 346 states: The verb means, 'to teach, instruct,' and the noun means, 'instruction, direction, precept.'

[154] Ibid.

[155] There were righteous kings before Hezekiah, like Asa (911-870 BC) and Jehoshaphat (870-848 BC), but their attempts at reform didn't last any longer than Hezekiah's (2nd Chron. 14:1-15:19; 17:1-20:23).

[156] Kittel, *Theological Dictionary of the New Testament*, vol. VI, p. 586.

pictures Yahweh (sic) as the husband of Israel. For example, Israel and Judah are depicted as faithless sisters who
play the harlot, being unfaithful to their Beloved (see esp.
Jer. 3:1-3 and Ezk. 23). The deep religious significance of
such a figure is apparent when we see the *close connection between idolatry and religious prostitution*. To de-
monstrate the faithlessness of Israel, Yahweh commanded
the prophet Hosea to take a wife who had been a harlot.
Unable to break the habit of her former life, she became a
living representation of Israel's faithlessness to Yahweh.
Hosea filled the role of God, who was always willing to
forgive.'[157]

God's faithfulness and forgiveness have been from Creation. They didn't
begin with Jesus, but were magnified and culminate in Him.

The Hebrew language and perspective are very concrete, and therefore,
very simple. The abstract is brought into the physical realm so that all can
plainly understand what God is speaking about. Yahveh remonstrates His
people for worshiping *idols of wood and stone*. This refers to cult prostitution. *TDNT* states,

"In Isaiah 1:21, the 'city of Jerusalem, once faithful and
the refuge of the righteous, has now become a harlot.' In
Jer. 3:1-4:4, the prophet 'accuses Israel and Judah of playing the harlot with many lovers (3:2), of committing adultery with wood and stone...(3:9), and of defiling the Land
by their πορνειαι'" (Greek *pornay'ai*, harlotry).[158]

The *Dictionary of Biblical Imagery* explains that,

"Israel chose to follow the cults God had warned against
(Psalm 106:35-39). Through Jeremiah, God notes the nation's resulting brazen and degraded state in his accusation: On every high hill and under every spreading tree,
you lay down as a *prostitute*. How can you say, 'I am not
defiled, I have not run after the *Baals*?' You are a swift
she-camel running here and there, a wild donkey accus-
tomed to the desert, sniffing the wind in her craving; in
her heat who can restrain her? (NIV Jer. 2:20, 23-24)"[159]

Can there be any doubt as to the devastating effect cult prostitution had

---

[157] Bromiley, *The International Standard Bible Encyclopedia*, vol. two, p. 617.

[158] Kittel, *TDNT*, vol. VI, p. 587. The *Greek* word, from the book of Jeremiah,
comes from the Septuagint (the Greek Old Testament made about 260 BC).

[159] Ryken, *Dictionary of Biblical Imagery*, p. 677.

upon ancient Israel? Both the northern and southern kingdoms were wiped out because of it. When Gentiles would come to believe in Jesus, would they be excluded from personal catastrophe if they indulged in cult prostitution? In First Corinthians and Ephesians we see Paul addressing this very issue with the Gentiles (1st Cor. 10; Eph. 5:3, 5).

Hosea ministered to the northern kingdom from 760-722 BC. Isaiah served the Lord from 740-700 BC, and Jeremiah prophesied in the southern kingdom of Judah (626-585 BC), which fell to Babylon in his day. *TDNT* says,

> 'In *Jeremiah as in Hosea* the charge of *infidelity* goes hand in hand with an uncompromising rejection of the practice of *sacral prostitution* as this was found in the Canaanite cult, Jer. 2:20; 3:6; cf. Hos. 4:12-14.'[160]

Time after time Yahveh sent His Prophets to plead and to warn the people against their sacrificial-sexual apostasy, but to little avail. This did not take God by surprise (Dt. 28:49-68; 31:16) and shouldn't be used by some to declare God's permanent severing of Israel (Jer. 16:14-16; 33:6-26; Hosea 1:10-11; Joel 2:18-19; Zephaniah 3:8-20; Rom. 9–11, etc.).

Many ancient peoples would leave their female babies by the roadside because they were seen as a liability to raise (food and clothing). Pagan priests would come along and raise them for cult harlotry. In contrast to many in the ancient pagan world abandoning their female babies, Yahveh speaks to Judah, through the prophet Ezekiel, saying that He found Israel abandoned like that, but had compassion for her. As she grew to womanhood she betrayed her Benefactor and lusted after other gods. This both saddened and angered Yahveh. God's anger toward Israel, because of her impenetrable heart and idolatrous harlotry, is visibly seen in Ezekiel 16. His love and pain for her can also be felt:

> [16:4]"As for your birth, on the day you were born, your navel cord was not cut, nor were you washed with water for cleansing. You weren't rubbed with salt or even wrapped in cloths. [5]No eye looked with pity upon you to do any of these things for you, to have compassion upon you. Rather you were thrown out into the open field, for you were abhorred on the day you were born. [6]When I passed by you and saw you squirming in your blood, I said to you while you were in your blood, 'Live!' Yes, I said to you while you were in your blood, 'Live!'"

> [7]"I made you numerous like plants of the field. Then you

---

[160] Kittel, *Theological Dictionary of the New Testament*, vol. VI, p. 587.

grew up, became tall and reached the age for fine ornaments. Your breasts were formed and your hair had
grown. Yet, you were naked and bare. [8]Then I passed by
you and saw you and behold! You were at the time for
love so I spread My skirt over you and covered your
nakedness. I also swore to you and entered into a
Covenant with you so that you became Mine,' declares
the Lord Yahveh."

[9]'Then I bathed you with water, washed off your blood
from you and anointed you with oil. [10]I also clothed you
with embroidered cloth and put sandals of badger skin on
your feet and I wrapped you with fine linen and covered
you with silk.'

[11]'I adorned you with ornaments, put bracelets on your
hands and a necklace around your neck. [12]I also put a ring
in your nostril, earrings in your ears and a beautiful crown
on your head. [13]Thus, you were adorned with gold and silver and your dress was of fine linen, silk and embroidered
cloth. You ate fine flour, honey and oil and were exceed-
ingly beautiful and advanced to royalty.'

[14]"'Then your fame went forth among the nations on account of your beauty for it was perfect because of My
splendor which I bestowed upon you' declares the Lord
Yahveh. [15]'But you trusted in your beauty and *played the
harlot* because of your fame and you poured out your *harlotries* on every passer-by who might be willing. [16]You
took some of your clothes, made for yourself colorful
*shrines* and *played the harlot*. Nothing like this has ever
been or ever shall be.'"

[17]"'You also took your beautiful jewels made of My gold
and of My silver, which I had given you, and made for
yourself *male images* that you might *play the harlot with
them*. [18]Then you took your embroidered cloth and
covered them and offered My oil and My incense before
them. [19]Also, My bread, which I gave you, fine flour, oil
and honey with which I fed you, *you would offer before
them* for a soothing aroma. So it happened,' declares the
Lord Yahveh."

[20]'Moreover *you took your sons and daughters,* whom
you had borne to Me, and *sacrificed* them to idols to be
devoured. Were your harlotries so small a matter?! [21]You

slaughtered My children and offered them up to idols by causing them *to pass through the fire!*'

[22]"Besides all your abominations and harlotries you did not remember the days of your youth, when you were naked, bare and squirming in your blood. [23]Then it came about after all your wickedness. 'Woe! Woe to you!' declares the Lord Yahveh!,"

[24]"that you built yourself a *shrine* and made yourself *a high place* in every square. [25]You built yourself a high place at the top of every street and made your beauty abominable and you spread your legs to every passer-by to multiply your whoredom!' (Ezekiel 16:4-25)

Yahveh was very upset and rightfully so. He charged Judah with ungratefulness, unfaithfulness, sacrificial idolatry, cult harlotry and child sacrifice, even though He had caused her to have life, fed her with the finest foods, and clothed her with the finest garments. As the door opened to sacrificial idolatry and cult prostitution, it also led to the casting of their infants into the fires of the pagan gods (vv. 20-21). Judah played the harlot in following all the nations, murdering her own sons and daughters in the process (Ezk. 16:15-16, 18-22, 24-25). This is something so repulsive and nauseating that it's sickening to even think about it. In following the other peoples around them they had lost all sense of their humanity.

Yahveh had given life to Israel and exalted her as a free woman, but she chose to be enslaved to other gods. Left unchecked, the abomination spread like wildfire through both kingdoms. God had to deal with them. Both kingdoms were destroyed because of Israel's lust for the flesh—cult harlotry.

Sacrificial-sexual idolatry caused Yahveh to annihilate the northern kingdom and He decimated the southern kingdom and brought them into Babylonian captivity. The punishment seems to have impressed itself upon the remnant that survived of the kingdom of Judah. After the Babylonian captivity (606-536 BC; see Jer. 29:10 and also 25:11-12), never again do the Jewish people engage in sacrificial idolatry, cult prostitution or infant sacrifice. God had finally brought judgment upon His people. He severely punished them for cult prostitution. They had walked in the ways of the nations around them and had found out that there was an end to God's grace and long-suffering.

This historical background figures prominently into why Yakov gave the four rules on sacrificial-sexual idolatry to the Gentile believers, many of whom continued to walk in their paganism, along with 'belief' in Jesus.

Yakov's use of *zinute* (prostitution) means 'cult prostitution.' The context, word definitions and history of Israel point directly to this and nothing else. That's not to say that common harlotry was non-existent, but the rule that Yakov presented to the Gentile believer *specifically* dealt with cult harlotry. Any other suggestion as to its meaning (e.g. sexual immorality, unchastity, adultery, or even common prostitution) negates the history of cult harlotry within Israel, the biblical usage of the word and the use of *zinute* (harlotry) right after the first rule on sacrificial idolatry (which spoke of not eating meat sacrificed to an idol at the time of the sacrifice). With the first two rules speaking of sacrificial-sexual idolatry, is it unreasonable to assume that the third and fourth rules would, too?

Yakov was concerned about Gentile believers thinking that they could worship Jesus on the Sabbath and go to the temple of Diana on Sunday. The Apostle Paul would deal with cult prostitution among the Corinthians and other congregations he established (e.g. 1st Thess. 1:9; 4:1-8) and the Lord Jesus Himself would come against it in Revelation (2:14, 20).

What had happened in Israel was happening among the Gentile believers in the days of Peter, Paul and John! If it could happen in ancient Israel, where God commanded Israel *not* to do the things that the Gentiles did (Dt. 12:28-32), it could certainly happen among 'former pagan' Gentiles, who had never known a God like Yahveh, nor His commandments.

Yakov knew the primary biblical meaning for *zinute* (cult prostitution), and he was well aware of the underlying realities of *Judah and Tamar, Israel and Baal Peor* and *Cult Prostitution in Ancient Israel*. Most likely, the Holy Spirit was bringing all this to his remembrance that day. On the one hand, it doesn't have anything to do with, 'what the Gentiles must do to be saved.' On the other hand, it has everything to do with it. *Cult Prostitution in the Ancient World* will reveal that *the entire ancient world* was infested with cult prostitution, and it'll reinforce why Yakov saw the need to prohibit it among the new Gentile believers.

# CULT PROSTITUTION

# IN THE ANCIENT WORLD

A brief sketch of cult prostitution in the ancient world will yield more understanding and depth concerning the vast extent of idolatry in the Gentile world. It will also help explain why Yakov wanted the converted pagan Gentiles to stay away from their former places of 'worship.'

One of Alexander Hislop's themes in his classic work, *The Two Babylons,* is that all the pagan religions had their prototype in ancient Babylon. The *names* of the gods and goddesses would change over time and with each nation, but their pagan rites would basically remain the same. Because of this they could easily be linked back to Babylon. It was in Babylon that cult prostitution began and would spread all over the Earth:

> 'The Chaldean (Babylonian) Mysteries can be traced up to the days of Semiramis, who lived only a few centuries after the Flood and who is known to have impressed upon them the image of her own depraved and polluted mind. That beautiful, but abandoned Queen of Babylon was not only herself a paragon of unbridled lust and licentiousness, but in the Mysteries, which she had a chief hand in forming, she was worshipped as Rhea, the great 'Mother' of the gods, with such atrocious rites as identified her with Venus, the Mother of all impurity, and raised the very city where she had reigned to a bad eminence among the nations as the grand seat at once of idolatry and *consecrated prostitution*.'[161]

Semiramis, known as both the Queen of Heaven and *Ishtar* (the origin of 'Easter') allowed the worst lusts within man to surface and be validated as 'worship.' Cult prostitution in the ancient world was not only rampant, it was the accepted, noble and 'godly' fixture of pagan life. *ISBE* states:

> 'The Code of Hammurabi allowed female prostitutes at any temple. The Gilgamesh Epic pictures such a woman in connection with the temple of Ishtar.'[162]

Hammurabi was King of Babylon when Father Abraham was alive (18th century BC).[163] One of the practices of the Babylonian religion consisted

---

[161] Hislop, *The Two Babylons*, p. 5.

[162] Bromiley, *The International Standard Bible Encyclopedia*, vol. two, p. 617.

[163] Sinclair, *Collins English Dictionary*, p. 699.

in *every teenage daughter* losing her virginity in 'honor' of the Babylonian goddess Venus. *ISBE* writes that,

> 'the Babylonians *compelled* every native female to attend the temple of Venus once in her life and to prostitute herself in honor of the goddess.'[164]

This was *religion* in the Gentile world. *TDNT* adds that,

> it 'was a national custom in...which even daughters of prominent families followed and to which no shame attached.'[165]

This was the ancient world, carnal and deceived. Hislop writes:

> "We find from Herodotus that the peculiar and abominable institution of Babylon in prostituting virgins in honor of Mylitta was observed also in Cyprus in honor of Venus. But the positive testimony of Pausanias brings this presumption to a certainty. 'Near this,' says that historian, speaking of the temple of Vulcan at Athens, 'is the temple of Celestial Venus, who was first worshipped by the Assyrians and after these by the Paphians in Cyprus and the Phoenicians who inhabited the city of Ascalon in'" Israel.[166]

The Athenian Venus came to Athens from Assyria, which had gotten its Venus from Babylon. Hislop states that,

> 'the Assyrian Venus...the great goddess of Babylon, and the Cyprian Venus were one and the same.'[167]

Pausanias, whom Hislop was quoting, hadn't realized that Celestial Venus had been worshiped before the time of the Assyrians in Babylon, but such was the case because the Assyrian religion was modeled after the Babylonian system:

> 'Tarsus, the capital of Cilicia, was built by Sennacherib, the Assyrian king, *in express imitation of Babylon*. Its religion would naturally correspond.'[168]

Mylitta, whom Herodotus speaks of, was just another name for Venus, the Babylonian Queen Semiramis deified.[169] One of the 'great' goddesses of

---

[164] Bromiley, *The International Standard Bible Encyclopedia*, vol. two, p. 617.

[165] Kittel, *Theological Dictionary of the New Testament*, vol. VI, p. 581.

[166] Hislop, *The Two Babylons*, p. 157. (Vulcan is another name for Molech.)

[167] Ibid.

[168] Ibid.

ancient Greece was Aphrodite, but she was just the Babylonian Queen by another name:

> "This Babylonian queen was not merely in *character* co-incident with the Aphrodite of Greece and the Venus of Rome, but was in point of fact the *historical original* of that goddess that by the *ancient world* was regarded as the very embodiment of everything attractive in female form and the perfection of female beauty; for Sanchuniathon assures us that Aphrodite or Venus was identical with Astarte, and Astarte being interpreted is none other than, 'The woman that made towers or encompassing walls' (i.e. Semiramis).[170] The Roman Venus, as is well known, was the Cyprian Venus and the Venus of Cyprus is histor-ically proved to have been derived from Babylon."[171]

> "On the testimony of Augustine, himself an eye-witness, we know that the rites of Vesta, emphatically 'the virgin goddess of Rome,' under the name of Terra, were exactly the same as those of Venus, the goddess of impurity and

---

[169] Ibid., p. 304. 'This, then, was the case with the goddess recognized as Astarte or Venus, as well as with Rhea. Though there were points of difference be-tween Cybele or Rhea, and Astarte or Mylitta, the Assyrian Venus, Layard shows that there were also distinct points of contact between them. Cybele or Rhea was remarkable for her turreted crown. Mylitta or Astarte was repre-sented with a similar crown (Layard, *Nineveh and its Remains*, vol. ii. p. 456). Lions drew Cybele or Rhea; Mylitta or Astarte was represented as standing on a lion (ibid.). The worship of Mylitta or Astarte was *a mass of moral pollution* (Herodotus, *Historia,* lib. i. cap. 199, p. 92). The worship of Cybele, under the name of Terra, was the same (Augustine, *De Civitate Dei*, lib. vi. cap. 8, tom. ix., p. 203).'

Ibid., p. 310: 'We have evidence, further, that goes far to identify this title as a title of Semiramis. Melissa or Melitta (Apollodorus, *Bibliotheca,* vol. i. lib. ii. p. 110)—for the name is given in both ways—is said to have been the mother of Phoroneus, the first that reigned, in whose days the dispersion of mankind occurred, divisions having come in among them, whereas before, all had been in harmony and spoke one language (Hyginus, *Fabulae,* 143, p. 114). There is no other to whom this can be applied but Nimrod; and as Nimrod came to be worshipped as Nin, the son of his own wife, the identification is exact. Melitta, then, the mother of Phoroneus, is the same as Mylitta, the well known name of the Babylonian Venus, and the name, as being the feminine of Melitz, the Mediator, consequently signifies the Mediatrix.'

[170] Ibid., see pp. 30-32, 296-297, 318. The encompassing walls signified her asso-ciation with her husband Nimrod who was the first to make *walled* cities. This provided men with protection from wild animals and human enemies, and be-ing grateful for that, many submitted to him as the first human king.

[171] Ibid., pp. 74-75.

licentiousness. Augustine elsewhere says that Vesta, the virgin goddess, 'was by some called Venus.'"[172]

The pagans gloried in *cult harlotry*. It was authorized by their gods. Only Yahveh, the God of the tiny Hebrew nation, came against the ancient world's worship of lust.

Many times, by tracing the passing of a name from one language to another, the original name can be detected. An example of this is the Greek goddess Hestia, and the Roman version, Vesta. Hislop says that,

'In Greece she' (Semiramis) 'had the name of Hestia, and amongst the Romans, Vesta, which is just a modification of the same name.'[173]

Each city-state in ancient Greece had its founding god or goddess, as well as the importation of other gods and goddesses. *ISBE* states that families,

'worshiped Hestia, goddess of the hearth, Zeus as protector of the courtyard and their own gods and heroes.'[174] 'Each state worshiped Hestia, and also the god credited with its founding. Therefore, Athenians worshiped Athena, but Spartans venerated Zeus.'[175]

For a Gentile to worship many gods and goddesses was not uncommon, it was *normal*. This is the reason for the four rules. Cult prostitution was everywhere, but *TDNT* states that Corinth was especially noted for it:

'the temple of Aphrodite with its 1,000 hierodules[176] was famous, and an inscription recalls that the goddess answered their prayers for the threatened fatherland in a critical hour.'[177]

Cult harlotry thrived in Corinth. This is important in understanding the Apostle Paul, when he writes about *fornication* (cult harlotry) in his letter to the Corinthians (1st Cor. 5, 6 and 10).

Of course Aphrodite was not the only goddess or god that offered cult prostitution in Greece and other lands. *ISBE* writes:

---

[172] Ibid., p. 76, note §. Augustine, *De Civitate Dei*, lib. ii. cap. 26.

[173] Ibid., p. 77.

[174] Bromiley, *The International Standard Bible Encyclopedia*, vol. two, p. 563.

[175] Ibid.

[176] Sinclair, *Collins English Dictionary*, p. 728: '(in ancient Greece), a temple slave, esp. a sacral prostitute...from Greek *hierodoulos*.' From *hiero* + *doulos* (slave). *Hiero*: 'holy or divine' that is to say, a holy slave or holy prostitute.

[177] Kittel, *Theological Dictionary of the New Testament*, vol. VI, p. 582.

'Dionysus was worshiped sometimes in orgiastic frenzy.' 'His attributes, that guaranteed fertility, closely parallel those of Demeter, who also seems to have controlled agricultural cycles.'[178] Demeter was the mother goddess.[179]

TDNT states that cult prostitution,

'was practiced by the class of hierodules whose payment accrued to the goddess. This type of prostitution was *widespread in Asia Minor* in cults of *mother* deities; it is also found, however, *in Syria and Egypt*. Through the *Canaanite cults* (Baal, Astarte), it penetrated into the religion of Israel.'[180]

IBD writes that statues have been found of naked goddesses:

'Numerous *nude* female figurines found throughout the Near East depict the goddesses who were venerated in *sacred prostitution*.'[181]

This is only a small part of the picture of cult prostitution in the ancient world. In that world women usually had no rights. Perhaps this, along with satanic deception, and the fact that carnal lust is a powerful urge of human nature, explains why cult harlotry was *the way of life*. The ancient peoples had a perverse understanding of life in relation to God's standard. Sex, like the appetites of hunger and thirst, wasn't seen as needing any restraint.[182] As was mentioned earlier, *female* babies in the ancient *civilized* world were seen as liabilities to be gotten rid of:

'Many cultures devalued female babies, so infant girls were often left to die and then picked up by people who raised them for prostitution.'[183]

Ancient cult prostitution not only exploited females, but men as well. Greece and Canaan weren't the only places where cult homosexual prostitution was practiced and condoned. *The Illustrated Bible Dictionary* speaks of it prevailing in the countries of Syria and Phoenicia as well:

'In the Ugaritic texts of temple personnel we find the qdsm' (*kedishim*, masculine plural for the singular, *ka-*

---

[178] Bromiley, *The International Standard Bible Encyclopedia*, vol. two, p. 563.

[179] Ibid.

[180] Kittel, *Theological Dictionary of the New Testament*, vol. VI, pp. 581-582.

[181] Douglas, *The Illustrated Bible Dictionary*, part 3, p. 1289.

[182] Kittel, *Theological Dictionary of the New Testament*, vol. VI, p. 582.

[183] Ryken, *Dictionary of Biblical Imagery*, p. 677.

*daysh*) 'who were...male cult prostitutes. Explicit references to sacred prostitution in Syria and Phoenicia are
found in the late texts of Lucian's De Dea Syria (2nd century AD). The prostitution of women in the service of
Venus at Heliopolis (Baalbek) is attested as late as the 4th
century AD.'[184]

Still, ancient Canaan *outdid the other lands* in terms of heterosexual, as
well as homosexual, cult prostitution. This, along with infant sacrifice,
was most likely what Yahveh meant when He said to Abraham that *the sin
of the land* hadn't been filled up yet (Gen. 15:16; see also Lev. 18:6-25,
esp. vv. 24-25), and why Joshua and the conquering Hebrews weren't to
take any captives (Dt. 20:16-18). *UBD* states:

'Fertility cults *nowhere controlled people more completely* than in Canaan.'[185]

The people of Canaan were totally degenerate and given over to wickedness. *DBI* explains the perverse symbolism behind cult prostitution:

'Fertility cults that worshiped Baal advocated intercourse
between worshipers and religious prostitutes, both male
and female, to encourage the gods to bestow greater fertility on land, livestock and people.'[186]

*TDOT* confirms that cult prostitution was part of the ancient lifestyle, both
of the pagans and of Israel:

'In Canaanite culture, extramarital relationships in connection with the fertility cult were common. Through
sacral prostitution the harlot and her lover became consecrated individuals.'[187]

Also, 'Apostasy from Yahweh was frequently connected
with participation in the Canaanite fertility cult with its
sacral prostitution.'[188]

*UBD* and *IBD* declare that Canaan was immersed in cult prostitution and
speak of the three major goddesses of fertility:

'The inhabitants of Canaan were *addicted* to Baal worship, which was conducted by priests in temples, and in

---

[184] Douglas, *The Illustrated Bible Dictionary*, part 3, p. 1289.

[185] Unger, *Unger's Bible Dictionary*, p. 512.

[186] Ryken, *Dictionary of Biblical Imagery*, p. 677.

[187] Botterweck, *Theological Dictionary of the Old Testament*, vol. IV, p. 101.

[188] Ibid., p. 100.

good weather, outdoors in fields and particularly on hill-
tops called 'high places.' The cult included *animal sacrifice, ritualistic meals* and licentious dances. Near the rock
altar was a sacred pillar or *massebah*, and close by, the
symbol of the *asherah*, both of which apparently symbolized human fertility' (i.e. ancient pornography). 'High
places had chambers for sacred prostitution by male prostitutes (*kedishim*) and sacred harlots (*kedishoth*; 1st Kings
14:23-24; 2nd Kings 23:7).'[189]

'...the worship of the major Canaanite goddesses, Ashera,
Astarte and Anath, involved sacred prostitution.'[190]

Canaan was saturated with this form of lustful worship. The reason given
to justify cult prostitution had to do with 'helping the gods' to bring life-
giving rain, and therefore, food for the people to live. To a people ignorant
of the true ways of God (i.e. His Law), this might seem reasonable:

'The rainfall of winter and the drought of summer were
believed to indicate that Baal had died and that there was
a need for him to be brought to life again by magic
rites.'[191] 'Similarly, the Canaanites believed that the gods
could be helped to bring about fertility of the soil *if the
people fertilized one another* in the places of worship.
Therefore, there was a crude sexuality in the name of religion. *Every Canaanite sanctuary* had its own prostitutes
for that purpose.'[192]

'Their votaries believed that they could stimulate the fertility of their crops by sympathetic magic when they engaged in intercourse.'[193] 'In the Baal cult, spring festivals
dramatized, in act, the mating of Baal with the goddess of
fertility. Archaeological discoveries have revealed that the
devotees of Baal practiced prostitution as a part of their
worship.'[194]

By linking Man's need for food (life) to cult prostitution, Satan elevated
lust to a divine duty. The Gentiles didn't have the knowledge of the God

---

[189]   Unger, *Unger's Bible Dictionary*, p. 413. (Baal is another name for Molech.)

[190]   Douglas, *The Illustrated Bible Dictionary*, part 3, p. 1289.

[191]   Ralph Gower, *The New Manners and Customs of Bible Times* (Chicago:
Moody Press, 1987), p. 335.

[192]   Ibid., p. 334.

[193]   Douglas, *The Illustrated Bible Dictionary*, part 3, p. 1289.

[194]   Pfeiffer, *The Wycliffe Bible Commentary*, p. 145.

of Israel and His standard concerning life and worship, so there was no re-straining guide to their 'religious' behavior. So completely different were Yahveh's requirements that, for many centuries, His own people ran to the sin of sacrificial-sexual idolatry, copying the pagans all around them.

In the days of James the third largest city in the Roman Empire was Anti-och, located in what was known as Syria, and is now in what is southern-most Turkey.[195] It was from this city that Paul and Barnabas were sent to Jerusalem to determine what the Gentiles were to do in order to be saved (Acts 15:2-3, 22, 30, 35). In those days it was known as Syrian Antioch, in order to distinguish it from Pisidian Antioch (in what is now central Turkey; Acts 13:14; 14:19, 21). In speaking about Syrian Antioch, F. F. Bruce, with typical British understatement, writes:

> 'The city's reputation for *moral laxity* was enhanced by the cult of Artemis and Apollo at Daphne, five miles dis-tant, where the ancient Syrian worship of Astarte and her consort, with its *ritual prostitution*, was carried on under Greek nomenclature.'[196]

The repugnancy of this *moral laxity*, as Bruce states, was dryly noted by the Roman satirist Juvenal, when he wrote that,

> 'the sewage of the Syrian Orontes has for long been dis-charging itself into the Tiber.'[197]

Even Rome, no paragon of virtue, could smell the stench of orgiastic cult prostitution that was pervading its Empire from the East. James Pritchard describes the sensuality of Astarte worship from the Ras Shamra texts found in Ugarit (45 miles southwest of Syrian Antioch):

> The 'holy trees, symbols of the life force...show stylized trees growing out of the navel or the pudenda' (vagina) 'of a formalized goddess. Sexual intercourse under these holy trees was thought to transmit the potency and vitality of the goddess (Hos. 4:13-14).'

> 'The female deity Asherah is referred to in the Bible as the consort' (wife or companion) 'of Baal (Judg. 3:7; 2nd Kgs. 23:4). These Asherahs and Astartes are often de-scribed as fertility goddesses. However, the female part-

---

[195] Bruce, *The Book of the Acts*, p. 224. 'Antioch on the Orontes (modern An-takya in the Hatay province of Turkey), situated some eighteen miles up-stream, was founded 300 BC by Seleucus Nicator, first ruler of the Seleucid dynasty, and was named by him after his father Antiochus.'

[196] Ibid.

[197] Ibid.

ner of the weather god appears to bare her breasts in an erotic pose rather than in a maternal gesture. Ancient Syrian seals, which depict her surrounded by stars as the queen of the heavens, baring her breasts to the weather god striding across the hills, seem to confirm this.'

'It is quite clear that prostitution was connected with the cult of Asherah (cf. 2nd Kgs. 23:7). In the same way, the goddess figurines found in' Israel 'from the 10th–6th centuries BC (described in the Bible as 'teraphim'), are to be regarded not only as 'nourishing goddesses'...but also as symbols of eroticism (see Prov. 5:19).'[198]

Turning west to Rome, the 'center of civilization' at the time of Yakov and Acts 15, it seems that all the gods of the conquered lands...had conquered the citizens of Rome. The city was a mixture of 'Italian, Etruscan, Greek, Egyptian and oriental' (i.e. Babylonian and Syrian, etc.) gods and goddesses.[199] *ISBE* states:

'The mysterious religion of Etruria first impressed the Roman mind, probably giving them the trinity of the Capitol (Jupiter, Juno, Minerva), which had come from Greece...Latium contributed the worship of Diana (from Aricia) and a Latin Jupiter. Two Latium cults, Hercules and Castor' were there, and 'the Sibylline Books' were treated as 'sacred scriptures for the Romans.'

'The Greek trinity of 'Demeter, Dionysus, and Persephone under the Latin names of Ceres, Liber, and Libera' was there 500 years before Yeshua was born in Bethlehem, and the Greek god Apollo came to Rome about 450 BC.

'Mercury, Asclepius, Dis, and Proserpina' were relatively new arrivals in the '3rd cent. BC,' but the 'craving for more sensuous worship' had the Greek deities entering 'wholesale and were readily assimilated.' In the 2nd century BC, 'Hebe entered as Juventas, Artemis as Diana' and 'Ares as Mars...It was the Orient, however, that supplied what they really wanted. In 204 BC, Cybele, known as the great Mother, came from Pessinus' (modern day Anatoli, central western Turkey near ancient Pisidian

---

[198] James B. Pritchard, *The Harper Atlas of the Bible* (New York: Harper & Row, Publishers, 1987), pp. 101-103.

[199] Bromiley, *The International Standard Bible Encyclopedia*, vol. four, p. 212.

Antioch). 'Her coming gave an impetus to the wilder and more orgiastic cults and the mysterious glamor that captivated the common mind. It struck a fatal blow at the old Roman religion. Bacchus with his gross immorality soon followed.' Although the 'educated classes sank into skepticism' concerning belief in the gods, 'the populace' was enthralled by 'superstition' and the pantheon of gods and goddesses.[200]

So much for the glory that was Rome. The entire 'civilized' world was enmeshed in sacrificial-sexual idolatry. The Book of Acts also attests to this. After proclaiming Yeshua as the Messiah (Acts 14:8-18), Paul sees a man in Lystra who was lame from his mother's womb. Paul heals him, the people of the town rejoice and the priest of Zeus wants to offer sacrifice to Paul and Barnabas as gods!

Of course, the two of them try as hard as they can to restrain the people from doing so, and just barely succeed. This same crowd, though, later led by some instigators, turns on Paul and actually stones him, leaving him for dead! The point of all this is that in Paul's day the reality of paganism was saturated upon the hearts and minds of the Gentile peoples—*all* the Gentile peoples. This, too, needs to be taken into account regarding the four prohibitions of Acts 15:20 to the Gentile believers in the Jewish Messiah.

Going through Athens, one of the most cultured and sophisticated cities of the world at that time, Paul observed that it was 'full of idols' (Acts 17:16). Confirming this lifestyle of idolatry and cult prostitution, the Scriptures declare that all Asia (modern day Turkey) and the world worshiped Artemis (Diana). Demetrius, a silversmith who made silver idols of Artemis (Acts 19:24), speaks of how Paul's preaching of Messiah Yeshua, as the one and *only* way, negatively affected his business and the worship of the goddess:

> 'And not only is there danger that this trade of ours fall into disrepute, but also that the temple of the great goddess Artemis will be despised, and that she whom all of Asia and the world worship, should even be dethroned from her magnificence.' (Acts 19:27)

Demetrius wasn't lying. The whole world worshiped Diana (in one form or another). This glimpse into the ancient world reveals that cult harlotry was a major reality in every biblical land, and morally upheld as proper. Into this milieu comes the God of Israel, in Yeshua, whose standard was quite radical, and as Demetrius attests, quite repulsive to many natives.

---

[200] Ibid., pp. 212-213.

Some of the Gentile believers in the days of the Apostles would not have considered cult prostitution a sinful act. Yakov was making sure that they understood what would be required of them *immediately*, or their very salvation would be in jeopardy.

Today, Western man doesn't go to temples to worship this way. He has thrown off the wooden idols for 'living idols' (Hollywood movies, TV, pornographic magazines and 'games,' etc.). These feed the same sexual lust and draw the same demons of harlotry. This kind of *worship* is openly flaunted and embraced by the Western world. Not much has changed since the days of ancient Canaan, Greece and Rome. Lustful sensuality is the religion of modern man and seen as 'normal' because 'everyone does it.'

The next chapter, *The Greek Perspective on the Second Rule*, will parallel the Hebraic and confirm that Yakov's second rule specifically addressed cult harlotry, and that all four rules are a conceptual package against sacrificial-sexual idolatry, not some random rules given for table fellowship. With table fellowship being seen as a false interpretation, the foundation is taken out from under those who teach that the Law isn't for the Gentile. This is because the four rules are a reflection of commandments found in the Law and pave the way for the Gentile to learn the other rules of Torah. These four rules were the first of many for the Gentile believers—the beginning of a *new* lifestyle for them. In learning Torah they would come to know the *entire* spectrum of Yeshua's godly standard for their lives, as the Apostle Paul confirms:

> '*All Scripture* is inspired by God and is profitable for teaching, for reproof, for correction and for training in righteousness so that the man of God may be perfect, *fully equipped* for every good work.' (2nd Tim. 3:16-17)

Even though some congregations of Paul's may have had a couple of his letters, the Scriptures that the Apostle refers to is the Old Testament.

# THE GREEK PERSPECTIVE

# ON THE SECOND RULE

*The Hebraic Perspective* on the second rule in Acts 15:20 revealed that Yakov was speaking of cult harlotry, and even though he spoke Hebrew at the Council, years later Luke would write it down in Greek.[201] Looking at the Greek word that Luke penned, and two other words associated with it, will bring out the scope of what the word means, which is *prostitution*, the same as it was for the Hebrew word. Context, and the ancient pagan culture, will continually reveal *cult* prostitution as its meaning in the New Testament, as it also did for the Hebrew word in the Old Testament. The Greek noun for the second rule is 'prostitution,' while the verb means 'to prostitute.' Another noun will speak of the person who is a prostitute.

At the very least, the second rule of Yakov should be translated into English as 'prostitution,' and as the other three rules relate to sacrificial idolatry, the only proper interpretation for the second rule is *'cult* prostitution.' *Biblical* fornication in the *Tanach* (OT), as we have seen, is first and foremost, cult prostitution. This carries over into the New Testament as well. Unfortunately, the use of the term 'fornication' for English translations must be ruled out, specifically for Acts 15:20, and in general for all other texts because its biblical definition is not understood today. Many wrongly think that *fornication* relates to adultery or illicit sex.

Placing 'fornication' or 'sexual immorality' or 'adultery' into the second rule of Acts 15:20 totally obscures what James meant for it, and for his theme of sacrificial-sexual idolatry. The second rule should be translated as 'cult prostitution' or 'cult harlotry' or 'cult whoredom.'

---

[201] Yeshua, the Apostles, and all the Jewish people in Judah and Galilee spoke Hebrew as their native language (see p. 22, note 68). It also seems that half the Book of Acts was originally taken from a Hebrew source. Bivin, *Understanding the Difficult Words of Jesus*, p. 5, states,

'The first 15 chapters of Acts show some of the same textual evidence as the Synoptic Gospels of being originally communicated in Hebrew. They deal with events in Jerusalem and are recounted in a Hebrew context. In Acts 15:36 there is a shift to Greek as Luke himself begins to describe Paul's missionary journeys.'

Yakov spoke Hebrew at the Assembly and it seems that the first half of Acts was originally recorded in the Hebrew language. This only emphasizes that the second rule should first be recognized as coming from a Hebraic context, with Greek confirming the meaning of the word for the second rule of Acts 15:20.

## *The Greek Noun Pornay'ah (Prostitution)*

The literal Greek word for the second rule in Acts 15:20 is the genitive πορνειας (*pornay'ahs*). Genitive speaks of possession and in English it's seen by either the word *of,* or an apostrophe *s* (*'s*) at the end of a word. For example, in the phrase 'the cane of John,' the word *of* tells us whose cane it is. We could also say 'John's cane.'

The Greek letter ς *sigma,* placed at the end of the word, forms the possessive (genitive) for it. It's the *s* sound in *pornay'ahs* that gives the 'of' in the phrase, '*of* (the) prostitution,' the literal rendering for v. 20. When the *sigma* is taken off the noun, it leaves the base of the noun: πορνεια (*pornay'ah*) prostitution.

Walter Bauer's classic Greek lexicon defines πορνεια (*pornay'ah*) as,

> 'prostitution, unchastity, fornication, of every kind of unlawful sexual intercourse...of sexual unfaithfulness of a married woman Mt. 5:32; 19:9.'[202]

*Pornay'ah* in Acts 15:20 is translated in most Bibles as 'sexual immorality' or 'fornication,' etc.,' but never 'prostitution,' yet, the very first word Bauer uses to define *pornay'ah* is 'prostitution.' English Bible translators don't use 'prostitution' because they may want to give *pornay'ah* as wide a definition as possible. They don't realize that the four rules deal with sacrificial idolatry, nor do they understand the theological dilemma in which they place themselves by declaring *pornay'ah* to be 'every kind of unlawful sexual intercourse' or 'sexual immorality.'

If Yakov had meant *sexual immorality*, what would have been the criteria for establishing what was moral and what was immoral? In ancient 'civilized' Greece homosexuality was lawful and morally upheld by society[203] (as it is today in 'civilized' countries). What standard would be used to define 'lawful and moral' for the Greek believer? If we leave it up to each

---

[202] Bauer, *A Greek-English Lexicon of the New Testament*, p. 693.

[203] Kittel, *Theological Dictionary of the New Testament*, vol. VI, p. 593 states, 'In the shameful vices of *unnatural* sex relations, *which spread like a plague in the Graeco–Roman world of his day,* Paul sees the outworking of a severe judgment of God,' Rom. 1:18f. Just because someone 'believed in Jesus' it didn't mean that homosexuality would be seen by him as sin. Even today there are 'Christians' who live lifestyles of homosexuality. Some churches even condone such lifestyles by the canard that they were 'born that way' and that 'we must not judge people, but only love them.' Torah condemns such 'lifestyle choices,' and so did Paul. Torah is the source from which Paul, a staunch proponent of grace, takes his warnings against homosexuality. He also says that leaders must judge those in the congregation, and he specifically states that homosexuals will not inherit the Kingdom of God (1st Cor. 6:1-11).

country or person, there's going to be a very wide range and diversity of what constitutes 'lawful and moral,' much of which God calls sin.

The criteria that establishes what 'lawful and moral' are *in God's eyes* is the Law of Moses (as understood and interpreted by Yeshua, not by the Pharisees or the Rabbis). Theologians and translators, offering the widest possible definition for *pornay'ah* in Acts 15:20, place themselves in a tremendous theological bind. If the Law has been done away with, as they teach, there's no moral standard or law to *condemn* homosexuality. Some- one might say, 'but Paul writes that it's wrong in Romans.' Was Paul making up his own law, or taking it from the Law (Lev. 18:22; 20:13)? If he *took it* from the Law, doesn't that mean that the Law was still in effect for Paul, and for all those to whom he was writing?

It's interesting that homosexuality and adultery are sins in the Old *and* the New Testament. Where did the New Testament get these from? Someone might say, 'If it's repeated in the New Testament then we have to abide by it,' but the point is that it's *established* in the Law of Moses *and* written of in the New *because of Gentile sins*. If Gentiles weren't sinning in homo- sexuality and cult prostitution these things would not have appeared in the New. Then someone would say, 'If it's not in the New, it's not a sin!' If a commandment, like the Sabbath, isn't specifically re-commanded in the New, it doesn't mean that God abolished it. Paul's moral compass for what constituted *sin* was the Law of Moses (Rom. 3:31; 7:7, 12, 14). Paul also spoke of Mosaic Law when the need arose to justify a point he want- ed to make. If the Law had been done away with (by him, as the Church teaches), he couldn't have used the Law 'to make his points.'[204]

The Church teaches that the moral laws weren't done away with. Aside from the fact that nowhere in the New Testament does it say that the moral law is the only thing that 'passes over' into the New Testament, we're right back at our starting point: who defines the moral law? Who de- fines what is moral and what is sin — God or Man?

If 'everyone is free and under Grace' then there's no standard that pro- claims sin except what is written in the New Testament. For things that the New Testament doesn't seem to command, like the 7th day Sabbath, Passover and dietary laws,[205] the Church *has made its own laws* (Sunday, Easter and ham, etc.) *to take the place* of God's laws. If morality is de- fined by obedience to God and His Word, then it's certainly immoral to keep Church laws that nullify God's laws, and also are not commanded in

---

[204] See p. 99, note 281 for cites in 1st Corinthians where Paul does this.

[205] An accurate reading of the New Testament will confirm that the Sabbath, Passover and dietary laws, to name a few major areas, are still valid. For more understanding see *Law 102* at http://SeedofAbraham.net/law102.html.

the New Testament. Man-made standards vary within each Christian denomination. Pentecostals and Baptists condemn the mere drinking of a glass of wine as sin, while others, such as Lutherans and Episcopalians uphold it. Who sets the standard? The Bible or the Church?[206]

There are five basic categories of sexual practices that are forbidden in the Law of Moses, each of which has the punishment of death:

1. Adultery: death as the punishment (Lev. 20:10; Dt. 13:6-11).

2. Homosexuality: death as the punishment (Lev. 20:13).

3. Incest: cut off, i.e. death (Lev. 18:6-29; see also Lev. 20:3-5).

4. Prostitution (common or cultic): death by fire for a daughter of a priest (Lev. 21:9). (For the common Israeli woman see point five.)

5. Sex outside of marriage: death by stoning (Dt. 22:13-21).[207]

All these sins can be forgiven today except cult harlotry because it severs the believer from Yeshua.[208] All other sexual sins are forgivable through His blood, revealing the depth of God's *grace* toward His creation (Jn. 8:2-11; Acts 13:38-39). One who says that she believes in Jesus, but plays the cult prostitute, has severed *her covenant relationship* with the God of Israel. She has cut herself off from the Lord by this sexually idolatrous act. She has chosen to worship and join herself to another god.

Bauer states that *pornay'ah* can be defined as 'fornication,' but what does he mean by this term? Is it conceptually the same as 'prostitution,' which was his first word, or is it defined by him as 'every kind of unlawful sexual intercourse,' which immediately follows 'fornication'? It's hard to tell.

---

[206] Alcohol isn't condemned in the Bible, but alcoholism is. Many mistake the two for the same thing, but they're not. To drink alcohol is not a sin and doesn't make one an alcoholic. If it were sin, it would be stated as such somewhere in the Bible (Dt. 14:26; Lk. 7:33-34; 1st Tim. 5:23). The point is that without the Law of Moses the Church has made up her own laws for sin, many of which contradict and nullify the Word of God (Dt. 14:26). Isn't this concept *exactly* why Yeshua told us to beware of the *teachings* of the Pharisees and the Scribes (Mt. 15:1-20; Lk. 11:52)? Who determines what is sin and what isn't—God or Man?

[207] An exception to this is if a man rapes a virgin who is not betrothed to another man (Dt. 22:28-29). He must pay her father fifty silver shekels and marry her (without the option of divorce) if the father consents (see also Lev. 19:20).

The punishment for one mating with an animal is death (Lev. 20:15-16), as well as one lying with a woman in her menstrual period (Lev. 20:18), but these aren't basic categories, but asterisks.

[208] This only speaks of one who is already a believer in Christ. If a cult harlot comes to believe in Yeshua, her sins will be forgiven and she will enter the Kingdom in purity, if she leaves off with her former lifestyle.

*The Companion Bible: The Authorized Version of 1611* uses 'fornication' for Acts 15:20, and this, as we'll see, indicates *cult prostitution.* 'Fornication' at one time seems to have referred to, or included, *cult prostitution.* *The Companion Bible's* comment for the second rule reveals this:

> 'In many cases the rites of *heathenism* involved uncleanness *as an act of worship.* Compare Num. 25:1-15.'[209]

Heathenism speaks of idolatry. Their comment on Num. 25:1 says that Israel committed *whoredom* with the daughters of Moab in honor of the pagan god Baal Peor. This, of course, was sexual idolatry. In the note on Num. 25:3, *The Companion Bible* states that the Israelis *prostituted* themselves to the god. 'Fornication' for *The Companion Bible*, specifically for Acts 15:20, is *cult prostitution.*[210] It links *pornay'ah* in Acts 15:20 to cult prostitution by using the word 'fornication.' It's possible that Bauer was defining it the same way, but it's hard to determine.

Another word Bauer uses to describe *pornay'ah* is 'unchastity.' *Unchastity* is the opposite of *chastity* or being *chaste. Chaste* means,

> 'not having experienced sexual intercourse; virginal ...abstaining from unlawful or immoral sexual intercourse.'[211]

*Unchastity*, then, is a term for one who has had immoral sexual intercourse and is no longer a virgin. The use of the word 'unchastity' for the second rule, though, opens up the interpretation to being seen as any kind of sexual immorality, or as Bauer states, 'every kind of unlawful sexual intercourse.' *Pornay'ah* is now being used in a general sense to describe, in a figurative way, one who goes beyond the biblical sexual norms. The Hebrew word also had this for its secondary meanings. It primarily spoke of prostitution, but could be used in a derogatory way to describe an adulteress, a wizard, or anyone who sold himself to something other than God.

Even though a cult harlot would be unchaste, this word wouldn't reveal what Yakov meant, for just in and of itself, no one would be able to understand that Yakov was speaking specifically of cult harlotry. Therefore, 'unchastity' is a false and misleading word when placed as the English translation for his second rule. This is also true for 'sexual immorality.'

Another serious theological problem arises when Bauer states that *pornay'ah* is 'sexual unfaithfulness of a married woman, Mt. 5:32; 19:9.'

---

[209] *The Companion Bible: The Authorized Version of 1611* (Grand Rapids, MI: Kregel Publications, 1990), p. 1617.

[210] In *Israel and Baal Peor* (p. 39f., above), this prostitution was specifically seen as cultic, centering around the worship of Baal (Num. 25).

[211] Sinclair, *Collins English Dictionary*, p. 273.

This, of course, is an adulteress. One could call an adulteress a 'harlot,' but this is a derogatory term for her. It's not the specific description of what she did. What Bauer defines as 'adultery' for both cites (*pornay'ah*, Mt. 5:32; 19:9) doesn't mean 'adultery' at all, but as we'll see, 'cult harlotry.'[212] Bauer falls into the same deep pit that most theologians do when they think that Jesus declared that 'only for adultery' can a biblical divorce take place. This isn't what Jesus said or meant—more on this in the chapter on *Jesus and Divorce* (p. 87f.).

In his initial definition Bauer gives no indication that the word can mean *cult* prostitution. He only presents 'prostitution.' However, in a veiled comment further on in the lexicon he speaks of 'idolatry...pagan cults' and 'sexual debauchery,' so, *cult* prostitution seems to be part of his definition for 'fornication' (*pornay'ah*), albeit, a hard to find part:

> '*fig.*, in accordance w. an OT symbol of apostasy from
> God, of *idolatry*; from the time of Hosea the relationship
> betw. God and his people was regarded as a marriage
> bond. This usage was more easily understandable because
> *many pagan cults* (Astarte, Isis, Cybele, et al.), were
> connected with *sexual debauchery* (cf. Hosea 6:10; Jer.
> 3:2, 9; Rev. 19:2).'[213]

The Greek word *pornay'ah* lines up with its Hebraic counterpart for both forms of prostitution. *Sexual idolatry* was the grand form of pagan worship. Bauer speaks of 'sexual debauchery' and links it with pagan cults (Isis and Cybele, etc.). When Israel did this they severed themselves or apostatized from God, as we saw in *Israel and Baal Peor* (p. 39f.) and *Cult Prostitution in Ancient Israel* (p. 47f.). Yakov wanted the Gentile believers to know this. Paul, too, admonished the Gentiles in Corinth for this very thing, using the example of Israel at Baal Peor. He said to them that it was written for *their instruction* and benefit. *TDNT* states,

> 'The judgment which smote the Israelites, the fore-fathers
> of Christians (1 C. 10:1), in the wilderness when they fell
> victim to *idolatry and lust*, and thus tempted God, took
> place as an *example*...10:8, 11.'[214]

The reference that *TDNT* makes to 1st Cor. 10:8 is the sacrificial-sexual idolatry of the Baal Peor affair. Paul, writing about it (fornication; KJV)

---

[212] The two Greek words for 'fornication' in Mt. 5:32 and 19:9 have one letter difference because 5:32 is in the genitive case, while 19:9 is in the dative case (indirect object), but they are the same Greek word, *pornay'ah* (prostitution).

[213] Bauer, *A Greek-English Lexicon of the New Testament*, p. 693.

[214] Kittel, *Theological Dictionary of the New Testament*, vol. VI, p. 593.

points directly to that specific orgy with his use of '23,000:'[215]

> [6]*"Now these things were our examples*, to the intent we should not lust after evil things, as they also lusted. [7]Neither be ye *idolators*, as were some of them; as it is written, The people sat down to eat and drink, and rose up to play. [8]Neither let us commit *fornication*, as some of them committed, and fell in one day three and twenty thousand.' (1st Cor. 10:6-8 KJV)

'Fornication' in 1st Cor. 10:8 should read 'cult harlotry.' Paul was admonishing the Corinthians, 'Neither let us commit cult harlotry!' It was a major problem among a number of Gentile believers. How could it not be?

Other lexicons also confirm 'harlotry' as the basic meaning of *pornay'ah*, which will contextually become 'cult harlotry' for most New Testament cites. Wesley Perschbacher writes that *pornay'ah* in Acts 15:20 means,

> 'fornication, whoredom, Matt. 15:19; Mark 7:21; Acts 15:20, 29.' 'adultery, Matt 5:32; 19:9; incest, 1st Cor. 5:1 ...from the Hebrew, put symbolically for idolatry, Rev. 2:21; 14:8.'[216]

'Fornication,' for Perschbacher, is seen with 'prostitution' (whoredom), as Bauer did. He notes that the second rule for Acts 15:20 is 'fornication' or 'whoredom.' It's unfortunate that translators don't follow suit and place 'whoredom' there. Even though it wouldn't be specifically what James had in mind, it would be a slight step up from 'sexual immorality' or 'unchastity.' Again, though, as with Bauer, it's hard to understand what Perschbacher means by 'fornication,' although with 'whoredom' following it, it would seem to suggest that it's similar, but not necessarily cultic. It also may just be a general reference for illicit sex and sexual immorality, etc.

Perschbacher writes of the Hebraic connection in Revelation 'symbolically' speaking of idolatry. Unfortunately, he also thinks the Greek word can be used for the term 'adultery,' citing Mt. 5:32 and 19:9. He falls into the same pit that Bauer did before him. It's not that an adulteress couldn't be *called* a *whore* or a *harlot* (in a derogatory way). The Greek definition expands to include those who are incestuous, adulterous or homosexual, etc., but only as a degrading slur upon them. He is wrong for translating *pornay'ah* as 'adultery' in Matthew. There's not one cite in the New Testament to validate the use of the word 'adultery' for *pornay'ah* (harlotry).[217] Timothy Friberg, in his lexicon, defines *pornay'ah* as,

---

[215] See p. 114, note 325 for why Paul says 23,000 and not 24,000 (Num. 25:9).

[216] Perschbacher, *The New Analytical Greek Lexicon*, p. 340.

[217] The Apostle Paul uses πορνεια (*pornay'ah*) in 1st Cor. 5:1 to describe the

'generally, of every kind of extramarital, unlawful, or unnatural sexual intercourse, fornication, sexual immorality,
prostitution...a synonym for μοιχεια' *moikay'ah* '(mar-
ital) unfaithfulness, adultery (Mt. 5:32)... metaphorically,
as *apostasy* from God through *idolatry* (spiritual) immorality, unfaithfulness (Rev. 19:2).'[218]

For Friberg, as with others, the word can mean any number of different
things, with 'prostitution' coming at the end (of his first sentence). *Pornay'ah* can be used to describe things other than prostitution, as we've
seen, but it's not the primary meaning of the word in the New Testament.

Friberg, too, falls into that same crowded pit that Bauer and Perschbacher
fell into before him. He thinks that *adultery* constitutes a biblical divorce
('Mt. 5:32') or as he states, is 'a synonym for' *adultery*. Revelation is a
book that speaks of actual cult prostitution among Christian believers, but
Friberg only mentions it in a metaphorical or figurative way, yet, in the
second chapter, Jesus Himself comes against cult harlotry in two assemblies in what is now western Turkey (Rev. 2:14, 20-21).

To understand what James meant when he gave the second rule, it's obvious that the primary meaning of the word should be used, since no secondary meaning can be inserted into it without first proving that the
primary meaning wasn't meant. Translators, however, have failed to follow this basic principle. The *Theological Dictionary of the New Testament*
also fumbles over *pornay'ah*. It states that the word,

'occurs only 3 times' (in Acts) 'in verses recording the
prohibitions of the apostolic decree, 15:20, 29 and 21:25.'
'There is no insistence on the Jewish Law, only on the observance of minimal requirements for the interrelationships of Jewish and Gentile Christians, 15:28.
Among these is the prohibition of fornication.'[219] 'The
whole decree is thus presented, not as a ritual order, but as
a short *moral catechism* which mentions negatively the
three chief sins (idolatry, murder and fornication').[220]

'The surprising combination of πορνεια' (*pornay'ah*, fornication: Acts 15:20) 'with dietary regulations is due to

---

man who had slept with his father's wife. Most theologians describe this as incest. It certainly was incestuous, but there's a twist to it—more on this in the
section on *Incest in Corinth* (p. 102f.).

[218] Friberg, *Analytical Lexicon of the Greek New Testament*, p. 323.

[219] Kittel, *Theological Dictionary of the New Testament*, vol. VI, p. 592.

[220] Ibid., p. 593.

the fact that the four prohibitions are based on Lv. 17 and 18. πορνεια᾽ (*pornay'ah*) 'here is marrying within the prohibited degrees, which acc. to the Rabbis was forbidden 'on account of fornication,' Lv. 18:6-18.'[221]

*TDNT* presents its *theology* of the passage as though it were the only possible interpretation. James made the decree as 'a short moral catechism' that had *no bearing on Gentile observance* of the Law (*There is no insistence on the Jewish Law*), and yet, *TDNT* mentions Lev. 17–18 (commandments from the Law) *as the basis for the rules!* Not marrying one's sister or aunt, etc., are very specific laws within the Law of Moses (Lev. 18:6-18). Witherington rightly rejects any connection to these prohibited marriages in Leviticus because the term *pornay'ah* 'is not used to describe these sexual sins' in the Septuagint.[222] *TDNT* doesn't have a biblical basis for linking *pornay'ah* in Acts 15:20 with the forbidden relationships of Leviticus 18, only a poor rabbinical basis. The Rabbis, like their Christian counterparts, didn't use the primary meaning of fornication, but one of the secondary meanings that came about more than a thousand years after Moses wrote the Torah. More on that in the section on *Jesus and Divorce* (specifically p. 90, and note 265).

*TDNT* presents table fellowship (*interrelationships*) as the reason why James gave the rules, but this interpretation is not based on a correct rendering of the four rules. *TDNT* also states that the *three chief sins* are idolatry, murder and fornication, but murder, as we'll see, cannot possibly be what Yakov meant by *blood*. This theological error negates that interpretation as well (more on this in the section, *The Fourth Rule: Blood*, p. 147f.). *TDNT* states that the four rules were the *only* rules for the Gentile (*minimal requirements for* fellowship), but this is a faulty interpretation of Acts 15:28. It speaks of not burdening the Gentile with anything more than these (four) necessary rules *because* the Gentile needed to know them *immediately,* in order to understand that sacrificial-sexual idolatry would nullify his salvation.

Bauer listed 'prostitution' first and might have used it for translating 'fornication,' and Perschbacher used 'whoredom' as the translation of the word in Acts 15:20, but we couldn't determine if he meant it literally or figuratively. Although these aren't fully accurate, they're better than what Bibles have now. Friberg muddied the waters by 'throwing everything in' about *pornay'ah,* so that all sexual sins were on an equal footing (e.g. 'every kind of extramarital' sex). He speak of 'prostitution,' but it seemed like an 'add on.' Unfortunately, none of them presented '*cult* prostitution'

---

[221] Ibid.

[222] Witherington, *The Acts of the Apostles*, p. 465.

as the *primary* definition of the biblical usage of the word because they didn't realize it. Yet, we'll see that it certainly is in the section on *Cult Prostitution in the New Testament* (p. 133f.).

*TDNT* tried to link *pornay'ah* (prostitution) with the forbidden marriages of Lev. 18, but if that was correct Yakov would have mentioned more relating to a possible marriage partner. At the very least, he might have mentioned that a believer should only marry another believer (1st Cor. 7:39). Furthermore, as Witherington pointed out, *pornay'ah* is never used in speaking of the forbidden marriages in the Septuagint. 'Incestuous relationships' isn't what Yakov meant for the second rule. *TDNT*'s theology of table fellowship and 'dietary regulations,' along with its interpretation that *blood* relates to murder, isn't what Yakov had in mind.

*The Companion Bible*, though, was accurate. From its cite in Acts 15:20 it pointed directly to the Baal Peor fiasco in Num. 25, exposing 'fornication' as 'sexual idolatry' (cult prostitution). This also brought out that, at one time, 'fornication' properly related to what *pornay'ah* meant.

The definitions in the Greek lexicons will narrow considerably when they speak of the *person* (*pornay*) who practices *pornay'ah* (a prostitute). It won't primarily mean adultery, incest, homosexuality or promiscuity. This, in turn, will allow *prostitution* to take its rightful place as the basic meaning for the second rule, with context, word usage in the Old and New Testaments, and Israeli and pagan history supplying the specific meaning of *cult* prostitution.

Incest, adultery and pre-marital sex are sins that can be forgiven, but cult prostitution technically cannot be. The only sins that cannot be forgiven are blasphemy against the Holy Spirit and apostasy (1st Tim. 4:1; Heb. 6:4-6). These are direct frontal attacks on the Person and work of the Holy Spirit. *Believers* who become, or use, cult harlots sever themselves from the covenant that they have with the Father through Yeshua. They have intentionally chosen to leave the Faith.

# *The Greek Verb Pornu'oh (to Prostitute)*

Walter Bauer writes that the Greek verb πορνευω (*pornu'oh*) means 'to prostitute, practice prostitution or sexual immorality.'[223] Using *pornu'oh* for 'sexual immorality' is more of a general 'catch-all' than an actual description of what a person might do, but Bauer describes the root of the word when he says it means, 'to prostitute, practice prostitution.'

Perschbacher is more focused with his definition. He says it means,

> 'to commit fornication or whoredom, 1st Cor. 6:18; 10:8...from the Hebrew, to commit spiritual fornication, practice idolatry.'[224]

Perschbacher opts for two descriptions of *pornu'oh*, which are the biblical meanings. With him having 'fornication or whoredom,' it refers to harlotry because he included 1st Cor. 6:18 and 10:8. Of course, it should be *cult* whoredom instead of just whoredom. 1st Cor. 6:18 addresses cult harlotry, while 10:8 speaks of the Baal Peor catastrophe. Thousands of Hebrews lost their lives because they ate the meat sacrificed to Baal, worshipped the god and committed cult harlotry.

Perschbacher also brings in the 'spiritual' aspect. This can relate to a person's walk with God; from actual cult harlotry to any one of a number of other things (e.g. magic, astrology, unfaithfulness, etc.). His use of *practice idolatry* speaks of cult harlotry.

Friberg states that *pornu'oh* means, metaphorically

> to 'generally practice sexual immorality, commit fornication, live without sexual restraint (1st Cor. 6:18)... metaphorically practice idolatry (Rev. 17:2).'[225]

Friberg again presents a broad definition with 'sexual immorality' first and to 'live without sexual restraint.' One is hard pressed to understand that 'harlotry' is the root of the word. His living 'without sexual restraint' can be taken to mean the general attitude of a harlot, and his use of *metaphorically* tells us he doesn't see the harlotry in Revelation as literal.

These men will change their general descriptions when they describe the person who is a biblical fornicator.

---

[223] Bauer, *A Greek-English Lexicon of the New Testament*, p. 693.

[224] Perschbacher, *The New Analytical Greek Lexicon*, p. 340.

[225] Friberg, *Analytical Lexicon of the Greek New Testament*, p. 323.

## *The Greek Noun Pornay (Prostitute)*

The Greek noun that is associated with Yakov's second rule is πορνη *(pornay)*. It describes the person who commits prostitution—a prostitute. The lexicons now become more focused. Bauer says that it's a,

> 'prostitute, harlot. 1 Cor. 6:15. fig. (Is. 1:21; 23:15f.; Jer. 3:3; Ezk. 16:30f.); as the designation of a government hostile to God and his people, Rev. 17:15f.'[226]

There's no reference to an adulteress or to someone promiscuous or any-one else that might be mistakenly placed into the category of 'sexual im-morality' or a 'sexual sin of any kind.' Bauer's definition is limited in not mentioning a *cult* prostitute, but his definition gives the basic meaning of *pornay'ah* (prostitution) as one who is a harlot. As we'll see, 1st Cor. 6:15 speaks of a cult harlot. He also speaks of its figurative use.

Perschbacher agrees with Bauer, adding 'whore,' but then writes 'an un-chaste female.' This clouds the issue for anyone looking at his definition, but when his cite is looked up, this 'unchaste female' is none other than a prostitute. He defines *pornay* as,

> 'a prostitute, whore, harlot, an unchaste female, Matt. 21:31-32; from the Hebrew, an idolatress, Rev. 17:1, 5, 15.'[227]

The 'unchaste female' of which Perschbacher speaks in 'Matt. 21:31-32' are prostitutes (NASB) or harlots (KJV):

> '"Which of the two did the will of his father?' They said, 'The first.' Jesus said to them, 'Truly I say to you that the tax collectors and *prostitutes* will get into the Kingdom of God before you. For John came to you in the way of righteousness and you did not believe him; but the tax collectors and *prostitutes* did believe him; and you, seeing this, did not even feel remorse afterward so as to believe him'" (NASB).

In translating *pornay* in Mt. 21:31-32 as an 'unchaste female,' Persch-bacher misses the Lord's point. Yeshua wasn't speaking about an unchaste female *per se*—these women were prostitutes as both the NASB and KJV bring out. 'Unchaste' describes their immoral character, but it doesn't de-scribe who they were.

Perschbacher does recognize, though, that 'from the Hebrew,' that the

---

[226] Bauer, *A Greek-English Lexicon of the New Testament*, p. 693.

[227] Perschbacher, *The New Analytical Greek Lexicon*, p. 340.

woman is an idolatress. This speaks of sexual idolatry (harlotry plus idolatry), which is cult harlotry and confirms what we saw from the Hebrew words. His 'idolatress' is also linked to the Harlot of Babylon (Rev. 17:1, 5), which is certainly a reference to cult harlotry (along with other forms of harlotry).

The biblical noun should not be watered down to include an adulteress or an unchaste female. L. Ryken speaks of the difference between a harlot and an adulteress:

> 'A prostitute, also called a harlot, is a person who provides sexual activity in exchange for material security. Generally a woman, she is distinguished from an adulteress by her lack of discrimination in partner choice.'[228]

It's the harlot's job to corral as many men as she can, and she certainly wouldn't say that she was choosing a partner or having 'an affair.' A common harlot also calls attention to herself by the way she dresses and acts so that she will attract as many men as she can.

On the other hand, the adulteress is not looking for anyone to detect her. The adulteress usually confines herself to one man in any given time period of her adultery, but even if she has many lovers, she is usually very secretive about it.

An adulteress shouldn't be labeled a prostitute except in a derogatory way. This is the way the Scriptures speak of Israel in relation to Yahveh. When Israel practiced cult prostitution she was called an adulteress by Yahveh because she was in a covenant-marriage with Him, but the actual practice of what she did was cult prostitution in the midst of sacrificial idolatry.

Friberg writes that *pornay* means,

> to 'sell...literally, a woman who practices sexual immorality as a means of making a living; harlot, prostitute, whore, 1st Cor. 6:15).'[229]

Friberg reveals that his definition for 'sexual immorality' can contain paid harlots and prostitutes. There's no mention of an adulteress. All three lexicons speak of 1st Cor. 6:15 referring to common harlotry, but upon closer examination we'll see that it's cult harlotry that Paul wrote about.

The Greek lexicons, once searched out, present the primary meaning of πορνεια (*pornay'ah*), and two other associated Greek words, as *prostitution* (cultic or common), and those who practice it (*prostitutes*). An adul-

---

[228] Ryken, *Dictionary of Biblical Imagery*, p. 676.

[229] Friberg, *Analytical Lexicon of the Greek New Testament*, p. 324.

teress can be classified under *pornay'ah*, but only in a derogatory way.

From authoritative Greek and Hebrew sources, Yakov's second rule is *prostitution*. With his first rule speaking of idolatry, Yakov's 'prostitution' points directly to cult prostitution.

# SCHOLARSHIP AND THE SECOND RULE

The understanding of the four rules addressing sacrificial-sexual idolatry hinges upon the second rule being *cult* prostitution. Four scholars affirm this (Knowling, Bivin, Witherington and Hegg), while others consider it a possibility among other interpretations (Williams, *Wycliffe* and Stern).

It's very telling, though, that scholars of the caliber of I. Howard Marshall and F. F. Bruce don't even mention it. Bruce believes that fornication relates to the unlawful marriages in the Law of Moses. The second rule for him means that Gentiles,

> 'should conform to the Jewish code of relations between the sexes instead of remaining content with the pagan standards.'[230]

Bruce tries to explain how the Gentiles could be commanded to walk in the Law of Moses by saying that they kept the rules, not because they had to, but 'voluntarily' for table fellowship, however, this 'slight of hand' theology is unacceptable. First of all, Gentiles had no say in the forming of the Decree (to accept it voluntarily), and second, one can't be seen to be doing something voluntarily if it's commanded of him.

Marshall believes that the second rule should be translated as,

> 'unchastity, variously understood as illicit sexual intercourse or as breaches of the Jewish marriage law...which forbade marriage between close relatives, Lv. 18:6-18.'[231]

*TDNT* presented the same understanding for the second rule[232] as Marshall, but Witherington dismantled their interpretation by noting that the Septuagint never refers to those prohibited marriages as *pornay'ah*.[233] R. J. Knowling saw the theological conundrum that taking rules from the Law would entail—the Gentile would be on an unequal footing with the Jews who kept all the Law. He also negated the rules coming from the Noahide laws, as four of the seven laws of Noah aren't covered in the Decree.[234]

David Williams vaguely suggests the possibility that a connection exists between the first and second rules, but doesn't openly declare the second rule to mean cult prostitution. He, too, goes on to say that it might pertain

---

[230] Bruce, *The Book of the Acts*, p. 295.

[231] Marshall, *Acts*, p. 253.

[232] Kittel, *TDNT*, vol. VI, p. 592, and also, p. 74 above.

[233] Witherington, *The Acts of the Apostles*, p. 465, and also, p. 74 above.

[234] Knowling, *The Expositor's Greek Testament,* vol. two: *The Acts of the Apostles*, p. 335, and also, p. 11f., above.

to the forbidden marriages of the Law:

> 'there may have been an intended connection between these two' (pollutions of idols and sexual immorality) 'for idolatry often involved immorality; but immorality is sometimes taken to mean marriage within the forbidden decrees (cf. Lev. 18:6-18).'[235]

David Stern clouds the issue by listing *all* the possibilities, including cult prostitution, but suggests none as to what Yakov meant. With fornication being 'everything' it effectively ceases to be the rule that pulls all the rules together to form Yakov's conceptual unit on sacrificial-sexual idolatry. Stern says that the second rule,

> is 'any form of sexual immorality...sexual unions outside of marriage...along with homosexual behavior, temple prostitution and other improper practices.'[236]

*Wycliffe* sees *cult prostitution* as a possibility for the second rule in Acts 15:20. It says that it was *extremely common* in the world at that time, but does not stand by that analysis, stating that it might also speak of ordinary prostitution:

> 'fornication may refer to immorality in general or to religious prostitution in pagan temples. Such immorality was so common among Gentiles that it mentioned special attention.'[237]

Some scholars recognize that Yakov *could have* been speaking about cult prostitution, but R. J. Knowling, who wrote his *Acts of the Apostles* in 1900, presented the second rule squarely as such. He stated, 'the heathen view of impurity was' very 'lax throughout the Roman empire.'[238]

'Impurity,' as we'll see for Knowling, refers to cult prostitution. He wrote how some thought that the second rule referred to the forbidden marriages of the Mosaic Law, but he didn't accept that interpretation because of the way the word was *used throughout the New Testament:*

> 'An attempt has been made to refer the word here to the sin of incest, or to marriage within the forbidden decrees, rather than to the sin of fornication...but others take the word in its *general sense as it is employed elsewhere in*

---

[235] Williams, *Acts*, p. 266.

[236] Stern, *Jewish New Testament Commentary*, p. 277.

[237] Pfeiffer, *The Wycliffe Bible Commentary*, p. 1152.

[238] Knowling, *The Acts of the Apostles*, p. 324: 'cf. Horace, *Sat.*, 1:2, 31; Terence, *Adelphi* 1:2, 21; Cicero, *Pro Caelio* 20.'

Scholarship and the Second Rule

> *the N.T...*from the way in which women might be called
> upon *to serve impurely in a heathen temple...*to which *re-*
> *ligious obligation*, as Zockler reminds us, some have seen
> a reference in the word here...we see the need and the
> likelihood of such a *specific* enjoinder against the sin of
> *fornication.*'[239]

*Fornication* for Knowling meant cult prostitution. This was evident to him
from the way the word was used throughout the New Testament and from
how Gentile women were called upon to present themselves for service at
the 'heathen temple.' It's also seen in his statement that the pagan *reli-*
*gious obligation* dictated 'a specific enjoinder against the sin of fornication.' This could only be *religious* if it were cult harlotry, as opposed to
common prostitution.

David Bivin, even though he thinks that 'blood' and 'strangled' speak of
dietary regulations, believes that *pornay'ah* in Acts 15:20 should be,

> "cult prostitutes...'Unchastity' is a poor translation. The
> Hebrew equivalent of the Greek noun *primarily* has to do
> with *prostitution.*"[240]

Witherington states that the basic meaning of *pornay'ah* is *prostitution*,
and adds that cult prostitution is part of the basic meaning:

> 'the term πορνεια' (*pornay'ah*) '*in its most basic mean-*
> *ing* refers to prostitution, *including* so-called sacred pros-
> titution.'[241]

Witherington also writes that if James had meant adultery he would have
used the Greek word for adultery: μοιχεια (*moikay'ah*).[242] Hegg also believes that *pornay'ah* refers to cult prostitution.[243]

While Knowling and Bivin knew that the second rule meant cult prostitution, only Witherington and Hegg understood it to be cult prostitution, *and*
that the four rules were a unit on sacrificial-sexual idolatry. It's very sad
that over the last 1,800 years only a few have been able to see the second
rule as cult prostitution, while fewer still have understood the four rules as
the basic unit that it is. This *biblical* understanding, though, opens the theological door for the Law to come through, even though Witherington
didn't realize this aspect of it.

---

[239] Ibid.

[240] Bivin, *Understanding the Difficult Words of Jesus*, p. 109 and note *.

[241] Witherington, *The Acts of the Apostles*, p. 463.

[242] Ibid.

[243] Hegg, *The Letter Writer*, p. 279.

The majority of Christian scholars don't understand that *pornay'ah* in Acts 15:20 should be translated as cult prostitution. It certainly can't be for lack of definitions in the Hebrew and Greek lexicons, or its usage in the Scriptures. It's because of their preconceived theology that 'the Law isn't for Christians.' This excludes *cult* prostitution from their radar screen of possibilities, but even among those that understand *pornay'ah* as cult prostitution, their anti-Law theology prohibits them from understanding the four rules as a package deal on sacrificial-sexual idolatry. Knowling and Bivin fall into this category.

It's understandable, though, because Church teaching on the Law creates a dark veil over the eyes of most theologians. These scholars are experts in their field, and yet, they don't realize the heresy that they believe and propagate. *The power of heretical teaching is deception that leads to false practice.* This is why Messiah Yeshua came against it so strongly among His own people, the Jews (Mt. 15:1-20; Lk. 1:29-33; Rev. 22:16).

It's a massive theological shift to think about, let alone accept, that the Law of Moses is still valid. Only Hegg correctly understands that the Law isn't done away with by the decision of James and his four rules, yet unfortunately, Hegg also attaches a dietary interpretation to both 'strangled' and 'blood,' something that, as we'll see, isn't part of the correct theological interpretation for Acts 15:20. Much worse than that, though, is that Hegg teaches Gentile (covenantal) circumcision, which is a major heresy because it's the wrong sign for the wrong covenant.[244]

The second rule of James has nothing to do with prohibited marriages, adultery or pre-marital sex, etc. *Prostitution* is the correct general definition for the rule, and as seen from the Hebrew and Greek word meanings, the ancient pagan reality, and a few scholars, it directly speaks of *cult* harlotry. Unfortunately, the popular definitions of fornication, present the wrong understanding.

---

[244] For why it's biblically wrong for a male Gentile believer to be circumcised for religious reasons (i.e. to keep Passover and/or the Law) see *Gentile Circumcision?* at http://SeedofAbraham.net/Gentile_Circumcision.html or ask for its PDF. Covenantal circumcision, which is a physical circumcision that is done in order to keep Passover and/or the Law, is totally different from medical circumcision even though the two may look identical.

# *Popular Definitions of Fornication*

Although the ASV, KJV, NASB and the NRSV use the word *fornication* for Acts 15:20, popular definitions (and commentaries, etc.) of it make the English word very problematic to use. Even with scholarly lexicons, the proper definition is veiled more times than not. How much more for popular sources? *Unger's Bible Dictionary* states this about *fornication:*

> 'The worship of idols is naturally mentioned as fornication (Rev. 14:8; 17:2, 4; 18:3; 19:2) as also the defilement of idolatry as incurred by eating the sacrifices offered to idols (Rev. 2:21).'[245]

> 'At the present time, adultery is the term used of such an act when the person is married, fornication when unmarried.'[246]

*Unger's* first paragraph is much too general and misses the biblical reality of cult prostitution by saying that the 'worship of idols' and the 'eating of sacrifices' constitutes fornication because there's no mention of *sexual* idolatry as the basis for it. Most would think that pagan worship was like a church service. The second paragraph says that at 'the present time' sexual intercourse outside of marriage is 'fornication' ('fornication when unmarried'). This seems to be how many people use it today.

*UBD*'s definition excludes married people from the ability to commit fornication because they classify that as *adultery*. This doesn't line up with the biblical definition at all. Nowhere is that distinction seen. In other words, it doesn't matter if a person is married or not, they can still commit biblical fornication, which is cult prostitution.

*Unger's* also says that fornication can only be applied to single people ('when unmarried'), but this contradicts Yeshua. He says that only for *fornication* (KJV Mt. 5:32; 19:9) can a biblical divorce (between two believers) take place. Obviously, the fornicator can be married.

Unfortunately for *Unger's*, there's no mention of harlotry. As this is the meaning of the word, their definition falls far short and is very misleading. They give a definition for 'the present time' (adultery), which doesn't match the biblical reality. This is unacceptable for a biblical dictionary on something this significant.

*Webster's Dictionary* is another popular source to which people might turn in order to understand what *fornication* in their English Bible means. At this point, though, *Webster's* lacks biblical credibility. *Fornication* for *Webster's* is sexual intercourse between persons other than a man and his wife.[247] This would include both married and single people, but doesn't

---

[245] Unger, *Unger's Bible Dictionary*, p. 378.

[246] Ibid.

speak specifically of prostitution. *Fornication* for *Webster's* is either adultery or promiscuity (sex outside of marriage). The reality that *fornication* is cult or common prostitution is absent. The word has taken on a popular definition.

The failure of the first two is also seen in a third source. *Collins English Dictionary* states that *fornication* is 'voluntary secular intercourse outside marriage...between two persons of the opposite sex, where one is or both are unmarried.'[248] Again we find a definition that rests on promiscuity, which can also be adulterous. There's no mention of prostitution, and cult prostitution cannot fall into their framework because *Collins* speaks of '*secular* intercourse.' They further state that *fornication* is 'sexual immorality in general, esp. adultery.'[249]

The Internet encyclopedia *Wikipedia* says that the term *fornication* comes from the Latin word *fornicationis*, which means, 'an archway or vault,' and in Rome, harlots 'could be solicited there,' and so, the word became a 'euphemism for prostitution.'[250] Despite this, *fornication* for *Wikipedia* is,

> 'a term which refers to sexual intercourse between consenting unmarried partners. In contrast adultery is consensual sex where one or both of the partners are married to someone else.'[251]

*Fornication* may have been an accurate English representation of cult prostitution at one time, but it certainly isn't for today. The definitions are misleading and make it impossible for the word *fornication* to be used in an English Bible because there's no link to cult prostitution. Of course, for the same reason, *illicit sex*, *sexual immorality* and *unchastity*, as some Bibles translate the second rule, are also unacceptable.

It's to the discredit of these sources that they don't present the biblical definition of fornication somewhere in their definitions. This creates a serious problem for understanding what the ASV, KJV, NASB or NRSV mean when they use *fornication* as the second rule of Acts 15:20. This is why all English Bibles should use the precise term of *cult prostitution* (or *cult harlotry* or *cult whoredom*) for Yakov's second rule.

---

[247]  Woolf, *Webster's New Collegiate Dictionary*, p. 448.

[248]  Sinclair, *Collins English Dictionary*, p. 602.

[249]  Ibid.

[250]  *Wikipedia* at http://en.wikipedia.org/wiki/Fornication.

[251]  Ibid.

# JESUS AND DIVORCE

The chief, if not the only grounds for a biblical divorce in the Church has been adultery. This position rests primarily on interpreting *pornay'ah* as *adultery* in Matthew 5:32. Jesus said that whosoever,

> 'shall put away his wife, saving for the cause of *fornication*' (πορνειας *pornay'ahs*) 'causeth her to commit adultery' (μοιχασθαι *moikas'thay* to commit adultery)[252] 'and whosoever shall marry her that is divorced committeth adultery'[253] (*moikatai,* to commit adultery; KJV).

R. T. France states that the cause of divorce, *pornay'ah* (ASV and KJV fornication; NASB and NRSV unchastity), 'means adultery.'[254] Robert Mounce agrees and says it 'undoubtedly refers in this context to an adulterous liaison.'[255] *The Wycliffe Bible Commentary* says that adultery is 'the one cause for divorce allowed by Christ,'[256] and David Stern also sees *pornay'ah* as adultery, stating that a marriage,

> 'must not be dissolved for anything less than the most direct insult to its one-flesh integrity, adultery.'[257]

The most obvious questions to ask are, 'If Jesus meant that only for adultery could a divorce take place, why isn't the Greek word for *adultery* used as the *reason* for divorce? Why is the word, whose biblical meaning is cult prostitution, written as the reason? This is very troubling, especially when the Lord uses the Greek word for *adultery* in the very same sentence to speak of the one who is divorced for anything less than *pornay'ah!*

---

[252] The *NU* text has μοιχευθηναι *moiku'thae'nay*, to commit adultery.

[253] The *NU* text has μοιχαται *moikatai*, to commit adultery.

[254] R. T. France, M.A., B.D., Ph.D., Author; The Rev. Leon Morris, M.Sc., M.Th., Ph.D., General Editor, *Tyndale New Testament Commentaries: Matthew* (Leicester, England: Inter-Varsity Press, 2000), p. 123.

[255] Robert H. Mounce, Author; W. Ward Gasque, New Testament Editor, *New International Biblical Commentary: Matthew* (Peabody, MA: Hendrickson Publishers, 1995), p. 47.

[256] Pfeiffer, *WBC*, p. 938. *Wycliffe* places an appendage on the theme of adultery, saying it could also mean 'unfaithfulness during the betrothal period,' a time amounting to about a year in ancient Israel. In the Law (Dt. 22:23-27) if the woman was found to have had sex with another during this period, it would have been seen as adultery because the two were legally married (even though they hadn't yet consummated it). Betrothal was officially a part of marriage. One betrothed to another was seen as married, so much so, that if the couple wanted to break the betrothal a divorce would be necessary (Mt. 1:18-25).

[257] Stern, *Jewish New Testament Commentary*, p. 59.

It seems clear, in whatever language is used—if Yeshua had taught that a biblical divorce could take place for the sin of adultery, 'adultery' would have been written in the Greek New Testament (reflecting the Hebrew word for adultery).[258] The Greek word is πορνεια (*pornay'ah*, prostitution), not μοιχευω *(moiku'oh*, adultery).

*TDNT* states that the Greek word for adultery specifically means adultery, unlike the word *pornay'ah*, which can have other meanings:

> 'μοιχευω' (*moiku'oh,* adultery) 'is narrower than πορ-νεια' (*pornay'ah,* prostitution) 'and refers solely to adultery.'[259]

Bauer, too, says that *pornay'ah* is to be, 'Distinguished from μοιχευειν' (*moiku'ain*) 'commit adultery.'[260] If *moiku'oh* refers solely to adultery, why would the text have *pornay'ah* (prostitution) if Yeshua wanted to convey that only for adultery a divorce could take place?

The Septuagint reveals that the Hebrew and Greek understanding for the words *prostitution* and *adultery* remained constant. *TDNT* states,

> 'In the LXX' (Septuagint) 'the group πορνευω' (*por-nu'oh*) 'to play the harlot...is normally used for the root זנה' (*zanah*), 'while with equal consistency μοιχευω' (*moiku'oh*) 'is used for נאף' (*na'ahf*, adultery).[261]

The distinction between prostitution and adultery is not only found in Hebrew and Greek, but in English as well. A prostitute is not an adulteress and an adulteress is not a prostitute. These distinctions are self-evident. Adultery should not arbitrarily be forced into Yeshua's reason for divorce because He uses a word that means *prostitution*, not adultery (nor should it be imposed on Yakov's second rule for the Gentile).

*ISBE* also contrasts the harlot and cult prostitute with an adulteress:

> 'Harlot; play the harlot...*zana*' (Hebrew, to prostitute); '*pórne*' (*pornay*, the Greek word for a prostitute), 'whore, commit fornication...common whore, prostitute, temple-prostitute. A harlot is a woman who uses her sexual capacity either for gain or for pagan religious purposes. In

---

[258] Also interesting to note is what Yeshua says of a woman who is divorced for anything less than *pornay'ah* (Mt. 19:9). She becomes an adulteress, not a prostitute. In other words, she's still married to the original partner. This is also true for the man that puts her away for anything less than *pornay'ah*.

[259] Kittel, *Theological Dictionary of the New Testament*, vol. VI, p. 581.

[260] Bauer, *A Greek-English Lexicon of the New Testament*, p. 693.

[261] Kittel, *Theological Dictionary of the New Testament*, vol. VI, p. 584.

contrast to the adulteress she is promiscuous and usually shows no regard for who her mate might be.'[262]

*ISBE* rightly notes that 'temple prostitution' is associated with both the Hebrew and the Greek words for prostitution. It also states there's a difference between a prostitute and an adulteress, something that is obvious, but seems to have eluded the attention of the Church and most theologians at Mt. 5:32.

*TDNT*, though, blurs the distinction between prostitution and adultery with its Scripture cites. *TDNT* states:

> 'Examples show that זנה' (*zanah*, to prostitute), 'can be used of the married woman who is unfaithful to her husband (Hos. 1–2; Ezk. 16, 23), or of the betrothed who by law already belongs to her husband, Gen. 38:24. In content πορνευω' (*pornu'oh*, to prostitute) 'here is equivalent to…μοιχευω' (*moi'kuoh*, adultery).[263]

*TDNT* is not accurate when it states that 'in content' (to prostitute) 'here is equivalent to' adultery. It's not adultery that Tamar was accused of (Gen. 38:24), or specifically what Hosea's wife walked in, but cult harlotry.

In Ezekiel 16 and 23 the nation of Judah is accused by God of literally practicing sexual idolatry (cult harlotry) and worshiping (sacrificing) to pagan gods. Israel severed herself from her husband Yahveh. Figuratively, she was an adulteress, but her sin was cult harlotry. God would correct her through the destruction of Judah and captivity in Babylon for the remnant.

Hosea's wife was a cult harlot before Hosea married her. Her 'adultery' consisted in returning to cult harlotry. This is not a definition for an adulteress. Gomer didn't commit adultery with another man, but cult harlotry with many men. Gomer continued in her profession while married to Hosea, and symbolically pictured Israel's unfaithfulness to Yahveh.[264] Her whoring spirit pictured the cult prostitution of Israel that gave itself 'upon

---

[262] Bromiley, *The International Standard Bible Encyclopedia*, vol. two, p. 616.

[263] Kittel, *Theological Dictionary of the New Testament*, vol. VI, p. 584.

[264] Hosea's message of repentance was to the northern kingdom of Israel, steeped in cult prostitution and sacrificial idolatry. For the parallel and symbolism to be complete, and for the very reason why God chose *her*, she would have to have been a cult harlot for her to accurately reflect Israel. This is also hinted at in her name. Keil, *Minor Prophets*, p. 27, relates that her name means 'perfection, completion in a passive sense' and 'that the woman was *thoroughly perfected in her whoredom*, or that she had gone *to the furthest length in prostitution*.' The name of her parent, Diblaim, is also telling, as it occurs in 'Moabitish places in Num. 33:46.' The Moabites worshiped their gods through cult prostitution.

every high hill' to the pagan deities. Yahveh's wife was figuratively seen as an adulteress, but the *practice* the Israelis committed was cult harlotry. Israel would be obliterated because of it (2nd Kgs. 17:1-23).

Gomer is a symbol of Israel in its cult harlotry that would not repent, even given many chances by God. Judah, in Ezk. 16 and 23, is literally practicing cult harlotry as a nation. For *TDNT* to present these two examples as 'adultery,' without detailing their cult harlotry, is very misleading.

*TDNT*'s 'betrothed' of Gen. 38:24 is Tamar. The verse says that she had 'played the harlot' and was pregnant by 'harlotry.' Judah had promised (betrothed) her to Shelah, his third son (Gen. 38:5, 11, 14). *TDNT* is technically correct. Even though Judah thought that the one whom he had intercourse with was a cult harlot (as we saw in the section on *Judah and Tamar; p. 37f.*), he had no way of knowing *how* Tamar had gotten pregnant (through cult harlotry or adultery) and so, it seems that the use of 'played the harlot' and 'harlotry' for Tamar may have been used in a derogatory way for thinking that she was an adulteress.

In the days of Yeshua the word זָנָה *zanah* (to play the harlot, to prostitute oneself) had come to encompass a number of different sins in the eyes of the Rabbis. *Zanah* was not an actual definition of the sins, but a general, derogatory 'catch-all' for the word. *TDNT* states:

> 'Later Judaism gradually broadened the original usage to include adultery, incest, unnatural vice (e.g. sodomy), and unlawful marriages.'[265]

Even though these sins fall under the heading of harlotry in Rabbinic Judaism, it didn't mean that the adulteress would actually be doing the work of a prostitute, or that the one who committed homosexuality was actually a *zonah* (prostitute). In the eyes of the Rabbis, the people committing sodomy, etc., would be seen as walking at a similar level of unfaithfulness to Yahveh as that of a prostitute, but even with this, Rabbinic Judaism knew that fornication involved '*especially* the sin of *paganism*'[266] (i.e. cult harlotry).

Rabbinic Judaism's primary meaning for *zanah* was cult prostitution (and that, even over common prostitution). The Jewish hearers of Yeshua that day fully understood that He was referring to cult prostitution as the basis for a biblical divorce. It would be the same for those who heard Yakov give the second rule, *especially* after the first rule on *sacrificial idolatry*.

Bauer and Perschbacher weren't accurate in linking adultery with *por-*

---

[265] Kittel, *Theological Dictionary of the New Testament*, vol. VI, p. 587.
[266] Ibid., p. 588.

*nay'ah* (prostitution) for Mt. 5:32 (and 19:9), and France, Mounce, *Wycliffe* and Stern didn't pick up on the obvious difference between *pornay'ah* (harlotry) and *moikuoh* (adultery) as the reason for divorce. *Pornay'ah* in these cites (Mt. 5:32 and 19:9)[267] cannot be defined as adultery. It defies common sense that Yeshua would use *adultery* to *describe* the person, and yet, use an entirely different word meaning prostitution for the *cause* of divorce. *If Yeshua had meant adultery,* He would have used adultery as the cause for divorce. To force the meaning of adultery upon *pornay'ah* (prostitution) totally distorts what Yeshua was teaching.

Also, a major theological problem arises if adultery is seen as the grounds for divorce among believers. Adultery is a very grievous sin, especially to the spouse offended, but what of the sacrificial love and forgiveness of Jesus? Is not the blood of Jesus able to forgive the adulteress and to heal the wounded husband? What makes adultery 'the unforgivable sin'? Didn't God forgive King David for adultery (2nd Sam. 12:1-15)? Didn't Yeshua forgive the woman caught in adultery (Jn. 8:2-11)? If so, why would it be any less for believers in the Kingdom of Messiah (Acts 13:38-39)?

As both believing partners struggle to find Him, the one offended can offer forgiveness to the offender, and the offender, if truly repentant, will be humbled and brought back into the Fold. Why should adultery be seen as severing the marriage?

When a believing spouse commits cult prostitution, though, *then* there is biblical grounds, and need, for a divorce. Why cult prostitution, but not common prostitution? Because common prostitution, like incest, common homosexuality and even adultery, is a sin that can be forgiven by the blood of Yeshua. To not forgive these sins by a believing spouse (for a believing spouse) defies the concept of forgiveness that Yeshua heralds.

On the other hand, cult prostitution (the worship of another god through sexual intercourse) severs the believing spouse from God first, then from the spouse. Divorce becomes just the official recognition of this.

Yeshua used the word for harlotry to declare that His idea of marriage between two believers[268] can only be severed by cult harlotry (i.e. sexual idolatry, which reveals apostasy). If a believer divorces his believing wife

---

[267] In Matt. 19:9, Jesus says, 'And I say unto you, whosoever shall put away his wife, except it be for fornication, and shall marry another, committeth adultery: and whoso marrieth her which is put away doth commit adultery' (KJV). *Fornication* here (NASB *immorality*) is the Greek *pornay'ah*. The two Greek words for adultery in the verse is *moikatai*, the same verb used in Mt. 5:32. The argument used for Mt. 5:32 applies to Mt. 19:9 as well.

[268] Yeshua is speaking of life in His Kingdom, obviously among believing partners. His Standard (e.g. Mt. 5–7) is for everyone in His Kingdom.

for adultery or 'irreconcilable differences,' he is committing adultery if he marries another and causing her to be adulterous if she marries another.

Robert Mounce sees the superficiality of interpreting *pornay'ah* as adultery. He says that Jesus, in declaring adultery to be the only grounds for divorce in Matthew 5, *lacks spiritual punch*. Mounce states:

> 'Some writers consider this section the third antithesis' of what Jesus had been saying previously, but it's not 'clear in what way Jesus *intensifies* the law on divorce.'[269]

Bravo! Traditional Jewish thinking believes that when Messiah comes He will teach the commandments to Israel *on a deeper level*. It's interesting that Yeshua's teaching on divorce comes on the heels of some very powerful and radical ways of understanding the commandments (e.g. if you hate your brother you have already broken the commandment not to murder). Mounce correctly discerns that the way Messiah's view on divorce is understood by the Church is not much different from Dt. 24:1-4.

Indeed, Yeshua intensified His generation's understanding of the commandments, as only the Messiah could. The Law is the love of God in verbal form. In other words, it's God's definition of love. The Law is also the written reflection of Yahveh's awesome deeds and holy character (Rom. 7:7, 12, 14). There's a tremendous amount of grace in Mosaic Law (the promises to the Fathers, Passover, Exodus, Red Sea, the Commandments, and the subsequent fulfillment of the blessed life in Canaan).

Yeshua is *the* Word of God (Jn. 1:1-3; Rev. 19:13) and as such, He is the *living* Torah. Now, the Father extends through His Son a greater promise: eternal life in the New Jerusalem, and because Yeshua is the *living* Law, He was able to reveal, during His days in Israel, the depths of the Law in a way that no one else could. In His Teaching on the Mount, Yeshua revealed the *essence* of the Law: 'Love your enemies!,' and 'turn the other cheek!'[270] This is such a radical understanding that many today say,

> 'It can only apply in Heaven. No one can seriously consider living like that here on Earth.'

Who will hit you on the cheek in Heaven, though? What enemies will you have there to love? His words must apply to His followers today, as He Himself demonstrated. Unfortunately, His words are so far from the accepted norm, so against our carnal nature, that many don't even consider living that way. Mounce, though, correctly questions that if Yeshua's position on divorce hasn't changed much from Dt. 24 (and is similar to the

---

[269] Mounce, *Matthew*, pp. 46-47.

[270] Ex. 16:1-5; 17:1-7; 23:4-5; 32:1-6, 30-32; Lev. 19:17-18; Num. 12:1-15.

world's) how can it be God's righteous, perfect and holy standard?

All those who say *pornay'ah* in Mt. 5:32 (and 19:9) refers to adultery, line up with the Jewish sage Shammai. He lived a generation before Yeshua, and in seeking to understand what God meant by listing 'uncleanness' as the cause of divorce in Dt. 24:1 (KJV 'uncleanness;' NASB 'indecency') he stated that *only for adultery* could a man divorce his wife.

His opponent in this, and many other debates, was Hillel. By the time of Yeshua the view of Hillel had been adopted over that of Shammai. Hillel said that, 'even if she burns his toast' the husband has biblical grounds for divorce,[271] as this could make the wife unclean in his eyes.[272] The point is that there is no intensification of the grounds for divorce on Yeshua's part if one thinks that adultery justifies divorce. Yeshua would only have been affirming Shammai.

Yeshua, though, was stating something much more radical than Shammai (and the interpretation the Church has given it), and more in line with His other foundational concepts of Torah. Isn't this understanding also hinted at with the Apostles' response the second time Matthew writes of it?

> 'And I say unto you, Whosoever shall put away his wife, except it be for fornication (*pornay'ah*) and shall marry another, committeth adultery (*moikatai*, to commit adultery), and whoso marrieth her which is put away doth commit adultery.' (*moikatai;* Mt. 19:9 KJV)

> 'His disciples say unto Him, 'If the case of the man be so with his wife, it is not good to marry.' (Mt. 19:10 KJV)

Yeshua declared that except for cult prostitution a man (in His Kingdom) could not get a divorce. This meant the Apostles 'were stuck' with their wives! In the days of Yeshua, many, like today, were tossing their spouses away 'for burning their toast' so that they could marry the next slice of bread that came along.

Why would the Apostles think that it wasn't good? Because they were still

---

[271] In this area Hillel was right, not that burnt toast was cause for divorce, but regarding the *attitude* behind it. The reason is obvious. Mosaic Law commanded the stoning to death of any adulteress (Lev. 20:10). Divorce wouldn't be necessary. 'Indecency' from Dt. 24:1 should be understood as an attitude and/or actions which were not in line with holiness. If a woman was vengeful, contentious, flirtatious or dressed provocatively, these would be Mosaic grounds for divorce. This was a concession to their hard hearts (both men and women) because they hadn't been given the Holy Spirit. With the Holy Spirit, though, one can pray for the spouse, and one's own heart, to be softened toward each other, something that just might cause the adulteress to repent.

[272] Stern, *JNTC*, p. 59; from the Mishna: *Gitin* 9:10.

carnal men. They hadn't been filled with the Holy Spirit, yet. The Scriptures speak of their hearts being hard (Mk. 6:52; 8:17). This is seen in their quarreling among themselves as to who was the greatest among them (Luke 22:24-27), and in their thinking that Yeshua was talking about literal bread when He told them to beware of the leaven (teaching) of the Pharisees and Sadducees (Mt. 16:5-12). It's further seen in their telling the blind man to stop pestering Jesus as He walked by (Luke 18:35-43), and also, in Yeshua's stern rebuke to Peter, and immediately after that, in His warning to the others about dying to self if they wanted to follow Him (Mt. 16:22-38). Finally, their unbelief is graphically revealed when they were told that Yeshua had risen from the dead (Mk. 16:9-15; Lk. 24:11).

Cult harlotry is the very simple, and yet, profound explanation for what *pornay'ah* means in Mt. 5:32. It reveals Yeshua's radical concept of marriage and divorce (and why the Apostles were so shaken up). It's also consistent with what Yeshua requires of people in His Kingdom: *sacrificial* love, death to self, forgiveness, *long-suffering* and reconciliation.

Some might question the specific use of cult prostitution over common prostitution, as *pornay'ah* can theoretically mean either one. Is it common prostitution, cultic, or both, of which Yeshua speaks? It has to be the one that's idolatrous. If a believer is a cult prostitute she has already cut herself off from the covenant with God (apostasy) and severed her relationship with her earthly partner. It's not as though God couldn't forgive the person, but when a person reaches this state, as a believer, God knows that she will never repent—she's gone over a red line. The official act of divorce ratifies what has already happened—high-handed rebellion against the Living God and the tearing apart of the one flesh (Gen. 2:24).

This kind of sin stands in a class all by itself. The person has willfully bound himself or herself to another god. There's no longer union with Yahveh or His people and this is why the plague in Num. 25 took 24,000 sons of Israel. When one has a believing partner that practices cult prostitution, divorce is not only justified, it's absolutely necessary.[273]

Common prostitution doesn't fall under this category. As wicked as it is, it can be forgiven because it doesn't involve the sexually idolatrous worship of, and joining to, another god. All *sexual* sins can be forgiven except the one that involves idolatry. Just as there is hope for a believer who commits adultery, incest or common homosexuality, there is also hope for res-

---

[273] This helps us to understand Paul's teaching on the marriage of an unbeliever and a believer, in 1st Cor. 7:12-16. The unbeliever who is *pleased* to dwell with the believer is not continuing in pagan practices which would corrupt the believer, and isn't fighting the believer as she walks in the things of the Lord, and is certainly not physically or emotionally abusing her.

toration if a believer becomes, or uses, a common prostitute because the soul has not merged with another god.

Another reason why Yeshua is referring only to cult prostitution is because of His infrequent use of *pornay'ah*. *TDNT* writes; the question,

> 'of πορνεια' (*pornay'ah*) 'is seldom dealt with in the preaching of Jesus and the primitive community; *it arises more frequently in Paul*. As compared with the different judgment of the Greek world and ancient *syncretism*, the concrete directions of Paul bring to the attention of Gentile Christians the incompatibility of πορνεια' (*pornay'ah*, cult prostitution) 'and the kingdom of God.'[274]

Why is there a difference between Jesus, the 'primitive community' (the community of Jews in Jerusalem that believed in Yeshua), and Paul? The only reason Yeshua mentions it is to display the radical standard of marriage and divorce for believers. R. T. France writes that divorce was all too freely practiced by His (Yeshua's) 'contemporaries.'[275] Yeshua was establishing His sole criteria for divorce (outside of other, non-cultic forms of apostasy, which would also be grounds for a biblical divorce).

Yeshua wasn't warning His Jewish followers about practicing cult harlotry, for that had been expunged from them by the Babylonian captivity. He was showing them the Kingdom standard. That's why the Apostles were worried. In their carnality they wanted to be able to divorce their wives if they didn't want them any longer. With Yeshua's radical teaching on marriage and divorce they realized that they didn't have that option, and neither do believers today if they're married to a believer.

The only reason why *pornay'ah* is mentioned three times in the Jewish 'primitive community' (in Acts) is as a warning *to the Gentile believer!* It's actually the same warning of Acts 15:20 being replicated in 15:29 and 21:25. The Jewish believers didn't need to be reminded of what cult harlotry would do to their relationship with God the Father and Yeshua the Son—they knew all too well their sinful Family History concerning cult harlotry and what it had done to their Fathers. On the other hand, the Gentile believers needed to be warned, and this is *exactly* what Acts 15:20 is all about. Yakov gave notice to the Gentiles that if they engaged in cult prostitution, their faith in Jesus would be null and void.

Paul addresses the issue a number of times because cult harlotry was actually taking place among some of his Gentile *believers*. Paul rebuked them for practicing cult harlotry (KJV 1st Cor. 6:13-20; 10:7-8; 2nd Cor. 12:21;

---

[274] Kittel, *Theological Dictionary of the New Testament*, vol. VI, p. 593.

[275] France, *Matthew*, p. 280.

Gal. 5:19-21) saying that 'those who practice such things will not inherit the Kingdom of God' (KJV Eph. 5:3-5; Col. 3:5; 1st Thess. 4:3-8).

Yeshua's sole cause for divorce among His followers was cult harlotry, not adultery, as these four reasons bring out:

1. It doesn't make any sense: *pornay'ah* means harlotry, not adultery. If Yeshua had meant adultery He would have used it. This, coupled with Messiah's use of 'adultery' in the very same sentence, for the description of the wife divorced for anything less than harlotry, confirms that He didn't mean adultery.

2. No intensification: Yeshua intensified and revealed the depth of the commandments of the Law, and in essence, the very nature and will of God. Having adultery as the grounds for divorce does not intensify the criteria for divorce and presents God as not wanting to, or unable to, forgive the adulteress (or adulterer).

   • It also doesn't allow God to redeem the sin in the life of both the adulteress and the offended spouse so they can struggle with forgiveness and become 'more like Jesus.' This is called 'the furnace of affliction' or God's refining Fire and the Holy Spirit uses it to pierce hard hearts and make them like the heart of Yeshua.

3. The Blood of forgiveness: the adulteress (or adulterer and prostitute) can be forgiven. The believer who is a cult prostitute cannot be restored to fellowship (although one must follow the leading of the Holy Spirit in each case). The cult harlot has left the covenant for another god. In this, Yeshua is *conceptually* spring-boarding off of Dt. 13:6-11: 'wife of your bosom...to go serve other gods...you must surely kill her.'

4. The rare use of *pornay'ah*: both Yeshua and the primitive Jewish believing community, by their infrequent use of *pornay'ah*, as contrasted with Paul, reveal that cult harlotry was not a common practice among the Jewish people at that time. Yeshua used it to present the Kingdom standard for biblical divorce, a very radical concept, which essentially excludes divorce among believers.

The sexually idolatrous worship of another god severs the believer from his covenant with the God of Israel. The difference between Mosaic divorce, or that of Shammai and the Church today, is that Yeshua's standard is *infinitely* higher. Yeshua wants us to realize our own hard hearts and our need for Him in the midst of this world of darkness. Only with His heart and power can we walk in His Kingdom the *way* He did.

*Under Mosaic Law* a man could divorce his wife for 'uncleanness' (Dt. 24:1-4; see also Prov. 12:4). It was variously interpreted in the days of

Yeshua as to what exactly constituted uncleanness. That it couldn't have been sexual idolatry is understood from Mosaic Law in that the punishment for cult (or common prostitution) was death, and therefore, divorce wasn't necessary.[276] Yeshua says that the reason why God gave divorce to Israel through Moses was because of the hardness of their hearts:

> "He said to them, 'Because of your hardness of heart, Moses permitted you to divorce your wives, but from the beginning, it wasn't this way.'" (Mt. 19:8, also Mk. 10:5)

In other words, they weren't able to forgive their wives for the 'uncleanness' that they saw in them. It could have been something as serious as a rebellious heart toward her husband or God, or as innocent as an inability to please a hard husband, but this hardness must give way to life in the Spirit when one is saved to serve his wife and to pray for forgiveness in one's heart toward her for any 'uncleanness' that he sees. In contrast, for cult harlotry, there is no recipient to forgive—the wife has intentionally severed her covenant with God and her husband. All that is left for the husband to do is to officially and spiritually divorce her. The relationship is already severed.

One must enter a marriage upon due reflection that it's of God, and for life, so that in the midst of troubles and storms, one has no option for divorce unless the spouse is a cult harlot. In other words, marriage among believers in Messiah should never end in divorce unless the other is a cult harlot (or apostatizes another way). That's what the new heart is all about (Ezk. 36:26). The theme of the parable of the unjust steward who wasn't able to pay his master (Lk. 16:1-13) clearly reveals to what extent Yeshua wants us to forgive others. Because the servant's master forgave him much, it would be unthinkable for him not to forgive one who owed him much less.

If our spouse sins by being adulterous, who are we, lustful creatures that we are, to withhold forgiveness? Yeshua has forgiven us for so much more. It's in this life that we must seek the Lord for His heart that is able to forgive, even those who crucify us. That's why bad things happen to us—so we can see our own hard and vengeful heart and cry out to Yeshua for His heart (Dt. 30:6; Jer. 31:31-34; Ezk. 36:24-27; Mt. 11:28-30).

Yeshua forbids divorce except upon the grounds of cult prostitution. The bar has been raised to the highest of the Heavens. This opens up a new understanding concerning what constitutes biblical grounds for a divorce

---

[276] Ex. 34:15-16; Lev. 20:1-6; Num. 25:1-9f.; Dt. 31:16-17 and by inference, Lev. 20:10; Dt. 22:18, 20, 22, 25. That the uncleanness wasn't adultery is seen in that the punishment for adultery was also death (Lev. 20:10; Dt. 22:22). Shammai was wrong and so is the Church.

among professed believers.[277] In Yeshua, reconciliation of all differences can take place...all differences except that of having another god and sexually acting it out.

Theologically, divorce can only take place between two believers when one partner permanently severs his relationship from Yeshua. Such is the case with cult prostitution, and of course apostasy, which although possibly harder to recognize, also severs the covenant with God.[278] All other sins are forgivable in His mighty and incredibly awesome Name.[279]

---

[277] Yeshua's statements relate to two believers in His Kingdom. When the Apostle Paul deals with divorce between a believer who is married to an *unbeliever* the criteria changes for that situation (1st Cor. 7:12-16).

[278] Apostasy is the falling away from Yahveh, never to return. It's not that the person has backslidden or has become a prisoner of Satan, but on the contrary, it implies that the person is now working for Satan and against Messiah Yeshua. It doesn't mean that they will automatically relinquish their 'tag' of 'Christian,' either. Some will keep it to deceive believers and family members. Satan is a master of lies and deception. Yeshua doesn't mention apostasy as a reason for divorce, but concentrates on the specific apostate practice of cult prostitution, yet apostasy of any kind is also biblical grounds for divorce. An apostate will never return to the Lord because the person has totally rejected Yeshua, and so, the apostate conceptually lines up with being a cult harlot, having sold himself to something other than the God of Israel, despising the salvation that is offered in Messiah Yeshua.

[279] One should separate from a believing partner that is a habitual offender in things like adultery, prostitution, incest, physical abuse and emotional abuse, etc. Separate, but don't divorce (unless the Lord leads you to divorce). Separation should be used as a chastisement for teaching the offender, with an eye to having him set his life in order with the King and not to be enslaved to his carnal passions. It's also a time for the one who separates to pray and intercede for her spouse, to pray until deliverance and healing come, or the Lord releases you.

# CULT PROSTITUTION

# IN THE CORINTHIAN ASSEMBLY

The letters of the Apostle Paul are not only filled with rich theological gems, but also with stern rebukes to local believers for sins they were committing.[280] Sometimes the Gentile believers weren't even aware of it (1st Cor. 10:21-22) or if they were, they didn't exhibit anything that led them to change (1st Cor. 5:1-2). Many of those problems would never have arisen if they had had a foundational knowledge in the Law of Moses. That's not to say that they weren't being taught the Law,[281] but just as mature belief in Messiah Yeshua doesn't happen overnight, so too, it takes a while for the Law to become part of a believer's understanding and walk. That's why Yakov gave the initial filter of the four rules first (Acts 15:20) and spoke of Gentiles going to the synagogues every *Shabat* (Hebrew for Sabbath) to learn the Law as they grew in Yeshua (Acts 15:21).

There are three texts in First Corinthians that speak of cult harlotry, two of which aren't normally associated with it (5:1; 6:12-20) although the word *pornay'ah* is used in both. The third text is chapter ten where Paul specifically speaks of *pornay'ah* in relation to the cult harlotry of Num. 25. Translators generally see 1st Cor. 5:1 as only incest, and 6:12-20 as common harlotry. These two texts have been overlooked as places where the Apostle addressed cult prostitution.

---

[280] Some problems that Paul wrote of in his letter to the Corinthians included divisions and strife (1:10-13; 3:1-9); pride (4:7-21); the Elders not rebuking a man who had slept with his father's wife (5:1-8); lawsuits against one another (6:1-9); cult harlotry (5:1; 6:18; 10:8); idolatry (8:1); the worship of demons (10:20); the eating of sacrifices to demons and the drinking of blood (10:21); men who would completely cover their heads in the assembly, and women who would not (11:4-16); their perverse way of coming to the Lord's Supper (11:17-22); their lack of discernment for His Body (11:29-30); and chaos in the assembly when the Holy Spirit would manifest (14:1-19, 27-28, 33-34).

[281] There are a number of places in First Corinthians where Paul uses the Law to establish his point. This would be meaningless if the Law had been done away with: **1.** Paul encourages the Corinthians to keep 'the Feast' (1st Cor. 5:6-8). This can only be Passover as he's just spoken about unleavened bread (Ex. 12:8-20; Lev. 23:6). **2.** He sums up his ability to receive funds from the Corinthians by citing the Law (9:8-9f.). **3.** He tells them that women should not speak in the assembly, again citing the Law (14:34-35). **4.** In 16:8 Paul speaks of staying at Ephesus until Pentecost, which is the Greek word for the Law's holy day of *Shavu'ot* (the Feast of Weeks; Lev. 23:15-22; Dt. 16:9-10, 16). Why would Paul 'note time' to *Gentiles* by an 'outdated' Jewish feast unless he still kept the Law and taught it to them (Phil. 3:17; 4:9)?

Corinth, the capital of Roman Greece, was the fourth largest city in the Roman Empire in the days of Paul.[282] With a population of approximately 650,000 people (400,000 of which were slaves) Corinth was a significant city where Paul founded the Corinthian assembly.[283] Corinth was also steeped in cult harlotry. Many gods 'inhabited' the city. There was Poseidon the sea god, and Isis from Egypt, along with Serapis, etc., but Aphrodite was the favorite and with good reason. She satisfied the lust of the flesh. So common was this 'worship' that to 'Corinthicize' someone was seen as a 'euphemism for' cult 'whoredom.'[284] *Shrines* of Aphrodite 'were *everywhere*' in Corinth.[285] Aphrodite was seen as the 'patroness of harlots'[286] and was known for her 'great army of prostitutes.'[287] At her *main* temple, which 'crowned the Acrocorinthus,' there were over a thousand cult priestesses (i.e. temple prostitutes) to accommodate the Corinthians in their religious fervor 'to worship' the goddess.[288]

There wasn't a great distinction between a cult priestess and a common harlot, either. Whenever the city was in danger, or in matters of 'grave importance,' common prostitutes were pressed into the service of the goddess to gratify the need for beseeching her favor.[289] Paul's *Gentile* converts, both slave and free, seem to have made up the bulk of the congregation in Corinth.[290] Most of them would have been immersed in the mindset of paganism. That's why Paul had so many problems with the Corinthian believers. G. G. Findlay notes that many of the Gentile *believers* were '*steeped* in pagan vice' and bound up 'with *idolatry*,'[291] which points directly to cult prostitution.

We also know that Paul had a number of Jewish converts in Corinth,[292] but

---

[282] G. G. Findlay, B.A., Author; W. Robertson Nicoll, M.A., LL.D., Editor, *The Expositor's Greek Testament*, vol. two: *St. Paul's First Epistle to the Corinthians* (Peabody, MA: Hendrickson Publishers, 2002), p. 730.

[283] Leon Morris, The Rev. Canon, M.Sc., M.Th., Ph.D., *Tyndale New Testament Commentaries: 1 Corinthians* (Leicester, England: Inter-Varsity Press, 2000), p. 18, note 5.

[284] Findlay, *St. Paul's First Epistle to the Corinthians*, p. 734.

[285] Morris, *1 Corinthians*, p. 18, note 3.

[286] Ibid.

[287] Ibid.

[288] Findlay, *St. Paul's First Epistle to the Corinthians*, p. 734.

[289] Morris, *1 Corinthians*, p. 18, note 3. See also Num. 31:1-4, 12-18 for ordinary women being 'pressed into' the service of cult harlotry 1,400 years earlier.

[290] Findlay, *St. Paul's First Epistle to the Corinthians*, p. 730.

[291] Ibid., p. 731.

[292] In Acts 18:8 Crispus, the leader of the Corinthians Jewish synagogue, and his

they most likely wouldn't have been involved in cult harlotry because they would have known Torah and their Family History. As with any small minority in an assembly today, they wouldn't have been able to affect the behavior of the Gentiles in the assembly who wanted to continue in their pagan ways, thinking that it was alright.

Some of the Corinthians would radically change their understanding of practicing cult prostitution when they would hear Paul's letter, but some of them would continue to practice it, as is seen from what Paul writes in 2nd Corinthians (6:14-18; 12:21; 13:5). Habits learned over a lifetime and sanctified by one's culture are not only very hard to break, but all too often, seen as 'normal and right.' Because of this 'normalcy' we catch a rare glimpse of a young congregation where the gross sin of cult prostitution walks hand in hand with 'belief in Jesus.' What James warned the Gentiles against in Acts 15:20, Paul actually had to battle!

In presenting these three sections of Paul's first (preserved) letter to the Corinthians (1st Cor. 5:9-11) the Apostle didn't outline it with chapter and verse numbers, nor keep everything 'in order.' His raising of a concern in one section will continue in another form in a later section as he would think of further things to support his previous words, and other things that needed to be addressed on the topic.

The problem of cult prostitution is first addressed in chapter five. In chapter six there's a conceptual discourse against it, which is further developed in chapter ten using the history of Israel. In chapter ten Paul speaks not only of cult harlotry, but also of the 'table and cup' of demons. Three of the four prohibitions of Yakov are actually mentioned by Paul, being practiced by Corinthian Gentile believers in Jesus:

1. the drinking of the raw blood of a sacrifice,

2. the eating of the sacrificial meat at the time of the sacrifice in the pagan temple,

3. and the 'worship' of the god or goddess through cult harlots, all in the Name of Jesus.

---

household, left the synagogue and assembled with the believers. It's not unreasonable to assume that a number of Jews followed him. See 1st Cor. 1:14-16 where Paul immersed not only Crispus, but Gaius and Stephanas, who may have been Jewish as well. Also, Paul was in Corinth for a year and a half (Acts 18:11) reasoning with the Jews, etc., about Yeshua being the Messiah (Acts 18:4). It's not unreasonable to think that a number of other Jews came to believe in their Messiah, too.

## *Incest in Corinth: 1st Cor. 5:1-5*

Most Bible commentators understand *pornay'ah* in 1st Cor. 5:1 to mean 'incest,' since the Gentile Christian man had intercourse with his stepmother. So say Morris ('Paul draws attention to a case of incest'),[293] Findlay (the 'Case of Incest')[294] and *Wycliffe* ('the fornication was incest').[295]

It certainly was an incestuous affair, but most likely something much worse—incestuous cult prostitution. This is based upon Paul's own words, and his use of *pornay'ah* (fornication; prostitution). Commentators have failed to pick up on its uniqueness. Paul writes:

> 'It is reported commonly that there is fornication *(pornay'ah)* among you, and *such* fornication *(pornay'ah) as is not so much as named among the Gentiles*, that one should have his father's wife.' (1st Cor. 5:1 KJV)[296]

When Paul states that this fornication was such that it was 'not so much as named among the Gentiles,' it must have been a very exceptional case. Note that the woman wasn't related to the man by blood, but by marriage. She wasn't his mother, nor his stepmother, but as Paul speaks of it, 'his father's wife.' The father most likely married her later in life when his son was already a man. The wife wouldn't have been a stepmother who had raised him, but just 'another woman' to him. There would be no childhood emotions attached to this woman, as might be found with a stepmother, which would make their sin 'that much less' *incestuous*.

In most incestuous relationships there *is* a blood relationship between the two parties, which truly makes it incestuous, but for there *not* to be one here would make it a far less exceptional incestuous case than otherwise. It's hard to believe that Paul would think that this kind of incest was so unique as to write that it wasn't found among the Gentiles. It should be obvious that the reason wasn't because the woman was his father's wife.

The woman was most likely a practicing cult harlot. This would account for Paul's use of *pornay'ah* (prostitution) and make the incestuous relationship part of an idolatrous sexual rite. If she were 'only' a common harlot, again, it wouldn't make it that exceptional. Her being a cult harlot

---

[293]  Morris, *1 Corinthians*, p. 83.

[294]  Findlay, *St. Paul's First Epistle to the Corinthians*, p. 807.

[295]  Pfeiffer, *The Wycliffe Bible Commentary*, p. 1236.

[296]  Substituting 'cult prostitution' for 'fornication,' it becomes clearer as to what Paul was addressing: 'It is reported commonly that there is *cult prostitution* among you, and such *cult prostitution* as is not so much as named among the Gentiles, that one should have his father's wife' (1st Cor. 5:1).

would not only be unique, but also part of the theme of cult prostitution that Paul will develop from this point on and speak against in chapters six and ten. Here is a Christian worshiping another god through a cult harlot who is his father's wife! This must have been a *first* for the Apostle! The Law's punishment for sleeping with his father's wife, even if she wasn't a cult harlot, is death (Lev. 20:11).

Paul's use of the Greek word for harlotry (*pornay'ah*), his astonishment at the actual deed, and the *punishment* he commands the Corinthians to carry out,[297] all suggest that the woman was a *cult* harlot and that she had intercourse at one of the pagan shrines with the son of the man to whom she was married.[298] If this is the case, and it appears to be, then the only place in the New Testament where *pornay'ah* has been seen as incest, and only incest, vanishes because it's incestuous cult harlotry, a truly unique sin in Paul's eyes. Of course, common harlotry can't be ruled out, but because of the uniqueness of the event according to Paul, and also the fact that he addresses cult harlotry in vv. 9-11 and the very next chapter, indicate that the woman was a cult harlot. Also, as we'll see in *Cult Prostitution in the New Testament* (p. 133f.) whenever *pornay'ah* is used in the New Testament, it continually points to cult harlotry, not common. Therefore, with Paul using *pornay'ah,* without qualification, it would have to be taken as cultic.

Cult prostitution with the wife of the believer's father must have been a first for Corinth, too ('not so much as named among the Gentiles'). What a horrendous 'witness for Christ' this must have been to the believers in the assembly, as well as to many unbelievers in Corinth, not to mention the cult harlot that he had intercourse with. This is a conceptual problem with 'freedom in Christ,' when it's not coupled to God's boundaries—His Law (Lev. 18:8; 20:11; Dt. 22:30; 27:20). Believers don't understand His will, and so, they sin against God and man unknowingly. This is why Yakov's second rule prohibits cult harlotry and why he gave the four rules to the Gentiles first.

---

[297] Paul speaks of handing him over to Satan to deal with his flesh (1st Cor. 5:5). He would be *severed* from his covenant with God, and the only fellowship in town, and if unrepentant, would spend eternity in Hell. The punishment seems to have had the desired effect (2nd Cor. 2:3-11), and is identical conceptually to being 'cut off from Israel' (Ex. 12:15, 19; Lev. 7:27; 17:14; 18:29, etc.).

[298] Paul speaks of the father in the present tense, and also, he doesn't say that the woman was a widow. The father doesn't seem to have been a Christian because he, too, would have been cast out of the assembly. Being a pagan he may have even initiated the event. It might have seemed good in his pagan eyes. Perhaps that's why the Christian man did it? To honor his father?

# *Cult Prostitution in Corinth: 1st Cor. 6:12-20*

In 1st Cor. 6:12-20 Paul speaks about what appears to be the sin of cult prostitution among the Gentile believers at Corinth. He initially tackles the Gnostic libertine heresy that says free men can do whatever they want. Because the Corinthian believers were 'free in Christ,' some united the two beliefs, logically seeing no need for sexual restraint. This reveals a problem with those who espouse 'freedom in Christ' and don't want to realize that it's freedom from sin, not license to sin. What is the Standard? Is it God's Law as lived out by Jesus, or whatever anyone thinks is right?

Most consider the harlot that Paul mentions twice (6:15-16) and the harlotry he speaks of three times (vv. 14, 18 twice) to be of the common variety, but can this be considering that Corinth was known throughout the ancient world for its cult harlots? Can Paul be writing about harlotry in Corinth, while it had nothing to do with pagan temples and cult harlots? There's nothing in the Greek words for *harlot* or *harlotry*, and nothing in the context of this passage to the Corinthians, that means that this harlot has to be a common harlot and not a cult harlot. If anything, those who think her to be a common harlot have the burden of responsibility to prove it. They should present clear evidence that the Apostle was speaking about common harlotry and common harlotry only, but this cannot be done.

Morris states that the philosophy behind the average Corinthian was a 'man who recognized no superior and no law but his own desires.'[299] In other words, he thought he could do whatever he wanted to do. Enter now some of them who accepted Christ as their Savior. Would their thought pattern change in this area? For some Gentiles, no.

Paul begins his argument against this 'freedom' by declaring that he, too, is free and then says what true freedom is—putting Jesus ahead of self:

> 1st Cor. 6:12: 'All things are lawful unto me, but all things are not expedient: all things are lawful for me, but I will not be brought under the power of any. [13]Meats for the belly and the belly for meats: but God shall destroy both it and them.'
>
> [14]'Now the body is not for *fornication*, but for the Lord; and the Lord for the body. And God hath both raised up the Lord, and will also raise up us by his own power. [15]Know ye not that your bodies are the members of Christ? Shall I then take the members of Christ and make them the members of an *harlot*? God forbid! [16]What?

---

[299] Morris, *1 Corinthians*, p. 19.

Know ye not that he which is *joined to an harlot* is one body? For two, saith he, shall be one flesh. [17]But he that is joined unto the Lord is one spirit.'

[18]'Flee *fornication!*[300] Every sin that a man doeth is without the body; but he that committeth *fornication* sinneth against his own body. [19]What? Know ye not that your body is the *temple* of the Holy Ghost which is in you, which ye have of God, and ye are not your own?'

[20]'For ye are bought with a price: therefore glorify God in your body and in your spirit, which are God's." (1st Cor. 6:12-20 KJV)

Paul states that 'All things are lawful' to him, and many take this as a cue that the Law has been done away with,[301] but the phrase obviously can't mean 'every–thing' because Paul comes against harlotry in Corinth after he's just spoken against thieves and adulterers, etc. (6:9-11). Therefore, 'all things' cannot mean '*every* thing.' Paul would never lie, nor break the Sabbath commandment, nor eat pig, etc., because they would be sin for him.

The phrase 'All things are lawful' can be equally translated 'All things are permitted.'[302] It seems to imply that Paul was speaking *rhetorically*, saying, 'I could also do what you're doing if I wanted to!' Paul was not coming against the Law of Moses. Stern thinks that the phrase wasn't a part of Paul's teaching, but that he was *echoing* a Gnostic libertine concept that was 'in use among a group of Corinthians.'[303] This version of Gnostic phi-

---

[300] The New American Standard Bible has, 'Flee immorality.' This totally distorts the meaning that Paul was writing about (i.e. cult harlotry).

[301] Paul uses the phrase twice here in v. 12. It's also used twice in 10:23 where there's a natural link to the cult harlotry about which Paul is speaking in chapter six. In 10:23 Paul deals with cult harlotry, the eating of the meat of the pagan sacrifice at the time of the idolatrous act and the drinking of the blood from the sacrifice. This would also align the two texts concerning what *type* of harlotry Paul was addressing here (cult harlotry).

[302] William Mounce, *The Analytical Lexicon to the Greek New Testament* (Grand Rapids, MI: Zondervan Publishing House, 1993), p. 194. Friberg, *ALGNT*, p. 155. It denotes 'that there are no hindrances to an action or that the opportunity for it occurs, it is possible...predominately as denoting that an action is not prevented by a higher court or by law it is permitted, it is lawful, it may be done.' Roman law permitted cult prostitution. This is most likely the 'freedom' that Paul was speaking of.

[303] Stern, *JNTC*, p. 451, says that it 'was not a central principle' of Paul's, 'but a saying in use among a group of Corinthians who would later have been called gnostic libertines.' On the other hand, Morris, *1 Corinthians*, p. 95, states, 'It looks like a catch-phrase the Corinthians used to justify their actions, possibly

losophy espoused that anything and everything sensual was permissible to free men (and even slaves were now 'free in Christ'). This attracted many with no moral compass and no desire 'to curb their flesh.'[304] They weren't interested in understanding what was right or wrong if it inhibited their sinful lifestyle. Just how many believers in Corinth walked this way isn't known. If it was a specific person, Paul would have addressed it as such, as he did in chapter five, with the man who had intercourse with his father's wife. Instead, it seems to be aimed at a group in the congregation (see 2nd Cor. 12:21).

Paul qualified 'all things' (παντα, *pahn'tah*) and the qualification was all things that edify and don't imprison one (v. 12, 'I will not be brought under the power of any'). Obviously, if one sins it's not edifying ('expedient') and not a 'freedom,' but an enslavement. The Apostle confined himself to the realm of a godly lifestyle. Just as God can do 'any–thing,' but restricts Himself to righteousness, so too, with Paul. He was free to do whatever he thought best in any situation, but he wouldn't use his freedom in Christ to justify sin (which is defined by the Law).[305]

Stern believes that Paul incorporates another libertine phrase[306] when he writes in v. 13, 'Meats for the belly, and the belly for meats.'[307] This speaks of the specific justification that the libertines used for their unrestrained sex. Leon Morris says that this phrase,

> 'looks like another expression used by the Corinthians. Eating is a natural activity and they apparently held that one bodily function is much like another. Fornication is as natural as eating.'[308]

Without an understanding of Torah (God's will) there wasn't any sexual restraint for them. If it's good to feed the body with food, a natural func-

---

one they would have derived from Paul's teaching.' Either way, some Corinthian believers were using this to philosophically justify their unrestrained sexual lust.

[304] Today, being 'free in Christ' means that many Christians walk as the world and don't even realize it. Many Christian women, following Hollywood, dress much more sensually than the ancient cult harlots of Corinth ever did. These Christian women don't seem to realize that their immodesty and ungodliness cause men to stumble. The same is true for how some Christian men dress.

[305] Ezk. 11:19-20; Zech. 14:16-19; Mt. 5:19; 22:34-40; Rom. 3:31; 6:1-4f.; 7:7; Jam. 2:9, 11; Rev. 12:17; 14:12.

[306] Stern, *Jewish New Testament Commentary*, p. 451.

[307] Or, 'Food for the belly and the belly for food,' *meat* being a KJV word for food or meal (grain). It's quite likely this also spoke of their gluttonous eating or feasting at the pagan shrines where cult harlotry took place.

[308] Morris, *1 Corinthians*, p. 96.

tion, why would it be bad to have sex with a cult harlot? The sexual desire is as natural as eating, so there shouldn't be any need for sexual restraint. Pagan thinking wasn't illogical, it was just ungodly. *Wycliffe* states that,

> 'the moral laxity that polluted the church, apparently' (was) 'caused by the application of the truth of Christian liberty to the sexual realm. The question is: If there are no restrictions in food, one appetite of the body, why must there be in sexual things, another physical desire?'[309]

Paul countered the libertine philosophy that stressed one's freedom to do whatever he sexually pleased, with what was *profitable* for him. He also pointed his readers to Judgment Day by saying that one day the body and food for it would come to an end (v. 13).

In relation to fornication and the harlot mentioned in the passage, Paul links his argument to idol worship, and therefore, to cult harlotry by contrasting true worship with pagan worship. He says that the body is 'for the Lord; and the Lord for the body' (v. 14) and building on this he says their bodies were members of Messiah (v. 15). The spiritual comparison between being members of Messiah, or members of a harlot, are parallel only if the harlot is a cult harlot.

Paul writes in v. 15, 'Shall I then take the members of Christ and make them the members of an harlot? God forbid!' The Greek for 'take' is 'take away.'[310] Gentiles who believed in Jesus would be 'taken away' and made members with this harlot. Something that is missing if this was just a common harlot is that Yeshua is God the Son. For the parallel to be complete, for them to be 'taken away' and given to *another*, Paul would have to be speaking of union with a harlot that could offer union with another god.

Leon Morris sees this and presents the possibility that Paul is writing about pagan temple prostitution. He first speaks of the typical understanding of 'union with a prostitute' being 'a horrible profanation of that which should be used only for Christ,' and then he goes on to say:

> '*This would be even more so* if the Corinthian prostitute *was connected with the temple*, for then the act would *form a link with the deity.*'[311]

Morris realizes that the words for *harlot* and *harlotry* also indicate cult

---

[309] Pfeiffer, *WBC*, p. 1238. No 'restrictions in food' is an anti-Law perception of the Good News. See 1st Tim. 4:4-5 where *the Word of God **and** prayer* qualify what food to eat. In other words, it's not just *prayer* that makes food acceptable for a believer to eat.

[310] Morris, *1 Corinthians*, p. 97.

[311] Ibid., pp. 97-98.

harlot and cult harlotry. With ancient Corinth infested with cult harlotry it would certainly point to this first.

In 1st Corinthians 6:16-17 Paul uses the word 'joined' twice:

> [16]'What? Know ye not that he which is *joined* to an harlot is one body? For two, saith he, shall be one flesh. [17]But he that is *joined* unto the Lord is one spirit.'

The Greek word that is translated *joined* is conceptually the same as its Hebrew counterpart in the idolatrous Baal Peor affair, in which cult harlotry played a major role. Coincidence? The Greek word is κολλαω (*kollah'oh*) and means to 'join oneself to, join, cling to, associate with.'[312] It also means to 'cleave to, to unite with'[313] and 'to attach one's self to.'[314]

Morris writes that Paul uses it to express the 'physical bond with the harlot,'[315] but there's more here that Paul speaks of than just a physical bond. The Apostle spoke of the spiritual bond the Corinthians had with Messiah, in v. 17. He used the same Greek word for *joined* in both verses (16-17). Again, the parallel is strongest if this were a cult harlot. There's nothing in the context to negate this, but on the contrary, many things that point directly to cult harlotry. Why can't this be happening in pagan Corinth? Why wouldn't the Gentile believer, steeped in pagan harlotry, be doing what the Hebrews had done when they came out of Egypt?

In v. 18 Paul cries out, 'Flee fornication!' What kind of prostitution is Paul addressing? It could certainly be both, as the word conveys both types, and if he had meant adultery or homosexuality, there are Greek words that he could have, and would have used to get his point across. That none of those words are mentioned means that the Apostle had harlotry in mind. That *harlotry* is what Paul was writing about is further seen from the noun which comes from *pornay'ah* (v. 18). *Pornay* (vv. 15-16) can only mean a *harlot* (common or cultic), not an adulteress, etc.

Paul states their Christian bodies were for the Lord and that the Lord Yeshua owned them (v. 14). Then he added that their bodies were *members* of Christ (v. 15). Now he tells them that their bodies are the temple or dwelling place of God (v. 19). It's here that the parallel draws closest to understanding that Paul was speaking of temple prostitution among the Corinthian believers:

> [18]'Flee fornication! Every sin that a man doeth is without

---

[312] Bauer, *A Greek-English Lexicon of the New Testament*, p. 441.

[313] Friberg, *Analytical Lexicon of the Greek New Testament*, p. 234.

[314] Perschbacher, *The New Analytical Greek Lexicon*, p. 243.

[315] Morris, *1 Corinthians*, p. 98.

the body; but he that committeth fornication sinneth against his own body. [19]What? Know ye not that your *body is the temple of the Holy Ghost which is in you,* which ye have of God, and ye are not your own?' (KJV)

Paul's use of the Greek word for temple ναος (*na'ohs*, v. 19) is defined as *the place where the deity dwelt,* in the inner sanctuary as opposed to in the outer courtyard.[316] Paul is saying that the believer's *body* is the dwelling place of God the Holy Spirit. By implication, believers should not go to *another* temple where *another god dwells* and *join themselves* to that god through *cult* harlotry.

*Cult harlotry* is further seen in the phrase in 2nd Cor. 6:14-16, that the body is 'the temple of the living God,' which is synonymous with Paul's use of 'the temple of the Holy Ghost' in 1st Cor. 6:19 above. In 2nd Cor. 6:14-16, though, it's absolutely clear that he's speaking of cult harlotry, and this, *to the same group of Corinthians:*

> 2nd Cor. 6:14: 'Be ye not unequally *yoked* together with unbelievers: for what fellowship hath righteousness with unrighteousness? And what communion hath Light with darkness?' [15]'And what concord hath *Christ with Belial?* Or what part hath he that believeth with an *infidel?*'
>
> [16]'And what agreement hath the temple of God *with idols?* For ye are the *temple of the living God;* as God hath said, 'I will dwell in them, and walk in (among) them; and I will be their God, and they shall be my people.'" (KJV)

The Apostle contrasts 'Christ with Belial' (v. 15) warning the Corinthian Christians not to be unequally *yoked* (v. 14) or joined to a cult prostitute who belonged to an idolatrous shrine.[317] He wouldn't use *Belial* if it were just a common prostitute, *as no religious significance* attaches to that kind of harlotry. Also, the use of the word *infidel* (v. 15) is only used in a religious context.

In 2nd Cor. 6:16 Paul speaks of the 'temple of God' and idols. This, too, can only be a contrast between the Lord and cult prostitution. The correlation with 1st Cor. 6 is seen in his use of the concept that God dwells in believers and that believers are the temple of God (1st Cor. 6:19; 2nd Cor. 6:16). It's also seen in his admonition to the Corinthian believers not to be

---

[316] Ibid., p. 99.

[317] Most today take this unequal yoking to mean that a Christian shouldn't marry a non-Christian. As correct as this concept is, the text is primarily warning Christians not to have intercourse with cult harlots.

unequally yoked with unbelievers (1st Cor. 6:15-16; 2nd Cor. 6:14).

In 1st Cor. 6:19 Paul states that they should glorify (worship) God through their body, the temple of God (v. 20) and not 'worship' *another* with their body. From the context, and the parallel to 2nd Cor. 6:16, it speaks of cult harlotry. True worship is within the believer's body, the temple or dwelling place of God. On the other hand, one goes to a pagan temple and gives his body to a temple harlot there 'to worship' the goddess. The wording of Paul is quite striking. Everything in the text points directly to temple harlotry, and not to common harlotry.

Paul writes many times of the Holy Spirit dwelling in believers, without mentioning that they are the temple of the Holy Spirit.[318] In contrast here, when speaking of *pornay'ah* (1st Cor. 6:13, 18 twice), which is either common or cult harlotry, and having used the word for harlot (*pornay*) twice (in vv. 15, 16), he chooses to employ the concept that believers are the dwelling place or Temple of the living God. This parallels the idea that those who use the harlot are going to the temple, or dwelling place, of another god. Paul's use of *pornay'ah* (harlotry) and *pornay* (harlot) then, in this context, should be seen as referring to cult harlotry and cult harlots.

What most scholars say about this passage in reference to it being common harlotry or that it was primarily about the common harlot is not acceptable. The parallels are strongest when the passage is taken first and foremost as an admonishment against cult harlotry, especially in a city noted for it throughout the ancient pagan world.

Paul was speaking about cult prostitution to the Corinthian assembly in chapter six. Here are six reasons that support this position:

1. The ancient city of Corinth in northern Greece was known the world over for its temple prostitutes. In Corinth, 'the temple of Aphrodite with its 1,000 hierodules[319] was famous.'[320]

---

[318] 2nd Tim. 1:14. See also Rom. 14:17; 15:13, 16; 2nd Cor. 13:14; Eph. 1:13; 4:30; 1st Thess. 1:6; 4:8; Titus 3:5.

[319] Colin G. Kruse, B.D., M.Phil., Ph.D., Author; Leon Morris, M.Sc., M.Th., Ph.D., General Editor, *Tyndale New Testament Commentaries: 2 Corinthians* (Leicester, England: Inter-Varsity Press, 2000), pp. 15-16. Kruse contests this figure of one thousand cult prostitutes in Paul's day. He writes that Strabo's statement (where the 'thousand cult prostitutes' is taken from) refers to the city of Corinth before the Romans destroyed it in 146 BC. The Romans rebuilt it one hundred years later in 44 BC (ibid., pp. 14-15). It's very possible, though, that Corinth in Paul's day had the same number of cult prostitutes for Aphrodite. In the Apostle's day the city was about a hundred years old and the 'capital for the Roman province of Achaia' (ibid., p. 16). It was also a chief city of commerce in the Roman world because of its location. Kruse even admits that there 'is no doubt that Corinth was regaining its wealth and prestige

2. The Greek words for 'harlot' and 'harlotry' equally mean 'cult harlot' and 'cult harlotry.' To say that it was only, or primarily, common harlotry that Paul addressed, would have meant that Paul was blind to a reality that pervaded the entire city.

3. Paul's use of the phrases, 'the body is the Lord's...members of Christ' and the 'temple of God,' imply a direct connection to idolatry. These, along with his use of *joined*, which conceptually links it to the Baal Peor fiasco, lend themselves to seeing the passage as a contrast between Yeshua and other gods, not just a common prostitute. Paul will also speak of the Baal Peor affair in chapter ten, which specifically deals with cult prostitution.

4. Paul's use of the phrase, 'All things are lawful unto me' is also repeated in 1st Cor. 10:23 where cult harlotry and sacrificial idolatry are specifically addressed. This lends itself to chapter six dealing

---

in Paul's time' (ibid.).

Kruse also writes that Corinth in Paul's day was infested with pagan worship and that Aphrodite was still the chief goddess: the 'new Corinth became a centre for the worship of many of the old Graeco–Roman gods. He' (Kruse speaking of the ancient writer Pausanias in 174 AD) 'refers to temples or altars dedicated to Poseidon, Palaemon, Aphrodite, Artemis, Dionysus, Helius, Hermes, Apollo, Zeus, Isis, Eros and others. Strabo recorded that in his time there was a small temple to Aphrodite on the summit of Acrocorinth, while' by the time of Pausanias, 'the ascent to the Acrocorinth was punctuated by places of worship dedicated to various deities including Isis, Helius, Demeter and Pelagian. On the summit there was still found the temple of Aphrodite with images of Helius, Eros and Aphrodite herself. Clearly then,' says Kruse, 'the new Corinth of Paul's day was still a center for the worship of Aphrodite, as the old city had been prior to its destruction in 146 BC' (ibid., p. 15).

Even if the new Corinth couldn't rival the old for its thousand cult prostitutes to Aphrodite, how many less did it have in Paul's day? Aphrodite was the chief goddess, as attested to by the fact that her temple was located on the highest point of the city, and Corinth was the fourth largest city in the Roman Empire at that time (Findlay, *St. Paul's First Epistle to the Corinthians*, p. 730). Morris (*1 Corinthians*, p. 18) writes, the 'new Corinth' would have 'an equally unsavory reputation.' There were probably a thousand or more cult prostitutes for Aphrodite in Paul's day. However, whatever their number, Paul and the Corinthian believers would still have had to deal with them and *all the other cult harlots* of the *other* gods and goddesses in Corinth. Whether Aphrodite had a thousand or just five, cult harlotry among the Corinthian believers was a major problem for Paul, and also, for the average sailor. Most likely what Strabo wrote of Corinth before the Roman destruction still pertained to Corinth in the Apostle's day: "Many sea captains squandered their money paying for the services of these cult harlots, so that the proverb, 'Not for every man is the voyage to Corinth,' was in use among them" (Kruse, p. 14).

[320] Kittel, *Theological Dictionary of the New Testament*, vol. VI, p. 582.

with the same problem with which chapter ten deals with, which is a further teaching against cult harlotry, an extension of the teaching that began in chapters five and six.

5. In an almost identical rebuke to the very same people, Paul, in 2nd Cor. 6:14-17, speaks against *cult* prostitution. In 1st Cor. 6:19 he writes of the believer's body being the temple of the Holy Spirit and the dwelling place of God. This he reiterates in 2nd Cor. 6:15-16 with the words 'Belial' and 'idols.' Paul comes against cult prostitution in 2nd Cor. 6. The parallel to 1st Cor. 6 is obvious.

6. As R. J. Knowling stated,[321] and as the chapter on *Cult Prostitution in the New Testament* (p. 133f.) will point out, the use of *pornay'ah* in the New Testament speaks first and foremost of cult prostitution, not common prostitution. For someone to suggest common harlotry over cult harlotry they would have to prove it, but this is not possible.

These six reasons reveal that the prostitution the Apostle spoke of in 1st Cor. 6 was temple prostitution, not common prostitution.

In relation to Torah, Paul is not doing anything in this passage that conflicts with the Law of Moses. He's not suggesting that one can break any of the laws of Moses, even with his use of the phrase, 'All things are lawful unto me.' On the contrary, he's calling the Corinthians to accountability in the area which Torah is most adamant, even though they are 'free in Christ' and 'under Grace.'

From both a textual and a sociological point of view, the Apostle's stern warning to the Corinthians in chapter six supports the understanding that *pornay'ah* in Acts 15:20 also means *cult* prostitution. Paul's opposition to it here is exactly what James spoke against in his Decree to Gentile believers. It's not a coincidence.

---

[321] Knowling, *The Acts of the Apostles*, p. 324; also, p. 82 above. Witherington, *The Acts of the Apostles*, p. 463. Witherington says of *pornay'ah* in Acts 15:20 that its 'most basic meaning refers to prostitution, *including* so-called sacred prostitution.'

# More Cult Prostitution in Corinth: 1st Cor. 10

The Apostle Paul begins chapter ten by speaking of the danger of walking in idolatry and how it can sever one from God. Ancient Israel in the Wilderness had much in the way of God's divine grace upon them, but failed to walk in faith when God tested them (Dt. 8:1-3). Paul cautioned the Corinthians against such things, writing specifically against cult prostitution in v. 8. The first four verses express the conceptual unity between ancient Israel and the Gentile Corinthian believers. Paul begins by showing them that the Fathers of Israel were their Fathers, too:

> 'For I do not want you to be unaware, brethren, that our Fathers were all under the Cloud and all passed through the Sea and all were baptized into Moses in the Cloud and in the Sea. And all ate the same spiritual food and all drank the same spiritual drink for they were drinking from a spiritual Rock which followed them[322] and the Rock was Christ' (1st Cor. 10:1-4).

The Apostle wanted the Corinthians to understand that Israel, too, was in covenant with Yahveh and that the 'Body of Moses' preceded, and was a picture of, the Body of Messiah. Both were chosen of God and both had God's gracious hand upon them, but people in both could sever themselves from that Grace. Morris sees this parallel and writes,

> 'the Israelites, without exception, received the tokens of God's good hand on them. The fact that most perished (v. 5) comes accordingly with greater force. The cloud was the means of divine guidance at the time of the Exodus (Ex. 13:21-22) when the people passed through the sea (Ex. 14:21-22).' Their 'participation in the great events of the Exodus brought the Israelites under the leadership of Moses.' They 'were united to him' in a *similar* way that we are to Messiah. They were all likewise sustained by the manna (Ex. 16:4, 13f.)...and spiritual drink...which refers to Christ and sees him as following the Israelites

---

[322] Paul's Pharisaic training comes to the forefront in 'the Rock that followed them.' It's not found in the Bible, but the Rabbis teach that a literal rock actually followed Israel. We see a similar thing when Jude writes that the Devil contended for the body of Moses (Jude 1:9; see Dt. 34:5-6). Nowhere in Scripture is that stated, either. Jude most likely got that from an apocryphal book of the first century BC called *The Assumption of Moses*. These are two instances of understanding from Paul, and a half brother of Yeshua, whose name is Judah in English (Latin: Jude) lived. They come into the New Testament as fact, but are only rabbinic traditions or fables (see also 2nd Tim. 3:8).

and continually giving them drink...Nevertheless... although God had given them such signal manifestations of
his power and goodness, the majority failed to enter the
Promised Land' and that Paul's warning now, 'against
*idolatry* is *very relevant to conditions in Corinth*.'[323]

Paul will go on to link the idolatry of the Corinthians with the debacle of
the Gold Calf orgy, and with the 'craving for food' that killed many in the
Wilderness (Num. 11:4-34). He'll then present Israel at Baal Peor and use
their unfaithfulness to God as a springboard to declare cult harlotry 'off-
limits' for the Corinthians. The Apostle will then bring the Family history
lesson to a close, warning the Gentiles that membership in the Body of
Messiah is not a guarantee—one can fall from Grace. Paul writes:

[5]"Nevertheless, with most of them God was not well
pleased for they were laid low in the Wilderness. [6]Now
these things happened *as examples for us*, so that we
would not crave evil things as they also craved. [7]Do not
be *idolaters*, as some of them were; as it is written, 'The
people sat down to eat and drink, and stood up to play.'
[8]Nor let us act immorally, as some of them did' (lit. 'Neither let us commit fornication as some of them committed
fornication')[324] 'and twenty-three thousand fell in one
day.'[325] (1st Cor. 10:5-8)

The reference to the people sitting down to eat and to play (the harlot) is a
direct reference to the Gold Calf (Ex. 32:6). Here cult harlotry was practiced in the Name of Yahveh, the Calf being being proclaimed as Yahveh
(Ex. 32:4-5, 8). 'To play' speaks of sexual misconduct. It's another way of
translating the Hebrew verb *zanah* (to prostitute—to play the harlot). Israel sacrificed to and worshiped the god of gold, indulging in idolatrous
sex in the Name of Yahveh.

Paul's second reference is to those that fell in one day ('Neither let us

---

[323]  Morris, *1 Corinthians*, pp. 139-140.

[324]  Brown, *The New Greek-English Interlinear New Testament*, p. 601.

[325]  This is a reference to Numbers 25:9. Even though Paul seems to be 'off' by
1,000, Keil (*The Pentateuch*, p. 792) states, 'The Apostle Paul deviates from
this statement in 1st Cor. 10:8 and gives the number of those that fell as
twenty-three thousand, probably from a traditional interpretation of the
schools of the scribes, according to which a thousand were deducted from the
twenty-four thousand who perished, as being the number of those who were
hanged by the judges' (i.e. at the command of Yahveh, Num. 25:4-5), 'so that
only twenty-three thousand would be killed by the plague; and it is to these
alone that Paul refers.' This is another example of Rabbinic influence in the
New Testament that doesn't have any Scripture to support it.

commit fornication…23,000 fell in one day' v. 8) and is rightly seen by Stern, Morris, Findlay and *Wycliffe* as the Baal Peor affair. Obviously, *fornication* here must mean cult harlotry. There would have been no reason to give these sexually idolatrous warnings if some Corinthian believers weren't engaged in cult prostitution. Paul continues:

> [11]'Now these things happened to them as an example, and they were written for our instruction, upon whom the ends of the ages have come. [12]Therefore let him who thinks he stands take heed that he does not fall. [13]No temptation has overtaken you, but such as is common to man; and God is faithful, who will not allow you to be tempted beyond what you are able but with the temptation will provide the way of escape also, so that you will be able to endure it. [14]Therefore my beloved, flee from *idolatry!*' (1st Corin. 10:11-14)

The *idolatry* from which Paul warned the Corinthians to flee from was sexual in nature (cult harlotry). The phrase, 'No temptation has overtaken you, but such as is common to man,' doesn't speak of just any temptation, but of cult harlotry (v. 8); idolatry (vv. 7, 14); tempting Messiah (v. 9, which involves disbelief and complaining about one's situation, as the fiery serpents sent among them spoke of Israel's belligerence over not having the food and water they wanted; Num. 20:5-9), and carnal lust for meat (v. 6). Paul told them that he realized that cult harlotry was a great temptation (craving or lust),[326] but he warned them and pointed out that as those Israelis fell, so would the Gentile believers who continued in sacrificial-sexual idolatry. Cult harlotry and belief in Yeshua were incompatible.

Not all idol worship involves prostitution. In some instances idol worship or idolatry is the burning of incense to a statue or astrology or ancestor worship or magic, etc. Israel entered into cult harlotry through idolatrous sacrifices and orgies (Ex. 32:1-6f.; Num. 25:1-13). Cult harlotry falls under the general heading of idolatry, being the *sexual* expression of idolatry. By telling the Corinthian believers to flee from idolatry in 10:14, Paul was reinforcing what he had written in 6:18.

Paul admonishes the Corinthians not to commit this abomination against God. The Greek word for fornication is *pornay'ah* (10:8). It's also used in

---

[326] Believers today are continually bombarded by the spirit of harlotry (Hos. 5:11; Rev. 17:1-6). Newspapers, billboards, television and movies are filled with men and women seductively dressed and lewd in their behavior, tempting all who happen to look their way. Pornography (a word from *pornay'ah*, prostitution) is everywhere and many believers are ignorantly emulating these shameful and corrupt human *idols*. The way that many in the Church dress today would be enough to make the bold-faced harlots of ancient Israel blush.

1st Cor. 5:1 (twice), 6:13 (once), 6:15-16 (twice *pornay*, prostitute) and 6:18 (twice, fornication). Why would *pornay'ah* be *cult* prostitution in chapter ten, but only common harlotry (or 'sexual immorality') in chapter six? Was Paul addressing two different groups of Christians within the assembly at Corinth, one for chapter six and the other for chapter ten? This could hardly be the case—he doesn't mention leaving off from one group to write to the other, but continually addresses them as one body in the midst of their cliques (1st Cor. 1:12-13; 3:1-4, 21; 10:17).

Chapter ten is the follow-up to chapters five and six. It's dealing with the same problem and the same people, but from a different angle. In chapter five Paul dealt with the specifics of the man involved in incestuous cult harlotry. In chapter six he resorted to a philosophical-religious approach ('All things are lawful' and the believer is 'the temple of God') to deal with the cult harlotry. In chapter ten the Apostle wrote of the history of Israel and how the Corinthians were part of Israel and should learn from them ('examples for us,' v. 6 and 'for our instruction,' v. 11).

In chapter seven, Paul told them to get married if they couldn't abstain (stating in 7:2 to avoid fornication by having a spouse). In chapter eight he spoke of the eating of idolatrous sacrifices and in nine he declared that he had every right to be paid by the Corinthians for the spiritual services he rendered, although he said he wouldn't take that right as it might interfere with the Great News (Gospel). Then he continued his thoughts concerning fornication from chapters five, six (and eight) into chapter ten.

Why didn't Paul write chapter ten immediately after chapters five and six (and include eight in the middle)? There's really no problem with Paul's discourse except that we see it in different chapters, but he didn't insert chapter and verse. Perhaps if he had had a computer he could have tidied it up a bit more. That it may not be the most logical sequence for some people doesn't allow for the fact that Paul was a human being writing a letter nearly two thousand years ago. Most likely, he was dictating his thoughts as they came to him (1st Cor. 16:21). It's not uncommon in his letters for him to wander off in another direction and then return to a previous thought and expound upon it, but even here, those who would discredit the Apostle concerning chapters five through ten don't do him justice. The chapters indeed reveal a development along the theme of Corinthian behavior in relation to cult prostitution, pagan sacrifices, and their attitude toward one another.

Leon Morris states that chapter ten is not a fresh thought for the Apostle Paul, *but a continuation of the Apostle's thoughts on cult prostitution:*

> 'This is not a new subject, for *fornication*…formed a part
> of much *idol worship*. Sacred prostitutes were found at

many shrines and Corinth had an unenviable notoriety in this respect. But Paul's *primary* reference is to the incident in which 'Israel began to indulge in' cult harlotry 'with Moabite women' and *'joined in worshipping* the Baal of Peor.'[327]

Morris rightly sees fornication here as cult harlotry ('idol worship... Sacred prostitutes...many shrines...worshipping the Baal of Peor') and that this wasn't the first time in the letter that Paul spoke about it ('not a new subject'). Paul was further addressing the problem from chapters five, six and eight, as the Spirit led him. This wasn't the first, nor the last time that Paul would address cult harlotry among his Gentile believers.

Also, Witherington finds in Paul's very first letter that the Apostle addresses *pornay'ah* (First Thessalonians 50 AD) which was written about a year after the Council of Acts 15 (48-49 AD). He notes the similarity between James speaking of the Gentiles *turning to God* (Acts 15:19) and therefore, needing to give up *idolatry*, and Paul saying that the Thessalonians had 'turned to God from idols' to serve 'a living and true God (1 Thess. 1:9).'[328] Paul also addresses *pornay'ah* in 1st Thess. 4:1-9, but Witherington says that,

> the 'fuller discussion of Paul's understanding of the decree comes however, in 1 Corinthians, especially chapters 5-10, where' (in 1st Cor. 10:7) 'ειδωλοθυτον' (*aedolothutone*) 'refers to meat sacrificed and eaten in the presence of idols.'[329]

Corinth wasn't an isolated incident.[330] A translation that would vastly improve understanding for 1st Cor. 6:15-16 would use 'temple harlot' or 'cult harlot,' instead of just 'harlot' or 'prostitute.' Without it, the translation gives the impression that the fornication from which Paul was telling them to flee from was just common harlotry (6:18) or 'sexual immorality.' Obviously, cult prostitution is sexually immoral, but who would be able to decipher 'sexual immorality,' either in Acts 15:20 (48-49 AD) or 1st Corinthians (52 AD) to understand that it was cult prostitution? No one.

---

[327] Morris, *1 Corinthians*, p. 142.

[328] Witherington, *The Acts of the Apostles*, p. 465. See also further in the letter where Paul seems to hearken back to both 1st Thess. 1:9 and Acts 15:20 when he speaks of the commandments he gave the Thessalonians (4:2), his use of *pornay'ah* (sexual idolatry) and sanctification (4:3), the passion and lust of the Gentiles (4:5), uncleanness (4:7) and the Holy Spirit (4:8). All these point to the theme of Acts 15:20: sacrificial-sexual idolatry.

[329] Ibid., p. 466.

[330] Paul also speaks of it in Galatians 5:19; Ephesians 5:3 and Colossians 3:5.

Some questions that some might ask are: 'Why didn't Paul appeal directly to the Law of Moses if the Law was still in effect?,' and 'Why didn't he just include the four rules from James?'

Paul appeals to the Law in chapter ten, relating that ancient Hebrew history was written *for Gentile Corinthian example and instruction*. He's giving the consequences of breaking the Law (in picture form; e.g. the Baal Peor affair) to impress upon them what could also happen to them.[331]

Paul dealt with the Corinthians in chapters six and ten, using their own terms and philosophy and the historical-spiritual reality of ancient Israel. Perhaps he saw this as a more powerful way to deal with them than to put forward the rules of James, which they most likely *already knew* (Acts 16:4-5), but hadn't been obeying. Findlay writes:

> 'To draw a hard and fast line in such questions and to forbid all participation in *idolothyta*, after the precedent of Acts xv, would have been the simplest course to take; but Paul feels it necessary to round the matter on fundamental principles.'[332]

Paul was dealing with a people steeped in cult prostitution and diabolical philosophy. As a shepherd he was dealing with it in the way that the Spirit was leading him, given the people and the situation. He was teaching them from different concepts the reasons for the rules and why they shouldn't be involved in cult prostitution. Knowling also sees this and adds that just because Paul doesn't mention the Decree, one shouldn't think that it did not happen or that Paul didn't recognize it:

> 'St. Paul's language in 1 Cor. 8:1-13; 10:14-22; Rom. 14, may be fairly said to possess the spirit of the Decree, and to mark the discriminating wisdom of one eager to lead his disciples behind the rule to the principle...there is no more reason to doubt the historical truth of the compact made in the Jerusalem Decree, because St. Paul never expressly refers to it, than there is to throw doubt upon his statement in Gal. 2:10, because he does not expressly refer to it as an additional motive for urging the Corinthians to join in the collection for the poor saints, 2 Cor 8:9.'[333]

Paul addressed the Corinthians in ways that we would like to be addressed

---

[331] See p. 99, note 281 for places in 1st Corinthians where Paul uses the Law to validate his points.

[332] Findlay, *St. Paul's First Epistle to the Corinthians*, pp. 731-732.

[333] Knowling, *The Acts of the Apostles*, p. 336.

if we were walking in darkness and thinking that it was the *Light*. His not mentioning the Decree of Acts 15 doesn't mean that it didn't happen or that Paul rejected it, or that he never gave it to the Corinthians.

The Law was valid for the Apostle.[334] In First Corinthians Paul uses a specific commandment in the Law of Moses to establish his authority and right to collect funds from them. He relates in 9:8-9 (and 1st Tim. 5:18) that the ox treading out the corn was not to be muzzled (a commandment of the Law; Dt. 25:4). He then goes on to draw the analogy between spreading the Gospel and receiving money from those who benefited from it. The Apostle gives analogies from various forms of work (soldier, farmer, etc.) and then turns to the Law *to cement his legal basis for this right*. As Morris states, Paul's use of the commandment is *authoritative* because *the Law settled the issue of Paul's right to funds:*

> 'Paul rejects the thought that the principle he is enunciating and illustrating from various fields of human endeavor rests simply on human wisdom (it is not a human point of view). He can show it in the *Law,*' which 'is *always regarded as authoritative.*'[335]

Paul used the Law to support his argument that he was entitled to financial support from the Corinthians. If the Law wasn't for Gentile Christians, Paul could not have used it.

The concern that James had in Acts 15:20, about cult prostitution in the Gentile community, was a stark reality that Paul faced among the Corinthian believers. That believers would do this, *thinking that it was alright,* reveals their spiritual condition. The blood of Yeshua forgives things that could not be forgiven under Mosaic Law, like murder and adultery (Acts 13:38-39; see also Joel 3:20-21). This, and the fact that the Gentiles were just learning to walk in Christ, enabled Paul not to sever them immediately from the believing community for their sacrificial-sexual idolatry (although he did act decisively with the Christian in 1st Cor. 5:1-5). Yet, is there anyone who would suggest that if those Corinthians continued in cult harlotry, that 'Grace' would cover them forever (Gal. 5:19-21)?

The significant places in First Corinthians where *pornay'ah* appears[336] reveal that cult harlotry is specifically what Paul meant when he wrote of *pornay'ah* (KJV fornication). Cult prostitution was primarily what Paul had in mind when he wrote chapters five, six, eight and ten.

---

[334] Rom. 3:31; 7:12, 14; 1st Cor. 5:6-8; 7:19, etc.

[335] Morris, *1 Corinthians*, p. 132. *Italics* are those of Morris.

[336] The reference in 1st Cor. 7:2, where the Apostle offers marriage as a viable option to fornication, can mean cult and/or common prostitution.

First Corinthians provides biblical and historical support for how Yakov used the word *pornay'ah*, even if his context wasn't seen as sacrificial idolatry. Being listed with three other rules on idolatry only strengthens the position that Yakov was warning the Gentiles to not engage in sacrificial-sexual idolatry. It had nothing to do with table fellowship and cannot be used to prove that the four rules were 'the only rules for the Gentile.'

In the days of Paul, going to pagan temples and cult harlots was as acceptable and honorable to the Gentiles as going to church is today for Christians. There was no social or moral stigma attached to it. Aside from Israel when she was faithful, that's the kind of darkness that was over *the whole world*.[337]

Yakov instituted the four rules as a filter for Gentiles who were entering into Yeshua's Kingdom. Most of them didn't have an understanding that temple harlotry and the worship of other gods was wrong. These rules were the most important laws for the Gentile to know immediately because it concerned his salvation, but obviously, not the only rules, just from the fact that these rules from the Law are given to the Gentiles.

The four rules of James prove that Torah is for every believer today. Grace must always be tempered with Law or people will do what they think is right in their own eyes. Many times, as we find with the Corinthians, this is sin in God's eyes (Dt. 12:8; Judges 17:6; 21:25; 1st Cor. 5–10).

The Corinthians had other problems revolving around sacrificial idolatry that needed to be addressed. The next two sections deal with the idolatrous practice of eating the meat and drinking the blood of the sacrifice to the idol. The first was addressed by Yakov. It was his first prohibition. The second was also addressed by him. It was his fourth rule in Acts 15:20.

---

[337] Hislop, *The Two Babylons,* pp. 14, 20, 57, 60, 77, 95, 133, 174, 199, 230, etc.

# Fellowship with Devils: 1st Cor. 10:16-22

In looking at another aspect of pagan worship from Acts 15:20, the drinking of blood (or a symbolic representation of the blood),[338] the Apostle Paul strongly rebukes some of the Corinthians for partaking of the cup of demons![339] Can this really be? *Christians* drinking blood to demons and thinking that it's alright? Paul speaks of how it would make God feel (jealous) and what it would mean to them (they would be severed; cut off from Messiah). Both concepts recall Israel at Baal Peor. Paul writes,

> 'Is not the cup of blessing which we bless, a sharing in the blood of Christ? Is not the bread which we break a sharing in the Body of Christ? Since there is one bread, we who are many are one body; for we all partake of the one Bread. Look at the nation of Israel. Are not those who eat the sacrifices sharers in the Altar? What do I mean then? That a thing *sacrificed to idols* is anything or that an idol is anything? No, but I say that the things which the Gentiles sacrifice, *they sacrifice to demons* and not to God and I do not want you to become sharers in (partners with)[340] demons.' (KJV: 'and I would not that ye should have fellowship with devils.')

> 'You cannot drink the Cup of the Lord and the *cup of demons!* You cannot partake of the Table of the Lord and the table of demons! Or do we provoke the Lord *to jealousy?!* We are not stronger than He, are we?' (1st Cor. 10:16-22)

It's not a minor problem that Paul is addressing. His reference to *idols* and *jealousy* speaks of how Yahveh felt in the Baal Peor affair (Num. 25:11, 13). It means that Yeshua would cut them off just as Yahveh cut off those Israelis who sacrificed to Baal Peor. What God had done to His people Israel, He was capable of doing to His people Israel who were Gentiles.

Some Gentile believers were drinking the cup of demons and didn't realize that it was wrong. Their religious culture permitted them to include the

---

[338] Hislop, *The Two Babylons*, p. 5. An alternative drink could be made of 'wine, honey, water, and flour' as an intoxicant to dull the senses, arouse the passions and lead the pagan further on. Flour would make the mixture thicken so it would resemble blood all the more.

[339] 1st Cor. 10:16-22. The whole congregation wasn't doing this, but obviously some (many?) were. This is an example where, if they had been raised in the Law of Moses they would never have considered this.

[340] Brown, *The New Greek-English Interlinear New Testament*, p. 472.

worship of Jesus with the practices of their other gods. Paul told them they couldn't worship their idols *and* worship Yeshua. The history of Israel was to be a warning to them. He didn't want them unaware or ignorant of what would happen to them if they disobeyed.

Those Corinthian believers drank the blood of the sacrifice as part of the ritual of sacrificial-sexual idolatry. As to the seriousness of the matter, Findlay states,

> 'where the feast is held under the auspices of a heathen god and as a sequel to his sacrifice...participation under these circumstances *becomes an act of apostasy*, and the *feaster identifies himself with the idol* as distinctly as in the Lord's Supper he identifies himself with Christ.'[341]

The reference to the table of demons is the first rule of James: don't eat meat sacrificed to an idol *at the time and place of the sacrifice*. Three of the four rules of James are expressly pointed out by Paul in First Corinthians (cult harlotry, sacrificial blood and sacrificial meat). Also, this section is Paul's closure for chapter eight, where some might think he was condoning the eating of meat sacrificed to an idol in the temple (8:1-13).

In his article on *Sacrifices and Offerings in the NT*, T. R. Schreiner affirms that Paul was dealing with some incredibly perverse concepts of what it meant 'to believe in Jesus.' He writes,

> 'how can they sit at the Lord's table and participate in the benefits of the Lord's death and at the same time sit down in an idol's temple and participate in the benefits of that which was sacrificed to idols? Obviously, such behavior is completely incongruous and inappropriate. One cannot have it both ways, gaining the benefits of Christ's death and at the same time expose oneself to demonic influences (1 Cor. 10:20-22).'[342]

Schreiner doesn't seem to have an understanding of the Gentile (pagan) mentality. Be that as it may, this is why James prohibited *pollutions of idols* and *blood* (his third prohibition) in Acts 15:20. What's plain for all of us to see today, went directly against many Gentile Christians in Corinth because they were raised in paganism. The need for the four rules and the Law of Moses was very necessary in the Corinthian assembly.

---

[341] Findlay, *St. Paul's First Epistle to the Corinthians*, p. 732.

[342] Bromiley, *The International Standard Bible Encyclopedia*, vol. four, p. 277.

# Beef in the Market: 1st Cor. 10:23-28

The buying and the eating of meat in the marketplace for common consumption is a corollary to what Paul has been addressing. In 1st Cor. 8, Paul *seems* to allow the believer to enter the pagan shrine and eat the sacrificial meat. His reasoning? The 'idol is nothing.' This would seem to contradict James, but Morris rightly points out that chapter eight wasn't Paul's final word on the subject. It only brings out his thoughts that an idol is nothing (compared to Yeshua). Morris writes that Paul,

> 'is certainly not giving his own full idea on the matter, for he later says that what is sacrificed to idols is actually sacrificed to devils (10:20). There are spiritual beings behind the idols, though not the ones their worshippers thought. But here this is not the point. Paul is prepared to agree that the gods the heathen worship are no gods.'[343]

The Apostle also speaks of not causing one's brother stumble, if he sees him in the pagan temple (1st Cor. 8:7-13). By dealing with the issue of temple attendance this way, Paul is saying that the believer should not be seen in the temple, even though the idol is nothing. This is his way of prohibiting the eating of the meat at the pagan temple for the believer who thought that there was nothing wrong with doing it.

When Paul speaks of the sacrificial meat ('table of demons') in 10:21 he reveals his fuller thoughts on the subject by declaring that they weren't to do that. With 'meat in the market,' the *essential* difference is that the believer is *not a participant in the temple sacrifice*. This is an important distinction. In 1st Cor. 10:23-28 Paul writes:

> 'All things are lawful, but not all things are profitable. All things are lawful, but not all things edify. Let no one seek his own good, but that of his neighbor. *Eat anything* that is sold *in the meat market* without asking questions for conscience sake, for the Earth is the Lord's and all it contains.'

> "If one of the unbelievers invites you and you want to go, *eat anything* that is set before you without asking questions for conscience sake. But if anyone says to you, 'This is meat sacrificed to idols,' do not eat it for the sake of the one who informed you, and for conscience sake."

In chapter six the understanding that all things were lawful for Paul meant that, theoretically he, too, was able to do anything he wanted within Ro-

---

[343] Morris, *1 Corinthians*, p. 122.

man jurisprudence. For Paul, the phrase 'eat anything' *would fall within the boundaries* of 'anything' that God declared to be clean. He wouldn't eat a ham sandwich because he knew that it was a sin for him and for others.[344] The text is not speaking about clean vs. unclean meat, but about meat sacrificed to idols. Paul isn't authorizing the eating of unclean meat. He says that it's alright to eat meat, which had been sacrificed, and then sold at the market (or given for dinner in another's home) as long as the buyer/guest didn't know that it had been sacrificed.

From two important passages of Scripture (Acts 15:20; Rev. 2:20) it has seemed to some that Paul is contradicting both James and Jesus in allowing believers to eat meat sacrificed to idols, but James admonished the Gentile believers not to eat meat that was literally just sacrificed on the altar, as Witherington brought out,[345] specifically referring to it in Acts 15:20 as 'the pollutions of idols.' In 1st Cor. 10:16-22 Paul forbids the same thing. Eating from the table of demons spoke of eating the just sacrificed animal, the person actually participating in the sacrifice and worship of another god. (The same would apply to the drinking of its blood.)

In Rev. 2:20-21 Messiah Yeshua comes against the eating of the meat at the time of the sacrifice, and also, cult prostitution (*fornication*):

> 'Notwithstanding I have a few things against thee, because thou sufferest that woman Jezebel, which calleth herself a prophetess, to teach and to seduce my servants to commit *fornication* and *to eat things sacrificed unto idols.* And I gave her space to repent of her fornication; and she repented not.' (Rev. 2:20-21 KJV)

Those Gentile *Christians* at Thyatira were indulging in cult harlotry and eating animals sacrificed to idols. It seems that 'Jezebel' taught them that sacrificial-sexual idolatry was an acceptable Christian practice and that eating the sacrificial meat (at the sacrifice) was alright. Yeshua had earlier rebuked her for it, but she had not repented.

Paul allowed believers to eat sacrificial meat (1st Cor. 10:23-28), but not at the sacrifice to the god. It pertained to the Gentile in the market seeking to buy some meat. They're told by Paul not to ask if it had been sacrificed (1st Cor. 10:25), which means that all meat sold in the market didn't come from pagan sacrifices. This is how Paul could say what he does, and not be coming against James or Jesus. Paul allows the Gentile to eat this meat

---

[344] See 1st Tim. 4:4-5, and note well, the *two* qualifications for what makes food acceptable to eat: prayer *and* the Word of God (e.g. Scriptures like Lev. 11) *not just prayer.* See *Law 102* at http://SeedofAbraham.net/law102.html for why the Church's position on the Law of Moses isn't biblical.

[345] See Witherington, p. 20.

because 'idols are nothing' (1st Cor. 8:4, 7, 10) the Earth is the Lord's and everything in it (Ex. 9:29; Ps. 24:1; 1st Cor. 10:28) and they're not eating it at the time of the sacrifice.

Some of the meat in the marketplace would come from a pagan sacrifice, the pagan priests selling the excess to the vendors in the market. This was common. Morris states, 'The priests customarily sold what they could not use.'[346] Other meat might be 'blessed' by a pagan priest and then slaughtered in the marketplace by the 'butcher,' but not literally sacrificed on the pagan altar. With the blessing of the pagan priest the meat would be seen as 'fit for consumption,' having received the pagan 'seal of approval,' but it might concern some believers even though it hadn't been part of a sacrificial ceremony.[347] This is why Paul tells them that they can eat the meat in the market. They just shouldn't ask if it had been sacrificed.

Paul told them not to eat the meat if an unbeliever said it was from a pagan sacrifice, so as not to confuse the unbeliever in terms of being able to present the Great News to him. He's *not* saying, 'don't ask,' if someone puts pork chops in front of you. No, Paul is speaking of a non-Christian home, where meat may have been used in a pagan sacrifice, not *which* meat to eat (clean vs. unclean). In the year and a half that Paul taught the believers at Corinth (Acts 18:11) he most likely would have had a few classes on the dietary laws (Lev. 3:17; 11:1-47; Dt. 12:16, 23; 14:1-21).

Witherington notes Paul's different Greek word for sacrificial meat eaten in the home and writes:

> 'It was okay to eat food sacrificed in a pagan temple at home. Paul specifically chooses a different term to refer to food that comes from the temple and is eaten else-where—ειπoθυτoν' (*aepo'thutone*) '(1 Cor. 10:28). In short, Paul, like James, insists that pagans flee idolatry' and cult prostitution 'and the temple context where such things' were 'prevalent.'[348]

---

[346] Morris, *1 Corinthians*, p. 120.

[347] This is what Paul addresses in Romans 14, not clean vs. unclean meats (as some wrongly think). This practice also happens in South Africa today where Moslem 'priests' offer their blessing to Allah before the animals are slaughtered for market. At the supermarket this is the only meat one can buy (unless he goes to a kosher butcher). It has the religious seal of Islam on the wrapper, declaring that the meat was offered to Allah and is 'fit to eat.' A number of believers in South Africa have voluntarily refused to buy the meat, as a witness to others, that Allah is not the true God. They would be similar to the 'veggie' eaters of Romans 14:2f.

[348] Witherington, *The Acts of the Apostles*, p. 466.

Paul wasn't rebelling against James, in his allowing the Corinthians to eat meat from the market, even if it had been part of a sacrificial rite. His teaching complements what James wrote, addressing the issue of sacrificial meat in the market.

Paul's teaching in this area is what some might call *halacha*—how to walk out one's faith in a situation that isn't addressed in Mosaic Law. This situation would never arise in a land that kept the Law, like Israel was supposed to, because in such a land there would not be any pagan sacrifices (nor shrines or cult harlots). That's why there's nothing in Torah that specifically deals with the issue of eating meat from a market, which had been sacrificed to an idol. With the God of Israel coming to the Gentiles, in their lands that were steeped in paganism, this problem arose and Paul, led by the Spirit, dealt with it in a righteous and compassionate way.[349]

Along with the eating of sacrificial meat at the pagan altar and the drinking of the blood from the sacrifice, First Corinthians ten deals with cult harlotry and the fact that some Corinthian believers were engaging in it. Paul warns them to flee from it, presenting the Baal Peor affair to show the Corinthians that their salvation would be nullified if they continued in sacrificial-sexual idolatrous practices.

Yakov's rules were certainly needed in the Corinthian congregation. This section emphasizes the need for the Law of Moses so that the believer doesn't sin against God, thinking nothing of it. The Corinthian assembly *fell behind none of the other assemblies in the Gifts of the Spirit* (1st Cor. 1:4-7), yet their need for *instruction* in God's laws of righteousness is all too evident (2nd Tim. 3:10-17).

A number of places in First Corinthians that seemed to deal with common prostitution primarily spoke of cult prostitution. This problem wasn't an isolated incident, as Revelation 2:20-21 brought out. Corinth was in Achaia (modern-day northern Greece). Thyatira was in Asia Minor (modern-day western Turkey), but both were firmly rooted in ancient pagan ways of sacrificial-sexual idolatry.

---

[349] The decision and four rules of James in Acts 15 were also *halacha*. Gentiles coming *to believe in the Jewish Messiah* had no precedent in Torah: 'What must a Gentile do in order to be saved?,' was dealt with, as well as prohibiting the Gentiles from continuing in sacrificial-sexual idolatry.

# CULT PROSTITUTION IN REVELATION

There are many places in the New Covenant that use πορνεια (*pornay'ah*, fornication: cult or common prostitution), but none present as clear a picture of its cultic and symbolic use as Revelation does. In Rev. 2:20-21 and 2:14, in both Thyatira and Pergamos, the risen Savior is found rebuking *Christians* for practicing cult harlotry and for eating meat sacrificed to idols at the pagan temple at the time of the sacrifice. In the first passage it's a so-called prophetess within the congregation that was authorizing it. Yeshua warned the assembly at Thyatira:

> 'Notwithstanding I have a few things against thee, because thou sufferest that woman Jezebel, which calleth herself a prophetess, to teach and to seduce my servants to commit *fornication* and *to eat things sacrificed unto idols*. And I gave her space to repent of her fornication; and she repented not.' (Rev. 2:20-21 KJV)

It's hard to imagine that Christians would continue in this practice so many years after Acts 15 and Paul's letters to Corinth, etc., and this, in an area of western Turkey that Paul had once evangelized and taught in. More than 40 years after Acts 15, Jesus revealed to the Apostle John that *Christians* were still practicing cult harlotry and eating pagan sacrifices.

The fact that 'fornication' *and* eating 'things sacrificed to idols' are mentioned together means that they were part of the same pagan ceremony, the nature of which was union with the god (or goddess). Christians at Thyatira were being taught that fornication was acceptable, as a Christian. More subtle than all the beasts of the field is the Serpent. If asked if they 'believed in Yeshua' they, too, like their Hebrew counterparts in the Baal Peor Affair, would have said, 'Yes!'

Yeshua calling this prophetess *Jezebel*, was no light matter. Nine hundred years earlier a daughter of the King of Sidon named Jezebel became the wife of King Ahab. He ruled the northern kingdom of Israel for 22 years (1st Kings 16:29; 876-853 BC). Jezebel led Ahab and Israel astray by bringing in cult harlotry through her god Baal (1st Kgs. 16:31-33). Sacrifice to Baal also meant infant sacrifice. Jezebel had the true prophets of Yahveh murdered and wanted to do the same to Elijah.[350]

Everyone who knew Scripture would know what Yeshua thought of this new 'Jezebel,' and this, too, affirms her teaching as sacrificial-sexual idolatry because the original Jezebel was known for her cult harlotry (2nd Kings 9:21-22). Yeshua gave the Jezebel in Thyatira time to repent. In 1st

---

[350] 1st Kgs. 18:1-4; 19:1-3; also 1st Kgs. 17:29-33; 21:1-29; 2nd Kgs. 9:1-17.

Cor. 10 Paul did the same thing because the Corinthians didn't understand that Yeshua wasn't like Zeus and Aphrodite. The Gentiles hadn't been at Mt. Sinai or Baal Peor and they hadn't been taken into captivity to Babylon because of cult harlotry, but Yeshua's patience and grace has an end, too (2nd Cor. 12:21–13:6; Rev. 2:20-23).

Some might say, 'Well that's a lot different from when God killed 24,000 Hebrews.' That's true, but looking at the whole picture, the Lord also strove with Israel for *many centuries* concerning cult harlotry, sending His prophets to warn them (2nd Kgs. 17:1-23; Jer. 7:25; 35:15). *That* Israel hadn't crossed the Red Sea. *That* Israel hadn't heard the Voice and seen the Fire on the Mountain (Ex. 19:16f.), just like the Gentiles.[351]

Also, Yahveh's literal presence was with Israel in the Wilderness at the Baal Peor affair and the reality of Yahveh's presence existed after the resurrection for the body of believers in Jerusalem. All the Jewish believers heard about the untimely deaths of Ananias and Sapphira (Acts 5:1-11). Who killed them? The 'cruel God' of the Old or the 'loving God' of the New? The two of them had 'only' lied to Peter about how much money they had actually gotten from the sale of their property, but the Holy Spirit killed them. The Spirit would not do so in Jeremiah's day, nor at Corinth in Paul's day. The main difference, though, was the manifestation of the Lord, or the lack of it, which determined whether the punishment would be carried out immediately, or time given to repent.

That the Spirit of the living God wasn't manifesting in the same way for Paul is evident from all the problems that he had with the Corinthians. Many times he had to threaten them, particularly the ones who said that he was a powerful letter writer, but in person he was 'weak and nothing' (2nd Cor. 10:8-11; see also 1:23; 12:20f.). Can you imagine a Christian saying that about the Apostle Paul? If lying to Peter was enough for Ananias *and* Sapphira to be instantly killed by God, how much more those in Corinth who rebelled against Paul's authority and frequented temple harlots?

Yeshua also rebuked the congregation at Pergamos, another assembly in western Turkey, about 50 miles (80 kilometers) northwest of Thyatira. They were doing the same idolatrous things as Thyatira. Here, though, the Lord speaks to them of Balaam and Israel in the Wilderness. Balaam taught the daughters of Moab *to seduce the sons of Israel at Baal Peor.* Yeshua said to the Pergamos Christians,

> 'I know thy works and where thou dwellest, even where
> *Satan's throne is*, and thou holdest fast my name, and hast

---

[351] Even with the very Presence of God, Israel still sinned greatly, and many times the Lord exacted immediate punishment (Numbers 14:11-37f.; 25:1-9f.; 21:4-6).

not denied my faith, even in those days wherein Antipas was my faithful martyr, who was slain among you where *Satan dwelleth*.[352] But I have a few things against thee, because thou hast there them that hold the *doctrine of Balaam*, who taught Balak to cast a stumbling block before the Sons of Israel, *to eat things sacrificed unto idols* and *to commit fornication*.' (πορνευσαι *pornu'sai*; Rev. 2:13-14 KJV)

With the mention of Balaam, the fornication spoken of has to be cult harlotry, not common harlotry. The Baal Peor disaster is attributed to him via Balak (Num. 22–24). Numbers 31:16 states that Balaam caused Israel to sin at Baal Peor for which he was killed by Israel (Joshua 13:22).

Also, the ancient city of Pergamos was *especially* noted for sacrificial-sexual idolatry. The harlotry spoken of would have to be linked to cult harlotry even if the Lord only mentioned *fornication* in and of itself. The fact that they were eating things sacrificed to idols again confirms that the fornication was *cult* harlotry.

*Wycliffe* states that Pergamos was 'given to idolatry *more than all Asia*,' and that,

> the 'hill behind it was adorned with numerous temples, among which was the great temple to Zeus, who was called Soter Theos, the Savior God.'[353]

Explaining *fornication* and *things sacrificed* at Pergamos, Morris says,

> 'Feasting on sacrificial meat and licentious conduct were usual accompaniments *of the worship of idols,* both in Old *and* New Testament times.'[354]

David Stern realizes that the problem at Pergamos wasn't the same problem that Paul dealt with in Corinth when sacrificial meat was sold at the marketplace. He says that the 'issue here is not eating meat used in pagan

---

[352] Hislop, *The Two Babylons*, pp. 240-241. The Lord was literally declaring Pergamos to be the place where Satan had established his throne (headquarters). Just as Jerusalem is the home of Yahveh (Ps. 48:2), so ancient Babylon was the Throne of Satan. When Babylon was destroyed Satan transferred his headquarters to Nineveh, and after that, to Pergamos. It was in Pergamos, with the 'worship of Aesculapius, *under the form of the serpent*' that 'frantic orgies and excesses' were practiced 'that elsewhere were kept under some measure of restraint' (ibid.). After Pergamos Satan's throne was established in Rome.

[353] Pfeiffer, *The Wycliffe Bible Commentary*, p. 1504.

[354] Leon Morris, The Rev. Canon, M.Sc., M.Th., Ph.D., *Tyndale NT Commentaries: Revelation* (Leicester, England: Inter-Varsity Press, 2000), p. 67.

rituals, but actually participating in idolatrous feasts and sexual sin, thus violating the *mitzvot* laid down for Gentile believers at' Acts '15:28-29.'[355]

These two Christian assemblies in western Turkey, Thyatira and Pergamos, were criticized by Yeshua around 95 AD. They were walking in the same sins that Israel had walked in at Baal Peor 1,500 years earlier. Not much had changed in paganism in all that time. *TDNT* confirms this:

> 'For the author, the OT model for this is the doctrine of Balaam who led Israel astray in the same fashion, Num. 25:1ff.; 31:16. Along the same lines the church of Thyatira is charged with tolerating a prophetess who teaches the same practices, 2:20f.; the name of Jezebel is the OT reference in this instance, 2nd Kings 9:7, 22.'[356]

More than forty years after Yakov made his ruling, Yeshua had to speak against these idolatrous practices at two Christian assemblies in Asia Minor. It wasn't without divine foresight that Yakov gave those four rules under inspiration of the Holy Spirit (2nd Tim. 3:16-17; 2nd Pet. 3:15-18).

The diabolical scheme of Satan has been to beguile the world into worshiping him instead of Yahveh, even and especially in Israel among His own people. The core of that worship was cult harlotry. This came from ancient Babylon, the great seducer of Man's heart.

New Testament Babylon is the seducer of all the nations, causing the peoples to worship Satan, getting the Gentile and Jewish peoples to think they are worshiping the true God when in fact they are worshiping Satan in one of his many different guises. The Great Harlot is mentioned in nearly three identical passages (Rev. 14:8, 17:2 and 18:3) speaking about what she has given Mankind to drink—the wine of her *harlotry:*

> Revelation 14:8: 'And there followed another angel, saying, Babylon is fallen, is fallen, that great city, because she made all nations drink of the wine of the wrath of her *fornication.*' (πορνειας, *pornay'ahs*; KJV)

> Rev. 17:2: 'With whom the kings of the Earth have committed *fornication* (επορνειας, *eh'pornay'ahs*), and the inhabitants of the Earth have been made drunk with the wine of her *fornication.*' (πορνειας, *pornay'ahs*; KJV)

---

[355] Stern, *Jewish New Testament Commentary*, p. 796. The Hebrew term *mitzvot* means 'commandments' of God (through His authorized agents; e.g. Moses, Yeshua, Paul, Peter and James, etc.). Stern writes that the rules the Gentiles in Pergamos were 'violating' came from Acts 15:28-29, the recording of the rules in the letter sent to the Jewish and Gentile community of Antioch.

[356] Kittel, *Theological Dictionary of the New Testament*, vol. VI, p. 594.

Rev. 18:3: 'For all nations have drunk of the wine of the wrath of her *fornication* (πορνειας, *pornay'ahs*) and the kings of the Earth have committed *fornication* (επορ-νευσαν, *eh'pornu'sahn*) with her, and the merchants of the Earth are waxed rich through the abundance of her delicacies.' (KJV)[357]

All nations, Jewish and Gentile, have drunk of the wine of fornication of the Harlot of Babylon. That the term *fornication* here means more than cult harlotry is obvious. It should be just as obvious that it also includes it. *Fornication* in these passages takes in all spheres where one can prostitute the soul, from sacrificial-sexual 'worship' to financial greed, physical lust, political and even satanic power.

Babylon is the diabolical opposite of the heavenly Jerusalem where the true God is worshiped. *TDNT* speaks of Babylon and the Harlot as the antithesis of Jerusalem and God, and of her fornication as cultic:

'In the description of the world power and metropolis of Rome, the counterpart of ungodly Babylon…πορνη' (*pornay*, harlot) 'and πορνευω' (*pornu'oh*, harlotry) 'are used as comprehensive terms for its utter degeneracy. Like the city harlots of the day it bears its name on a gold-en headband, and this name declares its nature:'[358] 'And upon her forehead was a name written, Mystery, Babylon the Great, the Mother of harlots and abominations of the Earth.' (Rev. 17:5)

'It is the leading harlot of the world, the great seducer of the nations and their kings…They seek its favors politi-cally and economically. But the word embraces more than this. The nations ape the customs of the metropolis *even to whoredom in the literal sense.* Above all, the capital is called πορνη' (*pornay*, harlot) 'as the *center of paganism* with its harlot-like apostasy from the true God.'[359]

From the Book of Revelation, whether looking at Thyatira, Pergamos or the Great Harlot, the worship of another god or goddess through sex (cult prostitution) was a major part of what has shackled Mankind to Satan. The Gentiles never had a Father Abraham who worshiped the living God, or a

---

[357] The Textus Receptus and the NU text are identical in their usage of the Greek words concerning *fornication* (KJV), yet the NIV wrongly uses *adulteries* and the NASB *immorality* in these three cites from Revelation.

[358] Kittel, *Theological Dictionary of the New Testament*, vol. VI, p. 594.

[359] Ibid.

Moses who led the Sons of Israel out of Egyptian slavery under the mighty outstretched Arm of Yahveh. The Gentiles had no divine Lawgiver like Moses. Therefore, they had no godly boundaries to restrain their perverse feelings. With no Torah to restrain them, their lusts were directed by Satan and fueled by their carnal nature.

*All* the Gentile lands and peoples of the world were steeped in sacrificial-sexual idolatry. It permeated their thinking, their very being and their way of life. Part and parcel with this was the belief that one could have as many gods as he wanted. It would be very natural for a Gentile believer to *add* Jesus to his pantheon. Both First Corinthians and Revelation attest to this, the seriousness of the problem, and how widespread it was among professing Gentile Christians.

Of course, not all Gentile believers did this, for there were some 'God-fearers' like Cornelius who had been taught to stop practicing idolatry before they had come to Yeshua. There would also be others who would immediately stop when they found out what Yeshua required of them in this area because of the Decree of James, the letters of Paul and their learning of Torah every Sabbath.

Many of them, though, would sin in ignorance, while others would do it in their prideful and self-indulgent philosophy of 'freedom in Christ.' This is what the Apostle Paul dealt with at Corinth and this is why Yakov gave the four rules. The four rules have nothing to do with table fellowship, but with the placing of these important godly boundaries before the Gentiles.

Yakov would not only tell the Gentiles what they needed to do in order to be saved, but also what would sever them from their Savior. It was because the Gentiles needed to understand this—that they couldn't worship Yeshua *and* their others gods, that the four rules were issued. The Gentile religious world at the time of the Apostles was a world that was neck-deep in satanic quicksand—and thought nothing of it.

What compassion the God of Israel has for all peoples, in sacrificing His own Son for us. He's displayed a love that is infinitely beyond our ability to comprehend, but He does expect us to be faithful to Him.

# CULT PROSTITUTION

# IN THE NEW TESTAMENT

All the places in the King James Version New Testament where the word *pornay'ah* (fornication) and its noun derivatives occur will be listed in order to get a sense of *how* the words are used. *Fornication* is mentioned 32 times in the New Testament and all these times speak of cult prostitution or includes it. Five times it's found in lists with other sins, and with no context given, it could certainly be cultic as well as common harlotry.

## *Fornication: Cult Prostitution*

1. Matt. 5:32: 'But I say unto you, that whosoever shall put away his wife, saving for the cause of *fornication*, causeth her to commit adultery. And whosoever shall marry her that is divorced committeth adultery.'

2. Matt. 19:9: 'And I say unto you, whosoever shall put away his wife, except it be for *fornication*, and shall marry another, committeth adultery. And whoso marrieth her which is put away doth commit adultery.'

Yeshua declared that cult harlotry is biblical grounds for severing a marriage between two *believers*, not adultery, etc. Also, if this harlotry were common, it would be forgivable, hence, no need for a divorce.

3. John 8:41: "'Ye do the deeds of your father.' Then said they to him, 'We be not born of *fornication*; we have one Father, *even* God.'"

The context speaks of those whom Yeshua said were the offspring of another god (the Devil, v. 44). The Pharisees didn't answer saying that their earthly father wasn't involved in common prostitution or adultery, etc. Their speaking of *God* as their Father means that *fornication* here is to be understood as cult harlotry.

4. Acts 15:20: 'But that we write unto them, that they abstain from pollutions of idols, and from *fornication*, and from things strangled, and from blood.'

As we've seen, the text speaks of cult harlotry. Its biblical usage, Hebrew and Greek word definitions and its listing in the passage immediately after eating the meat of a pagan sacrifice at the time of the sacrifice, confirm this. The next two passages (#5-6) are references to Acts 15:20:

5. Acts 15:29: 'That ye abstain from meats offered to idols, and from

blood, and from things strangled, and from *fornication*: from which if ye keep yourselves, ye shall do well. Fare ye well.'

6. Acts 21:25: 'As touching the Gentiles which believe, we have written and concluded that they observe no such thing, save only that they keep themselves from things offered to idols, and from blood, and from (things) strangled, and from *fornication*.'

In Paul's very first letter (50-52 AD) he warns the Thessalonians to stay away from fornication. This comes about three years after Acts 15, and as there's no qualifier, it's primarily cult harlotry the Apostle is speaking of:

7. 1st Thess. 4:3: 'For this is the will of God, even your sanctification, that ye should abstain from *fornication*.'

This next *fornication* amazed Paul because it was *incestuous* cult harlotry:

8. 1st Corin. 5:1: 'It's reported commonly that there is *fornication* among you, and such *fornication* as is not so much as named among the Gentiles; that one should have his father's wife.'

As we saw, the next two verses primarily speak of cult prostitution:

9. 1st Cor. 6:13: 'Meats for the belly, and the belly for meats but God shall destroy both it and them. Now the body is not for *fornication* but for the Lord and the Lord for the body.'

10. 1st Cor. 6:18: 'Flee *fornication*! Every sin that a man doeth is without the body; but he that committeth *fornication* sinneth against his own body.'

This next verse falls between chapters five and ten of First Corinthians, an area which spoke of cult harlotry, although common harlotry would equally be included in this admonition:

11. 1st Cor. 7:2: 'Nevertheless, to avoid *fornication*, let every man have his own wife, and let every woman have her own husband.'

Number 12 refers to the Baal Peor disaster (Num. 25) and clearly speaks of cult harlotry:

12. 1st Cor. 10:8: 'Neither let us commit *fornication*, as some of them committed, and fell in one day three and twenty thousand.'

Paul continues to address cult harlotry in this next verse to the Corinthians who hadn't taken to heart what he wrote in First Corinthians:

13. 2nd Cor. 12:21: 'And lest when I come again, my God will humble me among you and that I shall bewail many which have sinned already and have not repented of the uncleanness and *fornication* and lasciviousness which they have committed.'

In number 14, Judah (Jude) speaks of homosexuality. He refers to the ancient cities of Sodom and Gomorrah, cities that God rained fire and brimstone down upon because of their wickedness (Gen. 18–19), but is this homosexuality *only* common homosexuality?

> 14. Jude 1:7: 'Even as Sodom and Gomorrah, and the cities about them in like manner, giving themselves over to *fornication*, and *going after strange flesh*, are set forth for an example, suffering the vengeance of eternal fire.'

Judah's phrase, 'going after strange flesh,' is a euphemism for homosexuality. Homosexuality was certainly a major part of the sexual appetites that plagued the people of Sodom (Gen. 19:5) and Gomorrah. The phrase, though, coupled with *fornication,* points to homosexual *cult* prostitution as the major sin.

The Hebrews, following the native Canaanites, would engage in homosexual *cult* harlotry when they came into the Promised Land.[360] Canaan was a land that *outdid* all the other ancient lands in its perversions and it was especially noted for its homosexual *cult* harlotry.[361] It's not unreasonable to think that Judah was speaking of cult (and common) homosexuality when he wrote of 'fornication and going after strange flesh.'

The problem of cult harlotry among *believers* wasn't easily remedied. The next three cites (15-17) explicitly speak of cult harlotry, and all the following texts would include cult harlotry, although common harlotry can certainly be said to also be part of the meaning:

> 15. Rev. 2:14: 'But I have a few things against thee, because thou hast there them that hold the doctrine of Balaam, who taught Balak to cast a stumbling block before the children of Israel, to eat things sacrificed unto idols, and to commit *fornication*.'

> 16. Rev. 2:20: 'Notwithstanding I have a few things against thee, because thou sufferest that woman Jezebel, which calleth herself a prophetess, to teach and to seduce my servants to commit *fornication*, and to eat things sacrificed unto idols.'

> 17. Rev. 2:21: 'And I gave her space to repent of her *fornication*; and she repented not.'

> 18. Rev. 14:8: 'And there followed another angel, saying, Babylon is fallen, is fallen, that great city, because she made all nations drink of the wine of the wrath of her *fornication*.'

---

[360] See page 47ff.

[361] See page 61f.

19. Rev. 17:2: 'With whom the kings of the Earth have committed *fornication*, and the inhabitants of the Earth have been made drunk with the wine of her *fornication*.'

20. Rev. 17:4: 'And the woman was arrayed in purple and scarlet colour, and decked with gold and precious stones and pearls, having a golden cup in her hand full of abominations and filthiness of her *fornication*.'

21. Rev. 18:3: 'For all nations have drunk of the wine of the wrath of her *fornication*, and the kings of the Earth have committed *fornication* with her, and the merchants of the Earth are waxed rich through the abundance of her delicacies.'

22. Rev. 18:9: 'And the kings of the Earth, who have committed *fornication* and lived deliciously with her, shall bewail her, and lament for her, when they shall see the smoke of her burning.'

23. Rev. 19:2: 'For true and righteous are his judgments: for he hath judged the great whore, which did corrupt the Earth with her *fornication*, and hath avenged the blood of his servants at her hand.'

The next five cites (24-28) use *pornay'ah* in lists and don't lend themselves to a specific form of harlotry (cult or common) due to a lack of context. Of course, as we've seen, cult harlotry should be given primary consideration whenever *pornay'ah* is used. Pagan worship, with its cult harlots, was practiced throughout the Roman Empire. Both Paul and John, who wrote the following verses, certainly saw this as a serious problem that they had to deal with. If they were addressing something other than harlotry (e.g. adultery) they would have used those specific Greek words. In Gal. 5:19 (#25), Paul does just that, the Textus Receptus having both adultery (*moikay'ah*) and harlotry (*pornay'ah*):

24. Romans 1:29: 'Being filled with all unrighteousness, *fornication*, wickedness, covetousness, maliciousness; full of envy, murder, debate, deceit, malignity; whisperers.'

25. Gal. 5:19: 'Now the works of the flesh are manifest, which are these; Adultery, *fornication*, uncleanness, lasciviousness.'

26. Eph. 5:3: 'But *fornication* and all uncleanness or covetousness, let it not be once named among you, as becometh *saints*' (Hebrew *kadosh*: holy ones; Greek *hagios*: holy ones).

27. Col. 3:5: 'Mortify therefore your members which are upon the Earth; *fornication*, uncleanness, inordinate affection, evil concupiscence and covetousness which is idolatry.'

28. Rev. 9:21: 'Neither repented they of their murders, nor of their

sorceries, nor of their *fornication*, nor of their thefts.'

Three of the cites above (24, 25 and 26) are most likely speaking of fornication as cult harlotry, not common harlotry, although a general spirit of
whoredom (promiscuity) might also have been meant. The latter deals not
with idols or the taking of money for sex, but with carnal sexual indulgence. This is extremely prevalent in Western society today. Cites 27 and
28 can also be said to include both forms of harlotry.

In the KJV New Testament the term *fornication* is used 32 times (in the
28 cites above). The majority of its usage (17 times) clearly speaks of cult
harlotry, while the other 15 would certainly include it. In other words,
every text in the New Testament that speaks of *fornication* addresses or
includes cult harlotry. Based on its word usage in the New Testament,
translating *pornay'ah* in Acts 15:20 as 'sexual immorality,' etc., is a major
linguistic error, as well as a severe theological injustice to those who desire to know what God is saying to them in His Word.

# *Fornications*

Only twice in the New Testament is the plural of *fornication* used. Both
times relate to the same teaching and can be seen as encompassing cult
and common harlotry, but certainly not adultery because adultery is mentioned in both instances:

1. Matt. 15:19: 'For out of the heart proceed evil thoughts, murders,
   adulteries, *fornications*, thefts, false witness, blasphemies.'

2. Mark 7:21: 'For from within, out of the heart of men, proceed evil
   thoughts, adulteries, *fornications*, murders.'

The plural of *fornication* is a way of emphasizing the number of times it
occurs in the heart. This is also seen with 'murders' and 'adulteries,' etc.

In the next section we'll see that the noun *fornicator* appears twice in the
New Testament. The first instance speaks of incestuous cult harlotry when
the believer slept with his father's cult-harlot wife (1st Cor. 5:1-5). The
second cite could speak of cult or common harlotry, as no context is
given.

# *Fornicator*

1. 1st Cor. 5:11: 'But now I have written unto you not to keep company, if any man that is called a *brother* be a *fornicator*, or covetous, or an idolater, or a railer, or a drunkard, or an extortioner; with such an one no not to eat.'

2. Heb. 12:16: 'Lest there be any *fornicator*, or profane person as Esau, who for one morsel of meat sold his birthright.'

With 1st Cor. 5:11 coming immediately after Paul spoke of the believer who laid with his father's cult harlot wife, *fornicator* seems to specifically point to him as the 'brother.' Hebrews 12:16, though, would primarily speak of one using a cult harlot, without excluding a common harlot.

# *Fornicators*

The plural of *fornicator* is mentioned three times. All of them occur in First Corinthians within 14 verses. They relate to those who go to temple prostitutes. This is one of Paul's themes in his letter and must have been a theme in his previous (lost) letter as well (1st Cor. 5:9):

1. 1st Cor. 5:9: 'I *wrote* unto you in an epistle not to company with *fornicators.*'

2. 1st Cor. 5:10: 'Yet not altogether with the *fornicators* of this world, or with the covetous, or extortioners, or with idolaters; for then must ye needs go out of the world.'

3. 1st Cor. 6:9: 'Know ye not that the unrighteous shall not inherit the Kingdom of God? Be not deceived: neither *fornicators*, nor idolaters, nor adulterers, nor effeminate, nor abusers of themselves with mankind,'

The first passage would seem to refer primarily to those who use *cult* harlots because it was Corinth. The second, also, as Paul has just commanded the man's removal from the assembly for incestuous cult harlotry (1st Cor. 5:4-5). The third (1st Cor. 6:9) also speaks of those who use cult harlots because it immediately follows chapter five, and only three verses later, in 6:12-20, he speaks of temple harlots and the temple of the living God.

From this survey of all the places in the KJV New Testament where *fornication*, etc., has been used, *fornication* speaks first and foremost of cult prostitution. From just this perspective on how *pornay'ah* (prostitution) is used in the New Testament it's plain to see that Yakov's second rule of Acts 15:20 should have been translated as *cult prostitution*. Yakov meant this when he issued the Decree, not sexual immorality, prohibited marriages, common homosexuality or even common prostitution.

There were 13 English words associated with *zanah* (harlotry) in the KJV Old Testament,[362] but in the New Testament there are only seven words. In the Old Testament the various terms for *harlotry* occurred 138 times in the King James Version. In the New Testament, which is only about a quarter of the number of pages of the Old (about 28%), and which centers around the proclamation of life in Messiah Yeshua, the noun *pornay'ah* (harlotry) and its derivatives occurs a surprisingly 51 times. Here, as in the Old, the words primarily speak of *cult* harlotry. These are the terms and times of use in English from the King James Version New Testament:

| Term | Occurs | Cultic | Either | Only Common |
|------|--------|--------|--------|-------------|
| **1.** Fornication | 32 | 17 | 15 | 0 |
| **2.** Fornications | 2 | 0 | 2 | 0 |
| **3.** Fornicator | 2 | 1 | 1 | 0 |
| **4.** Fornicators | 3 | 3 | 0 | 0 |
| **5.** Harlot | 4 | 4 | 0 | 0 |
| **6.** Harlots | 4 | 1 | 1 | 2 |
| **7.** Whore | 4 | 4 | 0 | 0 |
| **Totals** | **51** | **30** | **19** | **2** |

Of the 32 times that *fornication* is used in the KJV New Testament, 17 times it clearly refers to cult prostitution, while the other times certainly would include it.[363] The plural, *fornications,* is mentioned twice in a list and includes both cult and common harlotry.[364]

*Fornicator* is mentioned twice, the first one seeming to refer to the man who slept with his father's wife, a cult harlot. The second could refer to one who used either a cult or a common harlot.[365] The plural *fornicators* is used three times and reflects the situation of cult harlotry in Corinth.[366]

---

[362] See p. 34 above.

[363] *Accordance Bible Software*; *Fornication* as cult harlotry: Mt. 5:32; 19:9; John 8:41; Acts 15:20, 29; 21:25; 1st Cor. 5:1 (twice); 6:13, 18 (twice); 10:8; 2nd Cor. 12:21; 1st Thess. 4:3; Rev. 2:14, 20-21.

*Fornication* as cultic or common harlotry: Rom. 1:29; 1st Cor. 7:2; Gal. 5:19; Eph. 5:3; Col. 3:5; Jude 1:7; Rev. 9:21; 14:8; 17:2 (twice), 4; 18:3 (twice), 9; 19:2.

[364] Ibid. *Fornications* as either cult or common harlotry: Mt. 15:19; Mk. 7:21.

[365] Ibid. *Fornicator* as one who uses a cult harlot: 1st Cor. 5:11. *Fornicator* as one who uses either a cult or a common harlot: Hebrews 12:16.

The four times that the KJV New Testament speaks of a harlot (*pornay*) all refer to a cult harlot.[367] Of the four times that it speaks of *harlots*, two are common harlots (Mt. 21:31-32), one can be either (Lk. 15:30), and the fourth is primarily cultic as it speaks of *religious* Babylon the Great the 'mother of harlots.'[368] The reason why I assign *common* harlotry to the two times that Yeshua mentions it in Mt. 21:31-32 is because cult harlotry among the Jewish people in His day was basically non-existent, God having purged it out of the Jewish people through the Babylonian captivity, and the harlots that Yeshua refers to would seem to be Jewish.

The four times that *whore* is mentioned are all in Revelation and speak of the 'Great Whore.' She is certainly *the* cult harlot.[369]

This overview of the KJV New Testament's use of *fornication* (Greek *pornay'ah*, prostitution/harlotry) and words associated with it reveals that its primary meaning in the New Testament is cultic. Of the 51 times the words are used, 30 times (58.8% of the time) it specifically speaks of *cult* harlotry. Adding the 19 times that the words can be cult and/or common harlotry makes it 49 out of 51 times (96% of the time) that the New Testament speaks of cult harlotry when the words associated with *pornay'ah* (harlotry) are seen. This is only slightly less than the percentage that was seen in the Old Testament (98.6%).[370]

The New Testament's use and primary meaning of the word follows the Old Testament's word usage and primary meaning. As Joseph said to Pharaoh about his two dreams: 'The dreams of Pharaoh are one' (Gen. 41:25). The two Testaments complement one another. Yakov's word, in Hebrew or Greek, has the same primary biblical meaning. When the Greek New Testament speaks of *pornay'ah* (KJV fornication) as the second rule of Acts 15:20 there's no doubt that it means *cult* harlotry, especially coming after the first rule on the eating of idolatrous sacrificial meat at the time of the sacrifice.

---

[366] Ibid. *Fornicators* as users of cult prostitutes: 1st Cor. 5:9-10; 6:9.

[367] Ibid. *Harlot* as cult harlot: 1st Cor. 6:15-16; Heb. 11:31; James 2:25.

[368] Ibid. *Harlots* as cult harlots: Rev. 17:5.

Harlots as either cultic or common: Lk. 15:30.

Harlots as common harlots: Mt. 21:31-32.

[369] Ibid. *Whore* as *the* Cult Harlot: Rev. 17:1, 15-16; 19:2.

[370] See page 36.

# THE THIRD RULE:

# THINGS STRANGLED

The third rule in Acts 15:20 is 'things strangled,' but some think Yakov never said it. The *Interlinear* has a footnote to the verse, "Other ancient authorities lack, 'and from whatever has been strangled.'"[371] Marshall explains why some manuscripts don't have the third rule, but why he thinks that Yakov did indeed give it:

> 'As the RSV mg. indicates, later scribes re-worded the list
> of forbidden things; the omission of 'things strangled'
> leaves three words which can be understood in a moral
> sense—idolatry, unchastity and murder ('blood'). This al-
> teration was probably made by scribes who no longer un-
> derstood the first century situation; in course of time the
> need for the prescriptions about food acceptable to Jewish
> Christian consciences disappeared.'[372]

With 'later scribes' re-wording the text it appears that Yakov gave the rule. Marshall's explanation that some scribes saw the three rules as 'a moral package deal' is interesting. This is because those Christian scribes not only hid a rule of James (*strangled*), but erroneously presented *blood* as murder, and *unchastity* as the meaning for cult prostitution. The next section will reveal why 'blood' in Acts 15:20 cannot be equated with murder. As noble as this moral lesson sounds it wasn't what Yakov addressed, nor was he presenting 'food acceptable to Jewish Christian consciences.'

Wesley Perschbacher says that strangled means 'strangled' or 'suffocated' and that it's,

> 'the flesh of animals killed by strangulation or suffo-
> cation, Acts 15:20, 29; 21:25.'[373]

Friberg agrees and interprets it as the blood not being drained:

> 'choked; of animals killed by strangling so that the blood
> is not drained from them.'[374]

---

[371] Brown, *The New Greek-English Interlinear New Testament*, p. 473. It states this for every passage where the four rules are mentioned (Acts 15:20, 29; 21:25). The NRSV has it, but says that 'some ancient authorities' lack it.

[372] Marshall, *Acts*, p. 253, note 1.

[373] Perschbacher, *The New Analytical Greek Lexicon*, p. 334.

[374] Friberg, *Analytical Lexicon of the Greek New Testament*, p. 319.

Bauer states that the word 'strangled' wasn't found,

> 'in the Septuagint nor in Hellenistic Jewish writings,' but in Acts 'it plainly means strangled, choked to death...of animals killed without having the blood drained from them whose flesh' (meat) 'the Jews were forbidden to eat...Lev. 17:13f.'[375]

It's true that Yahveh didn't want His people Israel to eat meat with the blood in it (Lev. 19:26; Ezk. 24:1-24). To allow the blood to remain within the animal corrupts the meat by its very presence, as many toxins or poisons are carried by the blood and remain in the meat if it's not properly drained. Most hunters know this, and upon killing an animal, slit its throat and hang it upside down as soon as possible so that the blood drains out. The Greeks also knew this. Bauer states that,

> 'the Pythagorean dietary laws forbid' meat from 'animals that have not been properly slaughtered.'[376]

Ancient man knew to take the blood out of the animal before eating it. In other words, it most likely wasn't a *common* practice to sell meat in the marketplace that hadn't been properly slaughtered, but even if some meat wasn't properly drained of blood, this isn't what Yakov was addressing.

Howard Marshall logically, but erroneously, lumps together the third rule (*strangled*) with the fourth (*blood*) and says that strangling the animal,

> 'meant that the blood remained in the meat, and the fourth item was blood itself.' These 'food regulations resemble those in Lev. 17:8-13.'[377]

*Wycliffe* also believes it pertains to 'Meats from which the blood had not been properly removed.'[378] Bruce thinks the,

> "prohibition against eating flesh with the blood still in it (including the flesh of strangled animals) was based on the 'Noachian decree of Gen. 9:4.'"[379]

Stern says it meant 'meat from animals not slaughtered in a way that allows the blood to flow out.'[380] Knowling writes that a law against strangling can't be found in the Law of Moses, but agrees that eating meat with

---

[375] Bauer, *A Greek-English Lexicon of the New Testament*, p. 680.

[376] Ibid.

[377] Marshall, *Acts*, p. 253.

[378] Pfeiffer, *The Wycliffe Bible Commentary*, p. 1152.

[379] Bruce, *The Book of the Acts*, p. 296.

[380] Stern, *Jewish New Testament Commentary*, p. 277.

blood in it would be offensive to a Jew. He writes that the rule pertains to,

> 'beasts as had been killed through strangling, and whose
> blood had not been let out when they were killed. For this
> prohibition reference is usually made to Lev. 17:13; Dt.
> 12:16, 23...But on the other hand, Dr. Hort contends that
> all attempts to find the prohibition in the Pentateuch quite
> fail, although he considers it perfectly conceivable that
> the flesh of animals strangled in such a way as not to al-
> low of the letting out of blood would be counted as un-
> lawful food by the Jews.'[381]

David Williams also believes that *strangled* means one shouldn't eat meat with blood in it.[382]

Most think that the rule *strangled* means not to eat meat that was strangled and/or has blood in it. One can only begin to wonder why, if Christian scholars believe this, the Church doesn't practice it today? Why is there no teaching from the pulpit that one shouldn't eat strangled meat or blood? Scholars like to connect *strangled* with the fourth rule, *blood*, but however reasonable this may seem it's not what Yakov meant.

Although these rules might *resemble* food regulations, as Marshall wrote, one would be hard pressed to understand why James didn't include *which animals* could be eaten when properly slaughtered *so as not to offend the Jews*. After all, that's what the rules were allegedly for. If James was going to caution against not eating animals that had been strangled, and therefore, had blood in the meat, he failed to tell the Gentiles *which animals God prohibited Israel to eat* (Lev. 11; Dt. 14). Could such a major part of the rule have escaped his attention? Perhaps at the time of the ruling (Acts 15:20), but certainly not until the end of the Book of Acts, and nothing is mentioned anywhere else in the New Testament about *strangled* pertaining to a food regulation or about it being connected to the fourth rule on *blood*. No, the rule doesn't concern a dietary regulation even though it does speak of strangled animals.

*Strangled* relates to sacrificial idolatry and only Ben Witherington and Tim Hegg have rightly understood this.[383] The rule points to an animal sacrificed to a god by being strangled.[384] It has nothing to do with blood

---

[381] Knowling, *The Acts of the Apostles*, pp. 324-325.

[382] Williams, *Acts*, p. 266.

[383] Witherington, *The Acts of the Apostles*, p. 464. Hegg, *The Letter Writer*, p. 277. Unfortunately, Hegg also thinks it's a dietary regulation (no meat from a strangled animal because of blood being in it), but obviously, this cannot be.

[384] Strangled is defined as 'suffocation' or 'choking.' The concept includes the wringing of the neck of a bird as well as the breaking of the neck of a larger

remaining within the victim for the general public to eat. The 'animal' in this case would most likely be a bird. Doves and pigeons were *often* used as a sacrifice, not only to the God of Israel,[385] but to other gods as well. Birds were plentiful, inexpensive (Lk. 12:6), and therefore, the 'perfect' sacrifice for the common people to bring.

*Strangling* wasn't necessarily limited to birds. In Isaiah 66:3 the prophet speaks of an Israeli who sacrifices a lamb, being like one who breaks a dog's neck, something that would certainly fall under the concept of *strangling*. The *Theological Dictionary of the Old Testament* says the polemic of the prophet attacks the '*simultaneous engagement* in both legitimate and pagan cults.'[386]

In other words, Isaiah is speaking about the dual practice of many Hebrews: sacrificing the required sacrifice to Yahveh (the lamb), but also sacrificing an unclean animal (a dog) to a pagan god. The relevant point is that the breaking of a dog's neck was part of a pagan sacrificial rite in the days of Isaiah, 700 years before James gave the four rules. Would it be unreasonable to assume that in the days of Yakov pagans continued this practice of strangling dogs for some of their gods?

The God of Israel also commanded that larger animals would have their necks broken (twisted or strangled). In response to refusing to redeem a donkey with a lamb,[387] the neck of the donkey would be broken. In the ritual attached to an unsolved murder in an open field in the land of Israel, an animal as large as a heifer had its neck broken (Dt. 21:1-9).[388]

It's well attested in ancient literature that Gentiles sacrificed dogs to their gods.[389] There were dog cults in ancient Egypt and Mesopotamia.[390] Gula,

---

animal by twisting it.

[385] Leviticus 1:14-17; 5:7-10; 12:6-8; 14:1-8, 22-32, 48-53; 15:13-15, 28-30; Mt. 21:12; Luke 2:21-24; Jn. 2:14-16. The priests of Yahveh wrung the neck off the bird and didn't leave the blood within it, draining it at the Altar. The priests didn't eat the dedication sacrifice (whole burnt offering; Lev. 1:14-17), but did eat the birds of the sin sacrifice (Lev. 5:1-10; 6:24-26).

[386] Botterweck, *Theological Dictionary of the Old Testament*, vol. VII, p. 155.

[387] Exodus 13:13: 'But every first offspring of a donkey you must redeem with a lamb, but if you do not redeem it then you shall break its neck. And every firstborn of man among your sons you must redeem.'

[388] Dt. 21:4: 'and the Elders of that city shall bring the heifer down to a valley with running water, which has not been plowed or sown and shall break the heifer's neck there in the valley.'

[389] Howard F. Vos, *Nelson's New Illustrated Bible Manners and Customs* (Nashville, TN: Thomas Nelson Publishers, 1999), p. 611, speaks of Rome's Lupercalia on Feb. 15th (now known as St. Valentine's Day). It was a 'purification and fertility' feast with much sexual revelry. The priests, 'called *lu-*

the goddess of healing in Mesopotamia, had dogs sacrificed to her. *TDOT* says that 'dogs were sacrificed to the goddess' and there's 'evidence of buried dog skeletons.'[391]

Philo (20 BC to 50 AD), a Jewish philosopher born in Alexandria, Egypt, who lived during the time of Messiah Yeshua and Yakov, confirms that in his day, 'pagans were sacrificing animals by means of *strangulation.*'[392] Witherington confirms this and says,

> there is 'evidence that the choking of the sacrifice, stran-
> gling it...transpired in pagan temples.'[393]

Citing the *Magical Papyri*, Witherington writes that with the strangling of the animal the pagans believed that the 'life breath or spiritual vitality *went into the idol.*'[394] Both this concept and the strangling of a pagan sacrifice are seen in the *Magical Papyri,* where the pagan priest is instructed:

> 'Take also on the first day seven living creatures and
> *strangle them*; one cock, a partridge, a wren...Do not
> make a burnt offering of any of these; instead, taking
> them in your hand, *strangle them*, while holding them up
> to your Eros[395] until each of the creatures is suffocated

---

*perci* sacrificed goats and a dog on the Palatine Hill...Because of this festival's popularity, the church absorbed it instead of abolishing it. Pope Galesius
V in 494 made it the Festival of the Purification of the Virgin Mary.'

[390] Botterweck, *TDOT*, vol. VII, pp. 148-149.

[391] Ibid., p. 150.

[392] Hegg, *The Letter Writer*, p. 277, note 588: Philo, *The Special Laws*, iv: xiii.
122. Hegg presents the four rules as a 'prohibition of idol worship in the pagan temples' (p. 269), but he wrongly thinks that *strangled* also refers to
'blood within the meat' (of meat from the pagan temples), p. 277. If that were
the case Yakov would have included the dietary laws from Lev. 11 and Dt.
14, etc., as part of his rules. Even if a Gentile had properly slaughtered and
hadn't strangled the animal he would have to know which meats couldn't be
eaten (i.e. which were clean and which were unclean [forbidden] and also, not
to eat any fat; Lev. 3:17; 7:23-25). Yakov never addressed these issues, so
*strangled* cannot possibly relate to *blood* in meat (a dietary prohibition), but
only to an idolatrous sacrifice where the animal or bird is strangled.

Jonathan Gray, *Ark of the Covenant* (Rundle Mall, South Australia, 2000), pp.
48-49. Today, the Jivaro tribesmen of the Amazon headwaters sacrifice pigs,
by strangling, to the fire god of Mount Sangay (an active volcano).

[393] Witherington, *The Acts of the Apostles*, p. 464.

[394] Ibid. The demons 'in back of the idol' might animate it (1st Cor. 10:20) giving
it the impression that the life of the sacrifice had indeed gone into the idol.

[395] *Encyclopedia Mythical* at http://www.pantheon.org/articles/e/eros.html. Eros
is the Greek counterpart to the Roman Cupid. Cupid's arrows speak of him as
Nimrod, the first 'mighty hunter' (Gen. 10:9). See Hislop, *The Two Babylons*,

and *their breath enter him*. After that, place the strangled creatures on the altar together with aromatic plants of every variety.'[396]

With the scant information given in Acts 15:20, the third rule, *if taken on its own*, would be impossible to definitively place within the category of sacrificial idolatry. *Strangled* can obviously be *interpreted* to mean the abstention from meat that has been strangled, but coming on the heels of two major rules pertaining to sacrificial-sexual idolatry it lends itself to also being part of that concept. Entirely lacking which animals couldn't be eaten, *strangled* can only point to a pagan ritual.

The third rule isn't a prohibition against eating meat with blood in it that had been slaughtered by strangling, as sinful as that is. It has to do with an idolatrous ceremony where a bird or an animal is strangled. Yakov included it among the rules because it was most likely a prolific pagan sacrificial practice in his day.

Most Christian scholars never thought of the possibility that *strangled* could relate to a pagan sacrifice. This points to a greater problem of interpreting Scripture from an *already preconceived* theological framework. Their perception of the rule, having to fall within only a certain category, food regulations for table fellowship (whether the prohibition against eating blood from Lev. 17 or the Noahide laws) is filtered through their false concept that the Law of Moses 'is done away with.' If scholars could tackle the Word of God, as Witherington did, they would have been able to see that the first two rules spoke of sacrificial idolatry, setting up a theme for *strangled* to also fit into that category.

*Things strangled* has nothing to do with Jewish dietary regulations or table fellowship. It was a prohibition against participating in an idolatrous pagan ceremony that used strangled animals or birds.

---

pp. 19-40, 187-191, 225-232, 313-316, for why Cupid is not an innocent little 'love boy,' but an infant-eating monster—Molech in another form.

[396] Witherington, *The Acts of the Apostles*, p. 464, note 423. *Magical Papyri* PGM XII. 14-95.

# THE FOURTH RULE: BLOOD

The Greek word in Acts 15:20 for the fourth rule of Yakov is 'αιματος (*hai'matos*; blood).[397] Perschbacher says it means 'blood; of the color of blood; bloodshed; blood-guiltiness; natural descent.'[398] Bauer states:

'of human blood...of the blood of animals...Its use as food is forbidden (compare Lev. 3:17; 7:26; 17:10) in the apostolic decree' Acts '15:20, 29; 21:25.' Some 'interpret this passage as 'a command not to shed blood.' Figuratively 'as the seat of life...blood and life as an expiatory sacrifice...especially of the blood of Jesus as a means of expiation...of the (apocalyptic) red color, whose appearance in heaven indicates disaster.'[399]

Friberg follows a similar line of thinking. He states that the word means,

'blood...human blood...by metonymy, human nature, physical descent...of sacrificial animals, blood...literally pour out blood, i.e. kill...menstrual flow, hemorrhage' 'literally fountain of blood, i.e. bleeding (Mk. 5:29)...by metonymy, of another's murder...of Christ's atoning sacrifice' (death) and 'in apocalyptic language, the red color of blood as symbolizing disaster.'[400]

There are a number of ways that one can interpret *blood* in Acts 15:20. It can literally mean blood from an animal sacrifice, blood in 'food' (meat) being 'forbidden' in the Apostolic Decree, as Bauer thinks, or sin (murder, i.e. bloodshed). It can also be the guilt of murder, one's lineage or even an apocalyptic disaster. How should it be interpreted for Acts 15:20?

Marshall interprets *blood* in Acts 15:20 as a food regulation, blood within the meat.[401] *Wycliffe* states that it,

"refers to the pagan custom of using blood as a food. The last two requirements' (of Acts 15:20) 'involved the same offense, for the Jew who believed that 'the life is in the blood' (Lev. 17:11) regarded the eating of any blood particularly offensive. This decree was issued to the Gentile churches not as a means of salvation but as *a basis for fel-*

---

[397] Brown, *The New Greek-English Interlinear New Testament*, p. 473.

[398] Perschbacher, *The New Analytical Greek Lexicon*, p. 8.

[399] Bauer, *A Greek-English Lexicon of the New Testament*, p. 22.

[400] Friberg, *Analytical Lexicon of the Greek New Testament*, p. 37.

[401] Marshall, *Acts*, pp. 243, 253.

*lowship*, in the spirit of Paul's exhortation that those who
were strong in faith should be willing to restrict their liberty in such matters rather than offend the *weaker* brother
(Rom. 14:1 ff.; 1st Cor. 8:1 ff.)."[402]

It seems strange that Yakov would make two rules (*strangled* and *blood*)
for the same offense when only one was needed (i.e. 'blood;' don't eat any
meat with blood in it). *Wycliffe* sees the rule as being for the 'weaker
brother,' the Jewish believer. It seems that *Wycliffe* thinks that eating meat
with blood in it is alright, but only for strong Gentile Christians.

Stern presents three possible meanings for *blood*. It could be literal,

> 'referring to *drinking animals' blood*, or failing to remove
> it from meat, or figurative, a metaphor for murder.'[403]

Stern realizes that *blood* can be referring to the actual drinking of it from a
pagan sacrifice, but he doesn't understand it as such for Acts 15:20, hence,
he offers three options from which to choose from without saying which
one he thought Yakov meant. At least the idea of drinking sacrificial
blood is brought into the arena of possibilities.

Stern also offers a Jewish twist on what Marshall wrote, saying that if
*strangled* wasn't originally part of the text then one is left with the three
things that the Rabbis say a Jew was to die for rather than transgress. A
Jew could transgress all the commandments in order to save his (or another's) life, but not 'idolatry, fornication or murder' (San. 74a).[404] This is the
'Jewish side' to the Gentile scribes' interpretation of the three rules 'on
morality.' Unfortunately, *blood* would have to be equated with murder.
Murder, though, is *not* a possible interpretation for *blood* in Acts 15:20.

Bruce also believes the rule reflects the prohibition against eating blood in
meat, but he thinks it comes from the Noahide laws. He, too, says it has to
do with table fellowship for Jewish and Gentile believers.[405]

Williams says the rule means 'not to eat any blood itself.' This must mean
for him that it's blood in meat because he fails to say that the practice of
eating (or rather drinking) blood was part of pagan sacrifices.[406]

Knowling also believes it was blood from meat, but suggests that the reason behind the rule had to do with the ancient fascination of what blood

---

[402] Pfeiffer, *The Wycliffe Bible Commentary*, p. 1152.

[403] Stern, *Jewish New Testament Commentary*, p. 277.

[404] Ibid., p. 278.

[405] Bruce, *The Book of the Acts*, pp. 295-296. The "prohibition against eating
flesh with blood still in it…was based on the 'Noachian decree' of Gen. 9:4."

[406] Williams, *Acts*, p. 266.

symbolized. He writes that it was,

> 'specially forbidden by the Jewish law, Lev. 17:10...and we may refer the prohibition...to the feeling of *mystery* entertained by various nations of antiquity with regard to blood, so that the feeling is not exclusively Jewish, although the Jewish law had given it such express and divine sanction...Nothing could override the command first given to Noah, Gen. 9:4, together with the permission to eat animal food, and renewed in the law.'[407]

Knowling brings out the reverence that the ancients had for *blood* (mystery) and says it was universal, not just among the Jews. This accounts for pagan sacrifice as well as Hebrew sacrifice in that blood was seen to contain the life of the animal or person.

Knowling further comments, though, about *blood* not being able to be equated with murder in Acts 15:20 because of,

> 'the collocation[408] with πνικτου' (*nik'too,* strangled) being 'against any such interpretation.'[409]

He cites Cyprian and Tertullian as first recognizing this. This means that *strangled* and *blood*, because of their being one right after the other in the rules, are part of the same theme (i.e. not eating meat containing blood in it). This would rule out blood being equated with murder for him, but unfortunately, it fails to answer why Yakov didn't tell the Gentiles what animals were acceptable to eat if properly slaughtered and cooked.

Witherington says that Gentiles drank (and tasted) blood at their pagan temples,[410] but he errs in thinking that it could also double as murder. Hegg sees *blood* as 'something not uncommon in idol rituals,' but wrongly thinks that *strangling* prohibits the eating of meat with blood in it.[411]

The fourth rule is *blood*. Christian scholarship says that it means not to eat meat that has blood in it. Stern and Williams suggested that it could be blood that was drunk, but they weren't sure about it. Only Witherington and Hegg thought it related to a pagan sacrifice in which sacrificial blood was ingested. Stern and Witherington brought up that it could also refer to murder and Hegg believed *blood* also meant not eating meat that hadn't

---

[407] Knowling, *The Acts of the Apostles*, p. 325.

[408] Sinclair, *Collins English Dictionary*, p. 316. *Collocation* means 'a grouping together of things in a certain order, as of the words in a sentence.'

[409] Knowling, *The Acts of the Apostles*, p. 325.

[410] Witherington, *The Acts of the Apostles*, p. 464.

[411] Hegg, *The Letter Writer*, p. 276-277.

been properly slaughtered.

The proper slaughtering and roasting (or cooking) of an animal, so there wouldn't be any blood left in the meat, is a biblical reality.[412] Although both of these, murder and the eating of blood within the meat, are considered sin by God, there's absolutely no evidence for either of them being what Yakov meant when he spoke of *blood* in Acts 15:20.

What Yakov meant cannot be determined from the word itself, as the different authorities display. This is where common sense and context come in. Common sense tells us that murder has to be ruled out because murder was a very serious crime in the Roman Empire and everyone knew it. The need for a Jewish man in Jerusalem to make a ruling on murder wasn't necessary. After all, how many Gentile Christians were running around murdering people and *thinking that it was alright?* The rules are prohibitions on things that the Gentiles thought were alright to do in their new faith.

Another obvious point is that there's no mention of which meats could or could not be eaten. The same reason that *things strangled* couldn't be a food regulation also applies to *blood*. If James had meant that Gentiles couldn't eat meat with blood in it, so as not to offend Jewish sensitivities, he never once addressed which animals weren't to be eaten (e.g. pigs).

Theoretically, one could slaughter a pig properly, so that the blood was removed and the pig roasted until it was 'well done,' but sitting down with a Jewish believer and offering him some hot pork chops would definitely offend his Jewish sensibilities. This also torpedoes the traditional interpretation of the rules dealing with 'fellowship toward the weaker brother.' Yakov, in not indicating which animals weren't to be eaten, renders the Christian interpretation of *table fellowship* impossible. Scholars should have known that the eating of bacon, even 'well done,' next to a Jewish believer, would certainly offend him, as *all* the Jewish believers continued to keep the dietary laws and the Law of Moses *after* the resurrection.[413]

On the other hand, the need to prohibit the Gentile from not drinking the blood from sacrifices offered to idols was very necessary. The eating of the flesh of the sacrifice and the drinking of its blood were major themes of sacrificial idolatry. This is the pagan counterfeit to eating the flesh and drinking the blood of Messiah Yeshua. Pagans believed that the eating of the flesh of the sacrificial victim and the drinking of its blood gave them *the life of the victim. ISBE* says it's,

> 'significant that eating blood was prohibited in earliest

---

[412] Lev. 3:17; 7:26-27; 17:10 19:26; 1st Sam. 14:31-34; Ezk. 33:25.

[413] Acts 21:20, 24; 22:12; 24:14; 25:8; Rom. 3:31; 1st Jn. 5:1-3; Rev. 14:12, etc.

Bible times (Gen. 9:4). The custom...*prevailed* among heathen nations as a religious rite.'[414]

The *custom* to which *ISBE* is referring to is the drinking of fresh blood from an animal sacrifice. That it's not the eating of meat with blood in it is seen from it being 'a religious rite.' There are no pagan religious rites that speak of eating blood in rare roast beef. Paul warned the Gentile Corinthian believers against *drinking* the cup of demons (1st Cor. 10:21).[415] *Obviously,* the prohibition against drinking blood at a pagan sacrifice was very necessary for Gentile converts to the God of Israel.

The *Theological Dictionary of the Old Testament* states that the concept of blood among the pagan nations was very powerful. Blood,

'is thus understood as the *essence* of the personal powers that are at work in man and beast.'[416]

This *essence* is what motivated the pagans to drink the blood because they desired the essence or power of the creature whose blood they were drinking. Animals were also a representation of the god they were worshiping, and so, the psychological power derived from such a sacrifice took on enormous value for them, just as drinking Yeshua's blood does for us. The pagans weren't wrong in their understanding of the life properties within blood—they were just deceived as to Whose blood they needed. In *Manners and Customs of the Bible*, James Freeman writes that,

'Hindoo devotees drink the reeking blood from newly killed buffaloes and fowls.'[417]

The Hindoos that Freeman describes were not the ancient temple worshipers of Zeus, Adonis or Baal in Greece or Canaan. They do, however, present us with the fact that the drinking of blood in Freeman's day (1870) was still part of paganism. Alexander Hislop reveals that the religion of the Hindoos originally came from Babylon.[418] *The International Standard*

---

[414] Bromiley, *ISBE*, vol. one, p. 526. See also Psalm 16:4.

[415] Most likely, the Jewish believers at Corinth weren't drinking blood. They had been raised in the Law and knew how offensive it was to Yahveh. Their coming into the Kingdom of Yeshua would only heighten that understanding.

[416] Botterweck, *Theological Dictionary of the Old Testament*, vol. III, p. 237.

[417] Rev. James M. Freeman, *Manners and Customs of the Bible* (Plainfield, NJ: Logos International, 1972), pp. 106-107, section 192.

[418] Hislop, *The Two Babylons*, p. 96. 'Hindoo Mythology...is admitted to be essentially Babylonian' (see also pp. 15-16, 27, 36-37, 60-61, 65, 70-71, 101, 159, 187, 230, 243-244, 272, 282, 319). For those concerned with Ralph Woodrow's critique of Mr. Hislop, see my critique of Mr. Woodrow at http://SeedofAbraham.net/2babreb.htm.

*Bible Encyclopedia* states that blood was also used in other ways:

> a 'blood friendship is established by African tribes by the mutual shedding of blood and *either drinking it* or rubbing it on one another's bodies.'[419]

In ancient Egypt the gods drank the blood of the sacrificial animals.[420] Could the priest and the people be far behind?

As King Solomon once said, 'There's nothing new under the sun' (Eccl. 1:9b). Paganism takes many of its principles from the God of Israel and His Kingdom and perverts them. In idolatrous sacrifices the drinking of blood could 'be commanded ritually' and one could also be initiated into a pagan cult with 'a baptism of blood.'[421]

*ISBE* further writes that Mithraism was of 'great antiquity in the East,' and it was widespread in the days of the Apostles. The,

> 'initiate was placed in a pit covered with boards on which a bull was slain in such a manner that the blood flowed through and drenched the worshiper below,' and 'he was thereby filled with the strength and other qualities of the beast.'[422]

This was Satan's way, through man, of dealing with issues like sin, salvation and eternal life. Conceptually, it's similar to the way Israel was baptized into the Covenant at Sinai. In Exodus 24:6-8, Moses,

> "sent young men of the Sons of Israel and they offered burnt offerings and sacrificed young bulls as peace offerings to Yahveh. Moses took half of the blood and put it in basins and the other half of the blood he sprinkled on the altar. Then he took the Book of the Covenant and read it in the hearing of the people and they said, 'All that Yahveh has spoken we will do and we will obey!' So Moses took the blood *and sprinkled it on the people* and said, 'Behold the blood of the Covenant which Yahveh has made with you in accordance with all these words.'"

There's something extremely powerful about blood in the spiritual realm. The reality behind the Mosaic sacrificial system was the sacrifice of Ye-

---

[419] Bromiley, *The International Standard Bible Encyclopedia*, vol. one, p. 526.

[420] Ibid., vol. three, pp. 237-238.

[421] Ibid., p. 237.

[422] Ibid., vol. two, p. 681. From an online dictionary: 'Mithraism—the cult of the god Mithras, which became popular among Roman soldiers...and was the main rival to Christianity in the first three centuries AD.'

shua. This ultimately gives divine power and authority to *blood*. In Lev. 17:11 it states,

> 'For the life of the flesh is in the blood and I have given it to you upon the Altar to make atonement for your souls. For it's the blood by reason of the life that makes atonement.'

Substituting 'His' in certain places of the verse, the tremendous significance of Yeshua's sacrifice can be seen:

> 'For the life of His flesh is in His blood and I have given it to you upon the Altar to make atonement for your souls. For it's His blood by reason of His life that makes atonement' (for you).

This is how the blood of Messiah Yeshua deals with sin, sin nature and how believers will be glorified and become exactly like He is now (except that He was always God the Son, while believers will be created to be like Him). This is the New Creation, the New Jerusalem coming down from the Heavens, the Bride of Messiah Yeshua (Eph. 5:32; Rev. 19:7; 21:1-2, 9, etc.) which will make the first Creation pale in splendor.

The eternal life and sinless character that *is* Yeshua is in His blood. His blood makes *new creatures* of Adam's descendants. *Everything* that *is* Yeshua is in His blood (and body) and we are given access to this because of His sacrifice (Gal. 3:13-14). This is what He meant when He said, 'I tell you the truth. It's for your good that I go' (John 16:7) referring to His sacrificial death.[423]

It's also written that 'the life of every creature is its blood' and that 'the blood is the life' (Lev. 17:14; Dt. 12:23). The ancient peoples understood the connection of the blood and the life being interwoven. That's why they ate the animal flesh and drank its blood in their pagan ceremonies.[424]

Many times God warned Israel not to eat blood.[425] That's why most of the Jews left Jesus that day in Capernaum when He said to them,

> 'Truly I tell you, unless you eat the flesh of the Son of Man and drink His blood, you have no life in you. Those who eat My flesh and drink My blood have eternal life and I will raise them up on the Last Day.' (John 6:53-54)

In Dt. 12:16 it states, 'you must not eat the blood! You are to pour it out

---

[423] For where Torah pictures Messiah as a human sacrifice, see *Human Sacrifice and Yeshua* at http://seedofabraham.net/Human_Sacrifice_And_Yeshua.html.

[424] Ibid., pp. 234-250.

[425] Lev. 3:17; 7:26-27; 17:12, 14; Dt. 12:16, 23; 15:23.

on the ground like water.' This pertains to the drinking of fresh blood from a slaughtered (or a sacrificed) animal. It's different from eating blood in 'rare meat' (e.g. Lev. 19:26). They're both sins, but only one is idolatrous.

The pagans had the right idea, but were applying it to the wrong reality for even when Yeshua said what He did about eating His flesh and drinking His blood, He wasn't looking for Jews to begin chomping on His arms and legs. It's a spiritual reality that comes to us from Him through His sacrifice and the Holy Spirit.

The reason the fourth rule was given was to prohibit Gentile believers from drinking the blood of a pagan sacrifice. It had nothing to do with *blood* meaning *murder,* and thus nullifies the reason why *strangled* was removed from Acts 15:20 by some Gentile scribes, in order to present their moral catechism. Of course, it also doesn't speak of the three sins that a Jew should allegedly die for, in resisting idolatry, fornication or murder.

It's evident that the rule on *blood* doesn't mean 'blood within the meat' because Yakov never spoke of which meats would be considered unclean by the Jews. If 'Jewish sensitivities' were supposed to be the reason for the rule, a Gentile eating unclean meat in the presence of a Jew, even if the meat had been properly slaughtered and drained of its blood, would certainly fail the criteria of the scholars for 'not offending the Jew.' How can Christian scholars fail to see this?

*Blood* centers around what Yakov perceived the Gentile need to be, directly in relation to the issue of his salvation. Drinking blood as part of a pagan sacrifice was not a crime against Rome, but it was a gross idolatrous sin against the God of Israel. Yakov ruled that the drinking of sacrificial blood was forbidden. This rule obviously falls under the category of sacrificial idolatry and cements the four rules of Acts 15:20 as a conceptual unit on sacrificial-sexual idolatry. Now the way is paved for Acts 15:21 to be properly understood and implemented, but before that—*Acts 15: Some Concerns.*

# ACTS 15: SOME CONCERNS

Before we get to the section on *Yakov's Concern* (p. 218ff.) there are six points that I want to address concerning Acts 15. Five are found in Acts 15:10, 19, 21 (twice) and 21:25, and the sixth is the fact that the four rules don't appear in the same order the second and third time that they are recorded (Acts 15:29; 21:25). Many theologians interpret three of these cites (15:10, 19; 21:25) as proof that the Law is not for Christians today.

The first concern (15:10) has Peter speaking of a *yoke* that neither he, nor his Fathers, could bear. The second concern (15:19) is Yakov's statement about 'not troubling the Gentiles.' The third and fourth concerns (15:21) have Yakov stating that Moses is 'read in the synagogues every Sabbath,' and also speaks of those who *preach* Moses. The fifth concern deals with Yakov's admonition that the Gentiles 'observe no such thing' (Acts 21:25), and the sixth looks at the rules not being written in the same order (15:20, 29; 21:25) and why Yakov (or Luke) might have done this.

## *Acts 15:10—The Yoke*

The yoke that Peter speaks of in Acts 15:10 is the Law.[426] Many see the Law, in and of itself, as the yoke, but that's not what Peter meant. Here's what he said:

> 'Now, therefore, why do you put God to the test by plac-
> ing upon the neck of the disciples, a yoke which neither
> our Fathers, nor we, were able to bear?'

Bruce writes that 'a proselyte, by undertaking to keep the law of Moses' was said to 'take up the yoke of the kingdom of heaven,'[427] and that the Law was the burden that the Fathers 'found too heavy.'[428] Obviously, he wasn't thinking of *Father* David,[429] otherwise known as the greatest king the world has ever seen, outside of his Son Yeshua, of course. David said

---

[426] Knowling, *The Acts of the Apostles*, p. 320. It's a 'metaphor common among the Rabbis, and also in classical literature,' cf. Jer. 5:5; Lam. 3:27; Ecclus. 51:26 (Zeph. 3:9) and Matt. 11:29 (Luke 11:46) Gal. 5:1. '*Psalms of Solomon*' 7:8 cf. 27:32, "present undoubted instances of the metaphorical use of the term 'the yoke' for the service of Jehovah. In *Sayings of the Jewish Fathers*," 3:8, 'we have a definite...reference to the yoke of Thorah...It would seem therefore that...Peter uses an almost technical word' for the Law of Moses.

[427] Bruce, *The Book of the Acts*, p. 290.

[428] Ibid.

[429] David is called πατριαρχου (*patri'arku;* Patriarch, Father) in Acts 2:20 (see also Mark 11:10 and Acts 7:8-9).

many things about the Law, none of which seem to correspond with what Bruce thought of it. Here's a sample of what David wrote:

> 'The Law of Yahveh is *perfect*, restoring the soul. The testimony of Yahveh is sure, making wise the simple. The precepts of Yahveh are right, rejoicing the heart. The commandment of Yahveh is pure, enlightening the eyes. The fear of Yahveh is clean, enduring forever. The judgments of Yahveh are true, they are righteous altogether. They are more desirable than gold, yes, than much fine gold. Sweeter also than honey and the drippings of the honeycomb. Moreover by them Your servant is *warned*. In keeping them there is great reward.' (Psalm 19:7-11)

David clearly extols the Law as something that is godly and beneficial. His different ways of speaking about the Law (e.g. its precepts and judgments) are Hebraic.[430] David sings much of the praise of Yahveh's Torah (Ps. 1:2; 37:31; 40:8; 119:1, 77, etc.) because he knew the wisdom and understanding inherent in it (Dt. 4:5-8; 30:15, 19, 20; 32:47).

If the laws of God were holy and wise for Moses, David, Isaiah and Jesus, why wouldn't they continue to be after the resurrection for us? Why would they be any less holy and wise for a Gentile believer who has been grafted into Israel (Rom. 11:13–12:5; Eph. 2:1-22; Gal. 6:16)?

Yeshua kept the Law all His life, as did all the Jewish believers many years after the resurrection (Acts 21:20, 24; 24:18; 25:8; Rev. 12:17). Perhaps the Apostles didn't understand 'the yoke' as Bruce presents it? Bruce errs because of his 'law-free gospel' paradigm.[431]

In making the Law the burden, Bruce, and all those who espouse such an idea, make the God of Israel who gave it an evil taskmaster. The Jews were set them free from Egyptian slavery by the blood of the lamb (God's grace), only so He could enslave them to His burdensome Law?

Williams also misses the point when he states that 'any attempt to revert to a religion of law was to try to test God.'[432] Stern stumbles as well, but

---

[430] Words like *judgments* and *statutes*, etc., are synonymous with God's Law and speak of His holy Instruction or Teaching (Torah) to Israel (Dt. 4:44-45; 5:1-22; 7:11, etc.). For *testimony* equaling Torah see Psalm 78:5; 119:88; 132:12; Is. 8:20. For *testimonies* see Dt. 4:45; 6:17, 20; Ps. 25:10; 78:56; 99:7. For *judgments* see Lev. 18:4, 5, 26; 25:18; Dt. 4:1, 5, 8; 5:31. For *ordinances* see Ex. 21:1; 24:3; Lev. 19:37; 20:22; 26:15; Num. 9:3. For *statutes*, Ex. 18:20; Lev. 10:11; 18:4, 5, 26; 19:19; 20:8; Dt. 6:1. For *commandments*, Ex. 15:26; 16:28; Lev. 22:31; Num. 15:22; Dt. 6:17 and for *the fear of Yahveh* see Ex. 9:30; 18:21; 20:20; Lev. 25:17; Dt. 4:10; 5:29; 6:2, 13, 24; Mt. 10:28.

[431] Bruce, *The Book of the Acts*, p. 285.

rightly comes against the verse being used to disparage the Law of Moses:

> "Much Christian teaching contrasts the supposedly oner-
> ous and oppressive 'yoke of the Law' with the words of
> Yeshua, 'My yoke is easy and my burden is light.'"[433]

Stern also says that if a person thinks something is *pleasant* then one can't project onto him that it's not. This point, though, can't be used in defense of the Law because it's subjective. Most Christians see the Law as a burden, and *if subjectivity* is the criteria for judging, the Law, according to most Christians, is very oppressive. The criteria, though, is not how we think or feel about the Law, but what God says about it,[434] especially in the New Testament.[435]

Stern writes that the commandments are not 'an oppressive burden any more than Yeshua's yoke is,' and that the yoke of the Law is 'acknowledging God's sovereignty and his right to direct our lives,' and that if God has given commandments, 'we should obey them.'[436] All this is true. The Law is not a burden, God is sovereign and He does have the right to direct the lives of believers by His commandments, which reveal His will—but Peter called *something* unbearable.

Stern believes Peter's yoke was *legalism*—the 'detailed mechanical rule-keeping, regardless of heart attitude, that some' Pharisees had. He states it was this 'yoke of legalism' that was 'unbearable.'[437] As true as, 'man is not justified by *legalism*' is, what is *written* is that, 'man is not justified by the *works* of the Law' (Gal. 2:16; cf. 1st Tim. 6:18), even if done from the heart. One cannot be justified by doing good and holy deeds, and that's Paul's point. Peter's yoke wasn't 'mechanical rule keeping.'

Witherington also believes that the yoke was the Law. He states that Peter, as 'a Galilean fisherman,' may not have liked parts of the Law that would have been a burden to him, such as going to Jerusalem three times a year for the annual Feasts (Ex. 23:17; Dt. 16:16). According to Witherington it would have meant the loss of income to support his family.[438]

As logical as this may seem it totally misses the mindset of a Jew like Peter who was all too happy to leave his fishing nets for a week in order to

---

[432] Williams, *Acts*, p. 264.

[433] Stern, *Jewish New Testament Commentary*, p. 276.

[434] Dt. 4:1-8; 12:8; 29:29.

[435] Mt. 5:17-19; 22:35-40; Rom. 3:31; 7:12, 14, et al. (et al., means 'and others').

[436] Stern, *Jewish New Testament Commentary*, p. 276.

[437] Ibid.

[438] Witherington, *The Acts of the Apostles*, p. 454.

go to Jerusalem on God's 'holy vacations' and worship Yahveh in the midst of all his brethren. After all, it was God who had made him a fisherman and ultimately provided for him and his family. Every Jew knew this, but Witherington, in failing to understand the holiness of the Law and the joy of celebrating the Feasts, stumbles. He also says that the Gentile was being required to become a proselyte to Judaism.[439] This was true, but neither Peter nor his Fathers were proselytes, so that can't be the yoke, either.

Hegg believes the yoke was the Gentile becoming a proselyte, with the traditional interpretation of Torah *and* the cumbersome man-made rules the Pharisees had attached to God's commandments. The Gentile would have to be circumcised, become a proselyte and comply with all the Pharisaic laws in order to become part of Israel (to 'get in' to the '*saved* Jewish community' as E. P. Sanders wrote of). In this, *being part of Israel*, the Gentile would be saved. Hegg writes,

> the "yoke they are unwilling to place upon the backs of
> the Gentile believers is the yoke of man-made rules and
> laws that required a ceremony to 'get in' and submission
> to *untold number of intricate halachah*."[440]

---

[439] Ibid., pp. 453-454. He also speaks of the possibility that Peter spoke of the 'priestly requirements of the Law' that the 'Pharisees and the Qumranites' wanted all Jews to walk in, and suggests that Jesus may have thought the Law to be *heavy* (Mt. 11:30). It wasn't the glorious Law that Yahveh had given to Israel (Dt. 4:5-8; Rom. 7:12) that Yeshua called heavy, but the weight of sin and guilt from not keeping the Law (Mt. 11:28; Rom. 7:7, 17-24).

[440] Hegg, *The Letter Writer*, pp. 265, 280-282. *Halachah* means 'the way to walk.' The Rabbis use it to describe their rules for living in this world. Hegg is greatly mistaken when he teaches that Gentiles should be circumcised. He sees Timothy *as a Gentile* who was circumcised (ibid., pp. 113-114, 285) and builds upon this fanciful interpretation to present his heretical theology that Gentiles should be circumcised *for the right reason* (not to be saved, but to keep the law of circumcision; Gen. 17:10-14; Ex. 12:43-48). Yet, why would Paul circumcise a 'Gentile Timothy' if he taught against Gentile circumcision (Rom. 4:1-12; 1st Cor. 7:17-19; Gal. 1:6-9; 2:1-5; 5:2; Phil. 3:2-3f.)?

Timothy is *not* an example of Gentile circumcision. His mother was Jewish and so was he (Acts 16:1). Paul circumcised him because he didn't want Timothy's non-circumcision to hinder the Gospel *to the Jews*. Why would Paul circumcise a Gentile *for the Jews* in the region (Acts 16:3)? The Jews could care less about a Gentile being circumcised. Verse three only makes sense if Timothy was a Jew and that he hadn't been circumcised when he was eight days old (Gen. 17:10-14). Hegg makes an appeal to the Mishna and S. Cohen (ibid., p. 113, notes 232-233), but Witherington soundly refutes it (see *Gentile Circumcision?* at http://SeedofAbraham.net/Gentile_Circumcision.html). Judaism believes that if the mother is Jewish, the child is, too. Also, there is no 'second witness' in the New Testament for Hegg's position on either Timothy being a Gentile, or Gentile circumcision 'for the right reason.'

The Pharisaic believers who wanted the Gentiles circumcised (Acts 15:1, 5) were looking for them to become proselytes. That a proselyte was considered a part of the Jewish people is seen in Nicolas being counted as such (Acts 6:5). Alfred Edersheim says that the children of a proselyte were 'regarded as Jews,'[441] and that once the proselytes 'were circumcised, immersed in water and offered a sacrifice,' they became,

> 'children of the covenant...perfect Israelites...Israelites in every respect, both as regarded duties and privileges.'[442]

Herbert Loewe (1882-1940) in *A Rabbinic Anthology* adds that a "proselyte can say 'God of our Fathers' because he is a full Jew."[443]

Unfortunately, Rabbinic Judaism is deceived—and Christianity and Messianic Judaism don't realize it. Nowhere in the Old, or the New, does God authorize a Gentile to become a Jew, even though he becomes part of Israel—in the Old, through physical, covenantal circumcision, and in the New, through the covenantal circumcision made without hands. Judaism, Christianity and Messianic Judaism accept the rabbinic conversion of a Gentile, making him a Jew, but this is not found in Scripture, and there-

---

Nowhere does the New Testament teach that a Gentile (or his newborn son) should receive circumcision if he understood that he wasn't doing it in order to be saved. On the contrary, it states that the Gentile *wasn't* to be circumcised (Acts 15:1-32; Romans 2:26-29; 3:30; 4:1-12, 16-18; 1st Cor. 7:17-19, 24; Gal. 2:3, 12; 5:2, 11; 6:12-17). Didn't God realize, though, what He had said to Abraham and Moses about circumcision (Gen. 17:14; Ex. 12:48)? Obviously, He did, but the 'circumcision made without hands' (Phil. 3:3; Col. 2:11), pictured in Dt. 30:6, has superseded physical covenantal circumcision *for the Gentile* and brings both Jewish and Gentile believer into Messiah's Kingdom. Despite Hegg's claim of just wanting to obey the Law, circumcision was given as the *sign* of the Abrahamic covenant, but Yeshua came with the New Covenant (Jer. 31:31-34; Mt. 16:19; Heb. 7:1–8:13; Gal. 6:16). Physical circumcision for the Gentile is the wrong sign for the wrong covenant.

With Timothy being circumcised, boys born to a Jewish woman should be considered Jewish, but even if 'only' the father is Jewish, the child should still be circumcised. This transcends rabbinic tradition, where only the mother determines if the child is Jewish, but Asenath was an Egyptian (Gen. 41:50-52), yet both her sons, Efraim and Manasseh, literally became two of the Tribes of Israel (Gen. 48:1-5; Num. 1:10). Sons born to anyone with Jewish lineage should be seen as Jews and circumcised on the eighth day (see Ruth 4:13-22).

[441] Alfred Edersheim, *The Life and Times of Jesus The Messiah* (Peabody, MA: Hendrickson Publishers, 2000), p. 1015.

[442] Ibid., p. 1014.

[443] C. G. Montefiore and H. Loewe, *A Rabbinic Anthology* (New York: Shocken Books, 1974), p. lxxxv. Loewe was an Orthodox Jew.

fore, it's not God's will. It was truly the leading of the Holy Spirit that prohibited Gentile circumcision in the New Testament.

The Gentile believer in Messiah Yeshua is part of the Commonwealth of Israel, but that doesn't make him a Jew, Hebrew, Israeli ('Israelite'),[444] or a so-called 'spiritual Jew.'[445] Yes, the Gentile believer is part of the Seed that Father Abraham was promised, and he has also been grafted into the Olive Tree (Israel; Romans 9–11), but that doesn't change his racial identity into a Jew or a Hebrew anymore then when a man marries a woman. The man and his wife become 'one flesh' (Gen. 2:24), but the woman doesn't become a man. The Jewish and Gentile believers are 'one in Messiah,' but the Gentile doesn't become a Jew.

Another illustration from the natural realm will help explain what it means for a Gentile to be part of the Commonwealth of Israel (Eph. 2:1-12).[446] Ireland is part of the British Commonwealth, and consequently, all Irishmen are part of that commonwealth, but an Irishman is not an Englishman, or a Brit, as many Englishmen now like to call themselves. In other words, the Irishman is still an Irishman. He was an Irishman before Ireland came into the Commonwealth of Great Britain, and also after that. Being part of the British Commonwealth means that both the Irishman and the Brit have the same king (or queen) and that their rule of life (law) is built upon the same foundation of English law (the Magna Carta, etc.), but it doesn't mean that the Irishman is no longer an Irishman, or that he becomes a Brit.

Now for its spiritual application. Any Gentile, like Ruth, who became part of the Covenant that God gave to Abraham, Isaac and Jacob and their Seed, *remained a Gentile* and became part of the covenant people (i.e. Commonwealth) of Israel. Ruth, after she said that she was 'one with Naomi, Naomi's people and her God' (Ruth 1:16-18) became part of Israel (without rabbinic conversion or approval, as it didn't exist back then), but Ruth remained a Moabitess all the days of her life,[447] and all the divine laws of Moses that applied to Jewish women also applied to her.

Looking at Ittai, the *Gentile* general who served King David, will reveal

---

[444] The term *Israelite* is an archaic term from the Greek New Testament, hence, my use of *Israeli*. For an article on how the term *Jew* constitutes 'Israel,' ask for the PDF, *Jews, Israel and the Jews Today*.

[445] Romans 2:28-29 isn't speaking of a Gentile as a 'spiritual Jew.' Ask for the PDF *Is the Gentile Now a Jew?* or read it at http://www.SeedofAbraham.net/ Is_The_Gentile_Now_A_Jew.html.

[446] The ASV, KJV, NASB, NKJV and the NRSV have *Commonwealth*, while the HCSB, NET and the NIV have *citizenship*. Either is acceptable.

[447] Ruth 1:22; 2:2, 6, 21; 4:5, 10.

that Ittai remained a Philistine all the days of his life. In other words, Ittai didn't become a Hebrew even though he was 'one' with David and Israel, and even though he lived in Israel, and obviously, had left his own people.

When David fled from his son Absalom, who wanted to murder him and assume the kingship over Israel, David and his entourage hurriedly left Jerusalem. In stopping to reconnoiter who was with him David saw Ittai and Ittai's men:

> 'And the King went out with all the people after him and stopped at the outskirts. Then all his servants passed before him, and all the Cherethites, all the Pelethites, and all the Gittites, six hundred men who had followed him *from Gath* (Philistines!), passed before the King. Then the King said to *Ittai the Gittite,*'

>> 'Why are you also going with us? Return and remain with the King (Absalom), for you are a *foreigner* and also an exile from your own place. In fact, you came only yesterday.[448] Should I make you wander up and down with us today, since I go I know not where? Return and take your brethren back. Mercy and truth be with you.'

> 'Ittai answered the King (as Ruth did to Naomi) and said,'

>> 'As Yahveh lives, and as my Lord the King lives, surely in whatever place my Lord the King shall be, whether in death or life, even there also your servant will be.'

> "So David said to Ittai, 'Go and cross over.' Then Ittai the Gittite and all his men and all their children who were with him crossed over." (2nd Sam. 15:17-22)

Ittai the Gittite's loyalty to King David is exceptionally commendable because Ittai was a Philistine from the Philistine city of Gath, as the *Hebrew-Aramaic Lexicon of the Old Testament* brings out.[449] Ittai served the King of Israel and his God, but he remained a Philistine all the days of his life

---

[448] David doesn't literally mean that Ittai had come 'only yesterday,' but chooses that phrase to show Ittai that it was alright for him and his men to leave, but in this we see Ittai's great loyalty to David.

[449] Ludwig Koehler, Walter Baumgartner, J. J. Stamm (authors), M. E. J. Richardson, (editor, translator), *The Hebrew and Aramaic Lexicon of the Old Testament* (Accordance Bible software) 2001; vol. 1, p. 206. "גתי (*Giti*)...of גת (Gath) הגתי (*haGiti*) from Gath; Jos. 13:3 2S 6:10f; 15:19-22; 18:2; 21:19; 1C 13:13; 20:5; pl. הגתים (*haGitim*) 2S 15:18."

(2nd Sam. 18:2), as this passage brings out when David says to him, 'you *are* a foreigner,' not, 'you *were* a foreigner.' Ittai was still a Gentile.

Even though as a Philistine Ittai should have been a mortal enemy of David he was truly part of the Commonwealth of Israel and would receive benefits, both temporal and eternal, because of his love for King David and David's God.[450] Ittai is a picture of the Gentile in the New Testament, while King David is a picture of Messiah Yeshua.

Rabbinic conversion *artificially* makes a Gentile into a Jew. There's nothing in the Old Testament, nor the New Testament, to support this change of racial identity. Nowhere in the New Testament do we see any Gentile being referred to as a Jew or a Hebrew. A Gentile who comes to believe in Yeshua, the King of Israel, doesn't become a Jew, but remains a Gentile.

All believers are in Messiah's Kingdom, but not all are Jews, yet, all are part of the Commonwealth of Israel, the Olive Tree and the Seed of Abraham. Gentiles, like Ittai, could live in Israel, and so, by citizenship they could say that they were Israeli, to say, an Egyptian or a Roman, but they weren't an Israeli or a Hebrew or Jew by race, anymore than a Russian man living in Greece, and possessing Greek citizenship, becomes a Greek by race. A Jew is a Jew by race.

Of course, there are some who twist Scripture (e.g. Eph. 2:11), to try and interpret it otherwise, but the word *Jew(s),* in both the Old and the New Testaments, *always* refers to a person who was racially born from the Seed of Abraham, Isaac and Jacob.[451] God cements this concept in the New Covenant by saying that the Gentile believers weren't to be physically covenantally circumcised like the Jews (Acts 15, etc.). The Pharisees who believed in Yeshua wanted the Gentiles to (artificially) become Jews via physical, covenantal circumcision (Acts 15:1-6f.), because that's what they believed should happen, but God, through Paul, Barnabas, Peter and James, overruled them (and rabbinic conversion), reestablishing the biblical concept that Gentiles don't become Jews.[452]

If a Gentile wanted to be part of Israel before Messiah, he could do that by being covenantally circumcised (Exodus 12:43-48), but he still remained a

---

[450] See also Uriah the Hittite, one of King David's champions, as another example of a foreigner residing within Israel who was *one* with Israel, but wasn't seen as a Jew or a Hebrew (1st Sam. 26:6; 2nd Sam. 11:3, 6, 17, 21, 24; 12:9; 23:39; 1st Kgs. 15:5).

[451] Gentiles who mistakenly convert to Judaism via the Rabbis are called proselytes and even though the Rabbis say that 'they are now Jews,' they are not Jews according to the Word of God, but remain Gentiles.

[452] See Acts 15:7-10, 14, 16-17, 19, especially v. 23 where these Gentile believers are still called Gentiles, and also, 1st Thess. 4:1-5 (especially v. 5).

Gentile, or in Hebrew he would be called a גֵּר (*ger*).[453] Proselytism, which artificially makes a Gentile into a Jew, is another rabbinic invention that goes against the Word of God. There is nothing in Scripture to support a Gentile becoming a Jew.

Peter's *yoke*, though, wasn't about becoming a proselyte to keep the 'man-made rules.' Peter wasn't a proselyte and he didn't keep 'man-made rules' (Mt. 15:2 by inference). This wasn't the *burden* that he spoke of. The yoke that neither Peter nor his Fathers could bear was the keeping of the Law for *eternal life* (salvation: justification before God). *This* is what *circumcision* (and proselytism) ultimately implied and this is what the Council struck down—*the false teaching that the Law was a vehicle for salvation.*[454] The *yoke* has nothing to do with 'legalism,' as has been defined by Bruce and Witherington, nor 'intricate *halachah*,' or 'mechanically' keeping the Law. Stern, Hegg and most Christians also miss it. Marshall, however, rightly perceives that Peter's yoke was the Law *used for justification:*

> '*The point here* is not the burdensomeness or oppressiveness *of the law*, but rather the inability of the Jews to gain salvation through it, and hence, its irrelevance *as far as salvation is concerned.*[455]

Exactly, but since the days before Yeshua, the keeping of the Law, for justification, is how the Jewish people thought they earned eternal life, despite the view of the New Perspective, which presents Judaism as a *faith-based* religion that 'doesn't look to the Law for salvation.' This 'new perspective,' brought into Christianity by Sanders, Dunn and Wright, follows one 'party line' of rabbinic thinking, believing that the Jew wasn't concerned about salvation because he was part of the Chosen People, *which guaranteed him salvation,* hence, the Jew didn't keep the Law for salvation. This, however, is an imaginary ideal based upon a false, non-biblical hope about what it meant to be part of the Chosen People—nowhere in the Law does God plainly speak of eternal life for the Chosen People, let alone guarantee it. God does hint at eternal life in the Prophets and Psalms, but the *method* of attaining it (faith in Messiah Yeshua) is never explained.[456]

---

[453] For how a *ger* differed from other *Gentiles* living in Israel see p. 268ff.

[454] Marshall, *Acts*, p. 250. Also, 'What the legalists were trying to do was to place the yoke of the law on the Gentiles, a yoke which the Jews themselves had never been able to bear successfully…as far as salvation is concerned.'

[455] Ibid.

[456] See Prov. 10:25; Is. 33:14; 35:10; 45:17; 51:11; 55:3; 56:5; 60:15, 19-20; Ezk. 37:26; Daniel 12:2.

Scot McKnight summarizes some of the New Perspective on Judaism by saying that,

> 'Israel was elected by God, brought into the covenant and
> given the law *to regulate how covenant people live.*'[457]

That's so good to hear! Israel was given the Law so that she could know how God wanted her to live out her faith in Him. It's shocking, though, that this 'new perspective' has taken 1,900 years to appear in Christianity.

James Dunn, though, speaking of Sanders' position, fails to understand that the Law was also a way of gaining God's favor or blessing. He states,

> 'the commandments are not a way of earning God's favor
> but a way of showing how the people of God should live.
> That's the basic point that had to be made in terms of the
> new perspective.'[458]

Sanders seriously errs if he thinks that the Jewish people didn't look to the commandments to earn God's favor. The Law clearly states that *obedience equals blessing,*[459] which the Rabbis rightly emphasize. It's actually *the* way of receiving God's favor and blessing (Lev. 26; Dt. 28). Conversely, one is cursed by God if he doesn't obey the commandments, which are like the law of gravity. Say that gravity doesn't matter and leap off a ten story building. Whether in ignorance or arrogance, if one doesn't keep the commandments, they still effect him.

Also, the idea of the Rabbis, that eternal life was given if one was part of the Chosen People, is false, too. There is no Scripture to validate it and it's not what is *practiced* in Judaism. Loewe states that Judaism,

> 'like Hellenism or Islam, can be expounded and under-
> stood *without being followed in practice.*'[460]

Rabbi Akiva (50-135 AD), who is revered in Judaism, even though he, by endorsing a false messiah, caused the Jewish people to lose their nation for more than 1,800 years, realized the danger of relying on 'being a covenant member' to automatically guarantee Paradise. It's said of him,

> that he 'seemed to hold that the future life is a privilege to
> be gained through positive upright living, rather than an
> inherent right *which can only be forfeited as a penalty.*

---

[457]  McKnight: http://blog.beliefnet.com/jesuscreed/2007/08/new-perspective-4.html.

[458]  Wright; *The Paul Page* at http://www.thepaulpage.com/Conversation.html. This teaching was given on Oct. 25th, 2004.

[459]  Dt. 11:26-28; 28:1-2, 15, 45, et al.

[460]  Montefiore, *A Rabbinic Anthology,* p. lvii.

> Sometimes he asserted God's mercy to be such that a sin-
> gle *meritorious act* will win a man admission to the future
> world.'[461]

Akiva realized that the afterlife could be forfeited by any Jew of the Chosen People. He also thought that meritorious acts or good deeds (of the
Law) were *necessary* for eternal life *even* if one were 'in covenant.' Here
we see a well known rabbi stating that being part of the Chosen People
was not enough to enter into eternal life, and that Paradise was attained by
keeping the Law.

In 'the New Perspective on Judaism and Paul,' *works of the Law* takes on
the connotation of being specific *Jewish* works, such as keeping the Sabbath and circumcision. The *works of the Law* for Dunn are 'sociological
markers' of the Jewish community, and so, they're *not seen* as 'merit-
seeking works,' but 'boundary-marking works.'[462] N.T. Wright agrees and
says they *aren't* the,

> 'moral works through which one gains merit, but the
> works through which the Jew is defined over against the
> pagan.'[463]

Wright adds that the 'works of the Spirit' are those things that show that
one is 'in Christ' (e.g. bringing people into the Kingdom).[464] Contrary to
this pristine, myopic evaluation of first century Judaism, 'works of the
Law' are both sociological boundary markers (for what nation other than
Israel keeps Passover and Tabernacles?) and *all* the good, moral works
that stem from the *doing* of the Law. It is equally Sabbath observance as
well as taking care of the poor, the widow and the orphan (compassion,
justice and love of neighbor),[465] *and* the mighty works or miracles that
Yeshua did (Mt. 11:2; Jn. 5:36; 15:24, etc.), which sprang forth from the
love, redemption and *freedom* pictured in the 7th day Sabbath and the
Year of Jubilee.[466] *All* these stem from the Law and are an organic whole.

The Father says of Yeshua, 'You are My Servant *Israel* in whom I will be
glorified (Is. 49:3).'[467] Yeshua is the quintessential Israeli (Rev. 22:16). He

---

[461] Ibid., p. 664, note 13.

[462] McKnight: http://blog.beliefnet.com/jesuscreed/2007/08/new-perspective-2.html.

[463] N. T. Wright; *New Perspectives on Paul* at http://www.ntwrightpage.com/
Wright_New_Perspectives.htm; Aug. 25-28, 2003.

[464] Ibid.

[465] Ex. 22:22; Lev. 19:18; Dt. 10:18; 14:29; 16:11; 24:17, 19; 26:12; Mt. 5:16;
26:10f.; Gal. 2:10; 1st Tim. 5:10; 6:17-19; Titus 2:11-14; 3:8, 14; Rev. 19:8.

[466] Exodus 23:4-5; Lev. 25:8-10; Is. 61:1-2; Lk. 4:18-19.

[467] John 14:10-12; 12:28; 16:14; 17:1, 5; 21:19.

is the Example *par excellence* of what being 'in the Spirit' means, one thing of which is that He *did* all the Law that applied to Him. Torah is the verbal expression of Yahveh—Who He is, what He's done for Israel, what He wants to do for Israel, *and* His will for Israel. God has magnified and glorified His Law, through Yeshua ('Yahveh was pleased for the sake of His righteousness to *magnify His Law and make it glorious;'* Is. 42:21).

How did Yahveh *magnify* His Law? Yeshua was like a prism through which the Law and the Holy Spirit were magnified and seen (1st Jn. 1:1f.) He is the *living* Torah, *the* Word of God (Rev. 19:13) who walked out the Law of Moses the way God intended it to be walked out. The teachings and merciful healings Yeshua did, as well as His observance of the Sabbath and Passover, etc., sprang from the Law and Spirit within,[468] and are our example of how God wants us to live out our faith in Yeshua. The Holy Spirit is able to empower believers so that we can do all the works of the Law, as Yeshua did,[469] through the *power* and *fruit* of the Spirit (Gal. 5:22-24). Torah forms the internal framework so that one can be *'fully* equipped *for every good work'* (2nd Tim. 3:16-17). The Holy Spirit is the *life* of the Law, who also seeks to write the Law upon the tablets of our heart, so that both God, and His will, have a living place within us.

Claude Montefiore (1858-1938), a noted Jewish scholar, writes that even though the Rabbis can stress the 'joy of the commandment,'[470] and that 'the Law must be fulfilled for its own sake and for the love of God, and *not* for reward,'[471] says that when it comes right down to it, the Jew must keep the Law *in order to be saved.* In summing up Judaism's concept of righteousness and the *reward* of eternal life, Montefiore states,

> 'There is no rigid or worked-out doctrine about Works and Faith. On the whole, the theory of *justification by works* is *strongly pressed.*[472]

This is (attempted) justification (salvation) through the Law, through the works of the Law, which is a rabbinic perversion of what God intended the Law to be used for. Montefiore also speaks of the individual Jew being regarded as a,

> 'bundle of *deeds.* If he has done 720 good deeds and 719 bad ones, he is more righteous than wicked (with due con-

---

[468]  Matthew 11:4-6; 23:23; John 5:36; 9:3-4, etc.

[469]  Mt. 5:16; Jn. 14:12; Acts 4:8; 8:6-7; Eph. 2:10; Titus 2:14; 1st Pet. 2:12, etc.

[470]  Montefiore, *A Rabbinic Anthology*, p. 202.

[471]  Ibid., p. xxxvi. *Italics* are Montefiore's.

[472]  Ibid., p. xxxv.

sequences as regards divine punishment and reward).'[473]

'At the judgment in the world to come, paradise or hell is given *according to the majority of good deeds or evil.*'[474]

Is this a concept of Judaism that wasn't there in the days of Yeshua and Paul? Has Judaism 'gone backwards' in its thinking? Once they were saved by just 'being in covenant,' but today it takes the works or deeds of the Law to save them?

The New Testament offers a number of places where *official* Jewish understanding, as to what constituted eternal life for the Jew, is seen. One place is Acts 15. Did the Gentile need 'to become a Jew' and keep the Law of Moses, symbolized in physical, covenantal circumcision, *along with faith in Jesus* for eternal life? The Law is seen as necessary for salvation by the believing Pharisees and Scribes (Acts 15:1, 5), who weren't any different, at this point, than their non-believing counterparts.

'Moses' hadn't placed this yoke upon the necks of Peter and his Fathers—the Pharisees had! This is what Peter and his Fathers (his genealogical fathers as well as the Elders of Israel) had been *deceived* into believing—that God would give them eternal life *if they kept the Law*. This is the yoke that no one could bear (Rom. 3:20, 28; Gal. 2:16-17), as Marshall brought out, and this is exactly what Yeshua says when He speaks to the Jewish authorities (Jn. 5:10f.), and the Jewish people, who looked for salvation by keeping the Law. Yeshua said in John 5:39:

'You search the Scriptures because you *think that in them you have eternal life*, but it is they that testify of Me.'[475]

Yeshua, the highest authority in any matter, speaks of Jewish *expectation* for eternal life residing within Torah. This is confirmed when the Pharisaic leaders in the Sanhedrin said that the common Jewish people were cursed because *they didn't know the Law*—'this multitude, which doesn't know the Law, is accursed!' (John 7:49)

All those 'cursed folks' were Jews *in covenant*, but Jews that didn't know the Law, or rather, keep it the way the Pharisees and Scribes did, and so, were obviously not candidates for Heaven. This is a biblical insight into what the Pharisees and Scribes, the highest Jewish authorities who be-

---

[473] Ibid.

[474] Ibid., p. 596.

[475] Edersheim, *The Life and Times of Jesus the Messiah*, p. 322. Writing of John 5:39 he says: 'Their elaborate searching and sifting of the Law in hope that, by a subtle analysis of its every particle and letter, by inferences from, and a careful drawing of a prohibitive hedge around its letter, they would possess themselves of eternal life,' but they were *'utterly self-deceived.'*

lieved in an afterlife, and who would evolve into the rabbis of today, thought how eternal life was attained, as we saw with the believing Pharisees in Acts 15.

Obedience to the Law *was* righteousness, as the Law and Paul state (Dt. 6:25; 24:13; Rom. 10:5), but extending that obedience to earning eternal life wasn't God's way for eternal life, hence, Peter's yoke in Acts 15:10. Also, in that same Sanhedrin, whose high priest was a Sadducee who didn't believe in an afterlife, the man born blind, whom Yeshua had given sight to, was despised and rejected. One of them, perhaps the high priest, said to the former blind man,

> 'You were completely born in sins and are you teaching
> us?! And they cast him out!' (John 9:34)

The Sanhedrin, the highest religious authority in the days of Yeshua, reveals *official* Jewish understanding of which Jews would be saved and which wouldn't. The man 'born in sin,' even though he was obviously a Jew, circumcised on the eighth day and part of the Chosen People, didn't qualify despite the fact that his answers to them were extremely perceptive—*as the religious authorities* the Sanhedrin was supposed to know 'where a man was from,' meaning, was Jesus from God or Satan?![476]

What we see here is of far greater value than what some rabbis, in idealizing Judaism, wrote. According to the New Testament, Judaism believed that eternal life was attained through the keeping of the Law. This dismantles the New Perspective thinking on the Jewish perception of salvation.

The Rabbis knew that all Israel wouldn't be saved, even though God had saved all Israel from Egyptian slavery. They knew Israel's history was permeated with wicked Israelis, some of whom Yahveh had destroyed and many of whom Scripture calls evil.[477] The Rabbis knew this side of Israel,

---

[476] See John 9:13-34, esp. v. 30. The Sanhedrin was confronted with the Messiah and they knew it. That's why they made doubly sure that the man had been *born* blind (by asking his parents to come; Jn. 9:18-23). There was a teaching at that time that the spittle of a righteous man could open the eyes of a blind man, but *only the Messiah* could open the eyes of one *born* blind. Now, here was this man who had been born blind looking right at them, while they tried to discredit Yeshua (see also Mt. 21:24f.). It shouldn't be overlooked, though, that some members of the Sanhedrin (perhaps Nicodemus and Joseph of Arimathea) voiced their godly objections. Even though it was the Sabbath when the miracle was done, because the miracle was so incredible, these men questioned the 'party line' that Yeshua was a sinner (Jn. 9:16).

[477] Ex. 32:1-35 is the sin of the Gold Calf; Num. 16:1-40, esp. v. 26, is the sin of Korah; Num. 16:44-45 is the sin of Israel in wanting to stone Moses and Aaron, saying that *they* had murdered Korah; Num. 13:1–14:45, especially 14:26-38, is the sin of the entire Camp (except for a few) in believing the ten spies and turning Israel against Yahveh and His promise to bring them into

too, and believed that obedience to the Torah was the key to eternal life, as Yeshua spoke of that day to the Jewish people (Jn. 5:39). Yes, the Pharisees had added many other rules to the Law, but the concept of earning salvation through the Law was the foundation of their misguided hope.

A rabbinic story reveals the problem the Rabbis faced with this concept. A great rabbi lay dying on his deathbed. All his students gathered around him and noticed that he was very sad. They asked him why. He said,

> "'I am soon going to be before the Holy One and *I don't know if I will be accepted.*' They said, 'But you are a great rabbi! You have taught us how to walk in Torah *and have kept Torah all your life!*' Whereupon he answered them, 'To you I am great, but in the eyes of the Holy One every wicked thing is seen.'"

The story reveals the pathetic problem with trying to use the works of the Law as a gauge to determine one's fitness to stand in God's presence on Judgment Day. No amount of good deeds (the holy works of the Law) can give one eternal life, nor the assurance thereof.

It also brings out that being 'part of Israel' wasn't enough, even for a great rabbi. The *Gentile,* 'getting into' the 'covenant-saved people,' would still be expected to keep the Law *for eternal life* (Rom. 2:17, 25; Gal. 5:4). *This* was the burden that neither Peter, nor his Fathers, could bear. After Peter spoke of the yoke, his very next words, in Acts 15:11, confirm this by saying that the Gentiles were saved *just as he himself had been:* 'But we believe that they' (i.e. the Gentiles) *'are saved just as we are,* by the grace of the Lord Jesus.' In other words, Peter could also have said,

> 'We used to think that keeping the Law entitled us to Heaven (Jn. 5:39), but we've come to see that this was a perverse concept the Pharisees gave to God's holy Law.'

The Council met because some believing Pharisees wanted to make Jews of the Gentiles (circumcision) *and attach the Law to faith in Yeshua* for salvation (Acts 15:1, 5). Salvation for those Pharisees, or entry into the Kingdom of Yeshua, consisted of faith in Yeshua *plus* the keeping of the Law (symbolized in circumcision). They hadn't realized that faith in Yeshua had made them a new creature (2nd Cor. 5:17; Gal. 6:15) and circumcised their heart (Dt. 30:6), and that keeping the Law and physical

---

the land of Canaan, for which they wandered (and died) in the Wilderness for 40 years (see also Num. 17:5, 10; 18:5). Also, there were the sins of all the kings of the northern kingdom of Israel for which Yahveh finally annihilated it through the king of Assyria in 721 BC, and the sins of most of the kings of the southern kingdom of Judah, with most of the population being destroyed and a tiny remnant (4,600; Jer. 52:28-30) led away into Babylon captivity.

circumcision had nothing to do with entry into Messiah's Kingdom or being Born Again. This is what Peter was addressing. He wasn't speaking against the Law or its good works. He was coming against circumcision and the Law being *added* to faith in Yeshua for salvation.

This was a new concept for those believing Pharisees and for most everyone else there. That's why the Council convened. The congregation in Antioch had wanted to know what was required for Gentile salvation. It was logical for the believing Pharisees to think the way they did—Gentiles became part of Israel, before Messiah Yeshua, by being circumcised (Ex. 12:48) and keeping the Law (Ex. 12:49; Lev. 19:34; 24:22), but this was the New Covenant and a new way of entering into it. There was *no precedent* in Torah for Gentiles coming into Messiah's Kingdom. In this Kingdom Yeshua performs *the circumcision made without hands* (Col. 2:11) that Torah pointed to (Dt. 30:6).

Only after much debate in Jerusalem did the outcome that we read of prevail (Acts 15:7). It most likely took several hours. Then Peter stood up and declared the counsel of God. It seems that Paul and Barnabas already understood this (Acts 15:1-2), but it certainly wasn't 'a given.'

Yes, the Law had also become enmeshed with *the Traditions of the Elders* (also known as the Oral Law, which would become the written Talmud), but the main point that Peter made was that the Law, symbolized in physical covenantal circumcision, could not be attached to Jesus for salvation. Peter and the Apostles had only come to see this *after* they realized how God had given them *and* Cornelius (Acts 10) eternal life—through faith in His Son *plus nothing else*. This was the entry point, the middle point and the end point. Led of the Holy Spirit, the commandments and good works of the Law of Moses are a spiritual by-product of how one walks out his faith in Yeshua.[478] Once in the Kingdom does it matter if one sins against the King or not? Here is where the Law comes to the forefront. It declares what is right and holy, sin and abomination, according to the King, for both Jew and Gentile.

Before Peter and Paul had known Jesus, they too, had been deceived into thinking that the keeping of the Law would merit them eternal life, but now, in Acts 15:10, Peter was setting the record straight, something that Paul would do in Romans 3:31, where he writes of *establishing* (the place of) the Law for every believer. The 'place of the Law' is *not* for eternal life, as he had previously thought, unregenerate Pharisee that he had been, but for holy *lifestyle* 'in Messiah.' The Law is the criteria for knowing

---

[478] Jer. 31:33; Ezk. 36:26-27; Mt. 25:31-46; Rom. 2:5-8, 13; Eph. 2:10; 1st Tim. 2:10; 5:9-10, 25; 6:18; 2nd Tim. 2:21; 3:14-17; Titus 1:16; 2:6-7, 13-14; 3:1, 8, 14; Heb. 10:24; James 2:14-26; Rev. 2:2-5, 9; 13:13, et al.

God's view on what is sin and what is right living (Rom. 7:7, 12, 14; 1st Cor. 7:19). Paul didn't write the letter of Romans to the Jews in the Sanhedrin, but to mostly *Gentile believers* in Rome who needed to know the place of the Law and the Law's value in the midst of God's grace.

Religious doctrines that nullify God's Word are very hard to perceive when one grows up in them. This was true for those Jewish believers back then and it's true for many Christians today. Tradition blinds people into thinking that their doctrine is of God. When we look at the Pharisees, locked in mortal combat with God the Son, we see how the 'doctrines of men' can blind one to God Himself. Only the Spirit of Yeshua can open blind eyes to reveal the deception and produce a desire for godly change.

Paul fought this false teaching on salvation (of combining the Law with faith in Jesus) in his letter to the Galatians. His conclusion of the matter, on using the good deeds of the Law (symbolized in circumcision) for justification, is seen in Gal. 5:4:

> 'You have been severed from Christ, you who are *seeking to be justified by Law!* You have fallen from grace!'

Paul wasn't coming against the Law, but its perverse use. Some of the Galatians were seeking to be justified by faith in Messiah *and* the Law (symbolized in circumcision), but adding anything to Yeshua's sacrifice denies the sufficiency of who He is and what He did. Once in the Kingdom, though, we should obey the King's rules. The laws of Moses are meant to be for our lifestyle in His Kingdom, just as they were for Paul.

The commandments of Moses are for our protection and blessing (Lev. 26; Dt. 28–30), and also set us apart (i.e. makes us holy and distinct) from the people of darkness around us. God didn't give the Law to Israel because He hated her or wanted to enslave her, but because He wanted Israel to be a wise and a blessed people. He wants that for us, too.

In the days of Yeshua, the keeping of the Law was the Pharisaic vehicle for Paradise, as it remains today. This is a perverse, conceptual use of the Law, which is works righteousness or legalism. As we've seen, though, legalism, when applied to the Law, can be wrongly defined. Many say that it's the Law itself that is legalism, but the Law is certainly not legalism, nor a burden, nor oppressive. The Law is God's holy Gift from Above, in verbal form (Lev. 18:5; Dt. 4:5-8; Rom. 7:12), the verbal reflection of God the Son who became flesh (John 1:1-3, 14).

God never intended that the keeping of His Law would be a means of eternal life. Nowhere in the Law, or any other place in the Old Testament, does He say that if it's obeyed the reward will be eternal life. The Law gave Israel the holy rules for covenant relationship with Yahveh and with their fellow Hebrews *after* they had been saved (set free) from Egyptian slavery. Once we are justified in Messiah and set free from Satan's Kingdom of sin and death, the Law becomes the divine guideline for how Gentiles and Jews are to live out their faith in Messiah Yeshua.

The yoke that neither Peter, nor his Fathers could bear wasn't the Law. Peter loved the Law. It wasn't circumcision. Peter was circumcised, and neither he, nor his Fathers found that unbearable. It wasn't being a Jew. Peter and his Fathers were Jews, and that didn't change after they came to the Jewish Messiah. They knew that God had been very gracious to the Jewish people and had chosen them out of all the peoples on the face of the Earth.[479] The yoke that neither Peter nor his Fathers could bear was the keeping of the Law for salvation, symbolized in circumcision. This was the tremendous burden of the dying 'great rabbi.' Works righteousness always nullifies faith in the person and work of Messiah Yeshua.

Acts 15:10 cannot be used to prove that the Law, in and of itself, is the yoke that Peter spoke of, and therefore, 'not for the Gentiles.' It's a verse that reveals the bankruptcy of trying to keep the Law for salvation (Rom. 9:30-32). Peter wasn't doing away with the Law, but the keeping of the Law for salvation, which was a yoke that neither he nor his Fathers could bear—for Peter had found the True Yoke (Mt. 11:28-30).

---

[479]  Exodus 8:22-23; 9:4, 6, 26; 10:21-23; 11:7; 12:12-13, 23-33; 13:5, 8-9, 11-15, 21-22; 14:4, 8, 13-14, 16, 17, 18, 19-20, 21, 22, 24, 25, 26, 27, 28, 29, 30; 19:5; 33:12-17; 34:8-11; Lev. 20:24, 26; Num. 33:50-56; Dt. 4:7-8, 33-37; 7:6, 14; 10:15; 14:1-3; 26:18-19; 28:9-10, 12-14; 32:9-13; 33:3, 29; 1st Kings 8:53; 2nd Kings 21:7-8; Psalm 132:13-18; 135:4; 144:15; 147:19-20; Isaiah 27:2-6; 41:8-9; 42:1; 43:3, 4, 15, 20, 21; 44:21, 22; 45:4, 17, 19, 25; 46:3, 4, 13; 49:14-16; 52:8-12; Jer. 46:27-28; 50:11, 18-20, 33-34; 51:19, 24, 45, 49; Ezk. 20:6; 34:23-31; 37:28; Zech. 2:8; 8:2-8; Rom. 9–11, etc.

# *Acts 15:19 — Don't Trouble Them!*

In Acts 15:19, Yakov says not to 'trouble those who are turning to God from among the Gentiles.' Many take this phrase to mean that the Jews shouldn't trouble the Gentiles with the Law of Moses.

David Williams states, 'nothing more than faith should be asked of them as necessary for salvation.'[480] This is true because salvation isn't based on doing the Law, but he alters his thinking when he says, 'once in the kingdom *certain things* could fairly be asked of them.'[481] He's speaking of the four rules of Yakov in relation to his understanding of table fellowship.

Bruce and Witherington see the *troubling* that Yakov spoke of was aimed at those who wanted the Gentiles to be circumcised.[482] *Wycliffe* says,

> they 'should no longer trouble the Gentiles by demanding that they accept circumcision and the law of Moses.'[483]

Tim Hegg thinks the *troubling* of the Gentiles has to do with not giving them all the rabbinic traditions, just the four rules, which he believes come from the Rabbis.[484] Of course, the Pharisaic concept of the Law included the (oral) Tradition of the Elders (Mt. 15:2, 6; Mk. 7:1-13), but that's not the point. The four rules weren't given to the Gentiles as a trade-off in lieu of all the Pharisaic traditions. They were the first of God's rules that the Gentiles needed to be aware of in relation to his salvation.

Three of the four rules come from the Law. In Ex. 34:12, Yahveh warns Israel not to make any covenants with the pagans in Canaan. He says in v. 14 that He won't tolerate worship of another god, and He specifically warns them, in vv. 15-16, not to play the harlot, worshiping other gods through (1) *cult harlotry* or (2) eating of the sacrifice, which would *include* both the *eating of the meat* and the (3) *drinking of the blood*.

In the Ten Commandments (Ex. 20:5), Yahveh forbids Israel to worship (which is synonymous with sacrifice; Ex. 10:25-26) another god. In Leviticus 17, Israel is told that they *weren't to sacrifice to demons, play the harlot* (v. 7) *or drink the blood* of the sacrifice (vv. 10, 12-14). In the Baal Peor debacle (Num. 25) Israel sacrificed to Baal, *ate of the sacrifice* and *played the harlot*. Within just these cites, three of Yakov's four rules are seen: not to eat meat sacrificed to idols (at the time of the sacrifice), not to drink the sacrificial blood and not to lay with the cult prostitutes.[485] By in-

---

[480] Williams, *Acts*, p. 266.

[481] Ibid.

[482] Bruce, *The Book of the Acts*, p. 295. Witherington, *The Acts of the Apostles*, p. 441.

[483] Pfeiffer, *The Wycliffe Bible Commentary*, p. 1152.

[484] Hegg, *The Letter Writer*, pp. 281, 275-282.

cluding *strangling,* Yakov was exercising his divine right to *legislate* (to enact a rule which would be considered as if God had commanded it). Yeshua gave this to His Body, and set this in motion, saying to Peter,

> "I will give you the Keys of the Kingdom of Heaven and
> whatever you bind on Earth will be bound in Heaven and
> whatever you loose on Earth will be loosed in Heaven"
> (Mt. 16:19; see Mt. 18:18 where this authority is also giv-
> en to the Apostles).

'The Keys of the Kingdom' spoke of the authority that God had given to the priests to forgive sin (Lev. 4:20, 26, 31; 6:7), teach the Torah (Lev. 10:8-11; 14:57; Dt. 31:9-13), *legislate* (make new rules) and adjudicate (judge situations between one man and another, etc. (Dt. 17:8-13; Ezekiel 44:20-24). To *bind* and *loose* were terms for *forbidding* or *allowing* something, respectively, usually in a court setting. The last three 'keys' had been usurped by the Pharisees in the days of Yeshua, but Yeshua was giving all of them to His Apostles,[486] and be extension, to Yakov.

Yakov didn't need to explain what he meant. Everyone understood.[487] He also didn't go to the Sanhedrin to formulate or authorize his rules. He knew about sacrificial-sexual idolatry from his own Family History Book (the Hebrew Bible) and the state of pagan affairs. The four rules concisely spelled it out for the Gentile believer—no sacrificial-sexual idolatry!

The *troubling* that James addressed had to do with those Jewish believers who had previously gone to Antioch and stirred up the controversy. They weren't officially sent from James, but were part of the believers in Jeru-salem (Acts 15:1, 24). They had told the Gentiles that they needed to be circumcised (i.e. keep the Law) along with faith in Yeshua for salvation (15:1, 5). This *troubling* can be seen to relate to both the human trouble-makers *and* their troublesome theology.

Yakov told everyone that the arguing was over (Acts 15:19). He had

---

[485] *Strangling* is not literally written in the Law, but the point is that the Gentiles were given three laws from the Law, showing that the Law was valid for Gen-tile believers, and Yakov commanded yet another rule to those 'under Grace.'

[486] Forgiveness of sin was given in John 20:23. The Apostles taught Scripture and Messiah (Acts 5:25; 15:35; 18:11; 28:31; 1st Cor. 4:17; 1st Tim. 3:2; 6:2-3). Acts 15 was legislation: Yakov gave the four rules. Acts 15 was also judgment: Yakov determined what the Gentiles needed to do in order to be saved. Cornelius was the first Gentile came into the Kingdom (Acts 10:28, 34; 11:1-3, 18), and Gentiles coming into the Kingdom had never happened be-fore. The ability to judge is also seen when Paul speaks of the Corinthians judging their Flock (1st Cor. 6:1-6; see also Lk. 22:28-30).

[487] See Witherington and Hegg, p. 48 above.

*judged* the issue and had come to a ruling. R. J. Knowling says that Yakov was the 'president' of the meeting and that this was even known in the days of Chrysostom (347-407 AD).[488] That Yakov was *the* authority is also evident from his use of the emphatic 'I' (εγω, *eh'go*) in, '*I* judge.'[489] Witherington says the Greek construction for 'I judge,'

> "makes the ruling more emphatically one of James's in particular—'*I myself judge*/rule'[490]...This way of putting it is equivalent to the familiar Latin phrase *ego censeo* used by Roman rulers and judges."[491]

Bruce thinks the Council voted on the Decree, but Witherington negates Bruce's perspective on what happened, giving the decision to James:

> "Bruce is quite wrong that James is putting forward a 'motion' to the assembly. Various parties have spoken and conferred, and now James will conclude the matter. We are indeed dealing with a decree or ruling from a recognized authority."[492]

Witherington further relates that verse 22,

> 'is about the decision to send representatives of the Jerusalem church with Paul and Barnabas with the decree. It is not about confirming the decree by the assembly's consent[493]...In other words, James is portrayed as more than just another rhetor; he is...*a judge or authority figure* who can give a *ruling* that settles a matter.'[494]

Yakov's authority is also seen by the way Paul speaks of him, along with two other chief Apostles (Peter and John) in Gal. 2:9, and also, by the way Luke writes about him.[495] Yakov, because he was the oldest half-brother of Yeshua, commanded an authority that was second to none, including that of the Apostles. Bellarmino Bagatti writes that,

> 'James...was superior to Peter and Paul, because he was a descendant of David, of the same blood as Jesus, and therefore the legitimate representative of the sacerdotal

---

[488] Knowling, *The Acts of the Apostles*, p. 323.

[489] The KJV has 'my sentence' and the NASB has 'my judgment.'

[490] Witherington, *The Acts of the Apostles*, p. 467.

[491] Ibid., note 437.

[492] Ibid., p. 467.

[493] Ibid., p. 451.

[494] Ibid.

[495] Ibid., see Acts 12:17; 21:18. Also 1st Cor. 15:7; Gal. 1:19; 2:9, 12.

race.' No 'apostle could claim such prerogatives.'[496]

Yakov was the second son of Yosafe (Joseph) and Miryam (Mary).[497] He was 'next in line' to the Throne of Israel, after his elder brother Yeshua, having been born before his other brothers (Mt. 13:55: Josi, Simon and Judah). This is why Yakov was the *Nasi* or Prince ('President') over all the Jews that believed in Yeshua, including the Apostles.[498]

The debate about what a Gentile needed to do in order to be saved had ended. Yakov had come to a decision and would not have the Gentiles attacked or troubled by a perverse teaching and perverted teachers. Verse 19 officially put an end to the desire among the believing Pharisees for the Gentiles to be circumcised and keep the Law, along with faith in Jesus, for eternal life. The ruling of Yakov assured the Gentile full partnership with the Jewish believer without his having to be circumcised. This is seen from what Peter and Yakov say in vv. 7-19, and none of this negates the Law as a way of life for the Gentile to walk out his faith in Messiah.

The next verse (v. 20) laid down the litmus test. Yakov gave his four authoritative rules for the Gentiles. If the Holy Spirit was directing him, and Scripture declares such (Acts 15:28),[499] then these four rules can rightly be called commandments from Jesus to all the Gentile believers through the Prince of the 'Mother Church' in Jerusalem.[500]

The four rules were the filter though which every Gentile had to pass in order for his faith in Yeshua to be seen as biblically genuine. Then Yakov said something that still bewilders most theologians 2,000 years later.

---

[496] Samuele Bacchiocchi, *From Sabbath To Sunday* (Rome, Italy: The Pontifical Gregorian University Press, 1977), p. 145, quoting Bagatti, *The Church from the Circumcision*, 1971, p. 70.

[497] Yeshua had four younger brothers (Mt. 13:55; Mk. 6:3) and two of them, Yakov (James or rather Jacob in English) and Yehuda (Jude or rather Judah) wrote letters that are authoritative (i.e. Scripture). As Yakov is mentioned first in both passages (Mt. 13:55; Mk. 6:3) and he's the Prince of the Council in Acts 15 and 21 it's not unreasonable to think that he was the first son born after Yeshua. (Also, Paul mentions Yakov as Yeshua's brother; Gal. 1:19).

[498] See Acts 12:17; 21:18; 1st Cor. 15:7; Gal. 2:9; also Jude 1:1.

[499] Conceptually, what is presented for Acts 15:19 can also be applied to v. 28 ('to lay upon you no greater *burden* then these necessary things').

[500] See Acts 16:4-5; also 1st Cor. 14:37; 2nd Cor. 8:8 (by inference); 1st Tim. 6:14; 2nd Peter 3:2, 14-16.

# Acts 15:21—Go to the Synagogue?!

Acts 15:21 is another example of Scripture not being correctly interpreted by Christian theologians due to prejudice against the Law of Moses. The verse isn't understood by scholars, although some are honest enough to say that it's an enigma. In an anti-Law environment this verse doesn't make any sense. Marshall realizes this and initially writes that 'James's concluding statement is puzzling.'[501] The verse reads,

> 'For Moses from ancient generations has in every city those who preach him, being read in the synagogues every Sabbath day.'

Why did James end his decision with that? Marshall posits two possibilities as to what James meant. First he proposes,

> 'since there are Jews everywhere who regularly hear the law of Moses being read in the synagogues, Christian Gentiles ought to respect their scruples, and so avoid bringing the church into disrepute with them.'[502]

On the surface, respect for one another is a godly ideal, but it has nothing to do with the verse. First of all, Marshall seems to be speaking about Jews who didn't believe in Jesus ('Jews everywhere'). *Those* Jews could have cared less about what some Gentiles were doing believing in a crucified Jewish man.

If Marshall meant the *believing* Jews, Yakov didn't give enough rules for there to be no dispute among the two groups. A Jewish believer would be very offended by a Gentile believer who didn't keep the Sabbath day holy, a rule not mentioned by James, but obviously kept by the Apostles and all the Jewish believers.[503] Jewish believers would also be offended by a Gentile believer eating pork, another rule not mentioned by James. Respect for Jewish believers cannot possibly be the reason for this verse.

In another stab at an explanation, Marshall says something very ironic:

> 'if Christian Gentiles want to find out any more about the Jewish law, they have plenty of opportunity in the local synagogues, and there is no need for the Jerusalem church to do anything about the matter.'[504]

Why would any Gentile Christian want to find out about the 'antiquated

---

[501] Marshall, *Acts*, p. 254.

[502] Ibid.

[503] It's obvious that the 7th day Sabbath was still considered holy by all the Jewish believers since they all kept the Law (Acts 21:20). This would certainly include the 7th day Sabbath. Also, James speaks of it in this very verse (Acts 15:21) as the day when Moses is read (and all assemble to hear him).

[504] Marshall, *Acts*, p. 254.

Law' if it only placed men in bondage and Christ came 'to do away with it'? If James was offering this bit of information to the Assembly, with the understanding that the Gentile could, if he so chose, go to the synagogue to learn of Moses, it can only be understood as one going to a prehistoric museum to see the fossils of dinosaurs in order to know what was in the past, but was now no more. The Gentile would come to the synagogue to gape at how all the Jews, believers included, were still following a way that held absolutely no relevance for the Gentile believer.

Marshall is groping in the dark. To throw out the Law, on the one hand, and then offer tips on how to get information about it, on the other, is very strange thinking. It does show, though, the utter futility of Christian scholarship in its attempt to give the verse meaning devoid of the Law.

Marshall realizes that 'Jewish Christians...continued to live by the Jewish law'[505] and that, according 'to Luke, many Jewish Christians continued to keep the law.'[506] He also states that James, 'In later literature...was typified as a law-abiding Jewish Christian.'[507] With this knowledge, and the fact that the whole believing Jewish community was keeping the Law (Acts 21:20), Marshall is still unable to see past his theological paradigm that wrongly nullifies the Law for every believer (Mt. 5:18-19; 15:9).

The Church teaches that the Apostles and all the Jewish believers didn't understand that the Law had been done away with. Did God forget to tell them? As far as the Book of Acts is concerned they never seemed to grasp this 'truth,' not even Paul.[508]

Samuele Bacchiocchi wrote a brilliant work on why the 7th day Sabbath is still holy and valid for believers today, but he also failed to understand the full implication of it. He states that the *old ways* (i.e. the Law) of the Jews were too difficult for Jewish believers 'to leave behind.' The,

> 'attachment of the Jerusalem Church to Jewish religious customs may perhaps perplex the Christian who regards the Mother Church of Christendom as the ideal model of his religious life. One must not forget, however, that Christianity sprang up out of the roots and trunk of Judaism. The early Jewish converts viewed the acceptance of Christ *not as the destruction of their religious framework,* but as the *fulfillment of their Messianic expectations* which enhanced their religious life with a new dimension.

---

[505]  Ibid., p. 243.

[506]  Ibid., p. 250. Actually, they all did (Acts 21:20-24), not just 'many.'

[507]  Ibid., p. 251.

[508]  Acts 21:20-24; 24:14-17; 25:8; 26:22-23; 28:17-24; see also Rom. 3:31; 7:7.

> The process of separating the shadow from the reali-
> ty…was gradual and not without difficulty.'[509]

Bacchiocchi recognizes that all the Jewish believers followed the Law and that Jerusalem was 'the Mother Church,' and therefore, the ideal model of faith, but he failed to realize that if it was right for all of them, if they could believe in Jesus and keep the Law, then why would it be wrong for the Gentile? Weren't the Gentiles grafted into Israel (Rom. 11:17f.)? Isn't Jesus, who kept the Law, *their* Example, too (1st Jn. 2:6; Rev. 14:12)?

Bacchiocchi writes that the Law faded away, albeit 'not without diffi-culty,' yet we never read in Scripture or church history of the Jerusalem believers, or their spiritual descendants, ever renouncing the Law as wrong or 'gone.' Just the opposite is true, as Bacchiocchi himself reveals. The Jewish Nazarenes, the spiritual descendants of the Jewish believers of apostolic Jerusalem, also kept the Law of Moses down to at least the fourth century. Epiphanius, bishop-historian of Salamis and Metropolitan of Cyprus,[510] brands them as heretics — for keeping God's holy Law:

> 'The Nazarenes do not differ in any essential thing from
> them (i.e. Jews), since they practice the custom and doc-
> trines prescribed by the Jewish law, except that they be-
> lieve in Christ…They preach that God is one and that Je-
> sus Christ is his Son.' They 'differ…from the Jews and
> from the Christians…from the former because they be-
> lieve in Christ; from the true Christians because *they ful-
> fill till now* Jewish rites as the circumcision, the Sabbath
> and others.'[511]

As Bacchiocchi rightly points out, the picture of the Nazarenes 'matches extremely well that of the Jerusalem Church' of the first century (i.e. the Apostles and other Jewish believers). He writes that,

> 'The *possibility exists*, therefore, that the Nazarenes repre-
> sent the survival of both the ethnic *and theological* legacy
> of' the apostolic community of Jerusalem.[512]

---

[509] Bacchiocchi, *From Sabbath To Sunday*, pp. 149-150.

[510] E. A. Livingstone, *The Concise Oxford Dictionary of the Christian Church* (Oxford, England: Oxford University Press, 2000), p. 193. Salamis is a Greek island 10 miles (16 km) west of Athens. Epiphanius lived from 315-403 AD.

[511] Bacchiocchi, *From Sabbath To Sunday*, p. 157. Epiphanius, *Adversus haere-ses* 29, 7, PG 41, 402.

[512] Ibid. Bacchiocchi also notes, 'The fact that they retained Sabbath keeping as one of their distinguishing marks shows persuasively that this was the original day of worship of the Jerusalem Church and that no change from Sabbath to Sunday occurred among' the Jewish believers even after the destruction of the

Possibility, indeed! They were following in the theological footsteps of all the Apostles and Jewish believers before them. If the Law of Moses was still valid and operative for all the Jewish believers throughout the Book of Acts, and three centuries thereafter, isn't it possible that *this is the correct understanding of the Law* for both Jewish and Gentile believers today?!

Many, not understanding why the Apostles still continued to walk in the Law so long after the resurrection, have the audacity to say that the Apostles didn't have the full understanding of what Yeshua's atoning death meant. Is that *possible?* God didn't tell the *Apostles* that they were wrong in this monumental area on their perspective on the Law? Certainly not in Acts 15 and Acts 21:20, 24, but didn't Paul differ from them? They can't prove that from Paul in Acts,[513] but they go to a couple of his letters where they think that Paul is 'doing away with the Law.' They do 'the Apostle to the Gentiles' an injustice. *ISBE* says that Paul's Gospel was *essentially the same* as Peter's (Gal. 2:9), and that there's no hint in Acts 21:20 of a different Gospel. Paul's anathema on those who preached a different Gospel (Gal. 1:8f.) is never pronounced upon the Apostles.[514] Peter (64 AD) affirms Paul as 'a beloved brother' whose letters are Scripture, even though they contain some things that are 'hard to understand.'[515]

The Church takes its position on the Law from only *some* of Paul's letters. Please note that it's *only* to the Apostle Paul that the Church goes for this false doctrine. It's *not to any of the other eight writers* of the New Testament, and it's *certainly not found* in the words of Jesus (Mt. 5:17-19; 22:38-40; Lk. 16:17). Those few Pauline texts that the Church holds up as proof of the Law's demise crumble under proper biblical interpretation, just as its interpretation of Acts 15:20 has done.

F. F. Bruce thinks that James spoke v. 21 to appease those Pharisees who 'lost out' on circumcising the Gentiles. He says that James really didn't mean that the Gentiles should go to the synagogue to learn about Moses because the Gentiles weren't the disciples of Moses and would never become such. He quotes R. B. Rackham to sum up his own position: 'Moses, so to speak, would suffer no loss, in failing to obtain the allegiance of those who had never been his.'[516] For Bruce, Acts 15:21 be-

---

city in 70 AD. The Apostles didn't change Sabbath to Sunday.

[513] See also *Paul & Acts* at http://SeedofAbraham.net/PaulAndActs.html.

[514] Bromiley, *ISBE*, vol. three, pp. 699-700.

[515] 2nd Pet. 3:15-16; see also Paul on Peter: 1st Cor. 3:21-22; 9:1-6; Gal. 2:1-10.

[516] Bruce, *The Book of the Acts*, p. 296, quoting Rackham, *The Acts of the Apostles: An Exposition*, (London: Methuen) 5th edition, 1910 (1st edition 1901). Knowling, *The Acts of the Apostles*, seems to have said that first (London:

comes the 'bone' that James threw to the disgruntled believing Pharisees, but this explanation is shallow because it makes James out to be a clever politician who wanted to pacify them. Yet, he didn't pacify them when it came to 'Jesus *and* circumcision' (the very ruling of Acts 15 that he struck down!) and there was no need for James to do so here, especially in light of his godly leadership. This interpretation doesn't fit with the character of James, nor with an honest reading of the text in question.

Second, it seems to pit Moses against Jesus, as though the two of them were at odds. Didn't Jesus walk in all the laws of Moses that applied to Him? Jesus, in a very real sense, was the greatest 'disciple' that Moses ever had. Aren't believers supposed to *follow* Jesus? To be *like* Him? Or is it just a spiritual thing? The Apostle John says that if one wants to be like Jesus he must keep himself from sin. *How* can one know what sin is?

> 'Beloved, now we are Sons of God, and...We know that when He appears, we will be like Him...everyone who has this hope fixed on Him, purifies himself, just as He is pure. Everyone who practices sin also practices *lawlessness...sin is lawlessness.*' (1st John 3:2-4; see also 2:1-6)

The Law reveals what sin is (Mt. 5:19; Rom. 7:7, 12). Without 'Moses' the Church fails to see some basic rules that Jesus wants His Bride to honor. She sins against Him by breaking His Sabbath day, not keeping Passover holy, and eating things that aren't meant for the Bride to eat, etc. This isn't the Way of Jesus. Without knowing 'Moses' one is a handicapped disciple of Jesus. The Master said this about those scribes who knew the Law *and* who would enter His Kingdom:

> '*every scribe* who has become a disciple of the Kingdom of Heaven is like a head of a household who brings out of his *treasure* things new *and* old.' (Mt. 13:52)

Yeshua doesn't denigrate the *old*, but speaks of its place and importance. The scribe, well versed in the Law, would better understand the New. It wasn't a contrast, but a complement. This is certainly what I've found to be true. Also, if Jesus came to do away with the Law, *where does He say that?* If the Sabbath and Passover (1st Cor. 5:6-8) are still in effect then the Law of Moses must be as well (Acts 21:20-24).

Knowling lists three possibilities for consideration for Acts 15:21. One, that Gentiles who had frequented the synagogue *before* coming to Jesus would more easily accept the rules after they had heard the Law. Two, that unless the Gentiles accepted the restrictions, the 'Jewish Christians' would not fellowship with them, and three, that James was telling the Jews 'not

---

Hodder and Stoughton, 1900), p. 325.

to worry about Moses; he wouldn't be neglected.'[517]

It's true that Gentiles, like Cornelius, who had frequented the synagogues before coming to Jesus, would more likely be able to accept the rules after hearing the Law, but why should they if the Law was gone? Also, what of the vast majority of Gentiles who hadn't been going to the synagogues?

Possibility two seems to stand out as a threat that James was giving to the Gentile believers, but there's nothing in Acts 15:21 that threatens the Gentiles with negation of fellowship. There's the presentation by James that they cease from pagan sacrificial rites, with the implication that if they didn't, they would lose their salvation, but this is not a threat—it's a divine warning that the worship of another god, along with Yeshua, would sever them from the Head *and* the Body, but that was in v. 20, not v. 21.

Point three of Knowling's is possibly where Rackham got his statement from—Gentiles would still come to Moses, but this wasn't a popularity contest between Moses and Messiah. James certainly wasn't concerned about Gentiles coming to Moses, but not Messiah!

Williams, too, offers a 'stab in the dark,' saying that since the Jewish believers were 'prepared to lay aside their long-standing prejudice against' the Gentiles, the Gentiles should give up something as well.[518] This makes Acts 15 more like the children's game than the epoch-making drama that it was.[519] There's nothing in the text to warrant this 'tit for tat' concept.

Williams states that because the Jews had walked in the Law so long, it was tough for them to 'lay it aside.'[520] Williams and Bacchiocchi make the Law out to be a nasty social habit that the Jew had picked up, but something the Gentile should just tolerate. This view presents the Jew caught up in something that he should really give up, but the Gentile will go out of his way to perform his Christian duty toward him (and not tell the Jew he's wrong?). Yet, the verse in question implies that *the Gentile* was to go to the synagogue. Why would a Gentile have go to a Jewish synagogue on the Sabbath day to appease the Jewish believers caught in the old Law?

Stern says it's 'a difficult verse.' He presents six options, saying that 'a good case can be made for any of the first four,' while also stating that 'it is hard to choose between' the four.[521] His first possibility was seen before with Marshall: Jewish 'scruples are to be respected.'[522] That is, don't of-

---

[517] Knowling, *The Acts of the Apostles*, p. 325.

[518] Williams, *Acts*, p. 266.

[519] See Bruce, p. 2 above.

[520] Williams, *Acts*, p. 267.

[521] Stern, *Jewish New Testament Commentary*, p. 279.

fend the Jews or the Pharisees. How this relates to a Gentile going to the synagogue, especially if he is not to walk in the Law, could only have the opposite effect of disturbing *all* the Jews (believers and non-believers).

Stern's second view was seen with Knowling and Bruce—Moses won't lose disciples from the Gentiles.[523] Stern says that there will always be disciples of Moses from the Gentiles, but just not from the Christian Gentiles. As we've seen, this view is not worth considering. It would seem that James would be more interested in Gentiles coming to Jesus than just to Moses. The only people that this would make happy would be Jews that didn't believe in Jesus!

His third view is that some Gentiles were already learning Torah in the synagogue, but hadn't chosen to convert to Judaism—don't press them to convert now.[524] That Gentiles didn't need to convert to become rabbinic Jews is true, that's a central point of Acts 15, but v. 21 implies that *all* the Gentiles were to go to the synagogue and learn the Law. There's nothing inherent in the verse that speaks of conversion.

Stern's fourth opinion says the Gentile Christians will continue to visit the synagogues to learn how to live a godly, ethical lifestyle. He also states that the Council's view was 'temporal' and only applied to the first century as 'Gentile Christians have long ceased to visit the synagogue in significant numbers.'[525] So, Gentiles don't need to learn, 'how to live a godly, ethical lifestyle,' now? Considering their punishments, keeping the Sabbath day holy is certainly more ethical than stealing or lying,[526] and no one writes that the Decree was temporal. The Law ('Moses') was to be learned on the Sabbath day, and the Law will be, as Yeshua said, until Heaven and Earth no longer exist (Mt. 5:18-19; see also Heb. 8:13; Rev. 12:17; 14:12).

Stern's fifth view states that the Gentile Christians going to the synagogue would 'eventually become Jews.'[527] As he points out, this view is contradicted in the New Testament. His sixth view is that the Gentiles, in going to the synagogue on the Sabbath, would keep on hearing the four rules of James 'emphasized over and over and will keep being sensitized to them' (as per Knowling). Aside from the fact that they wouldn't hear a prohibi-

---

[522] Ibid.

[523] Ibid.

[524] Ibid.

[525] Ibid.

[526] The Sabbath's greater moral value is seen in that the divine punishment for its violation (death) is greater than that of stealing or lying, two highly ethical commandments in and of themselves (Ex. 31:12-17; 35:1-3; Lev. 6:1-7).

[527] Stern, *Jewish New Testament Commentary*, p. 279.

tion against *strangling*, it stands to reason that they would hear and be sensitized *to many other rules* and wonder why they weren't keeping them, especially when they saw their Jewish brethren who believed in Jesus following the Law. This would certainly make for two different classes of believers, something Yeshua never intended in His Kingdom.

Witherington also slips here. He sees Acts 15:21 as a witness to the Jews in the synagogue that the Gentile believers were no longer practicing sacrificial-sexual idolatry.[528] How this can be read into the verse is hard to fathom. Could good Sabbath attendance at the Jewish synagogue negate Sunday sexual-worship of Aphrodite at the pagan shrine? Some Corinthian believers went 'to church' on the Sabbath and then visited the temple harlots on Sunday. No, the practice of sacrificial-sexual idolatry could continue even with good synagogue attendance on the Sabbath.

Witherington also states that, 'Avoiding idolatry and immorality was the heart of the Mosaic Law, as the Ten Commandments make clear,' so, *Moses* in v. 21 speaks of the Ten and the *Shema* (Dt. 6:4-5) because *'surely* it was the Ten...along with the *Shema* that one could...regularly ...hear read in synagogues.'[529] The problem with this is that nowhere in Scripture is *Moses* ever (only) equated with (just) the Ten, but all of the commandments. Also, the Rabbis didn't read the Ten every week, as Witherington implies, but only once a year, because they didn't want Jews to think that the Ten were 'all the commandments' that God required of them.

Others, seeing how shaky these interpretations are, come up with a linguistic twist to try and discredit the plain meaning of Acts 15:21. They say that the *only* reason *Moses* is *mentioned* is because James is telling everyone *where* he got the rules of v. 20 from (i.e. the Law). This teaching centers around the Greek word that links vv. 20 and 21. Their interpretation states that there's nothing binding on the Gentile except the four rules, which they wrongly see as rules for table fellowship, while also not realizing that *strangled* isn't in the Law. This is another fruitless attempt to discredit Torah for every believer. The Greek word that links Acts 15:20 to v. 21 is γαϱ (*gar*, 'for, because'). Friberg defines it as,

> 'a conjunction' (*for* or *because*) 'that basically *introduces an explanation* or an *exhortation* or a word that expresses cause or reason for, because' or 'an exclamation to point to *a self-evident conclusion*.'[530]

Bauer says that it can also mean that the phrase or sentence written after it

---

[528] Witherington, *The Acts of the Apostles*, p. 463.

[529] Ibid., p. 96.

[530] Friberg, *Analytical Lexicon of the Greek New Testament*, p. 96. 'γαϱ (*gar*) a conjunction basically introducing an explanation.' Bauer, *GELNT*, p. 151: a

is the 'tip of the iceberg' as to the author's thought on the topic:

> 'often the thought to be supported is not expressed, but
> must be supplied from the context, e.g. (he has truly been
> born) for we have seen his star.'[531]

Wright sums up the meaning of *gar* by saying that it's always that which
*explains* 'something that has just gone before' it.[532] The proponents of *gar*
would tell us that Yakov was *only* explaining in v. 21 that he took the
rules of v. 20 from the Law...*that's why Moses is mentioned.* To use *gar*
this way seems to defy common sense because there's no reason in their
explanation as to why Moses is mentioned 'from ancient generations...in
every city,' having 'those who preach him...being read in the synagogues
...on every Sabbath day.' Yakov didn't just *mention* Moses, he was *extremely* specific about him. Verse 21 hardly seems to be just a passing reference as to where Yakov may have gotten the four rules from.

Yakov tells everyone that Moses was preached 'from ancient generations.'
If he had only been telling the Assembly the source of the rules, there
would have been absolutely no need for him to tell the assembly of *Jewish*
believers[533] that Moses had those who preached him 'from ancient generations.' All the Jews there knew that.

If Yakov had only been telling the Assembly the source of the rules, there
would have been absolutely no need for him to tell the Jewish assembly
that Moses was preached 'in every city.' All the Jews knew that, too. Why
the need to mention *where* Moses was preached if Yakov was only mentioning Moses as the place from where he had gotten his rules from?

'Moses being preached in every city' cannot be used to say that James was
just giving Moses honor by mentioning him, as some others might think.
What would be the need for doing that, since he, more than any other, was
the symbol of the Law, which the Gentiles 'didn't need to keep'?!

---

'conjunction used to express cause, inference, continuation, or to explain.'

[531] Bauer, *A Greek-English Lexicon of the New Testament*, pp. 151-152.

[532] N. T. Wright: *Paul in Different Perspectives*, http://www.ntwrightpage.com/
Wright_Auburn_Paul.htm; Jan. 3rd, 2005. The 'function of *gar* always being
*to explain something that has just gone before.*'

[533] It remains to be seen if there were any Gentile believers from Antioch at the
Council, as the *other* members of the congregation that were sent from Anti-
och with Paul and Barnabas could have been believing Jews (15:2). Be that as
it may, whether there were a few believing Gentiles from Antioch at the
Council or not, it wouldn't affect the meaning of the verse or the fact that the
vast majority of those present were Jews. Acts 15:22-23 says that all the
Apostles, Elders and believing Jews were there, while Acts 15:6 speaks of the
Apostles and the Elders discussing the matter.

If Yakov was mentioning 'in every city' only for the Jews at the Council, this statement would also seem out of place for another reason. Most of the Jews at the Council lived in Jerusalem and although some would go to the synagogue, many would go to the Temple (Acts 2:46; 3:1, 3; 4:1; 5:20-21; 21:26). The Law wasn't read at the Temple on the Sabbath day, only in the synagogues, yet all the Jewish believers knew and walked in Torah (Acts 21:20; 25:8).

Yakov saying that Moses was 'in every city' means that he knew that wherever a Gentile lived he would be able to learn Torah, the will of God for the Gentile in the Kingdom. This is especially brought out by Luke's use of the Greek word for 'preachers' in verse 21. More on that in the next section, *The Preachers of Moses.*

If Yakov had only been telling the Assembly the origin of the rules, there would have been absolutely no need for him to tell the Jewish assembly that Moses was 'read in the synagogues.' All the Jews knew that, too. Moses 'being read in the synagogues' meant that Yakov assumed that the Gentiles would learn the Law as they heard it read. Why go to the synagogue and hear the Law *if it wasn't meant to be applied to one's life?*

The Law was read in the synagogue every Sabbath. It wasn't like a church sermon that might use a few verses of Scripture and then close the Bible. Three to six chapters of the Torah were read in sequence, verse by verse, every Sabbath. From Genesis through Deuteronomy everyone heard the Torah and could apply it to their life. A rabbi might give a message on a part of what was read, but the synagogue service centered around the Law being read aloud every Sabbath. Most Jews didn't have Torah scrolls in their homes. To hear and learn the Word of God one *had to go to the synagogue every Sabbath day.* Where else could a Gentile go to hear and learn the Words of the living God to instruct him in the Way? Of course, at this time, there were no New Testament writings—none.

If Yakov had only been telling the Assembly the origin of the rules, there would have been absolutely no need for him to tell the Jewish assembly that Moses was 'read in the synagogues every Sabbath.' All the Jews knew that. Gentiles were welcome in the synagogue. This is well attested. Paul, whenever he went to a synagogue with his Message of Life, always addressed the Gentiles who were also there. They could be God-fearers (Acts 17:17; 13:46, 48; 14:1-2) or those who hadn't taken any official steps, but were attracted to the Jewish God and His way of living.

Yakov's mention of the Sabbath also reveals that the issue of Sabbath vs. Sunday hadn't begun yet. In other words, all believers, both Jewish and Gentile, continued to keep the Seventh day Sabbath holy until around 100

AD, when what would become the Roman Catholic Church changed it.[534]

If the believing Gentiles weren't *already* coming and being directed to the synagogue to learn Torah, why would James mention Sabbath, synagogue, Moses and *all the cities in the world?* Wouldn't it have been enough for him to just mention Moses? Or not to mention him at all, as everyone knew where the rules came from? Yakov could have said,

> 'I've taken three of the four rules from Moses and added one myself. The Gentiles needn't be concerned with any other commandments except to love God and neighbor.'

He didn't say that, though. What some do in using the Greek word *gar,* to project their theological bias against Torah into v. 21, discredits the plain meaning of the text and reveals how desperate they are to distance themselves from the holy Law of God. Those who use *gar* this way, use it not as a means to an end, to properly interpret the meaning of the verse, but to pervert and *suppress* the divine meaning of God's Word in favor of their man-made *tradition* (that the Law has been done away with).

The Greek word *gar* does absolutely nothing to disrupt the understanding that James wanted the Gentiles to go to the synagogue on the Sabbath and learn Torah. Actually, it's *self-evident* from the text, if one can cast aside anti-Law sentiments and just allow the text to speak for itself. Yakov's statement in v. 21 reinforces and caps his *filter* decision of v. 20, for *gar* truly *explains* why Yakov gave only four rules. Putting the three verses together presents an overview of the text. It's really just one long sentence:

> 'Therefore, I judge that we do not *trouble* those who are turning to God from among the Gentiles, but that we write to them that they abstain from the pollutions of idols and from cult prostitution and from what is strangled and from blood *for* Moses, from ancient generations, has in every city those who preach him, being read in the synagogues on every Sabbath day.' (Acts 15:19-21)

Yakov only gave the much needed four rules because he knew that the Gentile believers were already learning the rest of the rules (laws) as they went to the synagogues. There wasn't any need to *trouble* the Gentiles with *circumcision* for salvation—this is also brought out in v. 24, in the letter that's written to Antioch. Yet, the Gentiles *did* need to be immediately warned against sacrificial-sexual idolatry, hence, the four rules prohibiting those deadly sins. Yakov could have also said,

> 'I've given these four rules for the Gentiles, and no more, because we've all seen that the Gentiles have been going,

---

[534] Bacchiocchi, *From Sabbath to Sunday*, pp. 165-212ff.

and we believe, will continue to go to the synagogue on
the Sabbath to learn God's Law. This way they'll grow in
the knowledge of their Messiah and walk in the Way of
Life alongside their Jewish believing brethren.'

The Gentile believers were *already* learning the commandments at the
synagogues and Yakov had every reason to believe that the Gentile believers would continue to go to the synagogues to learn the Law. *Continue* to
go to the synagogue?

Verse 21 has Yakov speaking to the Jewish believers what they, and he,
had already seen in this area of Gentile salvation for at least eight years.
Yakov assumed the paradigm would continue and this is where *gar* comes
to the forefront as it *truly explains* why he gave *only* these four important
rules instead of many others (e.g. Sabbath and dietary laws, etc.). The
Gentile believers *were already learning Torah in the synagogues.*

Yakov had observed for eight years or more, from Cornelius in Acts 10 to
his Decree in Acts 15,[535] that the *traditional* synagogues continued to be a
place of assembly and learning for Jewish and Gentile believers. Cornelius, his family and friends, most likely kept going to the same traditional Jewish synagogue after they came to faith in the Jewish Messiah. There
were probably Jews there who also believed. Cornelius' new faith in
Yeshua would only enhance his life of learning Torah at the synagogue.
Many of the Jewish and Gentile believers in Israel and Syria, etc., would
continue to assemble in traditional synagogues until around 80 AD.[536]

---

[535] **Acts 10** took place about 40 AD. Acts 15 was about eight years later in 48
AD.

**Acts 10:** Witherington, *The Acts of the Apostles*, p. 347: 39-40 AD. Marshall,
*Acts*, p. 183: 'before 41 AD.' Knowling, *The Acts of the Apostles*, p. 250:
40-44 AD.

**Acts 15:** Douglas, *IBD*, part 1, pp. 281-283: 48 AD. Unger, *UBD*, pp.
486-488: 48 AD. Witherington, *The Acts of the Apostles*, p. 444, note 361: 49
AD. Bromiley, *ISBE*, vol. one, p. 692: 49 AD.

[536] The cardinal prayer of the synagogue is the *Amida*, which the congregation
stands to recite 18 prayers to God. About 80 AD, another 'prayer' was added
in order to ferret out believers, who by this time were considered heretics. By
132 AD, the disastrous *bar Kochba* rebellion against Rome began. Jewish believers fought alongside their Jewish brethren (who didn't believe in Yeshua).
About a year later, Rabbi Akiva proclaimed *bar Kosiba*, the general of the rebellion, to be the Messiah. Akiva also changed *bar Kosiba's* name to *bar
Kochba* (son of the star, a reference to the 'star of Messiah' prophecy in Num.
24:17). Jewish believers refused to fight for this false Messiah. Many were
tortured by *bar Kochba* and his followers and bitter feelings arose on both
sides. This caused further division. Rabbi Akiva, though, in proclaiming a
false Messiah, caused tremendous damage to the Jewish people.

All the Gentile believers who attended the congregation in Antioch would also have been learning Torah. This assembly originally consisted of only Jewish believers (Acts 11:19) and would be modeled after a traditional synagogue. Later, Gentiles joined them. Would the new Gentile believers change Sabbath to Sunday and Passover to Easter? Who was learning from whom? Who had come into a new religion and a new way of life?

By Acts 15 Paul had only gone on one missionary journey, about a year earlier in 47 AD, in what is today Cyprus and south-central Turkey.[537] His experience of having to leave some synagogues wasn't the norm (Acts 9:31). The congregations that Paul established, which many today would call 'house churches,' would in fact have been seen by the Apostles as 'house synagogues' (places of assembly) where they would teach Torah and speak of Yeshua. Note also that Paul didn't have a monopoly on establishing assemblies or 'house synagogues' (Acts 11:19; Gal. 1:22).

The word *synagogue* comes from the Greek and by definition can mean 'a *Christian* assembly.'[538] Yakov uses it in referring to Christian assemblies (James 2:2; see also Acts 9:1-2; 26:11). It would be used for the assembly of Jewish and Gentile believers at Antioch, other believing assemblies, and also, traditional Jewish congregations. In other words, both a synagogue of Jews that didn't believe in Jesus, as well as an assembly like Antioch, made up of (only) believers (Jewish and Gentile), could equally be called a *synagogue*. This adds to the understanding of what Yakov said in Acts 15:21, about Moses 'being read in the *synagogues* every Sabbath.'

Yakov *already* knew that the Gentiles were going to the synagogues. Ac-

---

After Rome crushed the rebellion and killed Akiva and *bar Kosiba*, Rome changed the name of the land to Philistina (Palestine) in derision of the ancient enemies of the Jews, and Jerusalem to *Aelia Capitolina* (naming it after one of their gods, *Jupiter Capitolinus*). They barred Jews from living in the city, restricting even their visits to only one day in the year, the Day of Atonement (Lev. 23:26-32), to mourn the wholesale slaughter of the Jews and the destruction of the city and the Temple. This was meant to further humiliate the Jewish people. In backing the rebellion against Rome and proclaiming *bar Kosiba* to be the Messiah, Rabbi Akiva caused the Jewish people to be without their own homeland for more than 1,800 years (from 135 to 1948).

[537] Acts 13:1–14:26. Unger, *UBD*, pp. 486-488: 45 AD. Douglas, *IBD*, part 1: p. 28: 46-47 AD. Bromiley, *ISBE*, vol. one, p. 692: 47-48 AD.

[538] Perschbacher, *The New Analytical Greek Lexicon*, p. 388. *Synagogue*: a 'collecting, gathering; a Christian assembly or congregation, James 2:2' (where *James* speaks of a *believing* synagogue, 'for if a man comes into your *synagogue* with a gold ring'). Mounce, *TALGNT*, p. 432, has exactly what Perschbacher has. Bauer, *GELNT*, pp. 782-783: a 'place of assembly...a *Christian assembly-place* can also be meant' (James 2:2). A 'meeting for worship, of the Jews...*Transferred* to meetings of *Christian congregations*.'

tually, the word 'church,' as a distinct entity separate from the Jewish people, wasn't in his or the Apostles' vocabulary.[539] He assumed they would *continue* to go to the synagogues to learn the Law on the Sabbath day. He was making a statement of observation, as well as one of expectation. Wherever Gentiles were there would be synagogues in which they could learn Torah—believing or non-believing synagogues.

Witherington thinks there were a number of Gentiles like Cornelius, both in the Promised Land and throughout the Roman Empire. He asks,

> 'Has Luke exaggerated the apparent prevalence of people like Cornelius and the importance of their involvement in the synagogues of the Diaspora and the holy Land?'[540]

> 'Luke is quite careful in the way he presents the progression of things. Cornelius is not a pagan, nor is this a story about a mission to those Gentile lands. Cornelius is seen as significant in that his case raises the questions about preaching to pagans and going not only into their homes but into their lands. In other words, he is cast as a bride figure standing at the boundary between Judaism and pa-

---

[539] The Greek εχχλησια (*eklaysia*), translated into English as 'church,' means an 'assembly' or congregation, but literally speaks of those 'called out.' Originally it pictured the Greek 'town meetings' of free men *called out* of the populace to vote on city matters. The spiritual aspect relates to believers being '*called out* of darkness into His marvelous *Light*' (1st Pet. 2:9) and may be one reason why Paul chose to use this word instead of *synagogue*. Believers are the 'Called Out Ones,' the Greek equivalent of the Hebraic, 'Chosen People.' Where it says, 'to the *church* at Corinth,' it should read, 'to the assembly (or congregation) at Corinth' or 'to the *called out ones* of Corinth.'

*Eklaysia* was first used of Israel 330 years earlier in the Septuagint. It speaks of 'the Church in the Wilderness' at Mt. Sinai (i.e. Israel; Dt. 4:10; 9:10; 18:16; also Acts 7:38). That's why Paul used *eklaysia* over the newer term *synagogue*. What God began at Mt. Sinai was continuing in Yeshua. In no way did his use of the word 'church' oppose Israel or Mosaic Law. The Church didn't begin in Acts 2 on Pentecost (the Mosaic holy day of *Shavu'ot*; Leviticus 23:15-21; the Feast of Weeks). Jewish believers were *filled* with the promised Holy Spirit on that day (Ezk. 36:27; see Acts 2:46-47; 5:11-12, 42 where 'the Church' met in the Temple). Paul's 'churches' were 'house assemblies' (1st Cor. 16:19; Phlm. 1:2; see also Rom. 16:5, 10-11, 14-15, 23), which Jews would call 'house synagogues.' Also, it doesn't seem that Paul began the congregations in Rome (1:13, 15), Ephesus (1:15; 3:1-4) or Colosse (1:3-4, 9) even though house churches are mentioned in two of those letters (Rom. 16:5; Col. 4:15). The assemblies in Rome were most likely begun by Jews from Rome who had been in Jerusalem for *Shavu'ot* (Acts 2:1-10f.), had come to believe in Yeshua and had returned to Rome to share the Good News.

[540] Witherington, *The Acts of the Apostles*, p. 341.

ganism, and living in a very Hellenized city full of Gentiles, yet, in the Holy Land.'[541]

'Often overlooked is the fact that Luke suggests that there were such Gentiles as Cornelius, not only in the Diaspora, but in Israel as well.'[542] 'What is important about these people for Luke is that time and again they are seen as the bridge between Judaism and Christianity, and on various occasions they are seen as the most likely of those who are within or associated with the *synagogue* to' give their lives to Messiah '(see 18:7-8).'[543]

"Luke's obvious interest in folks like a Cornelius or a Titus might be because he himself, and/or Theophilus, had been a 'God-fearer' before" coming to Yeshua.[544]

Yakov held up a paradigm that he knew all the Jews at the Council would be able to follow. Moses was proclaimed and taught in all the synagogues in every city on every Sabbath day and the Gentile believers were coming, and would continue to come, to the synagogues to learn the Law.

Hegg believes that the Gentiles would go to the synagogues every Sabbath and learn the rules of Moses so that they could walk in them.[545] He then poignantly asks, where else could the Gentile go to learn about the one true God?[546] There was no other place in all the world.

The Gentiles didn't need 'to become Jews' in order to be saved, but the Gentiles did need to be told what would disqualify them from membership in the Kingdom of Yeshua (v. 20). Yakov, and every believing Jew, knew that the Gentile believers were already going to the synagogues to learn of Moses, and Yakov assumed that it would continue (v. 21).

In declaring Acts 15:21 to everyone at the Council, Yakov was *specifically* thinking about the Law of Moses for the Gentiles. With that, he presents Torah as a lifestyle of sanctification for both Gentile and Jewish believers (e.g. Acts 21:20-24; 25:8; 28:17; see also Rom. 3:31; 7:7, 12, 14).

---

[541] Ibid., p. 340, note 46.

[542] Ibid., p. 341, note 51.

[543] Ibid., p. 344.

[544] Ibid., note 64: Most likely, 'Theophilus had been a prominent Gentile who was a synagogue adherent before his...conversion to' Jesus '(see, e.g. 17:4).'

[545] Hegg, *The Letter Writer*, pp. 73, 17-22.

[546] Ibid., p. 73. Gordon Tessler (*The Genesis Diet*; Raleigh, North Carolina: Be Well Publications, 1996, p. 116) also speaks of going to the synagogue to learn the Law, as well as that the Decree pertained to cult harlotry and the drinking of blood from a pagan sacrifice.

Torah was part of every Gentile's life back then, and therefore, it should be part of every believer's life today.

The need for the Law has not yet disappeared (Mt. 5:18-19; Heb. 8:13). Verse 21 is the 'period' at the end of that long sentence. It's the logical complement and explanation for vv. 19-20 and why Yakov gave *only* four rules. The Gentile would learn the rest of the Law at the synagogue. Verse 21 was *also* given to assure the Jews at the Council that Torah *would be* a part of Gentile life...just not the salvation part.

In the synagogue the Gentile would learn all the other rules of the Kingdom that pertained to him. Not every law of God applied to the Gentile, just as every law didn't apply to Yeshua or the Jewish believer. For example, Jesus didn't need to keep the laws pertaining to the offering up of the daily sacrifice (Ex. 29:38-42) because He wasn't a priest in the Temple (Heb. 8:4). He was not of the lineage of Levi and Aaron, but of Judah and King David.[547] Yeshua, though, kept all the commandments that applied to Him and if believers want to be like Him, shouldn't they also?

Praise God that Yakov didn't stop at verse 20, but went on to speak of Moses being taught in the synagogues on the Sabbath day. Because of verse 21 we know that there are more than four rules that God wants the Gentile believer to walk in. This verse authoritatively establishes that.

---

[547] Mt. 1:1-17; Lk. 1:27; 2:4; 3:23-28; Acts 13:22-23; Rom. 1:3; 2nd Tim. 2:8; Heb. 7:13-14; Rev. 5:5; 22:16.

# Acts 15:21 — The Preachers of Moses

Some theologians and commentators connect the phrase in Acts 15:21, 'those who *preach* him' (i.e. the *preachers* of Moses) to v. 19 ('don't trouble them') to try and explain it. The verse reads:

> 'For Moses has had throughout many generations those who *preach* him in every city, being read in the synagogues every Sabbath.' (Acts 15:21)

Their interpretation speaks of 'not troubling the Gentiles with the Law,' but both the *connection* and the *explanation* aren't biblical. The *Theological Dictionary of the New Testament* is an example of the connection and interpretation, saying,

> 'The verse is *probably* to the effect that we do not wish to burden Gentile Christians with the Law (v. 19). There are enough *preachers* of Moses. We desire to preach the Gospel.'[548]

*TDNT* admits that the interpretation of v. 21 is 'much debated'[549] (as we saw in the previous chapter). Their connecting it to verse 19, to explain it, though, opposes the understanding that James wasn't speaking about the *Law* as a burden or trouble, but about the *troublemakers* who had gone to Antioch and had caused strife among the believers with their *troubling theology* of 'faith in Yeshua *plus* circumcision.' Yakov wasn't contrasting 'Christian preaching' about Jesus with 'Jewish preaching' on the Law. Even with those believing Pharisees who 'wanted Moses,' it wasn't *just* Moses, but Moses (the Law symbolized in circumcision) *and* faith in Jesus (15:1, 5). It was never 'Moses vs. Jesus,' and preaching as to content (Moses or Jesus) was never brought up. Acts 15 was a theological gathering on what the *Gentiles* needed to do *in order to be saved*. It wasn't a pastors' conference on preaching the Gospel.

To contrast the 'preachers of Moses' with those who preached the Gospel is contrary to the meaning of the context, and also, to the meaning of the word for 'preach.' It has little to do with what we might normally associate with the word (i.e. a Christian preacher bringing a sermon in church). The Greek word that Luke used for 'those who *preach* him' (NASB) reveals that Yakov wasn't speaking about Jewish 'preachers' of the Law (i.e. the Rabbis), but the Jewish official of the synagogue who would go out into the neighborhoods and literally *call* the Jewish people to worship, *announce* the days of the feasts (they didn't have calendars like we have today) and *proclaim* synagogue news and events. In Hebrew the man was known as a *shamash* (*servant*, also called a *gabbai*). He's the model or

---

[548] Kittel, *Theological Dictionary of the New Testament*, vol. III, p. 705, note 43.

[549] Ibid.

prototype for the church *deacon*.

Luke used the word χηρυσσοντας *(kayrus'sontas;* an active participle), which would better be translated into English as those who *announce* or *proclaim*, not *preach*. The *shamash* had nothing to do with giving a Torah message in the synagogue (or anywhere else), and so, cannot be used to say that Yakov was speaking of those 'who *preach* Moses,' in counter-distinction to preaching Jesus.

Walter Bauer defines the verb χηρυσσο *(kay'ruso),* from which Luke's word stems, and reveals that even though it can be used of Christian preachers, *per se*, the man doing it would better be called a *herald:*

> '*announce, make known* by a herald...*proclaim aloud...*
> gener. *speak of, mention publicly...*of proclamation that is
> relig. in nature...of the proclamation or preaching of the
> older prophets...of contemporary preachers...of Jewish...
> the preaching of John the Baptist, and proclamation of the
> Christian message in the widest sense...*preach, proclaim*
> someth. Mt. 10:27.'[550] (emphasis his)

The only 'Jewish things' mentioned are the 'older' Prophets and John the Baptist, neither of which could be classified in the category of rabbis 'preaching' a sermon on Moses in the synagogue on the Sabbath. This 'announcer' was usually 'in the streets' *(publicly*, as a herald), not in the synagogue, which rules out the term applying to a rabbi in the synagogue.

Johannes Louw and Eugene Nida, in their Semitic domain lexicon, write that the primary idea behind *kay'ruso* is one who *officially* announces or proclaims something, acting as a herald:

> "to announce in a formal or official manner by means of a
> herald or one who functions as a herald—'to announce, to
> proclaim.'"[551]

---

[550]  Bauer, *A Greek-English Lexicon of the New Testament,* p. 431.

Friberg, *Analytical Lexicon of the Greek New Testament,* p. 230; 'the official activity of a herald; *announce, publicly proclaim*' (emphasis his).

[551]  Johannes Louw and Eugene A. Nida, editors, *Greek-English Lexicon of the New Testament based on Semantic Domains,* vol. 1 (New York: United Bible Societies, 1989), p. 412, section 33.206, χηρύσσω.

Joseph Thayer, *Thayer's Greek-English Lexicon of the New Testament* (Accordance Bible Software; Altamonte Springs, FL: OakTree Software, 2011), n.p., χηρύσσω; 'from Homer down...*to be a herald; to officiate as herald; to proclaim after the manner of a herald*' (emphasis his).

Perschbacher, *The New Analytical Greek Lexicon,* p. 238; '*publish, proclaim, as a herald,* 1 Cor. 9:27; *to announce openly and publicly,* Mark 1:4' (emphasis his).

The verb *kay'ruso* primarily speaks of the *act* of an official who proclaims or announces something as a *herald*. It doesn't include a rabbi who would bring a message from Torah. This is further brought out by the noun, which speaks of the *official* who *proclaims*. This *preacher*,[552] in Greek, is κηρυξ (*kay'ruks*) a masculine noun, which stems from κηρυσσο (*kay'ruso*) *to proclaim*.

The ancient pagan, Christian and Jewish meaning of *kay'ruks* is primarily an official herald who proclaimed something *in the streets* for the populace to hear and know, or he could be someone like the former demon possessed Gentile man telling his friends and neighbors what Yeshua had done for him (Mk. 5:20). Generally speaking, the man is an official proclaiming something, in the streets, for an authority (and that's how Paul could use it of himself). He would be someone like the old town criers, who officially announced various edits and public announcements to the people, walking from one neighborhood to another. Friberg says *kay'ruks* is a,

> 'herald, one who *proclaims public announcements, summons to assemblies*, carries messages, etc.; in the NT one who acts as God's official human messenger, *preacher, proclaimer* (1st Tim. 2:7).' (emphasis his)[553]

Thayer defines *kay'ruks* and confirms that the man is a herald who has official authority:

> 'common in Greek writings from Homer down; *a herald, a messenger* vested with public authority, who conveyed the official messages of kings, magistrates, princes, military commanders, or who gave a public summons or demand, and performed various other duties...In the N.T. God's ambassador, and the herald or proclaimer of the divine word...one who summoned to righteousness, of Noah, 2 Pet. 2:5; used of the apostles, as the divine messengers of the salvation procured by Christ and to be embraced through him, 1 Tim. 2:7; 2 Tim. 1:11.[554]

---

[552] The ASV, KJV, NASB and NKJV use *preach,* while the HCSB, NET and NRSV use *proclaim* for the Greek κηρυσσοντας (*kayrus'sontas*), which Luke uses in Acts 15:21.

[553] Friberg, *Analytical Lexicon of the Greek New Testament*, p. 229.

Bauer, *A Greek-English Lexicon of the New Testament*, p. 431: 'herald, whose duty it is to make *public proclamations...*in a relig. sense...*preacher, one who proclaims...*of Noah...2 Pet. 2:5. Of the apostle Paul...1 Tim. 2:7.'

[554] Thayer, *Thayer's Greek-English Lexicon of the New Testament*, n.p., κῆρυξ.

The ancient herald or proclaimer was held in high esteem in the days of Homer, as well as in the days of the Apostles. Aside from being dependable and loyal to the one who sent him to proclaim, *TDNT* states that the herald,

> 'had to have a good voice...if a herald does no have a powerful voice, he is useless. This condition is related to his task...the herald had *to declare official decrees and announcements.* He could do this only if he had the voice. He is like the heralds who...went through smaller villages with a bell and publicly read official proclamations with a loud voice.'[555]

*Official decrees and announcements...* although this *herald* can conceptually be linked to the term *apostle* (i.e. a *sent one,* which is what the Greek word *apostle* means), or an evangelist (*proclaimer* of good news), *TDNT* states that the New Testament 'manifestly avoids it' for the apostle and evangelist.[556] The reason for this, they say, is that the *preaching* or the *proclamation* of Yeshua's person and work is the central theme of the New Testament, not the earthly messengers (i.e. the preachers) who proclaim (preach) Him. *TDNT* states:

> 'For the true preacher is God or Christ Himself...hence there is little place for the herald.'[557]

In other words, even though it's used by the Apostle Paul, the emphasis in Christian preaching is not on the preacher, but on *who* is being proclaimed. The word is only used twice by Paul, speaking about himself (1st Tim. 2:7; 2nd Tim. 1:11) being a proclaimer of Christ, and once by Peter, relating that Noah was a *preacher* (proclaimer) of righteousness (2nd Pet. 2:5). In the Septuagint it's only seen in two places. Once, after Joseph has been elevated to second in command to Pharaoh, when riding in his chariot, servants (proclaimers/heralds) would *proclaim,* 'Bow the knee!'

> "And he had him ride in the second chariot which he had, and *they cried out* before him, 'Bow the knee!' So he set him over all the land of Egypt." (Genesis 41:43)

The only other time we see it in the Old Testament is when King Nebuchadnezzar had a gold statue of himself made, and commanded everyone to bow down and worship it when his favorite melody was played:

> "Then a *herald cried aloud:* 'To you it is commanded, Oh

---

[555] Kittel, *Theological Dictionary of the New Testament*, vol. III, p. 686-687.

[556] Ibid., p. 696.

[557] Ibid.

peoples, nations, and languages, that at the time you hear the sound of the horn, flute, harp, lyre, and psaltery, in symphony with all kinds of music, you must fall down and worship the gold image that King Nebuchadnezzar has set up.'" (Daniel 3:4-5)

It seems that the reason why Luke used the word that he did was to alert us to the fact that it wasn't the Jewish rabbi, who *preached* Moses in the synagogue, but the Jewish *herald* who proclaimed 'Moses' in the streets, calling the people to the synagogue. This is seen in the fact that the person proclaiming isn't necessarily preaching a theological message, but announcing public (and religious) news, and acting as a traditional herald.

Also, in Acts 15:21, Yakov speaks of the one who *preaches* Moses, *and* that Moses *is read* in the synagogue. The two phrases are not part of the same concept: 'those who *preach* him in every city' (the herald/*shamash*), and 'being *read* in the synagogues every Sabbath' (the one who reads from the Torah and might comment on it). The *preacher* (proclaimer) that Yakov spoke of, the *shamash*, could *proclaim* 'Moses' in the streets on any day of the week, while the one who 'read Moses,' read him on Shabat, in front of the congregation:[558]

> 'For Moses has had throughout many generations those who *preach* him in every city, *being read in the synagogues every Sabbath*.' (Acts 15:21)

The point here is that the *preacher* of Moses that Yakov spoke of is not 'preaching the Law,' as *TDNT* spoke of, but calling people to the synagogue for worship services and announcing times of Feasts, etc. He wasn't the one who gave the sermon, but was like *the town criers of old, who went through a town proclaiming news.*'[559] This *preacher* is very different from the concept of a Christian preacher or evangelist.

*TDNT* writes that the Rabbis 'make frequent reference to the herald,' who is 'to proclaim.' The Hebrew word they used is כָּרוּז (*karuz*). It means, 'crier,' and appropriately enough, is spoken of the *rooster,* 'who summons the faithful to wakefulness in the morning.'[560] They state that the Jewish herald or *shamash*, 'goes through the town and makes something known,'[561] like a rooster, by his crying out loud.

---

[558] The reading of Moses (the Law) in the synagogue would be done by several men called to read from the Torah scroll, not just one individual. These men were usually members of the congregation, with no official status. A rabbi, or some other man of learning, could give a sermon on the text, but this didn't always happen because many synagogues didn't have a rabbi.

[559] Kittel, *Theological Dictionary of the New Testament*, vol. III, p. 695, 3b.

[560] Ibid., 3a.

*Karuz* is directly linked to the Hebrew verb קָרָא *kara*, and Davidson says it means 'to cry, call out, shout...proclaim...invite.[562] The definition conceptually lines up with the Greek meaning of Luke's word. The *Theological Lexicon of the Old Testament* states of *kara:*

> "*to call* is common Sem(itism)...the noun...*procla-mation*....In Akk., where, as in Arab., the root...exhibits ...the specialized meaning *to invite*...The basic meaning ...is apparently *to draw someone's attention with the sound of the voice in order to establish contact*...The verb...has various nuances...i.e., *to call to, to call out, to commission, to call on, to announce, proclaim*...a genuine *proclamation* such as *Tomorrow is a feast for Yahweh!* (Exod 32:5). In the case of an official decree such as the one just mentioned' it 'usually means *to proclaim*, i.e., in the absolute sense of the *pronouncement of a proclamation* (Lev 23:21)...The meaning *to read* developed from the connotation *to proclaim, announce*, apparently because *reading* was originally *reading aloud* in public, e.g., *in the case of official decrees*.'[563]

This definition doesn't speak of a rabbi in a synagogue, but one who, by his voice, *draw's attention* to himself in order to proclaim something in the streets. Also interesting is that Yahveh specifically commands that His feasts are to be *proclaimed* to Israel, and this is exactly what the *shamash* does:

> "These are the feasts of Yahveh, holy convocations which you must *proclaim* at their appointed times." (Leviticus 23:4; see also vv. 2, 21, 37)

The Rabbis took the Lord seriously—*proclaiming* the Feast times was an official function of the *shamash*. He was an official assistant to the *nasi* (the *prince* or ruler of the synagogue). The *shamash* was the 'mouth, arms and legs' of the *nasi* (and by extension, that of the congregation) in providing for the physical needs of the faith community from the congregation's resources. He might collect funds and/or food from some of the

---

[561] Ibid., 3b.

[562] Davidson, *The Analytical Hebrew and Chaldee Lexicon*, p. 665.

Brown, *The New Brown, Driver, Briggs, Gesenius Hebrew and English Lexicon*, pp. 894-895: to 'call, *proclaim*...cry, utter a loud sound...make a proclamation.

Koehler, *The Hebrew and Aramaic Lexicon of the Old Testament*, vol. 3, p. 1129: to 'call, shout...proclaim...announce.'

[563] Jenni, *Theological Lexicon of the Old Testament*, Volume 3, pp. 1158-1162.

members during the week, to administer it to the poor and needy, and was available to serve the *nasi* in whatever needed to be done in the physical realm. He also officially announced the rulings of the synagogue, called the people to the Sabbath assembly, and proclaimed the days of the feasts, etc. The Christian counterpart to the *shamash* is the deacon.[564]

Just as the town criers of England, 300 years ago, would go through the neighborhoods of a city and announce royal and public news, similarly the Jewish *shamash* would make his rounds in the days of Yakov. He not only told the current news as such, but *called the people to the synagogue on the Sabbath* 'to hear Moses.' These Jewish *preachers* would be found, not only in Israel, but on the streets of every pagan city all over the world (in which there were Jewish neighborhoods). These men would be able to tell both visiting Jews, and curious and/or believing Gentiles, *where* the nearest synagogue was. Yakov was *specifically* pointing to these Jewish town criers in referring to 'those who *preach*' Moses (Acts 15:21). This is a far cry from 'Christian preaching on Jesus vs. Jewish preaching on Moses,' and also, from *just mentioning Moses,* as the source of Yakov's rules. It reveals that Yakov was clearly expressing that a Gentile, in whatever city that he lived or found himself in, would not have a problem finding out *where* the Law was read on the Sabbath day.[565]

---

[564] If the new believing assemblies were like the synagogue in terms of their structure and function, and they were, then there were no plates passed around on Shabat to collect tithes and offerings because in Israel tithes and offerings went to the priests in the Temple, not to the rabbi in a synagogue, if a synagogue even had a rabbi. The members of a community would support the synagogue with funds and/or crops, over and above their tithes and offerings (and the rabbi supported himself by working in a secular field, like Paul did; 1st Cor. 9:1-18) even though, of course, the people would give gifts to the rabbi in appreciation of him. Outside Israel, tithes and offerings would also be sent to the Temple, but this, in the form of money (not animals or crops; see e.g. 1st Cor. 16:3; 2nd Cor. 8:4, 19-20; 9:5) and the people would also support their synagogue with other funds and/or crops, which the *shamash* would pick up.

For more on believing assemblies being a reflection of the synagogue, ask for the PDF *Synagogue and Church Officials.*

[565] The fact that these Jewish *preachers* spoke in the streets about where Moses was read (i.e. the synagogue) is further brought out by *TDNT* in a passage that has a rabbi drawing a crowd to himself and then directing them to the Law (in the synagogue) to find out about life:

Rabbi Alexander cried out, '"Who desires Life?! Who desires Life?!' Then the whole world gathered round him and said, 'Give us life!' Then he spoke to them Psalm 34:12: 'Who is the man who desires life...? Keep your tongue from evil...avoid evil and do good...Perhaps someone will say, I have kept my tongue from evil and my lips from deceitful speech, I will now give myself to sleep, but it then says, 'Avoid evil and do good,' and by good is meant

Acts 15:21 reveals what Yakov and the believing Jewish community had seen over the past eight to ten years concerning the Gentiles. The Gentile believers had *already* been going to the synagogues (both believing and unbelieving synagogues) to learn about their new God and His ways through the Law of Moses, and Yakov assumed that this would continue into the future, which it did (until after the death of the Apostles). This means that Gentile believers should still be learning the Law today, so that they can walk in *all* the Lord's ways that He has for them.[566]

Should the Gentile go to the traditional Jewish synagogue today?[567] Perhaps, but the reason why Yakov directed them to the synagogue was to learn the Law of Moses. Everyone today has a Bible and can learn to walk in all the laws that apply to him or her. This is the essence of Acts 15:21.

Yakov was concerned about the Gentile. Not being raised in the Law the Gentile literally didn't know Adam from Eve, and he certainly would be ignorant of many of God's specific rules on how to love Him (e.g. keep the Sabbath holy), and his neighbor (e.g. not to charge interest on a loan; Ex. 22:25). Yakov wanted them to come to maturity in Messiah. How could they do that without the Word of God (the Old Testament; 2nd Tim. 3:14-17)? *Nothing* of the New Testament had been written when Acts 15 took place—neither Paul, nor anyone else, had written any letters,[568] and

---

the knowledge of the Law, for it is said in Prov. 4:2, 'For I gave you good doctrine, do not disregard My direction'" (instruction, Law). Kittel, *Theological Dictionary of the New Testament*, vol. III, p. 702.

The point here is that the rabbi wasn't preaching a sermon on the street, but *calling* the people to the synagogue to learn the Law, just as Yakov spoke of when he used the word 'preach' in Acts 15:21.

[566] Some might say that Acts 15:21 is not mentioned in the letter (vv. 15:22-32), but the Council sent two prophets, Judah and Silas (Acts 15:32) to relate by word of mouth (v. 27) to the believers in Antioch, *all* that had been discussed at the Council. It's highly unlikely that they forgot to relate the essence of v. 21. Besides, the Gentiles at Antioch were already learning the Law of Moses at the believing Jewish synagogue ('church') in Antioch. It would have been superfluous to have written it to them.

[567] With 2,000 years of Christian anti-Semitism, and Jewish apologetics against Messiah Yeshua, the Synagogue today can be extremely hostile to a believer because it's anti-Yeshua. Also, Judaism has taken into itself spirits of witchcraft in the form of *Kabbalah* and New Age, etc. The important thing to ascertain from Yakov's admonition to the Gentile, about going to the synagogue, is that the Gentile is to learn Torah *the way Yeshua lived it*. There is a vast difference between learning about the commandments from a traditional Jewish rabbi, and learning and living Torah with Yeshua's Spirit, as He Himself spoke of (Mt. 16:5-12, et al.). One is a very deep and dangerous pit, while the other is a divine treasure trove.

[568] There is a possibility that Yakov's letter (the book of James) had already been

the Gospels wouldn't be written for at least another decade. The Gentile believer would have to go to the synagogue to learn about his new God and *His* ways.

In stark contrast, everyone has Bibles today, and yes, Jewish and Christian Bibles are basically the same. One difference is that some of the books of the *Tanach* (Old Testament) are arranged in a different order, but they're all there. The words in an English Christian 'Old Testament' Bible are basically the same words that an English speaking Jew finds in his English *Tanach*.[569]

---

written, as both Acts 15 and Yakov's letter are dated at 48-49 AD.

[569]  Jewish translators of the Hebrew *Tanach* into English steer around prophecies of the Messiah that point directly to Yeshua. At these places they may alter some Hebrew word meanings so the Jewish person won't be able to make a connection 'to Jesus.' This is where their belief system 'takes over.' One place where this happens is the virgin who would conceive the Messiah (Is. 7:14). I explain why the current Jewish meaning for the English word 'virgin' is wrong in, *Isaiah 7:14 and the Virgin Conception of Messiah* at http://SeedofAbraham.net/virgin.html, and also, *Recognize this Man?* at http://SeedofAbraham.net/nltr23.html. Feel free to ask for the PDFs.

A literal case of a deliberate alteration of a Hebrew word (actually, one Hebrew letter) is found in Psalm 22:16, which speaks of Messiah's hands and feet being pierced (his crucifixion), but in the English *Tanach* (which takes its reading from the Hebrew text), it speaks of those surrounding the person that is afflicted, as being *'like a lion* at his hands and feet.' I address this in *Lion Hands* at http://seedofabraham.net/nltr25.html. Aside from this intentional and malicious change, the vast majority of the texts, for Jews and Christians, are identical.

Someone might say that this is unfair, and they would be right, but this also happens with Christian translations of Greek New Testament texts that point out the Law's validity. One such place is Hebrews 4:9. Both the Textus Receptus and the *NU* have the same Greek words for the verse, but the KJV and NKJV speak only of a 'rest' that 'remains for the people of God,' while the NASB and NRSV, as well as others, correctly speak of 'a *Sabbath* rest' that remains for the people of God. The Greek word is *sabbatismos*, a technical term found in ancient literature for *Sabbath observance*.

Samuele Bacchiocchi in *The New Testament Sabbath* (Gillette, WY: *The Sabbath Sentinel* magazine, 1987) says that the writer of Hebrews is teaching that a '"*Sabbath keeping* is left behind for the people of God.' The Greek word *sabbatismos* is found in 'Plutarch, *De Superstitione* 3 (Moralia 166A); Justin Martyr, *Dialogue With Trypho* 23, 3; Epiphanius, *Adversus Hacreses* 30, 2, 2; *Apostolic Constitutions* 2, 36, 7.'" Andrew Lincoln admits that 'in each of these places the term denotes *the observance or celebration of the Sabbath*. This usage corresponds to the Septuagint usage of the cognate verb *sabbatizo* (cf. Exodus 16:30; Leviticus 23:32; 26:34f.; 2nd Chronicles 36:21), which also has reference to Sabbath observance.'

Hebrews 4:9 speaks of striving by faith to enter into the eternal Sabbath rest (a

Today, believers can read the first five books of Moses (and the rest of the *Tanach*), asking the Spirit of Yeshua to open their eyes as to what God wants them to see and do. There are also house assemblies and congregations that keep Sabbath and Feast days, etc. They offer new Gentile believers a place to learn the fundamentals, but a word of warning: some of these congregations mix truth with gross error, which means that *that* kind of an assembly is not for you, even if it's 'the only one in town.'[570]

---

Sabbath rest *remains* for us to enter into), and with it 'matter of factly' speaking of the Sabbath, and not Sunday, it reveals that literal Sabbath observance and celebration were still being practiced, and that Sunday hadn't come into the faith community.

[570] Two major heretical teachings, that some 'Hebrew Roots' assemblies espouse, are the denial of the eternal deity of Messiah Yeshua as God the Son, and/or that the male Gentile needs to be physically circumcised in order to keep Passover (or Torah). The former is a false Yeshua, who has no power to save, while the latter is the deadly sin of presumption (Num. 14:25-45; 15:30-31; see also Dt. 1:19-45). If you're not sure about something, feel free to email me (see p. 293 for contact information).

# Acts 21:25—Observe No Such Thing!

Acts 21:25 is the third and last place where the four rules appear. The KJV states that the Gentiles should 'observe no such thing.' There are two possible Hebraic interpretations for what Yakov meant, and neither one of them negates the Law for the Gentile. The first interpretation is that the Nazarite Vow, which Paul was entering into (v. 23f.), wasn't to be taken by a Gentile. The second is that the Gentile was not to be circumcised.

Due to the two different Greek texts there are two different English translations for the verse. Only the Textus Receptus (KJV, NKJV) has the phrase *observe no such thing*. Without discussing which Greek text might be the one that Luke actually wrote, I'll deal with both of them. First, the two texts will be written out in English and then I'll comment on the NASB, which is translated from the Greek NU text, which doesn't have the phrase. After that the KJV translation will be explained because the *translation* of the Greek text seems to point to the Law's demise. These two Bibles reflect the differences in the two Greek textual traditions. The meaningful differences of the KJV are placed in *italics:*[571]

> NASB—Acts 21:25: 'But concerning the Gentiles who have believed, we wrote, having decided that they should abstain from meat sacrificed to idols and from blood and from what is strangled and from fornication.'

> KJV—Acts 21:25: 'As touching the Gentiles which believe, we have written and concluded that they *observe no such thing, save only* that they keep themselves from things offered to idols, and from blood, and from strangled, and from fornication.'

The NASB doesn't have the Greek phrase 'observe no such thing, save only' that the KJV (and basically the NKJV) has. The New Revised Standard Version (also NU based) reads much like the NASB and makes it clear that there was a letter sent. This will figure into the proper understanding of the verse:

> NRSV—Acts 21:25: 'But as for the Gentiles who have become believers, *we have sent a letter* with our judgment that they should abstain from what has been sacrificed to

---

[571] The New American Standard Bible and the New Revised Standard Version use the 1881 Westcott–Hort Greek New Testament. This was revised and updated as the NU text; the Nestle–Aland Greek New Testament–United Bible Societies third corrected edition, 1983; Brown, *NGEINT*, p. iv (page number not printed).

The KJV, and to a great extent the NKJV, are based on the Textus Receptus, which is a more authentic manuscript tradition than the NU, and therefore, a truer reflection of what was originally written.

> idols and from blood and from what is strangled and from
> fornication.' (See also Acts 15:30)

In both the NASB and the NRSV there's no phrase that seems to be saying that the Gentiles have only four rules ('save only'); James is just reiterating the decision of Acts 15:20. There's nothing in the verse in the NU
Greek text that lends itself to coming against a Torah lifestyle.

With the KJV's 'observe no such thing, save only' the term *save only*
seems to be saying that the four rules are the only rules that a Gentile has
to keep.[572] The problem with this is the translation of the Greek phrase εἰ
μη (*ae may*) as *save only*. Bauer says it means *except, if not* or *but*.[573] If we
place *if not* into the sentence it doesn't make any sense:

> 'that they should observe no such thing, *if not* that they
> keep themselves from things offered to idols...'

Placing *except* in the verse reads like this:

> 'As touching the Gentiles which believe, we have written
> and concluded that they observe no such thing, *except* that
> they keep themselves from things offered to idols, and
> from blood, and from strangled, and from fornication.'
> (Acts 21:25)

Both Berry's Greek *Interlinear* translation (of the Textus Receptus) of the
Greek phrase,[574] and the New King James Version use *except* in their
translation of v. 25. Using *except* not only makes the verse compatible
with what was *written* in Acts 15:29f., but changes the tone of the verse
from 'these are the *only* commandments a Gentile needs to do' to "even
though the Gentile *can't observe this* ('observe no such thing,' v. 25), they
can and should do the four rules." That's a major shift in understanding
from the Gentiles having *only* four rules.

Placing *but* within the verse further shows that James wasn't speaking of
*only* four rules. He was reiterating what the Gentiles needed to do in relation to what he had just said to Paul:

> 'As touching the Gentiles which believe, we have written
> and concluded that they observe no such thing, *but* that
> they keep themselves from things offered to idols, and
> from blood, and from strangled, and from fornication.'

---

[572] Be that as it may, how many Christians know anything about the four rules,
let alone keep them, even as the Church interprets them?

[573] Bauer, *GELNT*, p. 220; also Perschbacher, *NAGL*, p. 119.

[574] George Ricker Berry, Editor and Translator, *Interlinear Greek–English New
Testament* (Grand Rapids, MI: Baker Book House, 2000), p. 380, Acts 21:25.

Inserting *but* presents a much different thought from *save only*. It seems that James wanted the Gentiles to know that even though they couldn't do whatever it was that he was speaking about to Paul, they could and should keep the four rules.

As for the longer phrase, that they *observe no such thing*, Bruce uses this to come against the Law. He writes,

> 'The elders added the assurance that they had *no* thought of going back on the terms of the apostolic decree, and imposing legal requirements on Gentile believers. So far as they were concerned, said the elders, *all that was required of them* was that they should abstain from eating flesh that had been sacrificed...As for the Gentile believers, of course, we have already agreed that *nothing* is to be imposed on them apart from the abstentions detailed in the apostolic letter.'[575]

Bruce is certain that no other legal requirements from the Law were necessary for the Gentile. All 'that was required of them' was that they keep the four rules. Marshall takes a similar position, saying:

> 'the fact that Paul was being asked *to behave in this way* in no sense implied that similar demands would be made of the Gentiles. The *fundamental freedom of the Gentiles from the law* had been established at the meeting described in chapter 15 whose decision is now reaffirmed. It seems strange that the Jerusalem decree should be repeated verbatim (cf. 15:20, 29) to Paul who was well aware of its contents.'[576]

Paul's 'behavior' meant that he was entering into the Law's Nazarite Vow (NV), but according to Marshall, Bruce insists that Paul couldn't have taken it because it lasted for at least 30 days. Bruce thinks the vow of the four men was going to be complete in seven days.[577] He suggests that the four

---

[575] Bruce, *The Book of the Acts*, p. 407.

[576] Marshall, *Acts*, p. 346.

[577] Ibid., p. 345, note 1. Bruce is on the right track, but heading in the wrong direction. Perhaps the controversy and enigma over what Paul entered into with those four Jewish men (Acts 21:23-24) would be solved by suggesting that the seven-day purification rite (Acts 21:26-27) was just that: a seven-day period that one had to complete *before* he was able to enter into the 30, 60 or 100 day Nazarite Vow. In other words, it was a preliminary purification or cleansing rite that one did before he took the Nazarite Vow.

Acts 21:26-27 speaks of 'days of purification,' not 'days of separation' as is said for the Nazarite Vow in Numbers 6:2, 4, 6, 8, 12, 13, 21 twice, with vv.

men had contracted some 'ritual uncleanness during their vow' and that Paul was going to pay for their expenses, but as Marshall counters:

> 'Bruce apparently assumes that Paul could share in the rite although he had not shared in the defilement. This view does not explain the preliminary visit to the temple for' (Paul's) 'purification in verse 26.'[578]

Great point! Why would Paul need to be purified with them if he wasn't defiled? If he was just paying the expenses for their purification he would not need to be purified, but Paul says to Felix in Acts 24:18 that he *was*

---

18-19 speaking of the consecrated or set-apart head or hair (NKJV). One can only speculate as to why no information on a preliminary purification rite exists, but the fact is that there's no record of a seven-day Nazarite Vow, either. A seven-day purification rite, to be accomplished before taking the NV, was most likely what Paul and the four men were involved in.

Another possibility is that it may have been a special time of purification for Jewish men coming from *outside* the land of Israel (Judah and Galilee). This would deal with their perceived uncleanness of having been among the idolatrous pagans (i.e. the Gentiles). On the other hand, with more Jews living outside the land of Israel than within, and many hundreds of thousands coming to Israel for each of the three annual holy Feasts (Passover, Pentecost and Tabernacles) it would seem far too long a time for pilgrims to have to prepare for the Feasts (as well as the sheer numbers making it an 'impossible' practice).

If this was a seven-day rite of purification before one took the NV, on which Paul initially embarked (Acts 21:26-27), both the concept and the sacrifice that would have been offered for him and each of the four men at the end of their purification (Acts 21:24, 26) parallel the Nazarite rite of purification if he became defiled (Num. 6:9-12). A Nazarite would be defiled if someone suddenly died in his presence (Num. 6:9). He would have *to shave his hair* 'on the *seventh* day' (Num. 6:9; Acts 21:24, 27) and on the eighth day, bring either two turtledoves or two young pigeons to the priest as a *sin sacrifice* and a *burnt sacrifice* (Num. 6:10-11; cf. Acts 21:26) as well as a lamb for a *guilt sacrifice* (Num. 6:12). *Then* he would begin his vow anew. Here is not only a seven-day time frame of purification from defilement (Num. 6:9; Acts 21:26-27), but also the *shaving* of the hair of the head on the *seventh* day, spoken of as the day of his cleansing (Num. 6:9; in Acts 21:24, 26, *purified*, NKJV). With the sacrifices on the eighth day the man's head became sanctified again (Num. 6:10-11, 18-19) and he was able to begin the NV afresh, or in the case of the four men and Paul, to begin it.

This seven-day ritual of purification may very well have been adopted in Paul's day for any Jew wanting to take the NV. This understanding only emphasizes the central point of Acts 21:20-27—Paul was entering into (the preliminary stage of) a NV (the shaving of the hair, Num. 6:9; Acts 21:24). He would have offered *sacrifices* for himself and paid for the *sacrifices* of the others (Num. 6:10-12; Acts 21:24, 26) to show *everyone* that *he still kept the Law of Moses* (Acts 21:24) as a Christian, 25 years *after* the resurrection.

578 Marshall, *Acts*, p. 345.

purified (cf. 21:26-27). Of course, even if Paul *wasn't* taking the vow he would still be seen as supporting the Law *and* animal sacrifice because the four men were involved in both. If Paul thought that the Law had been done away with, his compliance with the suggestion to pay for the sacrifices of the men and be purified with them would certainly have gone against his theology, not to mention his conscience.

If Paul thought that the Law had been done away with, this would have been the perfect place for a showdown. Wouldn't it have been much better for Paul to tell the truth to James, and all the Jewish believers, that Jesus had done away with sacrifice and the Law? If Jesus wants believers to walk in His Truth,[579] and these *Jewish believers were walking in falsehood about the Law*, why wouldn't Paul have addressed the issue here in Acts 21:20-27? Paul wasn't shy when it came to standing up against Peter in Antioch when he thought that Peter was wrong (Gal. 2:11). Most people today don't see Peter as Paul's equal, but in his day Peter was the *chief* Apostle and recognized as such by *all* the believers in Jerusalem and beyond. Paul had enough fortitude with Peter in Antioch, so why not with James in Jerusalem—if he thought that the Law had ended?

The four men were under a Nazarite Vow, as no other vow entailed the shaving of the head (Num. 6:18; Acts 21:24). Although Marshall lines up with Bruce in the 'only four (rules) and no more Camp,' he says that for Paul to take the NV was not out of line. *He sees Paul as having kept the Law!* In relation to the vow, Marshall states that Paul's action,

> 'would make it clear that *he lived in observance of the law*, but many scholars have doubted whether the historical Paul would have agreed to this proposal.'[580]

It seems very strange for Marshall to speak of the 'fundamental freedom of the Gentiles from the law,' base it on Acts 15, and then turn around and say that Paul kept the Law. Be that as it may, many scholars disagree with 'the Paul' presented in Acts 21, saying that *their* Paul would never have done it, but the authority of James, the integrity of Luke, and the inspiration of the Holy Spirit all stand behind the facts of Acts—the historical Paul kept the Law and he gave the four rules *and more* 'to his Gentiles.' He also took the NV, which meant that he was going to offer *animal sacrifices* to God in the Temple at Jerusalem 25 years *after the resurrection.*

After centuries of the Church teaching against the Law, many are shocked

---

[579] Jn. 14:6; 15:26; Rom. 1:18; Eph. 4:24; 2nd Tim. 2:15; Heb. 10:26; 2nd Peter 1:2; 1st John 1:6; 4:6; 5:6.

[580] Marshall, *Acts*, pp. 345-346.

when they learn that Paul took a Nazarite Vow. The observance of the vow meant the sacrificing of at least *three animals for each man* (Num. 6:9-21). The Apostle agreed to pay for all the sacrifices for them *and* for himself (Acts 21:23-24) at the conclusion of the NV.

*The Wycliffe Bible Commentary* also teaches that Acts 15 meant that the Gentiles were 'free from the Law,' but should keep the four rules so that no offense would be given to the Jewish believers. They state that the four rules in Acts 21 were meant to emphasize that.[581] Williams agrees and writes that,

> 'no legal requirement was to be laid upon the Gentiles as necessary for salvation.'[582]

As true as that statement is, Williams then says that the four rules would be *required* of the Gentiles. He, too, says that it's odd and out of place that James would repeat the four rules verbatim, but he says it may simply have been a literary device of Luke's or done for the benefit of those present with Paul.[583]

Knowling cuts to the heart of the problem by saying that the Gentiles were 'on a different footing' from the 'Jews who became Christians,'[584] because *they couldn't observe **something*** that the Jews could. He says that James' repetition of the rules emphasized his commitment to the Decree and that he expected Paul to show that he had 'no desire *to disparage the law*.'[585]

Stern rightly states that the accusation against Paul (Acts 21:21) was a baseless lie. Paul was accused of teaching *Jews* not to circumcise their sons and to stop observing the Law. Obviously, others were misinterpreting Paul's letters before the 21st century (e.g. Gal. 2–5; cf. Rom. 3:7-8; 2nd Peter 3:14-17). Stern offers three points to refute it. One, Paul kept the Law: he circumcised Timothy (Acts 16:3); he observed the Feasts (20:16); he said that he believed in the Law (24:14) and had 'committed no offense against the Law' (25:8); and at the end of his life he stated that he had done nothing to offend the Jewish people or the Customs (i.e. Law) of the Fathers (28:17).[586]

Two, Stern says that Paul's teaching, that the Gentiles need not observe the Jewish Law, was never given to the Jewish believers (1st Cor. 7:18;

---

[581]   Pfeiffer, *The Wycliffe Bible Commentary*, p. 1165.

[582]   Williams, *Acts*, p. 366.

[583]   Ibid.

[584]   Knowling, *The Acts of the Apostles*, p. 450.

[585]   Ibid., p. 451.

[586]   Stern, *Jewish New Testament Commentary*, p. 303.

Gal. 5:2-6).[587] Here Stern wrongly sees that the Gentile was subject to a 'Law-free Gospel,' but this places the Gentile in a completely different faith category than that of the Jewish believer. Is this what *Grace* is all about? Stern creates two totally different Flocks for the Shepherd who came to make both Flocks one (John 10:16; Eph. 2:16; 3:6). Shouldn't God's holy Instruction apply to every believer? Except for religious circumcision, Paul makes no distinction in his writings.[588] James (2:8-12; 4:11-12) and John (Rev. 14:12), as well as the Lord Himself (Mt. 5:19) don't seem to differentiate between Jew and Gentile, either. In other words, aside from physical covenantal circumcision, the Gentile and the Jew should observe the same laws. There's no section in Paul's letters that is just for Jews and another that's just for Gentiles, with *different* rules. If the Jews were keeping the Law, while the Gentiles didn't have to, there would seem to have been a need for different sections specifically addressed to each group.

In his third point Stern presents the much overlooked fact that the New Testament doesn't need *to repeat truths already evident* from the Old Testament—it 'assumes them,' and so did Paul.[589] This is an excellent point. Just like a sequel to a good book, the New doesn't have to list every law of the Old in order for them to be considered valid. Many Christians think that the New is 'completely different from the Old,' and things not specifically stated in the New don't apply to them,[590] but being grafted into Israel (Rom. 11) means that the Gentile was to learn about his new Family History and *this Family's* way of *living* (Torah, Prophets, Writings and New Covenant). The New Covenant wasn't made with the Gentiles, but only with the House of Israel and the House of Judah (Jer. 31:31-34). The Gentiles becomes part of Israel (Is. 49:6; Rom. 11:11f.; Eph. 2:11f.) and his allegiance should be to the *Israel* of God (Gal. 6:16).

Stern believes that Paul's keeping of the Law was affirmed in Acts 21:24 with Paul's subsequent obedience to Yakov's suggestion of taking the vow (v. 26).[591] Those that don't want to see Paul like this, tacitly proclaim Luke to be a liar. As there's no indication that Luke was a liar, Acts clearly reveals that the Apostle Paul kept the Law, all his life, *as a Christian*.

Stern also writes that Mishna *Nazir* (Nazarite) says that the time of the

---

[587] Ibid.

[588] Rom. 3:31; 7:7, 12, 14; 1st Cor. 7:17-19; 2nd Tim. 3:16-17.

[589] Stern, *Jewish New Testament Commentary*, p. 303.

[590] Witness the church called the Church of Christ—they won't have any musical instruments in their church services because this practice *isn't specifically mentioned in the New Testament*.

[591] Stern, *Jewish New Testament Commentary*, p. 304.

Nazarite Vow was 'one to three months in length.' He states:

> 'clearly, the four men were poor; otherwise they could
> have bought their own sacrificial animals and gifts.' Paul
> 'as patron must do more than merely pay the expenses; he
> too must be accepted by the *cohanim*' (priests of the Tem-
> ple) 'and be *ritually purified*.'[592]

As patron and participant[593] Paul was in agreement that the Nazarite Vow,
and therefore, animal sacrifice *after* the resurrection of Jesus, were still
valid (and actually, this was Paul's *second* NV recorded in Acts).[594] Hegg
rightly discerns that there were 'no competing values between the death of
Yeshua and the offering of sacrifices in the Temple.'[595]

With *all* the Jerusalem believers keeping the Law of Moses (Acts 21:20),
many would sacrifice and take the NV on a regular basis to honor Jesus
because the NV pictured a special consecration to God, such as only the
High Priest of Israel had (Lev. 21:10-11; Num. 6:6-8). Of course, anyone
taking the Vow was seen to hold *God's Law* in the highest esteem. *This is
the reason* why James directed Paul to take the Vow—to prove to all the
believers (and providentially to us today!) that what they had heard about

---

[592] Ibid. Stern writes of Paul being *ritually purified*, which speaks of the seven
days of purification before Paul could begin the Nazarite Vow.

[593] Paul was a participant in the vow, walking alongside those who had just begun the purification rite. Paul was told in Acts 21:24 to 'take them and be *purified* with them,' and in v. 26, 'Paul took the men and the next day, having
been *purified with them*, entered the Temple to announce the expiration of the
days of purification, at which time an offering should be made for each one of
them' (NKJV). With the purification rite completed, Paul would have begun
the vow with the other men. Someone might say that God stopped Paul from
taking the vow because it was wrong, but there is no Scripture to support that.

Williams, *Acts*, p. 366, also believes that Paul was under the NV. Knowling,
*The Acts of the Apostles*, pp. 449-450, states that the Greek word 'certainly
seems to demand that' Paul 'place himself on a level with the four men and
take upon himself the Nazarite vow' (see also Acts 24:18).

[594] Acts 18:18 states, 'Paul, having remained many days longer, took leave of the
brethren and put out to sea for Syria, and with him were Priscilla and Aquila.
In Cenchrea *he had his hair cut, for he was keeping a vow*.' Scholars are per-
plexed that Paul would do such a thing, yet Marshall, *Acts*, pp. 344-345, believes it was a NV. Williams, *Acts*, pp. 321-322, says it was based on a NV.
Stern, *JNTC*, pp. 290-291, doesn't think Paul's vow of Cenchrea was a *strict*
NV, saying that it could only be done in Jerusalem, but Williams overcomes
Stern's objection by revealing that Josephus (*War* 2.309–314) writes that such
a thing was possible, and Marshall, *Acts* p. 300, citing Mishnah *Nazir* 3:6; 5:4,
says that the shaving of the hair for the NV was permissible outside Jerusalem
and Israel.

[595] Hegg, *The Letter Writer*, p. 289, note 564.

Paul was a slanderous lie, and that he still walked 'orderly, *keeping the Law*' (Acts 21:24; see also his admonition to the Gentiles; 1st Cor. 11:1).

The phrase *observe no such thing* doesn't refer to the nullification of the Law, but theoretically to the NV that Paul was entering into. Yet, if the Gentiles were to walk in the Law of Moses, why would James tell them not to observe the Nazarite Vow? Why shouldn't the Gentiles be able to observe the NV and sacrifice, if the Jewish believers did? Biblically they could have. The Gentile believers should have been able to keep the NV and sacrifice animals. God had ordained it from the days of Moses (Lev. 17:8; 22:17-19, 25; Num. 6:2f.; 15:14-16; Is. 56:6-7), but in Paul's day the Temple was in the hands of a wicked high priest and Sanhedrin. They were extremely anti-Yeshua[596] and they certainly weren't going to recognize believing Gentiles as part of the House of Israel. As a result of this the Gentile *wasn't able* to take and complete the Nazarite Vow.

Upon completion of the vow each person was to sacrifice three different animals upon the Altar of the Temple (Num. 6:13-20). This is something that the Gentile would not have been able to do, but not because sacrifice had been 'done away with.' It's obvious from this very passage that animal sacrifice was still taking place among all the Jewish believers, including the Apostle Paul, at *least* twenty-four years *after* the resurrection.[597]

The Nazarite Vow is one possibility as to what James meant when he said that the Gentiles should *observe no such thing* because he had just directed Paul to take the vow. The Gentiles weren't able to observe the vow at that time, but in Yeshua's Kingdom of a thousand years on this Earth in Jerusalem, both Jew and Gentile will be able to sacrifice in the Temple (Ezk. 43–48; Zech. 14:16-21; Rev. 20:1-10).

In this case *observe no such thing* may point to the NV, but certainly not to the Gentile being 'Law-free.' This understanding, coupled with the fact that 'save only' should be translated as 'except,' or 'but,' reveals that James didn't mean the Gentiles had *only* four rules. The emphasis shifts to the NV that the believing Gentiles *couldn't* observe. James wouldn't have directed the Gentile believers to the synagogue to learn the Law, in Acts 15:21, only to reverse himself in Acts 21:25 and not explain why.

---

[596] Mt. 26:57-68; 27:1-2, 11-14, 17-20, 39-43, 62-66; 27:11-15; Acts 4:1-22; 5:17-42; 7:1-60; 9:1-2.

[597] Bromiley, *ISBE*, vol. one, p. 692. Regarding the arrest of Paul in Jerusalem, which takes place in Acts 21:26-36, *ISBE* places this event in the year 54 AD.

Unger, *UBD*, pp. 486-488, thinks it took place in 58 AD.

Douglas, *IBD*, part 1, p. 281, has 59 AD. For *IBD*, Paul's arrest happened 29 years *after* the resurrection.

Having said all that, the correct interpretation of *observe no such thing* refers to the prohibition against Gentile circumcision. The context, as well as the way the sentence reads, points directly to this. The first indicator is the slander against Paul, that he was teaching *Jews* not to circumcise their sons (Acts 21:21). That, along with the fact that James says that they had *sent a letter* (NRSV) reveals that Gentile circumcision is the subject of what the Gentile wasn't to do. The KJV also speaks of the letter:

> 'As touching the Gentiles which believe, *we have **written** and concluded* that they observe no such thing...' (Acts 21:25 KJV; cf. Acts 15:23f.).

*Written and concluded* refers to the letter of Acts 15:23 that Yakov wrote to the assembly at Antioch, which was also circulated in other believing assemblies (Acts 16:4-5). The letter put to rest the question of *Gentile circumcision* for salvation. The phrase, *we have written and concluded*, as well as his reiteration of the four rules, and also, the slander against Paul, all point directly to Yakov's decision of Acts 15, six to eight years earlier, that Gentiles weren't to be circumcised (and nothing is ever given in Scripture for the Gentile to be covenantally circumcised 'at a later time').

Because of its sanctity, the lies against Paul were rectified when he took the NV. This reveals that Paul still kept the Law (and wanted the Gentiles to as well; 1st Cor. 4:16-17) and that he believed that circumcision was still required *for the Jewish believer* and his sons. *Observe no such thing* speaks of the *Gentile believer* (and his sons) *not* being circumcised.

Many have thought it out of place that Yakov repeated the four rules in speaking with Paul.[598] *On the contrary,* this was a most appropriate time for him to reiterate the rules. After having told Paul to take the vow, to declare that circumcision for Jewish infants was still intact and that Paul still kept the Law, Yakov immediately reveals that circumcision still doesn't apply for the Gentiles, but they do have to keep the four rules. It was *extremely* appropriate for James to reiterate the four rules. He *clarified what was most incumbent* upon the former pagan Gentiles after he had just spoken of what they *weren't* to do—circumcision.

The Gentile wasn't to be circumcised in order to become a Jew[599] and keep the Law for salvation. Circumcision was given to the Jew as the *sign*

---

[598] Marshall, *Acts,* p. 346; Williams, *Acts,* pp. 366-367, and Knowling, *The Acts of the Apostles,* p. 450.

[599] God *never* intended for a Gentile 'to become a Jew.' No Gentile is ever seen 'becoming a Jew,' in Scripture. Gentile conversion is a rabbinic perversion. For more on this see *Is the Gentile Now a Jew?* at http://seedofabraham.net/ Is_The_Gentile_Now_A_Jew.html or ask for its PDF. Also, see The Stranger and the Native Born on p. 268.

of the covenant relationship that he had with God because of the covenant that God made with Father Abraham (Genesis 17:1-14, 23-27). Many say that the New Testament is totally different from the Old, and so no one needs to keep the Law, but if that's true, why is the Jewish believer still required to circumcise his sons (Acts 21:20-24)?

We Jews are also adopted into the Family of Israel who love Messiah, just as the Gentiles are (Acts 15:7-11; Rom. 8:15; Gal. 4:1-5; 6:15). It's by *the circumcision made without hands* that we all enter in (Phil. 3:3; Col 2:11). The *sign* has changed. That's why Peter and Paul could say that religious circumcision wasn't necessary for the Gentile, but that all must keep the (other) commandments and statutes of Moses as they apply to them (Acts 15:1, 7-11; Rom. 3:20, 31; 1st Cor. 7:19).

Would non-circumcision make the Gentile less valuable than the Jew? Of course not (Acts 15:1-21f.; Rom. 10:12-13). The Gentile, by being Born Again, receives the circumcision made without hands, which does for him what physical circumcision symbolizes—the creation of a new nature (Dt. 10:16; 30:6; Ezk. 36:26). *This* makes the Gentile (and the Jew!) acceptable to God. Physical circumcision doesn't change the Adamic nature. It doesn't matter *spiritually* if one is physically circumcised or not (1st Cor. 7:17-20), only racially. Yet, wouldn't the continued circumcision of Jewish sons create a problem if Gentile sons weren't circumcised? After all, if both parents were to keep the Law, how could one be required to circumcise his son, while the other was forbidden to do so? The theological reason for this is because the Gentile was never part of the Abrahamic covenant, but the Jew is.

Yeshua said that He had *another* Flock and that the two would become *one* Flock (Jn. 10:16). Here's a hint of a 'marriage union,' with the Gentile taking the place of the (uncircumcised) wife in order to woo her husband, the Jew, to Messiah by her prayers and holy conduct. Gentile prayers and love for the Jew is happening today.[600]

---

[600] This concept, of how one enters Messiah's Kingdom (by being Born Again; John 3:3, 5), and the position of the Gentile to the Jew (like a Jewish husband to his wife), further refutes Hegg's position of Gentile circumcision 'for the right reason' (see p. 158, note 440). James declared that the Gentiles weren't to be circumcised—*period!* (Acts 21:25) Nothing is ever mentioned about it being possible, 'for the right reason,' in Acts or anywhere else. Acts through Revelation covers approximately 70 years (30-100 AD). During this time Gentile believers were having many sons, yet there's not a single reference in the NT *validating* religious circumcision for them. It's hard to believe that an alleged issue of this magnitude could have been overlooked by the nine writers of the NT (and the Holy Spirit!) 'if circumcision for the right reason' was a valid theological position. On the contrary, Paul expressly comes against it when he tells the Gentiles, who came to Messiah uncircumcised, to *remain*

Also, a by-product of not circumcising the male Gentile means that the racial Seed of Abraham, Isaac and Jacob is preserved for God's end-time purpose—to display His faithfulness and forgiving loving-kindness *to Israel after the flesh* (Is. 62:1-12; Jer. 23:5-8; Rom. 11:25-32).

*Observe no such thing* doesn't refer to the Nazarite Vow and still less to the Law—it refers to Yakov's decision that the Gentile wasn't to be circumcised (Acts 15:19-29). It fits well with Paul being accused of teaching Jews *not* to circumcise their sons, Yakov saying that he had *written* something, and also, his reiterating of the four rules (Acts 15:22-29; 21:25).

The reiteration of the four rules also reveals *exactly* what Yakov was referring to. In other words, if the four rules hadn't been reiterated, some scholars could say that there were *other* things 'written and concluded' that Luke didn't mention. It would open up endless speculation and other perverse interpretations. Thank God that Yakov reiterated the four rules!

*Observe no such thing* focused first on the Nazarite Vow to point out that animal sacrifice was still in effect for all the Apostles at the Temple in Jerusalem 25 years *after* the resurrection, and theoretically, for the Gentile believer as well. Just from the perspective of the Nazarite Vow, the Law of Moses is confirmed for every believer today.[601]

*Observe no such thing* cannot be used to teach that Yakov's four rules to the Gentiles were the only rules for them or that they didn't have to keep the Law. On the contrary, the Holy Spirit, through Yakov, was making sure that everyone knew *that Paul still kept the Law*, and by extension, that everyone else should, too. Yakov reemphasized the four rules of Acts 15 to make sure that the Gentiles knew what they *should* implement in relation to what they *shouldn't do*—religious circumcision.

---

*that way* (1st Cor. 7:18; see also Gal. 2:3), yet two chapters earlier he exhorts the Gentile Corinthians to keep the Feast (the Passover!; 1st Cor. 5:6-8). Gentile circumcision 'for the right reason' was never an option in Apostolic times. The circumcision made without hands (being Born Again) allows the Gentile (and the Jew!) to come into Messiah's Kingdom and keep Passover. Religious circumcision for the Gentile is the wrong sign for the wrong covenant and is a sin of presumption. For more on this see *Gentile Circumcision?* at http://SeedofAbraham.net/Gentile_Circumcision.html or ask me for its PDF.

[601] See *Sacrifice in the New Testament* at http://SeedofAbraham.net/ntsac.html or ask for its PDF.

# *Acts 15:20, 29; 21:25 — Switched Rules*

A brief profile of the three passages where the four rules are seen is both insightful and enigmatic: insightful in that it also confirms *blood* as sacrificial blood that is drunk;[602] enigmatic in that the order of the four rules changes after initially being spoken by Yakov in Acts 15:20. Rule two, *cult prostitution,* and rule four, *blood,* trade places with each other after Yakov first declares it in Acts 15:20:

Acts 15:20: "but to write to them

1. to keep away from the *pollutions* of idols

2. and of cult prostitution

3. and of things strangled

4. and of blood."

Acts 15:29:

1. "to keep away from meat *sacrificed* to idols

2. and blood

3. and strangled things

4. and cult prostitution, from which keeping yourselves you will do well. Goodbye."

Acts 21:25: "And concerning the Gentiles having believed, we wrote, having decided (that) they avoid *both*[603]

1. the meat *offered* to idols

2. and blood

3. and strangled (things)

4. and cult prostitution."[604]

The Greek word in Acts 15:20 for the first rule (ἁλισγημάτων—*pollutions of idols*) changes to a different Greek word in the letter of 15:29 and is reiterated in 21:25 (εἰδωλοθύτων—*meat offered to idols, i.e. sacrificed*). The change *emphasizes* that it's an *animal* sacrifice, not just *any* food offered to idols (and that eating it at the time of the sacrifice was prohibited).[605]

---

[602] Eating blood at any time is sin. The differentiation here is between blood that would literally be drunk at a pagan sacrifice (idolatry), and that which is found in a rare hamburger or steak (a dietary regulation).

[603] The King James Version does not have the word *both*. It's not found in the Textus Receptus, which is the basis for the KJV.

[604] Brown, *NGEINT*, pp. 472-473, 499. I've used 'cult prostitution' for the three passages instead of the nebulous 'sexual immorality' found in *NGEINT*.

[605] Bruce, *The Book of the Acts*, pp. 299-300. A report by Eusebius, *HE* 5.1.26,

215

Any food (grain, vegetables and fruit, etc.) could be given or 'sacrificed' to an idol (or a pagan priest as the idol's representative). The Greek word for the first rule in 15:20 could theoretically encompass these non-animal foods, but the Greek word for the first rule in Acts 15:29 and 21:25 specifically means *animals* sacrificed to idols *at the time of the sacrifice.*[606] Yakov was speaking of a major idolatrous animal sacrificial rite, not the giving of grain, fruit or baked goods.

Diverting from the original order listed in Acts 15:20, number two (*cult prostitution*) and number four (*blood*) are switched in the letter of Acts 15:29 and in Acts 21:25. Why does this happen? Perhaps because this is a more 'natural' or chronological order for the rules in which they were enacted. *Blood,* that would be drunk at a pagan sacrifice, is placed immediately *after* the sacrifice of the animal to the pagan god. It's the order of a pagan ceremony:

1. sacrifice the animal,

2. drink its blood, and later, after it's roasted,

3. eat the meat of the sacrifice,

4. and 'worship' the god or goddess through cult prostitution.

The Greek word for *both* in Acts 21:25 is το (*toe*). It means 'both'[607] in the sense that it,

> 'connects...clauses, thereby indicating a close relationship betw. them.'[608]

Yakov (or Luke?) most likely saw the close relationship or order of events between the animal being sacrificed and its blood being drunk, and wrote the letter, and reiterated it (Acts 21:25) accordingly. Yakov said to 'avoid *both*' the sacrificial meat *and* its blood. This excludes *blood* from referring to murder or blood in rare roast beef. The term *blood* is now *intimately*

---

reveals that later Christians understood *blood* in Acts 15:20 (15:29; 21:25) to refer to that which was drunk (rather than blood in rare meat, blood not properly drained, or blood shed by murder). It states that one of the martyrs of Vienne and Lyon, France (177 AD) protested his accusation by asking 'How could Christians eat children when they are *not allowed* even to drink the blood of brute beasts?' The only place in the New Testament that this prohibition could come from would be the rule on *blood* from Acts 15:20.

[606] In English the wording for the first rule in both Acts 15:29 and 21:25 may be different, but the Greek word is the same. It stresses that it's an animal sacrificed to idols, and that the meat was eaten *at the time of the pagan ceremony* (see p. 19f., and p. 125f., above).

[607] Perschbacher, *The New Analytical Greek Lexicon*, p. 403.

[608] Bauer, *A Greek-English Lexicon of the New Testament*, p. 807.

connected to rule one on sacrificial idolatry and speaks of the idolater drinking it after the animal was sacrificed.

The rearranging of the two rules could further be displaying the idolatrous nature of the Decree by taking the two primary rules (*animals sacrificed to idols* and *cult prostitution*) and making them standout as 'bookends,' with the drinking of the blood and the strangling of a sacrifice being 'enclosed' by the two major points. This ordering of the rules further affirms them as a unit or a 'package deal' on sacrificial-sexual idolatry.

*Switched Rules* emphasizes that the four rules of Yakov are a conceptual unit on sacrificial-sexual idolatry and that *blood* speaks of it being drunk from an animal sacrifice. Rules two and four seem to have been switched in order to better portray the conceptual theme of the rules by showing their natural order in a sacrificial-sexually idolatrous ceremony.

This new order also has the two most obvious sacrificial-sexual rules at the 'front and the back,' thereby ensuring that everyone would understand that the rules dealt with sacrificial-sexual idolatry. Also, with the word *both*, the sacrificial blood that would be drunk is grammatically tied to the animal that had just been sacrificed to the pagan god.

# YAKOV'S CONCERN

Most theologians see the four rules of Acts 15:20 as taken from the Law of Moses, with at least two rules being of a non-moral character (*strangled* and *blood*).[609] Others see the rules coming from the Noahide laws. Both groups think that the rules were given for *table fellowship* so the Gentile would not offend his Jewish counterpart who was still 'attached to the Law.' The interpretation of *table fellowship* will be discussed first, then the Noahide view, and then Yakov's concern: sacrificial-sexual idolatry.

## *Table Fellowship*

Scholars center their interpretation of Acts 15:20 around table fellowship even though it presents a theological dilemma for them.[610] They have to acknowledge that three rules come from the Law of Moses and that some are 'just ceremonial.' This is justified by saying that it was to assuage the sensitivities of the Jewish believers who still walked in the Law of Moses.

### Various Interpretations of the Four Rules of Acts 15:20

1. The First Rule: Pollutions of Idols
   1. Meat sacrificed to idols and eaten at the sacrifice, with the remains sold in the marketplace.[611]
   2. Meat sacrificed to idols and only eaten at the cult sacrifice.[612]
2. The Second Rule: *Pornay'ah*
   1. Sexual immorality.[613]
   2. Unchastity.[614]
   3. Adultery.[615]

---

[609] Williams, *Acts*, p. 266. The Decree touches 'on both the ethical and ceremonial aspects of the law.'

[610] Marshall, *Acts*, p. 243: 'fellowship at table with Gentiles.' Williams, *Acts*, p. 266: so the Gentile and Jew could 'live in harmony with one another.' It would be impossible for the Jew to 'have any dealing with the Gentile believers unless the latter observed these basic requirements.' Pfeiffer, *WBC*, p. 1152: 'fellowship between Jew and Gentile.'

[611] Bauer, *GELNT*, p. 221. Perschbacher, *NAGL*, p. 118. Friberg, *ALGNT*, p. 130. Marshall, *Acts*, p. 253. Bruce, *The Book of the Acts*, p. 295. *Wycliffe*, p. 1152. Williams, *Acts*, p. 267. Stern, *JNTC*, p. 277.

[612] Witherington, *The Acts of the Apostles*, pp. 461-463. Hegg, *The Letter Writer*, p. 275.

[613] Brown, *NGEINT*, p. 472. Stern, *JNTC*, p. 277.

[614] Marshall, *Acts*, p. 253, illicit sex or breaches of the Jewish marriage law.

    4. Fornication.[616]

    5. The prohibited marriages of Lev. 18:6-18.[617]

    6. Cult prostitution.[618]

3. The Third Rule: (Things) Strangled

    1. Proper animal slaughter and the draining of the blood (based on Lev. 17) so as not to eat meat with blood in it.[619]

    2. Prohibition against eating flesh with the blood still in it (based on the 'Noachian decree of Gen. 9:4').[620]

    3. A pagan sacrifice that was strangled.[621]

4. The Fourth Rule: Blood

    1. Murder.[622]

    2. The eating of meat with blood in it.[623]

    3. The drinking of fresh, raw blood from a pagan sacrifice.[624]

Everyone correctly understands the first rule, although most don't distinguish that Yakov only meant sacrificial meat *at the time of the sacrifice*. *Pornay'ah* (#2) wasn't seen by the Church as cult harlotry, which would have opened the possibility that the rules were a coherent unit, and therefore, rules three and four were assigned to food regulations.[625] The interpretation of the rules in this manner allows most theologians to present

---

[615] Unger, *UBD*, p. 378. Brown, *Collins English Dictionary*, p. 602, pt. 2.

[616] KJV. Brown, *NGEINT*, p. 472; the NRSV margin translation has *fornication*.

[617] Marshall, *Acts*, p. 253. Bruce, *The Book of the Acts*, p. 295. Williams, *Acts*, p. 266. Kittel, *TDNT*, vol. VI, p. 593.

[618] Knowling, *The Acts of the Apostles*, pp. 324-325. Bivin, *Understanding the Difficult Words of Jesus*, p. 109. Witherington, *The Acts of the Apostles*, pp. 463-464. Hegg, *The Letter Writer*, p. 279. Pfeiffer, *WBC*, p. 1152.

[619] Friberg, *ALGNT*, p. 319. Bauer, *GELNT*, p. 680. Marshall, *Acts*, p. 253. Williams, *Acts*, p. 266. Pfeiffer, *WBC*, p. 1152. Stern, *JNTC*, p. 277. Hegg, *The Letter Writer*, pp. 277, 281.

[620] Bruce, *The Book of the Acts*, p. 296.

[621] Witherington, *The Acts of the Apostles*, p. 464. Hegg, *The Letter Writer*, p. 277.

[622] Stern, *JNTC*, p. 277. Witherington, *The Acts of the Apostles*, p. 464, note 426, lists this as a second possibility. Marshall, *Acts*, p. 253, note 1: 'later scribes.'

[623] Marshall, *Acts*, pp. 243, 253. Bruce, *The Book of the Acts*, pp. 295-296. Williams, *Acts*, p. 266. Knowling, *The Acts of the Apostles*, p. 325. Pfeiffer, *WBC*, p. 1152.

[624] Witherington, *The Acts of the Apostles*, p. 464. Hegg, *The Letter Writer*, p. 276, also note 586.

[625] Knowling, *The Acts of the Apostles*, pp. 324-325. Marshall, *Acts*, p. 253; etc.

them as *table fellowship* and to continue to teach that the Law isn't valid.

If *blood* (#4) related to table fellowship (the prohibition against eating blood in meat) Yakov would have said *which* animal meat could be eaten and which couldn't, so as to prevent *offending* the Jewish believer. This, supposedly, was the purpose of the rules, yet no reference is ever made to any prohibited animals, but eating pig would certainly offend every Jew.

In other words, if Yakov was getting that specific, saying that blood should not be found within meat one was eating (a dietary regulation) and that the animal should be properly slaughtered and drained of its blood (i.e. not *strangled*, #3), he should have told the Gentiles which animals were acceptable meat to eat and which weren't. Theoretically, the situation arises that a Gentile can butcher a pig according to acceptable slaughter practices; slitting the throat, draining the blood, skinning it, etc., and then roasting it until it was 'well done,' but can you imagine a Gentile sitting down with his Jewish friend and offering him a hot slab of ham with his eggs? Great way to start a conversation!

It also begs the question that the pig is not the only meat that is forbidden by God and that would obviously offend every Jew at the table. What if the Gentile were to offer shrimp? It doesn't have any blood, nor need to be slaughtered properly, yet God forbids this creature along with cats, dogs, horses, catfish, squid, crab and shark, etc. (see Lev. 11; Dt. 14).

Yakov never addresses this in Acts 15, Acts 21, or any other place. No foods are ever mentioned that might offend a Jew. This is why *blood* cannot relate to dietary regulations of the Law, and this is why *table fellowship* is an extremely poor theological interpretation of the rules. *Blood* must be seen as the pagan ritual of drinking it as part of a sacrifice. The very idea that the rules were given so as not to offend the Jews boomerangs right back into the faces of those who declare them to be for 'weak Jewish sensitivities.' Witherington saw this and said:

> "The rules that James offers are *much too limited to regulate matters of table fellowship*, for, as Wilson says, 'they do not even guarantee that no forbidden meat or wine (for example, pork or wine from libations) is used.'"[626]

One might argue that the Gentiles would learn about the forbidden animals as they went to the synagogue and heard the Law read (Acts 15:21), but this misses the point. Aside from most theologians not wanting the Gentiles to go to the synagogue in the first place, it might take six months or longer for a Gentile to even hear Lev. 11 or Dt. 14 read, so as 'to learn' about the dietary laws. It's not as though the Gentiles had their own Bibles

---

[626] Witherington, *The Acts of the Apostles*, p. 465.

and could read them whenever they wanted. That's why the Gentiles were going to the synagogues in the first place—to hear the Word of God and to learn the laws that applied to them.

If a Gentile possibly didn't hear about the dietary laws for six months, did it mean that he wasn't to fellowship with the Jewish believers for that length of time? If so, is there any hint of that written in Scripture? No, *blood* can't relate to the dietary laws. As for *blood* equaling murder, every Gentile knew the punishment that Rome exacted for it. No believing Gentile needed to be admonished about murdering people.

In biblical law the eating of blood in rare meat is sin (Lev. 3:17; 7:26-27; 19:26; Ezek. 33:25), but not necessarily idolatrous. The 'eating' of blood that the Bible speaks of as idolatrous is seen as drinking it from a pagan sacrifice. Drinking the raw blood of an animal was part of the worship of many pagan gods and goddesses. This was done to attain the characteristics of the god and the benefits thereof, and as Paul found out, there certainly was a need for this prohibition (1st Cor. 10:20-21).

*Blood* and *strangled* are just two aspects of the four rules that have been misunderstood. Turning to rule two, some think that *pornay'ah* means not to marry within the prohibited relations of Lev. 18:6-18,[627] but *pornay'ah* cannot be interpreted as pertaining to 'prohibited marriages' because it always refers to prostitution in both the Old and New Testaments.

Witherington insightfully saw that Torah regulations found in Lev. 18 for 'prohibited unions between close relations' were *never* addressed in the Septuagint as *pornay'ah*.[628] This is another reason why the rule doesn't speak of 'prohibited marriages.'

Others see *pornay'ah* as sexual immorality, unchastity or fornication (popularly defined), but these water down the Greek word to the lowest common denominator and defy the biblical interpretation for the word, the context, and its historical environment. *Sexual immorality* can be made to mean anything sexual, and consequently, it means nothing specifically.

From both its Hebrew and Greek usage the definition of Yakov's second rule was seen as cult prostitution. The history of ancient Israel, and the world at large, confirmed this, as well as the use of *pornay'ah* as the only biblical grounds for divorce between two believers (Mt. 5:32). First Corinthians, Revelation, and the way the word is used throughout the New Testament further support this understanding.

Why don't most scholars translate the second rule as *cult prostitution*?

---

[627] Marshall, *Acts*, p. 253. Bruce, *The Book of the Acts*, p. 295. Williams, *Acts*, p. 266. Kittel, *Theological Dictionary of the New Testament*, vol. VI, p. 593.

[628] Witherington, *The Acts of the Apostles*, p. 465.

Placed right after the prohibition on not eating the meat of an idolatrous sacrifice at the time of the sacrifice, the context of sacrificial idolatry could have been recognized so much sooner than it was. Ben Witherington III (1998) seems to have been the first theologian to present the four rules as a *unit* on sacrificial-sexual idolatry.

The Church's anti-Law bias has blinded its scholars. That's why *pornay'ah*, *blood* and *strangled* weren't properly understood. Separating and annulling the Law of God from the New Covenant, scholars handicap themselves and fall into a major heresy. Their understanding blinds them to God's Word. Theological blindness is not confined to the Pharisees. It adversely affects hundreds of millions of believers today (most of the Body of Christ) in their walk with God.

With most theologians thinking that they are 'free from the Law' it's hard to imagine how they can present any rules as coming from the Law. Knowling was quick to point this out. If the Law was done away with, how could Yakov do this, and more importantly, *how could Paul allow it?* If the Law was done away with, why didn't Paul tell James? When would the Jewish believers learn this 'vital truth'? Furthermore, if the rules were only to be kept in the presence of the Jews, as some theologians say, the Jews, and especially the Jewish Apostles, would certainly have been offended when they found out about the hypocrisy.

There are other theological and practical problems with interpreting the rules for *table fellowship*. One is that it creates two separate and distinct groups of believers within the Kingdom of God with two *different* standards of sin. On what day will the two peoples (in the same congregation) assemble? Should majority rule or should they meet on both days? This is theologically absurd, and in practical terms, impossible. The Jew must keep the Sabbath day holy and if he doesn't it's a sin, but the Gentile doesn't have to keep it? Welcome to the Wall of Separation *in reverse* (Eph. 2:14)! Is the Kingdom of Jesus a democracy? Who makes up the rules for sin and how to live one's life — the Church or God?

This is a major reason why most Jews, who don't believe in Jesus, won't even consider Him a viable option for being the Messiah of Israel. Because of Sunday, Easter, Christmas and the eating of unclean meats, Jews see Christianity *as just another pagan religion*. They *know* that the Law is from God. They also believe, and rightly so, that the Messiah wouldn't change Sabbath to Sunday and do away with the Law, yet isn't that exactly how Christians present the Jewish Messiah to the Jewish people?

Theologians get around the Law being kept by all the Jewish believers (Acts 21:20) by saying that *they didn't realize* it had been done away with, but this creates a larger problem than it seems to solve. How could *all* the

Jewish believers think that the Law was still valid? Were they all, including the Apostles, who had walked with the risen Savior after the resurrection, just so slow to heed the teaching of the Holy Spirit in this vital area? What of Paul, the Church's 'No Law!' champion? He also kept the Law to the extreme point of *Nazarite Vow and sacrifice* 25 years *after* the resurrection! (Acts 21:20-26)[629] Nowhere in Acts (or anywhere else in the New Testament) do the Apostles *ever* say that the Law is not valid.

Having two theologically different communities of faith is totally foreign to God and His Word. A major theme of Torah is that there is one law for both the native-born Hebrew and the stranger.[630]

The Gentile believer in Yeshua has now become *one with Israel*. Messiah declared that even though there was another Flock (i.e. the Gentiles) the *two shall be one* and have one Shepherd:

> 'I have other sheep (Gentiles) which are not of this Fold (Jews). I must bring them also and they will hear My Voice and *they will become one Flock* with one Shepherd.' (John 10:16)

Wouldn't it seem strange for His Jewish sheep, but not His Gentile sheep, to observe the Sabbath? In this 'one Flock' it would be a sin for a Jewish believer to eat shrimp, but a Gentile Christian would be 'free' to eat it? What kind of a kingdom would that be? It would be a *divided* kingdom with diametrically opposed rules *for what constitutes sin*.

It also makes God out to be the one erecting a 'middle wall of partition.' There's nothing in Rom. 11:17-21, 24-27, where the Gentile is grafted into the cultivated olive tree (Israel), or Eph. 2:12-22; 3:6, where the Gentile is part of the Commonwealth of Israel and made into 'one new Man' with the Jew, to support a different theological lifestyle for the Gentile.[631]

*Table fellowship* is not why Yakov gave the four rules. Nowhere is table fellowship mentioned in Acts 15, nowhere is it the reason for their holding the Council, and nowhere in the Word of God is it said to be the reason

---

[629] **Acts 15:** Douglas, *IBD*, part 1, pp. 281-283: 48 AD. Unger, *UBD*, pp. 486-488: 48 AD. Witherington, *The Acts of the Apostles*, p. 444, note 361: 49 AD. Bromiley, *ISBE*, vol. one, p. 692: 49 AD.

**Acts 21:** Bromiley, *ISBE*, vol. one, p. 692: 54 AD. Unger, *UBD*, pp. 486-488: 58 AD. Douglas, *IBD*, part 1, p. 281: 59 AD.

[630] See p. 268f., *Two Different Kingdoms? The Stranger and the Native-Born*, for Scripture cites and a greater understanding of who this *stranger* is.

[631] Don't let some anti-Law English translations of Eph. 2:15 mislead you. This verse speaks about the laws that *separated* Jews from Gentiles, not the *entire* Law (Ex. 23:33; 34:12; Dt. 7:3-11; Josh. 23:11-15; Acts 10:28). Ask me for the PDF on Eph. 2:15.

for giving the four authoritative rules.[632] The commandments of Yakov[633] were given in relation to what a Gentile must do in order for his faith in Jesus to be seen as biblically genuine.

The Book of Acts tells us 'what happened.' It's very hard to argue with what it states about Paul, and all the Jews, keeping the Law of Moses 25 years after the resurrection (Acts 21:20, 24). Some realize the futility of trying to bend those two verses. They're honest and say they don't understand it. How could Paul take the Nazarite Vow if the Law was 'no more'?

Others teach that Paul was only being 'a Jew to the Jews.'[634] He was just

---

[632] Marshall, *Acts*, p. 255: 'the letter carries on with a firm tone of authority. The decision reached by the church was regarded as being inspired by the Spirit, who is throughout Acts the guide of the church in its decisions and actions.' Williams, *Acts*, p. 270: 'the council's decision had been reached under the guidance of the Holy Spirit (cf. 10:19; 13:2f.). This belief is made explicit in verse 28, where the form of expression does not mean that they put themselves on a par with the Spirit, but only that they were willing to submit to his guidance.' Bruce, *The Book of the Acts*, p. 299: 'The decree is regarded as binding in the letters to the seven churches of proconsular Asia (Rev. 2:14, 20). Toward the end of the second century it was observed by the churches of the Rhone valley (which had close links with those of Asia) and...Africa.'

[633] The biblical reality of the four rules of Acts 15:20 is that they are commandments from Yeshua. Yakov didn't make these up on his own and they're not suggestions. Just as the writings of Paul are to be obeyed, so too, the four rules of Yakov. Paul said, 'If anyone thinks he is a prophet or spiritual, let him recognize that the things which I write to you are *the Lord's commandments*' (1st Cor. 14:37; 1st Tim. 6:14; 2nd Pet. 3:2, 14-18).

[634] Knowling, *The Acts of the Apostles*, p. 451. Marshall, *Acts*, p. 346, citing Stahlin and including himself. Bruce, *The Book of the Acts*, pp. 406-408. Bruce argues that *the Elders and James* were lacking understanding as to *why* Paul followed their counsel and took the vow: 'Therefore, in their *naïveté*, they put a proposal to him' (p. 406). Bruce thinks that Paul was only going along with them as part of his stated policy—to be 'a Jew to the Jews' (1st Corinthians 9:20). 'Paul fell in with their suggestion,' relieving 'them of embarrassment' (because of what they had heard about Paul teaching Jews not to circumcise their sons). Bruce also writes that Paul 'cannot be fairly charged with compromising his own gospel principles.'

On the contrary, Paul most certainly would be charged with unethical behavior if his reasons were as Bruce has stated. Paul *expressly* took the NV *to show everyone that he kept the Law* (Acts 21:24). Keeping Torah doesn't mean to keep it only when in Jewish society ('He himself was happy to conform to Jewish customs *when he found himself in Jewish society;*' Bruce, p. 406). Bruce says that among the Gentiles, Paul would 'conform to Gentile ways.' What does that mean? What was the 'way of the Gentiles'? (See Ezk. 20:32; 1st Peter 4:3) Did Paul sacrifice to idols in Corinth? Did he eat pigs in Ephesus? Did he desecrate the 7th day Sabbath in Athens? Did he keep Sunday, Christmas and Easter in Rome?

observing the Vow so as not to offend the Jews. If this was the case, Paul would have been a chameleon, not an Apostle. Still others have the *hutz-pah* (Jewish for audacity) to say that Paul was 'afraid for his life,' from James and the Jewish believers! *This,* they say, was why the Apostle Paul did something that he never would have done on his own, but this makes Paul out to be a very weak and unprincipled man, something that Scripture does not bear out.[635] It also makes James and the other Apostles out to be more like 'the James Gang,'[636] than living examples of Yeshua's love and *way of life* for us.

Other scholars simply say it didn't happen! It was just *fanciful writing* on Luke's part. He made it up! These scholars say *the Paul* they know would never have allowed it, and that's true! *Their image* of Paul would never

---

Being 'among the Gentiles' also presupposes that there were *no* Jews among the Gentiles, but wherever there were Gentile converts to Yeshua there were also Jews who believed in Him (Acts 13:42; 14:1; 17:17; 18:4; 19:10, etc.). How would Paul walk *then*? Would he keep Torah or not? (See Rom. 3:8)

Bruce's Paul seems to be a deceiver of the highest order because the taking of the NV meant that Paul esteemed and walked in Torah *all the time*. Paul would not say to God that he would keep the Sabbath day holy among the Jews, but not among the Gentiles. Paul would have been extremely unscrupulous if he had taken the Vow *only to appease James* and the Jewish Apostles. The *stated reason* for Paul taking the Vow was so that '*all* will know that there is *nothing* to the things which they have been told about you, but that you yourself *also* walk orderly, *keeping the Law*' (Acts 21:24).

If Paul only took the Vow to appease James then *he was deceiving James* and all the other Jewish believers there, but Scripture records that Paul kept Sabbath and Torah all the time (Acts 24:14; 25:8; 1st Cor. 7:19). Also, in Acts 20:16 and 1st Cor. 16:8, Paul orders his life around *Shavu'ot* (the Law's Pentecost or Feast of Weeks; Lev. 23:15-21; Dt. 16:16; see also Acts 18:18; 20:6; 27:9).

What being 'a Gentile to the Gentiles' meant for Paul was that he would *associate with them*, something that he *never* would have done as an unbelieving Pharisee (Acts 26:5). This is why he rebukes Peter—for *not associating* with the Gentile believers when Peter knew better (Gal. 2:11-15; Acts 10:15, 28, 34-35). It doesn't mean that Paul or Peter ate unclean meat, as some wrongly teach. It also means that Paul *would relate to Gentiles on their own terms*, bringing the Gospel to them in ways that they could understand; see Acts 17:15-30f., where Paul doesn't voice his thoughts about their idolatry, but speaks of Messiah to them in a way that they could understand, not knowing Mosaic Law as the Jews did). It didn't mean that he would sin against God in the process, by breaking the Sabbath, eating pig, keeping Easter or 'living like a Gentile sinner' as he writes (Gal. 2:15; 1st Tim. 5:22).

[635] Acts 9:20-29; 14:19-22; 2nd Cor. 11:23-12:21; 2nd Peter 3:14-18.

[636] The James Gang was a band of notorious outlaws in the Old West who lived in the 1870s and were led by Jesse *James*.

have allowed it to happen. *Their Paul* set them 'free from the Law,' but the biblical Paul declares freedom from sin, not the holy Law of God.

With *some* of the words of Paul, theologians are able 'to theologize the Law away' because they mistake Paul's coming against the Law, in relation to salvation and circumcision, for his entire view on the Law. They're not convincing, though, when they try to explain why Paul elevates the Law (Rom. 3:31; 7:7, 12, 14; 1st Cor. 5:6-8; 7:19), and here in Acts, the only recourse some have is to declare Luke a liar! Marshall, in relation to Luke writing about Paul taking the NV, to show everyone that he kept the Law (Acts 21:24), states that,

> 'many scholars have doubted whether the historical Paul would have agreed to this proposal. A. Hausrath put the objection most vividly by saying that it would be more credible that the dying Calvin would have bequeathed a golden dress to the mother of God' (Roman Catholicism's allegedly sinless and deified Mary), 'than that Paul should have entered upon this action. Luke, it is claimed, *has invented the incident* to show that Paul was a law-abiding Jew. Even Stahlin...argues that Paul would never have accepted verse 24b.'[637]

These scholars seem to think that Luke *the Gentile* (Col. 4:10-14) had nothing better to do than to *fabricate* an Apostle Paul who kept the Law! Whatever possessed the good doctor to do such a monstrous thing?! In other words, what was Luke's motivation for doing it?

If the Law had been done away with, the *biblical* Paul would have voiced his opposition to James. In that he doesn't, we know that it wasn't. Paul still kept the Law and exhorted Gentiles to do the same, as he himself wrote in his letters of imitating or following Him as he followed Messiah Yeshua (Rom. 3:31; 7:7, 12; 1st Cor. 5:6-8; 7:19; 9:8; 11:1; 14:34).

David Williams, who espouses table fellowship, nevertheless writes that *Paul kept the Law all his life.* He also refutes those who say that Paul was against the Apostolic Decree of Acts 15:20-21 (by his not specifically presenting it in his letters; e.g. Rom. 14; 1st Cor. 8:10; Gal. 1–5). Williams says that 'there is nothing in all his writings to suggest that he disapproved of them.'[638] He states that Paul, 'believed that his own teaching *upheld the*

---

[637] Marshall, *Acts*, pp. 345-346. See *ISBE*, vol. one, pp. 43-44, for Luke's accuracy in historical details, which gives evidence of his overall trustworthiness. Luke, Ramsay states, 'should be placed among the very greatest of historians.' Acts 21:24b: 'and that all may know that those things of which they were informed about you are nothing, but that you yourself also walk orderly and *keep the Law.*'

*law* (Rom. 3:31)' and 'his epistles are full of exhortations *to live by the letter* no less than by the spirit of the law (cf., e.g. Rom. 13:8-10; Eph. 5:1, 3ff., 31; 6:2f.).'[639]

> 'Of course he knew now that obedience to the law could no longer be regarded *as the basis of salvation* (cf. Gal. 2:15), but for Paul the law remained *the authoritative guide to Christian living*...Broadly speaking, this was the conclusion reached by the Jerusalem council.'[640]

The Law of Moses is 'the authoritative guide to Christian living.' That's what God intended it to be (Dt. 4:5-8; Rom. 3:31), but if Paul didn't nullify the Law, who did? The nullification of the Law is the heretical teaching of the Roman Catholic Church, not the New Testament, and Protestants have followed in this heresy without questioning it. The Roman Catholic Church, around 100 AD,[641] threw out God's holy Sabbath and castigated the Law 'as Jewish,' and with their diabolical attitude toward 'the Jews,' gave birth to the oxymoron *Christian anti-Semitism*.

The nullification of the Law has done much to drive a wedge between Christians and Jews. It's not of God, but of Satan, as Daniel writes:

> 'And he shall speak pompous words against the Most High and shall *oppress the saints* of the Most High and think *to change times and laws*. Then the *saints* shall be given into his hand for a time and times and half a time.' (Dan. 7:25)

To *change the times* speaks of the observance of God's holy times (the Sabbath and Passover, etc; Lev. 23). The *laws* speak of the Law. Obviously, the nullification of the Law by the Catholic Church did not take God by surprise. It's the Catholic Church that has oppressed the saints with its persecutions of Christians, and also, its false doctrines and pagan ceremonies that came in 'to replace the Law.' It's unfortunate that the Reformers continued to follow this heresy of the Catholic Church (i.e. 'the Law has been done away with'), which came from Satan.

One of the places that the Church points to, to prove their theological position on the Law being annulled, is Mt. 5:17-18. The Lord Yeshua says that He came to *fulfill* the Law and that it wouldn't depart 'until all is *fulfilled:*'

---

[638]  Williams, *Acts*, p. 260.

[639]  Ibid., p. 261.

[640]  Ibid.

[641]  Bacchiocchi, *From Sabbath To Sunday*, pp. 152-157, 159-207, 211-212.

> <sup>17</sup>'Do not think that I came to abolish the Law or the Pro-
> phets. I did not come to abolish, but to *fulfill*.'

> <sup>18</sup>'For truly I say to you, until Heaven and Earth pass
> away, not the smallest letter or stroke shall pass from the
> Law until all is *fulfilled*.' (Mt. 5:17-18)

The Church explains that the meaning of *fulfill* is that Jesus did away with
the Law by His sacrifice and established 'love' as the criteria for His
Kingdom. This juxtaposes Law and love, or as many say, Law and Grace.
There is even Scripture that would seem, at first glance, to support their
interpretation:

> 'Love does no wrong to a neighbor. Therefore, love is the
> *fulfillment* of the Law.' (Rom. 13:10)

> 'Bear one another's burdens and thereby *fulfill* the law of
> Christ.' (Gal. 6:2)

Was Paul showing us 'a new way' when he spoke of *fulfill*? Hardly. To
*summarize* the commandments of God into a single concept was nothing
new to the Jewish people, of whom Paul was one all his life (Rom. 11:1).
In the Talmud (*Makot* 23b-24a) there are a number of such summaries
from the Scriptures:

> "Rabbi Simlai said, 'Six hundred and thirteen command-
> ments were given to Moses'" (a traditional 'count' of the
> number of commandments in the Law).

> "David came and reduced them to eleven (Psalm 15)."

> "Then Isaiah reduced them to six (Is. 33:15-16), Micah to
> three (Micah 6:8), and Isaiah...to two, as it is said, 'Keep
> judgment and do righteousness' (Is. 66:1)."

> "Then Amos reduced them to one, 'Seek Me and live'
> (Amos 5:4). Or one could say Habakkuk: 'the righteous
> shall live by his faith' (Hab. 2:4)."<sup>642</sup>

These reductions, or conceptual summaries of the Law of Moses, in no
way do away with any of the other commandments. They present a rally-
ing point around which the Jewish people can focus themselves. Paul does
the same thing with Romans 13:10 and Galatians 6:2.

In a well known rabbinic story that goes back a generation before Yeshua,
it's said that,

> "A pagan came before Shammai and said to him, 'Make

---

<sup>642</sup> Stern, *Jewish New Testament Commentary*, p. 96.

me a proselyte, but on condition that you teach me the
entire Torah while I am standing on one foot!' Shammai
drove him off with the builder's measuring rod, which he
had in his hand. When he appeared before Hillel, he told
him, 'What is hateful to you, do not do to your neighbor.
*That is the whole Torah.* The rest is commentary.' Now,
go and 'learn it!'"[643]

Obviously, neither Simlai or Hillel would have thought that he was 'doing
away with the Law' by summarizing it. Can 'fulfill' then, in Mt. 5:17, be
biblically interpreted to mean that 'Jesus fulfilled the Law' (so Christians
don't have to keep it), especially when Yeshua has just stated, in the very
same breath of Mt. 5:17, that He *hadn't* come '*to abolish* the Law'?

In Mt. 5:18, Yeshua again speaks of *fulfill*, this time in relation to the Law
remaining until 'all is fulfilled.' Here, too, the Church takes the position
that 'all was fulfilled' at the crucifixion. That the work of salvation that
Yeshua came to do, the giving of His life in sacrifice for all mankind, was
accomplished at the crucifixion, is above argument. In His death we find
life. In His death we have forgiveness of sins and are able to die to self
and attain a new nature — His. In His death we have access to the Spirit of
God. *All was fulfilled* concerning the *redemption* of Israel, but did that redemption mean that the Law was no longer valid?

Further establishing Yeshua's thoughts on the Law, in verse 18, He speaks
of the Heavens and the Earth departing *first*, before any *letter* of the Law
is nullified. As the Heavens and the Earth are still with us, and won't be
gone until the Day of Judgment, it's reasonable to say that *His view* of the
Law for us *today* is established. The need for the Law of Moses will no
longer be necessary after Judgment Day, when we become like He is now,
for then the Law will truly be written on our hearts (Jer. 31:33). The critical point, of believers in Yeshua walking in all the Law that applies to
them, is presented by Him in the very next verse:

> '*Whoever* then breaks one of the *least* of these command-
> ments, and teaches others to do the same, shall be called
> *least in the Kingdom of Heaven*, but whoever keeps and
> teaches them, he shall be called great in the Kingdom of
> Heaven.' (Mt. 5:19)

The Kingdom of Heaven didn't officially begin until *after* the sacrifice
and resurrection of Messiah Yeshua. His reference to it in Mt. 5:19 can
only mean that *in His Kingdom* the Law is still valid. In Yeshua's Kingdom where He is King, those who break the *least* of the commandments

---

[643] Ibid., p. 33. From the Talmud, *Shabat* 31a.

will be called *least* in His Kingdom. Conversely, those who keep the least of the commandments of the Law will be called great in the Kingdom of Yeshua. The choice is ours to make. This understanding of the validity of the Law for us today is from our Lord Himself.

The Church's interpretation of Matthew 5:17-19 is wrong, as well as their theology that the Law of Moses has been done away with. Here are five points that explain what Yeshua meant when He said that He came *to fulfill the Law:*

1. The most basic and elementary understanding of what *fulfill* means, which is also the most profound, is simply that Yeshua was referring to all the places in the Old Testament which spoke of a coming Messiah who would suffer and die for Israel — and there He was!

   a. After His resurrection, Yeshua expressly spoke of this *fulfillment* in Luke 24:44: 'These are My words that I spoke to you while I was still with you; that *everything written about Me* in the Torah, the Prophets and the Psalms must be *fulfilled*' (see also Luke 24:25-27, 45-49; Jn. 1:45; 5:39; Acts 3:18, 22-26; 4:2, 33; 13:29, 32, 38-39).

   b. *Fulfill* speaks of Yeshua satisfying the prophecies in the *Tanach* about a suffering Messiah. This would include prophecies concerning a Messiah who would be born in Bethlehem and beaten on the cheek with a rod (Mic. 5:1-2), and who would suffer and die an atoning death for Israel (Is. 53:1-12; Zech. 12:10; 13:1).

   c. Yeshua also *fulfilled* the words in the Prophets that spoke of His ministry of healing (Is. 35) and His ministry of teaching about the Kingdom of God (Is. 55:3; 56:5; 60:19; 61:7-8; Jer. 32:40).

   d. Yeshua came to *fulfill* the promise of God to Adam and Eve, that the Seed of the woman would crush the head of the Snake (Gen. 3:15). The Seed of the woman is Messiah Yeshua and His sacrifice fulfills this prophecy.

   e. Conceptually, Yeshua's use of *fulfill* has nothing to do with the nullification of the Law, but with the completing of what the Law pointed to — the Messiah of Israel (Gen. 3:15: 49:10; Dt. 18:18).

2. *Fulfill* also means that Yeshua presented Himself as the fulfillment of the pictures of the Messiah, which are called types and shadows.

   a. Yeshua *fulfilled* what the Passover lamb pointed to (Him). The First Passover paves the way for Yeshua to be the Passover Lamb of the Second Passover. The second Passover parallels the first: freedom from Egyptian slavery spoke of freedom from the Kingdom of Darkness (Col. 1:13-14; 1st Pet. 2:9).

    b. Yeshua's fulfillment of the Passover does not do away with the commandment to celebrate God's Passover (Ex. 12:14; 1st Cor. 5:6-8; Rev. 5:1-14). On the contrary, the meaning of the First Passover is now infinitely amplified. This concept also applies to all the other Feasts of Israel, as well as to the 7th day Sabbath.

3. Another area of *fulfill* is Yeshua's holy and sinless life. He fulfilled all the holy and righteous demands of God's Torah, and as such, became the quintessential Israeli, the Example *par excellence* of what it means to be a true Son of Israel, exemplifying what circumcision in the flesh means (Dt. 10:16; 30:6), full and unreserved submission to God. He's the model that every believer strives to emulate—fully consecrated to His Father, *keeping the Law from His heart* (Psalm 40:7-8). Should Christians strive for anything less? (1st Cor. 11:1; 1st John 2:4-6; 3:1-5)

4. Yeshua's sacrifice *fulfills* Israel's need to not only be forgiven of her sins, but to also be given a new nature (His nature). This is promised to Israel by God through His servants, Moses, Jeremiah and Ezekiel.

    a. Yeshua's sacrifice didn't nullify the Law, on the contrary, it put into motion God's ability to *fulfill* His word to Israel that He would actually *put His Law in her heart*, cause her to walk in His commandments and place His Spirit within her in order for her to keep His Law from a heart of love (Dt. 30:6; Jer. 31:31-34; Ezk. 36:24-26; Joel 2:28-29). How, then, could the New Testament do away with the Law of God? It would be the very opposite of what Yahveh had said about the New Covenant (Jer. 31:31-34).

    b. Yeshua's sacrifice for our sins didn't cancel the Law, it canceled our sin indebtedness (Col. 2:14) and changed our nature to walk in the Law's holy ways (Rom. 6–8), just as Yeshua walked (Jer. 31:33; 2nd Cor. 5:21; 1st Pet. 1:20-24).

5. *Fulfill* also speaks of Yeshua's death making an opening for the Gentiles to come into the New Covenant (Is. 42:6; 49:6). God's extending of the New Covenant to the Gentiles in no way negates His Law, nor His Word to Israel and Judah (Rom. 11:25-29).

In places where *love* is said to fulfill the Law, like Rom. 13:10, love is seen as the ultimate or central motivation for relationship, either with God or Man, but this cannot mean that the Law of Moses is annulled because *the core of the Law* is love of God (Deut. 6:4-5) and love of man (Lev. 19:18). All the other commandments of the Law are *God's way* of

*defining* what love of God and love of man is. The two great commandments of the Law are seen by the Lord Yeshua as the foundation, or the
two branches from which all the other commandments hang from:

> 'On these two commandments hang *all the Law* and the
> Prophets.' (Mt. 22:40)

In other words, every commandment, statute and ordinance, etc., has its
reason for existence in either the love of God or Man. If God were a tree
made up of two branches full of fruit on each branch, the names of the two
branches would be 'love of God' and 'love of man.' The *fruit* on the
branches would be all the commandments, for they tell us **how** *God* wants
us to love Him and man.

For the Church to juxtapose *love* against God's Law is an artificial theological perversion because the essence of the Law is love (Dt. 6:4-5; Lev.
19:18). The Law of Moses is a written reflection of God and His holy
character. The Law is God's holy Word to Israel as to what is sin and
what is pleasing to Him. The only way that we know another's will is by
his word. If a father tells his son to take out the garbage, the son knows
the will of his father by his words. Israel, both Gentile and Jew, knows the
will of her God by His Words, the commandments. Yeshua saying, 'love
one another as I have loved you' (Jn. 13:34) added a divine reality to the
commandment to love our neighbor as ourself (Lev. 19:18). God loved
His creation *as a man*, and now, the Apostles were to love one another as
they had been loved by the Father and the Son (Jn. 14:5-11).

The Law remains God's way of specifically showing us what is right and
what is wrong in His eyes. Torah has not been 'done away with.' It remains the Standard of Holiness (as Yeshua defines it), and will remain
with us until there are no more Heavens and Earth as we know them.

Witherington saw the four rules as a unit on sacrificial idolatry, but failed
to grasp the theological significance of Acts 15:20-21. He said that the
rules were given so that the Jews outside of Israel wouldn't be offended
by Gentiles continuing to practice idolatry 'by going to pagan feasts.'[644]
Yet, good church attendance didn't negate sacrificing to other gods and
laying with cult harlots, as Paul testifies to (1st Cor. 10; 2nd Cor. 6).

Witherington also states that the rules were for 'fellowship'[645] (and that it
was 'important to James,'[646] as a witness to non-believing Jews, that the
Gentiles were not practicing sacrificial idolatry any longer). How much of

---

[644] Witherington, *The Acts of the Apostles*, p. 463.

[645] Ibid., p. 439: 'so that both groups may be included in God's people on equal
footing, *fellowship* may continue, and the church remain one.'

[646] Ibid., p. 463.

a witness it was to non-believing Jews is debatable, but fellowship can't be the reason for the rules, as he himself states.[647] Because of his anti-Law theology he also confuses the Judaizers with Peter, Paul and James by saying that the Judaizers 'wanted Gentile Christians to be Torah observant.'[648] *The Jewish Apostles wanted* the Gentiles to be Torah-observant! That's what Acts 15:20-21 is all about. The Judaizers wanted the Gentiles to (artificially) become Jews and keep the Law (symbolized in circumcision) *in order to be saved.*

Hegg, following Witherington, sees the rules as a 'prohibition of idol worship in the pagan temple.'[649] He, too, wrongly thinks the rules were for table fellowship between the two groups, and for the prevention of 'accusations of idolatry' in the Jewish community. He believes that *strangled* also means a dietary restriction (i.e. no eating meat from an animal that had been strangled because of the blood being in it).[650] Clearly, however, James didn't give the rules for fellowship, non-believing Jewish approval, or as food regulations. Hegg does, though, correctly state that the Gentile was to learn and keep the Law of Moses.[651]

Acts 15 deals with the issue of salvation, not table fellowship. The four rules revolve around sacrificial-sexual idolatry. They were given as a filter to the Gentile so that his faith in Jesus could be seen as biblically genuine.

Traditional Christian scholarship, in trying to interpret Acts 15:20-21, exposes their flawed theological presupposition against the Law of Moses. Devoid of Torah, and actually anti-Law, these scholars, commentators and translators ingeniously invent their own seemingly biblical interpretations for passages in the New Testament that relate to the Law, and their explanations are backed up by all the 'machinery of scholarship' and two millennia of Christian interpretation. When understood from the Hebraic Perspective, though, their theological delusion is glaringly apparent.

The Church assigns the four rules to table fellowship and says that these were the *only rules* that a Gentile had to keep,[652] but this places the Gentile outside the Torah-observant *believing* Jewish community. The theological

---

[647] Ibid., p. 465. See also p. 220f., above.

[648] Ibid., pp. 647-648.

[649] Hegg, *The Letter Writer*, p. 269.

[650] Ibid., p. 281: Hegg writes of 'acceptance of Gentiles within the Torah community,' which speaks of table fellowship with Jewish believers and approval from the non-believing Jewish community. Also, p. 277 (for not eating strangled meat with blood in it).

[651] Ibid., pp. 73, 83, 288-290.

[652] Marshall, *Acts*, pp. 242-243.

nightmare this presents was seen at the picnic table.

The interpretation of 'table fellowship' separates the Gentile from the Jewish believer (and the traditional Jew)[653] by placing him in a different category in relationship to God and sin. What the Messiah has brought together, the Church has cut asunder. Table fellowship was not what Yakov had in mind when he gave the four rules, as important a concept as that is.

> 'For I have not shunned to declare to you the whole counsel of God. Therefore, take heed to yourselves and to all the flock among which the Holy Spirit has made you overseers, to shepherd the assembly of God, which He purchased with His own blood. For I know this, that after my departure, savage wolves will come in among you, not sparing the Flock. Also, *from among yourselves* men will rise up, speaking perverse things, to draw away the disciples after themselves. Therefore, watch and remember that for three years I did not cease to warn everyone night and day, with tears.' (Acts 20:27-31)

---

[653] If the Church had been walking in the Law all these centuries, they would have truly seen the Jewish people as their relatives, and not as their enemies ('Christ killers!'). Persecution of the Jews would never have happened 'in the Name of Jesus' and the Jewish people would have seen Gentiles both loving them and keeping the Law of Moses. This would have led them into finding out more about Jesus as their Messiah.

Tragically, the very opposite has happened. More Jews have been persecuted in the 'name of Jesus' than all other 'names' combined. Jews have been murdered, infants literally ripped out of the arms of their screaming mothers, and synagogues burned to the ground *with the Jewish people of the town inside them*...all in the name of Jesus. Is it any wonder that the name of Jesus is a curse word in the Jewish community? The history of the Church toward the Jewish people has been demonically cruel and devoid of God's love.

If you're not familiar with the persecution of the Jewish people by the Church over the last 19 centuries you might want to read Max Dimont's, *God, Jews and History*, or any Jewish history book, starting from the time after Jesus.

# Noah and Acts 15:20

F. F. Bruce writes that Yakov's four rules came from the Noahide laws.[654] This interpretation also seeks to circumvent the fact that the rules come from the Law, but interesting questions and problems arise from this perspective on Acts 15:20. First, though, what are 'Noah's laws' for the Gentiles? The Gentiles were required to be,

1. 'practicing justice and
2. abstaining from blasphemy,
3. idolatry,
4. adultery,
5. bloodshed,
6. robbery and
7. eating flesh torn from a live animal' (and 'also not to drink blood taken from a *live* animal.' The last part was added at a later date.)[655]

All four rules of Yakov could conceivably fall under Noah's third category of idolatry: eat no meat at the idolatrous sacrifice, don't practice cult harlotry, keep away from strangled animal sacrifices and don't drink the blood of a sacrifice. Yet, the Noahide people don't see all of Yakov's rules as pertaining to idolatry. Also, no law of Noah specifically speaks of any of Yakov's rules.

If Yakov's first rule on not eating sacrificial meat was placed under idolatry (#3), and *pornay'ah* was seen as adultery (#4), and *blood* was seen as murder (#5), there's still no place for *strangled*.[656] In all this, only three of Noah's seven laws have been touched, but this is how Bruce and others might align Yakov's rules with Noah. Of course, Yakov's rule on *blood* cannot be equated with murder, and so this negates it from being Noah's 'murder' (#5), and Yakov's rule on *pornay'ah* doesn't mean adultery (#4).

Some might suggest that *strangled* from Acts 15:20 be placed in #7, but the Rabbis created #7 to prohibit the Gentile from literally severing a limb from a *living* animal and eating it raw. *Strangled* doesn't fit here.

The added comment to #7 (not to drink the blood from a *live* animal) referred not to drinking it at a pagan sacrifice, nor to eating blood in half-cooked meat, but of eating the blood in the severed limb of a *living animal* (along with the raw meat). Today, though, it seems that the Rabbis inter-

---

[654] Bruce, *The Book of the Acts*, pp. 295-296.

[655] Stern, *Jewish New Testament Commentary*, p. 278. The Noahide laws are listed in the Talmud, *Sanhedrin* 56a–60a.

[656] Some might try to place *strangled* in #3 (idolatry), but those who espouse the Noahide laws, like Bruce, see it as a dietary regulation.

pret it to mean not drinking or eating blood, which can be seen as both a dietary regulation and a prohibition against idolatry.[657]

Isn't it strange that Yakov would *seem* to use only three of Noah's seven categories for the Gentiles? The Rabbis say that 'a righteous Gentile' was to do *all* of Noah's laws, but Yakov never mentions justice (#1), blasphemy (#2), or robbery (#6). If the four rules were taken from the Noahide laws, why didn't Yakov just give the Gentles *all* the Noahide laws? Also problematic for those who think that the rules came from Noah is the fact that the name of Moses is mentioned in Acts 15:21, not Noah's.

People who follow the Noahide laws say that all Gentiles should observe them. Not that the laws of Noah are bad, but this can't be justified from Acts 15:20 or anywhere else in the New Testament.[658] One has to really *stretch* Yakov's four rules into being *taken* from the Noahide laws, even under a false interpretation.

Unfortunately, it's not possible to give Scripture cites where God gave the seven laws to Noah for the Gentiles (except for murder and not eating 'live flesh' with its blood; Gen. 9:4-6), *because they come from the Talmud*. The idea that God gave these laws to Noah, and therefore, to the Gentiles, so some could be righteous and 'go to Heaven,' *comes from the Rabbis*.

Nowhere in Scripture are the seven Noahide laws seen as being given to Noah in the same way that Yahveh gave the Law to Moses for Israel. It's ironic, though, that the laws Noah did know, clean and unclean animals, are *not* part of the *rabbinic* Noahide laws,[659] and Noah was a Gentile!

What is the theological purpose of F. F. Bruce and all those who espouse

---

[657] JAHG–USA (Jews and Hasidic Gentiles–United to Save America) *The Noahide Laws* at http://www.noahide.com/lawslist.htm. 'Hasidic Gentiles' is a term for Gentiles who keep the Noahide laws.

[658] Gentiles who follow the Noahide laws are deceived into believing that it's *all* a Gentile needs to do for eternal life. These Gentiles don't believe in Jesus as their Savior. They're called *Bnei Noach* (Sons of Noah). This position, while rabbinic and false, found a staunch adherent in Noahide leader Vendyl Jones, a former Baptist minister whom many label as an apostate. Having personally met Mr. Jones in Jerusalem in 2005, I can attest to his apostasy. Among other things, he denies both the deity and the atoning work of Yeshua, and he actively seeks to destroy a believer's faith in Messiah Yeshua.

Messiah Yeshua is *God the Son* (http://SeedofAbraham.net/yeshua.html), but this is considered blasphemy and idolatry by the Rabbis. Anyone who believes in the biblical Jesus must not even consider becoming a so-called *Bnei Noach*. See more on the deity of Yeshua in the article, *Yeshua—His Deity and Sonship* at http://SeedofAbraham.net/Yeshua-His_Deity_and_Sonship.html.

[659] Gen. 7:2, 8; 8:20.

Yakov's rules as coming from the so-called Noahide laws? Those that place the rules of Yakov within the framework of the Noahide laws are saying that God gave certain rules for the Gentile, through Noah, *before* the Law was given to Israel at Mt. Sinai. Hence, Yakov was only relating to the Gentile believers what they should be observing. Theologically for Bruce, this means that the rules *didn't come from the Law*, and so, Church theology, that the Law isn't for the Christian, is intact. This interpretation, though, is just another ingenious attempt at explaining Acts 15:20 so that the Gentile doesn't have to keep the Law of Moses.

When one starts out from a false premise (that the Law is not for the Gentile or that it's no longer valid) and tries 'to fit Scripture into it' (Acts 15:20), the result is heretical teaching. Aside from the problems that have been seen with the four rules of Yakov trying to fit into the Noahide laws, this is just table fellowship with a different twist. The same theological problems arise, though: there would be two totally different faith communities; one for the Jew (who kept the Law), and the other for the Gentile (who didn't have to keep the Law). Also, 'law is still law.' If the Gentile is free from the Law, how can Bruce say that Gentiles are to keep some of, or all of, the *laws* of Noah? Of course, the scene at the picnic table is still a mess: 'Chitlins and gravy, anyone?!'

Although Edersheim speaks of the Noahide laws being in force at the time of James,[660] both Witherington and Hegg prove that they didn't exist in the days of the Apostles.[661] This latter view places a Noahide interpretation of Acts 15:20 outside the realm of possibility. Some might say that Yakov gave it to the Gentile believers first, before the Rabbis thought it up and began giving it to the Gentiles, but it's hard to believe that the Rabbis would *follow* James the Jewish-Christian in this. Witherington says that there is no Jewish background or 'parallel to the enumerating of these four items together.'[662] Also, neither James in his canonical letter in the New Testament, nor Paul, ever speak of Noah, let alone any Noahide laws.

If properly interpreted, the four rules of James can only be placed into one Noahide law, idolatry. If not properly interpreted, as Noahide people teach, the rules may be squeezed into three or four Noahide laws.

Although this concept finds 'a way around' the Law of Moses as the origin of the rules, it doesn't account for the rules being given so as not to of-

---

[660] Edersheim, *The Life and Times of Jesus The Messiah*, p. 1014.

[661] Witherington, *The Acts of the Apostles*, p. 464, note 428: 'There is no real evidence that these seven were already viewed in NT times.' Hegg, *The Letter Writer*, pp. 266-268 and note 570. Nothing 'even remotely akin' to Noahide Law 'is found in the…Mishnah' (about 300 BC–200 AD).

[662] Witherington, *The Acts of the Apostles*, p. 465, note 429.

fend the believing Jews. The rules cannot rightly be assigned to table fellowship as is evident from the picnic table fiasco, and even though Noah knew clean from unclean animals, there are no rules about clean and unclean animals in the Noahide laws. If one wanted to believe that the seven rules of Noah were for the Gentile believers, it still wouldn't deal with the problem of offending the Jewish believers who ate only clean meat, not to mention their keeping of the Sabbath and the Feast days.

Also a problem with the Noahide position is that Noah's laws are still *law*. Even if just a *few* were given to the Gentile, it would place the Gentile 'under law' and in a separate and certainly unequal category with his Jewish counterpart. This would make the Gentile 'a second class citizen,' which is something God never intended.

Someone could now reject the view that the rules were ceremonial, realizing that the four rules prohibit sacrificial-sexual *idolatry*. This, he would say, takes them out of the ceremonial realm of the Law and places them in the moral realm (the worship of another god). Therefore, the Law isn't for the Gentile because the four rules are like any other moral laws that come into the New from the Old. The problems with this position is that sacrifice is generally acknowledged as ceremonial. Also, as we've seen, Gentiles were *already* going to the synagogues to learn the Law (Acts 15:21). The four rules were the most important rules that the Gentile needed to know in order for his faith in Yeshua to be seen as genuine. He would learn the rest of the laws as he went to the synagogue every Sabbath. Whether the issue is moral or ceremonial is debatable, but Acts 15:21 reveals that the Law is for every believer.

God's rules are either for both Jew and Gentile or they're for neither. Either the Sabbath is still holy or it's not, but it cannot be holy for the Jewish believer,[663] while 'just another day' for the Gentile. The Body of Christ is one Flock called Israel, but the Church has built an heretical wall of separation teaching its 'Law-free Gospel.' Yet, the Lord has always had His righteous remnant in Israel (1st Kings 19:1-18; Rom. 11:1-32). Jews and Gentiles that believe in Yeshua are part of that righteous remnant. There aren't two different sets of laws for them. As the Apostle Paul said,

> 'Do we then make void the Law through faith? Certainly not! On the contrary, we *establish* the Law.' (Rom. 3:31)

---

[663] Acts 21:20; Rom. 7:12; 1st Cor. 7:19; Rev. 1:10.

# Sacrificial-Sexual Idolatry

Ben Witherington III writes that it's 'no exaggeration to say that Acts 15 is the most crucial chapter in the whole book.'[664] It certainly is, but not only because the Gentile didn't have to be circumcised and keep the Law for salvation, as significant as that concept is. With a proper biblical interpretation of verses 20-21, the Law of Moses is validated and authorized for every Gentile (and Jewish) believer today.

Sacrificial-sexual idolatry was the satanic scourge of the ancient world and the way of life for the Gentile. Yakov dealt with the major issue first. Eighteen years after the resurrection[665] the assembly at Antioch sent Paul and Barnabas to Jerusalem because of the conflict over what constituted Gentile salvation (Acts 15:1-4).

The Apostles and other Jewish believers assembled and listened to the arguments presented. After 'much dispute,' or arguing (Acts 15:7), Peter stood up and told his story about how the *first* Gentile, Cornelius, had been saved (Acts 10:1–11:18). He said that the Gentiles had received salvation in the same way as the Jews had, 'through the grace of the Lord Yeshua the Messiah' (15:11). Everyone was silent. The Holy Spirit had spoken through Peter. The rabbinic concept of keeping the Law for salvation was dealt the death blow it deserved. God had never intended the Law to be used as a vehicle for eternal life (Acts 15:10; Rom. 3:31; 8:3-4).

Then Yakov, the literal half brother of Yeshua, arose and affirmed what Peter had said, adding his own insight (Acts 15:13-18). God was raising up the fallen 'Tabernacle of David' (the Kingdom of David that had laid in ruins for more than 600 years), through His/his Son, and was inviting the Gentiles to be a part of it (Is. 42:6; 49:6; Amos 9:11).

As Prince of the Council, Yakov sealed the decision (Acts 15:19) and issued the four rules (v. 20). Why the four rules? Why didn't he just declare that the Gentiles were saved by faith in Messiah Yeshua without needing to become circumcised, and let it go at that?

Yakov was concerned that Gentile believers might think that they could continue to practice sacrificial pagan rites *along with* 'faith in Jesus.' This would seriously affect their salvation. The four rules he presented to the Gentiles were the essence of idolatrous temple practices. Yakov exercised his judicial acumen and warned the Gentiles about something that would jeopardize their very salvation. Yakov's concern was valid. The Apostle Paul had to deal with sacrificial-sexual idolatry among some of his Gentile believers in Corinth (1st Cor. 6:19-20; 10:21) as well as in other cities,[666]

---

[664] Witherington, *The Acts of the Apostles*, p. 439.

[665] See p. 223, note 629 for the time frame.

[666] Gal. 5:19; Eph. 5:3; Col. 3:5; 1st Thess. 4:3.

and the risen Messiah had to rebuke two of the seven assemblies in Revelation for practicing it as well (2:14, 20).

Gentile *continuance* in sacrificial-sexual idolatry was the reason Yakov issued the four rules. It had nothing to do with table fellowship. As a Jew he knew the history of ancient Israel, as well as the past and current conditions in the pagan world. He also knew that the Father desired for His people to be totally devoted to Him through Yeshua. If Gentiles continued worshiping other gods, along with belief in Yeshua, it would cost them their eternal life. The four rules were a salvation issue for the Gentiles, the very reason the Council of Acts 15 was convened.

Israel committed cult prostitution with the women of Moab (Num. 25), yet they 'still believed' in Yahveh, even after they had joined themselves to, and become 'one' with, Baal Peor through the sacrifices and orgies. It's this walking in both the Camp of God and the Camp of Satan that Yakov addressed in Acts 15:20. In a very real sense, Yakov's ruling took care of 'the two *pluses:*' He said,

> Jesus *plus* the Law couldn't earn salvation, and
>
> Jesus *plus* Zeus wouldn't be tolerated.

The first three commandments of the Ten Commandments address idolatry. Other commandments reveal the punishment. *Unger's* writes:

> 'The individual offender was devoted to destruction (Ex. 22:20); his nearest relatives were not only bound to denounce him and deliver him up to punishment (Dt. 13:2-10), but their hands were to strike the first blow when, on the evidence of at least two witnesses, he would be stoned (Dt. 17:2-5). To attempt to seduce others to false worship was a crime of equal enormity (Deut. 13:6-10).'[667]

Sacrificial-sexual *idolatry* was Yakov's concern when he issued the four rules to the Gentiles. God addressed ancient Israel in a similar vein when He took her out of the darkness of Egypt. The eating of unclean meat, as sinful as that is, was not the primary thing that made the Gentile defiled in the eyes of the Jewish people. In Acts 10:28, Peter told Cornelius and the Gentiles gathered in his house, 'You yourselves know how *unlawful* it is for a man who is a Jew *to associate* with a Gentile or to visit him.'[668]

---

[667] Unger, *Unger's Bible Dictionary*, p. 515.

[668] It was this way from the beginning. Joshua said to Israel, 'Be strong then, to keep and to do all that is written in the Book of the Law of Moses so that you may not turn aside from it to the right hand or to the left, so that you will *not associate* with these nations, these which remain among you, or mention the

Peter spoke of the mere association with Gentiles as being off-limits. This was not just a rabbinic tradition. It was Gentile pagan 'worship' that defiled the soul of the Gentile. This made them spiritually unclean and would continue to defile believing Gentiles if they practiced it, even if they said that they 'believed in Jesus.' Witherington writes,

> "Jews believed that the chief source of Gentile impurity was their contact with 'the defilement of idols,' not their contact with non-kosher food."[669]

The four rules were to be observed immediately by the Gentiles, in response to salvation, not for table fellowship with Jewish believers. Was Gentile faith in Messiah Yeshua genuine? These rules would reveal that at a very basic and crucial level.

Most of the Gentiles coming into the Kingdom of Yeshua didn't have any idea who the God of Israel was and what He required. Where would they find out that worshiping other gods was wrong? Where would they find out how God wanted them to walk out their new-found faith? *This* is where the synagogue and the Law of Moses come in. Acts 15:21 assumes that the Gentile believer was to live a lifestyle of Torah so that he could truly be one with the House of Israel[670] *and* not offend his believing Jewish brother—nor the God-Man who died for him.

There's a parallel with the Hebrews entering the Promised Land and the Gentiles entering the Promised One. It has to do with worshiping God and God alone. This was Yakov's concern in giving the four rules. In the Ten Commandments it's written, 'You must have no other gods beside Me' (Dt. 5:7; see also Ex. 20:3; 22:20).

In Dt. 12, Yahveh begins to define what it means not to have any other gods. Among other things, Israel wasn't to have anything to do with pagan altars, other than to destroy them (vv. 2-3), and they weren't to eat the blood of any sacrifice (vv. 16, 23). In speaking of the pagan altars and the eating of blood, conceptually, the three other rules can be placed right alongside them (the eating of the meat sacrificed to the god at the altar, the strangling of a sacrifice and cult prostitution). All four rules would be acted out around a pagan altar.[671]

---

name of their gods or make anyone swear by them or serve them or bow down to them, but you are to cling to Yahveh your God, as you have done to this day' (Joshua 23:6-8; see also Dt. 7:3; Ezra 9:12–10:4f.).

[669] Witherington, *The Acts of the Apostles*, p. 462.

[670] The Gentile believer is grafted into Israel (Rom. 11:13-31) and part of the Commonwealth of Israel (Eph. 2:11-22; see also p. 189, notes 538-539.)

[671] See p. 173f., where the three major rules are seen before Deuteronomy.

When Yahveh was leading His people Israel into the Promised Land He wanted them to know what would jeopardize their covenantal relationship with Him. God was doing the same thing for the Gentiles through Yakov. This is further seen even to the extent in how Yahveh closes Deut. 12 and how Yakov closes his letter to the Gentiles. In Dt. 12:28, Moses says,

> 'Be careful to listen to all these words which I command you so that it may be well with you and your sons after you forever, *for you will be doing what is good and right in the sight of Yahveh your God.*'

In his letter to the Gentiles, Yakov writes,

> 'that you abstain from things sacrificed to idols and from blood and from things strangled and from cult harlotry. *If you keep yourselves free from such things you will do well!* Shalom to you!' (Peace to you! Acts 15:29)

The parallel between Dt. 12 and Acts 15:29 is seen in both what is commanded about sacrificial idolatry and in the closing, 'that it would be well' with each group to obey the commandments. Both Moses and Yakov were warning the people what would *not* be tolerated. Did it mean that God wasn't going to give any more commandments to Israel after Dt. 12? Or that Dt. 12 was all the commandments that God had for them? Hardly. Acts 15:20 is not the last of the commandments for the Gentile, either.

Deuteronomy 12 is the first place in Deuteronomy where Yahveh explains or defines in a greater way His commandment not to have any other gods except Him.[672] This is the reason why Yakov gave his ruling. The Gentiles were well known for having many gods and goddesses in their pantheon and the *inclusion* of Jesus *would have posed no problem for many of them.* This was seen at Corinth, Pergamos and Thyatira. That's why these four rules were singled out. They had to be obeyed immediately. The rest of God's rules would be learned later. With the warning of Yakov, the Gentiles would understand that their faith must be in Yeshua and in Him alone. *ISBE* describes the pagan mindset of the Gentile *believer:*

---

[672] There's mention of breaking down altars (Dt. 7:5), an admonition not to forget Yahveh by bowing down and following other gods (Dt. 8:19), and a warning against being enticed to turn away from Yahveh (Dt. 11:16), coming before Dt. 12, but Dt. 12 begins the formal teaching of what it means to follow Yahveh, in relation to other gods, as well as how to observe His other commandments. Before Dt. 12 God speaks of commandments, statutes, judgments and ordinances, preparing Israel to receive His Instruction, but He doesn't fully *explain* what His commandments, statutes, judgments and ordinances are. Of course, in Dt. 5 there are the Ten Commandments, where the first three speak of not worshiping any other gods, but in Dt. 12ff., it's more fully addressed.

They 'would gladly have accepted Christ along with
Mithra and Isis and Serapis...*The same person* might be
initiated into the mysteries of half a dozen pagan divini-
ties and also be a priest of two or more gods. Some had
not the slightest objection to worshiping Christ along with
Mithra, Isis and Adonis.'[673]

Yakov knew the pagan mindset and that Yeshua could breach no rivals.
With knowledge of God's standard comes His wisdom and discernment as
to what is pleasing to Him and what is sin (Dt. 4:5-8; Rom. 7:7, 12, 14; 1st
John 3:1-5). When God's wisdom is lacking, all sorts of heresies can enter
(e.g. 'the Law is abolished; the rules were given as a concession to Jewish
sensitivities;' Sunday assembly instead of Sabbath holiness, etc.).

Without a standard from God in these areas the way is open for pagan
holy days and pagan ways to be 'baptized in the Name of Jesus,' with
everyone doing what *appears* to be right in his own eyes.[674] The Church
has sanctified pagan holy days *in opposition* to the holy days of God! Baptizing a pagan celebration to an idol (e.g. Easter) doesn't give it biblical
legitimacy, but it does make for a tradition of the Church that nullifies
God's Word. Moses warned Israel about this kind of thing:

> "*Be careful to obey all these words* that I command you
> today so that it may go well with you and with your sons
> after you forever because you will be doing *what is good
> and right in the sight of Yahveh your God.* When Yahveh
> your God has cut off before you the nations whom you
> are about to enter to dispossess them, when you have dis-
> possessed them and live in their land, *take care that you
> are not snared into imitating them* after they have been
> destroyed before you. Do not inquire concerning their
> gods saying, '*How did these nations worship their gods? I
> will also do the same.*' **You must not do the same for
> Yahveh your God** because every abhorrent thing that
> Yahveh hates they have done for their gods. They even
> burn their sons and daughters in the fire to their gods. *You
> must diligently observe everything that I command you.
> Do not add to it or take anything away from it.*" (Deut.
> 12:28-32)

What has the Church done in 'baptizing' pagan Sunday, Easter, Thanks-

---

[673] Bromiley, *The International Standard Bible Encyclopedia*, vol. four, p. 214.

[674] This phrase is used to denote Israel going astray after other gods (Dt. 12:8;
Judges 17:6; 21:25). The opposite is to do what is right in God's eyes (Dt.
13:18; 1st Kings 15:5, 11; 2nd Kings 22:43).

giving and Christmas? The Church has taken celebrations to gods and goddesses and incorporated them into the worship of Jesus. The Church truly has a dark veil over her eyes. She's caught in her traditions that nullify God's Word and doesn't even realize it's sin! When it is brought to the attention of church officials it's usually rationalized away: 'Oh, we don't worship Nimrod or Adonis. We worship the birth of Christ.' *Where has God given the Church authority* to sanctify pagan holy days 'for Jesus'?! Also, where does Scripture say to celebrate the birth of Jesus? The Church greatly errs because it has thrown out God's holy standard—the Law of Moses.

The need to know what comprised salvation for the Gentile caused the Assembly in Jerusalem to convene. It was established that the Gentile was saved in the same way that the Jew was. Yakov declared the four rules and then uttered one verse of Scripture that reveals that believing Gentiles were already learning and keeping Torah.

Yakov didn't *command* the Gentiles to go to the synagogue because he knew that for more than eight years the Gentile believers were learning Torah in the Jewish congregations in which they worshiped.[675] These congregations were also called synagogues. The one in Antioch, where the term 'Christian' is first mentioned (Acts 11:26), was an assembly of Jewish and Gentile believers who obviously kept the Law (Acts 21:20, and by inference 20:6, 16; 22:12; 27:9), and Paul's Gentiles assembled in 'house churches/synagogues' and also learned the Law,[676] along with their believing Jewish brethren. The Gentile believers were already going to synagogues and learning the Law *before* Acts 15, and Yakov realized that, so there was no need to compel them to go.

Also, all the assemblies met on the Sabbath day and celebrated Passover.[677] This is ancient Church history. Sunday and Easter, ham and 'no Law,' didn't enter the Body of Messiah for more than 30 years after

---

[675] A powerful example of Gentile observance of the Law is seen about 195 AD. All the congregations in what is now Turkey, Syria and Israel kept the Passover. This angered Bishop Victor of Rome (whose office would soon become that of the Pope). The Bishop *demanded* that those congregations celebrate Easter instead of the Jewish Passover, but Polycrates, the bishop of all the assemblies in Turkey, 'claiming to possess the *genuine apostolic tradition* transmitted to him by the Apostles Philip and John, refused to be frightened into submission by the threats of Victor of Rome.' Bacchiocchi, *From Sabbath To Sunday*, pp. 198-199ff. If Gentile believers weren't learning Torah in the days of Acts 15:21, why would all those congregations be keeping Passover a hundred and fifty years later?

[676] Acts 20:20; Rom. 16:5; 1st Cor. 16:19; Col. 4:15; Philem. 1:2 (see also p. 189, notes 538-539).

[677] Rom. 3:31; 7:7, 12, 14; 1st Cor. 5:6-8; 7:19.

Paul's death. *No Gentile believer* was assembling on Sunday or keeping Easter in Paul's day. None. That wouldn't begin until about 100 AD.[678] These Christian traditions are easily seen to be unbiblical in that there are no Scriptures stating that believers should observe either of those days, and of course, pagans kept them both, in honor of 'their Christ,' more than a thousand years before Yeshua was born in Bethlehem.

# *Conclusion*

Yakov's second rule in Acts 15:20 was seen in both the Hebrew and the Greek words to mean *prostitution*, with the biblical emphasis on cult prostitution. The second rule, appearing immediately after the prohibition of eating sacrificial meat at the sacrifice, raised the theme of sacrificial idolatry. *Things strangled* and *blood* followed suit.

The Hebrew word for Yakov's second rule (*zinute*; prostitution), and its derivatives in the Old Testament, overwhelmingly spoke of cult harlotry. *Judah and Tamar* revealed cult harlotry being practiced in Canaan in the days of the sons of Jacob, and the Baal Peor affair at the time of Moses revealed how easily the Sons of Israel were seduced and the devastating consequences that cult harlotry had upon Israel.

In both Israel's history, and that of the ancient world, cult harlotry was rampant. It was *the* sin that brought down both the House of Israel and the House of Judah. Yakov was certainly aware of his Family History, and that of the pagans. He didn't want the Gentile believers to wrongly think that they could continue in sacrificial-sexual idolatry unscathed.

In the sections on Corinth and Revelation both Paul and Yeshua rebuked Gentile believers for practicing cult harlotry. Those *Christians* thought it was alright to do it. In the survey of the Greek word *pornay'ah* (harlotry) and its derivatives in the New Testament, its use was overwhelmingly seen as referring to cult harlotry, not common harlotry (and especially not adultery, sexual immorality, unchastity, or sex outside of marriage, etc.).

Once the smoke screen of scholarship was blown away, the four rules of Yakov were seen as a conceptual unit on sacrificial-sexual idolatry. Yakov's admonition was very simple: tell the Gentiles what would sever them from Jesus (Acts 15:20) and encourage them to walk in God's ways by learning His Torah (Acts 15:21).

Today there aren't many Christians going about thinking that eating meat and drinking blood sacrificed to idols, or lying with cult harlots, would be acceptable to Jesus, but great is the importance of correctly understanding

---

[678] Bacchiocchi, *From Sabbath To Sunday*, pp. 165-198.

Acts 15:20-21. It can no longer be used by the Church to teach that Gentiles had only four rules to obey, and it cannot be spoken of as given for table fellowship, out of Gentile consideration for the weaker Jewish brother. *Acts 15:20-21* exposes the satanic deception of a 'Law-free Gospel.'

The goal is understanding the Hebrew Bible (Genesis through Revelation) from its Hebraic Perspective.[679] God chose Abraham, not Socrates. He bound Himself (covenant) and interwove His ways (Torah, Prophets, Writings and New Testament) amongst Israel, not Greece. He revealed Himself in power (the Passover and Exodus; Yeshua crucified and resurrected) to Israel, not Rome. His reality and character are reflected in the *words* of the Hebrew Bible, not the Koran. *IBD* describes language as a reflection of a *nation's cumulative experiences:*

> 'it is an axiom of linguistics that any culture, no matter
> how primitive, develops that vocabulary which is perfect-
> ly adequate to express its thought and desires.'[680]

*Only Israel encountered* the God of Creation. Only Israel was freed from Egyptian slavery, walked through a divided and dry-bed Red Sea, heard the Voice of Yahveh as a nation (Ex. 19:16ff.) and was given the wisdom of God (the Law!; Dt. 4:5-8). No other nation was promised a land or entered into a covenant with God (Dt. 10:15; 29:1), and both the New Covenant and the Messiah were promised to Israel (Jer. 31:31-34; Micah 5:2). The Hebrew Scriptures need to be understood for what they are saying, as *The Lifting of the Veil* has revealed. The Scriptures are Israel's privileged possession (Rom. 3:1-2; 9:1-5) and belong to every believer:

> 'Ask now about former ages, long before your own, ever
> since the day that God created Adam on the Earth. Ask
> from one end of the Heavens to the other: has anything so
> great as this ever happened or has its like ever been heard
> of? Has any people ever heard the voice of God speaking
> out of the midst of the Fire as you have heard and lived?'

> 'Or has any god ever attempted to go and take a nation for
> himself from the midst of another nation, by trials, signs
> and wonders, by war, by a mighty hand and an outstret-
> ched arm and by terrifying displays of power, as Yahveh
> your God did for you in Egypt, before your very eyes? To

---

[679] The Hebraic Perspective centers around the place of the Law of Moses in our lives (Rom. 3:31) as interpreted by Yeshua, not by the Rabbis, Talmud or *halacha.* Yes, there are some insights that can be learned from them, but many who study them, not grounded in Messiah, have shipwrecked their faith on the rocks of the Rabbis (Mt. 16:6-12; 23:1-33; Lk. 11:27-28, 37-54; Titus 1:9-16).

[680] Douglas, *The Illustrated Bible Dictionary*, part 1, p. 306.

you it was shown so that you would acknowledge that Yahveh is God—there is no other besides Him! From the Heavens He made you hear His voice to discipline you. On Earth He showed you His great Fire, while you heard His words coming out of the Fire, and because He loved your Fathers, He chose their sons after them.'

'He brought you out of Egypt with His own presence, by His great power, driving out before you nations greater and mightier than yourselves to bring you in, giving you their land for a possession as it is still today. So acknowledge today and take to heart that Yahveh is God in the Heavens above and on the Earth beneath—there is none other! *Keep His statutes and His commandments,* which I am commanding you today, *for your own well-being and that of your sons after you* so that you may long remain in the Land that Yahveh your God is giving you for all time.' (Dt. 4:32-40)

Yahveh gave *His will* to Israel when He gave her His Law. Keil says, the

'object of the glorious manifestation of His holy majesty upon Sinai' was the giving of 'the Law through Moses to the congregation of Jacob as a *precious* possession,' and 'Israel was distinguished *above all nations* by the possession of *the divinely revealed Law.*'[681]

In the Beginning, the Gentiles learned the Law until the door was closed in their face by what would become the Roman Catholic Church, but in the End, the Spirit of Messiah Yeshua is opening the door that no church can shut! The Gentile (and Jew) is learning Torah again! Praise Yeshua!

This understanding is a radical departure from Church theology. With a proper Hebraic understanding of Acts 15:20-21, Church theology on the Law is completely shattered. Many Gentiles have seen this and are walking in their ancient Hebraic heritage as part of the Commonwealth of Israel (Eph. 2:11-22). Theologians can try and theologize Acts 15:20-21 away, but it's a losing cause for them because they're fighting the Lord.

Yeshua is lifting the veil of deception from the eyes of His Bride so that she can see more clearly who He is.[682] Thank God for *Yakov's Concern!* Because of it believers are beginning to walk in the freedom of God's perfect Law of Liberty:

---

[681] Keil, *The Pentateuch*, p. 875.

[682] Daniel 7:25; Acts 20:28-30.

'May Your forgiving loving-kindnesses also come to me, Oh Yahveh, Your salvation according to Your word. So I shall have an answer for him who reproaches me, *for I trust in Your word*. Do not take *the word of Truth* utterly out of my mouth, because I wait for Your *ordinances*. I will *keep Your Law* continually, forever and ever, and I will walk at *liberty* (freedom) for I seek Your precepts. I will also speak of Your *testimonies* before kings and shall not be ashamed, and I shall *delight* in Your *commandments*, which I love. I shall lift up my hands to Your commandments, which I love, and I will meditate upon Your *statutes*.' (Psalm 119:41-48)

'But one who looks intently at the perfect Law, the Law of *Liberty* (Freedom) and abides by it, not having become a forgetful hearer *but an effectual doer*, this man will be blessed in what he does!' (Yakov 1:25)

'I would not have come to know sin except through the Law.' (Rom. 7:7c)

"whoever says 'I abide in Him' *ought to walk just as He walked*." (1st John 2:6)

'And the Dragon was enraged with the Woman, and he went to make war with the rest of her offspring, *who keep the Commandments of God and* have the testimony of Yeshua the Messiah.' (Revelation 12:17)

There's much for all of us to learn about our God in the Hebrew Scriptures, both Old and New.[683]

---

[683] Even though the words are Greek, the underlying thought process and concepts of the New Covenant are Hebraic in nature.

# IS ACTS RELIABLE?

Is the Book of Acts a reliable document from which to draw theological understanding? Being inspired by the Holy Spirit and part of the New Testament one would assume that, but some say it's a poor historical account and not to be trusted. That, though, is just a smoke screen for those who don't want to believe what Luke writes about Paul. In my article, *Paul & Acts*, it reveals the Apostle to be a Jewish man who kept Torah all his life.[684] It's quite a jolt to those who think that Paul did away with the Law. That's why they say that Acts 'can't be trusted.'

Those who attack both Luke and his Book of Acts use the unscrupulous tactic of character assassination, while their scholarship is questionable at best. Acts, though, is a very trustworthy document. Luke has faithfully recorded the essence of the speeches in Acts, including Paul's. Both F. F. Bruce and I. Howard Marshall confirm this. Neither of them uphold the Law for believers today, so no one can accuse them of furthering their own theological agenda when they speak of the accuracy and reliability of Acts, specifically of 'Luke's Paul.' Writing of Acts, Bruce states,

> 'even if there are aspects of…Paul at which we might scarcely guess if we did not have his letters, the picture of him that Luke gives is *ineffaceable*.[685] And in giving us this picture…Luke has made a great, indeed, a unique contribution to the record of early Christian expansion. His narrative, in fact, is *a sourcebook of the highest value for the history of civilization*.'[686]

Bruce praises Acts and also says that without Acts we would be at the behest of those who denigrate the Jews and the God of Israel. He writes,

> 'The importance of Acts was further underlined about the middle of the second century as a result of the dispute to which Marcion and his teaching gave rise. Marcion of

---

[684] See *Paul & Acts* at http://SeedofAbraham.net/PaulAndActs.html.

[685] Sinclair, *Collins English Dictionary*, p. 787. *Ineffaceable* means 'incapable of being effaced; indelible.' As the Mafia might say, Luke's Paul can't be 'rubbed out.' What's written of Paul in Acts accurately reflects both what he entered into (the Nazarite Vows) and his theological position on the Law.

[686] Bruce, *The Book of the Acts*, p. 16. Bruce quotes Tertullian (p. 14, note 58) as having said of the Book of Acts, 'Those who do not accept this volume of scripture *can have nothing to do with the Holy Spirit*, for they cannot know if the Holy Spirit has yet been sent to the disciples, neither can they claim to be the church, since they cannot show when this body was established or where it was cradled' (Tertullian, *Prescription against Heretics* 23).

Sinope was an exceptionally ardent devotee of Paul who nevertheless *misunderstood* him. About AD 144 he promulgated at Rome what he held to be the true canon of divine scripture for the *new age inaugurated by Christ.* Christ, in Marcion's teaching, *was the revealer of an entirely new religion*, completely unrelated to anything that had preceded his coming (such as the faith of Israel documented in our Old Testament). God the Father, to whom Christ bore witness, had never been known on earth before: *he was a superior being to the God of Israel*, who created the material world and spoke through the prophets. Paul, according to Marcion, was the *only* apostle who faithfully preserved Christ's new religion in its purity, *uncontaminated by Jewish influences.* The Old Testament could have no place in the Christian canon. The Christian canon, as promulgated by Marcion, comprised two parts: one called *The Gospel* (a suitable edited recension of the third Gospel), and the other called *The Apostle* (a similarly edited recension of Paul's nine letters to churches and his letter to Philemon).'[687]

The Church has misunderstood Paul, just like Marcion. Even if it doesn't faithfully adhere to every jot and tittle of Marcion's beliefs, it nevertheless conveys that they are an entirely different religion, not the continuation that God intended with Yeshua. Bruce says that because of Marcion the leaders of the faith felt compelled to define the canon of Scripture with greater clarity to ensure the true promulgation of God's Word:

'For them, *The Gospel* comprised not one document only but four, and those four included the full text of the one which Marcion had published in mutilated form. For them, *The Apostle* included not ten but thirteen Pauline letters, and not Pauline letters only, but letters of other 'apostolic men' as well. And, linking *The Gospel* and *The Apostle* was now seen to have greater importance than ever, for not only did it validate Paul's claims but it validated the authority of the original apostles; those whom Marcion had repudiated as false apostles and corruptors of truth as it is in Jesus. The position of Acts as the *keystone* in the arch of the Christian canon was confirmed.'[688]

Bruce further states that Luke's vindication of Paul, as a true Apostle, was

---

[687] Ibid., p. 4.

[688] Ibid., pp. 4-5.

not his primary purpose in writing Acts:

> "Luke does in passing, show that Paul's commission was as valid as Peter's, and that both men were equally faithful to their commission. But these secondary aspects of his work acquired special importance in the second century, in view of the Marcionite's tendency to claim Paul peculiarly for themselves, and also in view of tendencies in other quarters to play down Paul's record in the interests of Peter's or James's. Tertullian, for example, points out the inconsistency of those sectarians (the Marcionites in particular, no doubt) *who rejected the testimony of Acts but appealed so confidently to the unique authority of Paul.* 'You must show us first of all who this Paul was,' he says to them. 'What was he before he became an apostle? How did he become an apostle?'"[689]

> 'Paul in his letters gives his own answer to such questions, but for the independent corroboration one would naturally appeal to Acts, when once that work had been published. But this the Marcionites could not do: Acts did vindicate the claims made by and for Paul, indeed, but since it simultaneously vindicated claims made by and for Peter, its testimony was unacceptable. Acts shows...Peter and the rest of the Twelve were true and faithful apostles of Jesus Christ (which the Marcionites denied).'[690]

Those who say that Acts cannot be trusted as a faithful theological witness to what it records are part of the family of Marcion, whether they know their distant relative or not. They, like Marcion, discredit Luke to suit their own false theology and 'run to Paul!'—yet Bruce, to his eternal credit, even with his anti-Law theology, sees Paul in the Book of Acts as fully Law-observant. He writes:

> 'Christianity' for Luke is 'no innovation *but the proper fulfillment of Israel's religion.* He is at pains to present Paul *as a loyal and law-abiding Jew.* This comes out particularly in the speeches made by Paul in his own defense in Jerusalem, Caesarea, and Rome.[691] In those apologetic speeches...Paul claims to believe *everything* in the law and the prophets and to have done nothing contrary to Israel's ancestral customs. The *one point at issue* between

---

[689] Ibid., p. 14.

[690] Ibid.

[691] Acts 22:3-21; 23:6; 24:10-21; 25:8, 10-11; 26:2-23; 28:17-20.

him and his accusers is the *resurrection faith*: by this he means the faith that Jesus rose from the dead...Jesus' resurrection is for him *the confirmation of the Jews' national hope.*'[692]

F. F. Bruce couldn't find the 'Paul of the Church' in the Book of Acts, but he helps to confirm that Mosaic Law is for every Christian. With Paul being Torah-observant all his life, how can anyone possibly think that it's theologically wrong to keep the Law, especially when Paul writes of 'imitating' or 'following' him *as he followed Christ?*[693]

Marshall also believes that the Book of Acts is very reliable, but first he states that Luke has taken a lot of ungodly criticism (character assassination) because of his presentation of Paul as Law-observant. In speaking of Ernst Haenchen's 'mammoth commentary on Acts,' Marshall writes,

> 'Anyone who may have thought that R. Bultmann represented the ultimate in historical scepticism in regards to the New Testament was in for a shock...The result was that Luke's historical accuracy was apparently torn in shreds; the narrative was claimed to have little basis in tradition, and to be full of historical inconsistencies and improbabilities, and to be basically the product of the fertile mind of a historical novelist with little or no concern for such tiresome things as facts.'[694]

Marshall refutes Haenchen's claim from a number of authoritative sources and states that Luke's historical background was exceptionally accurate:

> 'One of the major contributions of Ramsay to Lucan study was his demonstration that on matters of detailed historical background *Luke shows remarkable accuracy.*'[695]

Marshall then cites the work of A. Sherwin-White who speaks of Luke's reliability in relation to Rome and her culture. He says Acts demonstrates,

> 'that for the most part Luke portrays the first-century Roman scene accurately. The conclusion to be drawn is that if Luke is right about the details of the story, he is

---

[692] Bruce, *The Book of the Acts*, pp. 9-10.

[693] 1st Cor. 4:14-17; 11:1; 2nd Cor. 12:18; Phil. 3:15-17; 4:9; 1st Thess. 1:6-7; 2nd Thess. 3:7, 9.

[694] Marshall, *Acts*, p. 35. It's very telling, though, that no one questions Luke's integrity or accuracy in his Gospel.

[695] Ibid., p. 36. *Italics* are Marshall's.

likely *also to be right about the main episodes.*[696]

Marshall goes on to say that although the speeches in Acts are not verbatim, as no one had recording devices in that day, they are nevertheless accurate portrayals of what Peter, Paul and the rest said:

> 'British scholarship has in general defended the view that the various speeches placed in the mouths of Peter, Paul and others were, if not verbatim accounts of what was actually said, at least compositions based on tradition and expressing the structure and the details of the earliest Christian preaching.'[697]

We may not know every word that was literally spoken, but we can be sure that what Luke writes is an accurate representation of the *substance* of the speeches, and therefore, what is written about Paul in Acts, regarding his Nazarite Vows and his position on the Law, confirm that Paul kept the Law of Moses all his life. In zeroing in on 'the problem' (Paul's Law observance), Marshall writes:

> '*It is **this** point, perhaps more than any other*, which has led to skeptical estimates of the historical value of Acts. The case against Luke is summarized in an essay by P. Vielhauer which argued that Luke's presentation of Paul's attitude to natural theology, *to the Jewish law*, to Christology and to eschatology was quite inconsistent with the picture that we get from Paul's own letters.[698] This article has had an extraordinary influence in persuading scholars of the unhistorical character of Acts. In fact, however, the case has been strongly criticized, and in our opinion *convincingly destroyed,* in a brief discussion by E. E. Ellis.[699] Some general observations by F. F. Bruce confirm the point.[700] This is not to say that there are no points of tension between Luke's portrait of Paul and his own writings; it is to affirm that in our opinion they are not so sub-

---

[696] Ibid., pp. 36-37.

[697] Ibid., pp. 39-40, note 1: C. H. Dodd, *The Apostolic Preaching and its Developments* (London, 1936); F. F. Bruce, *The Speeches in the Acts of the Apostles* (London, 1943).

[698] Ibid., p. 42, note 1: P. Vielhauer, *On the 'Paulism' of Acts*, in *SLA*, pp. 33-50. Cf. Haenchen, pp. 112-116.

[699] Ibid., pp. 42-43, note 1: E. E. Ellis, *The Gospel of Luke* (London, 1974), pp. 45-47.

[700] Ibid., p. 43, note 2: F. F. Bruce, *Is the Paul of Acts the Real Paul?* BJRL 58, 1976, pp. 282-305. Cf. Hanson, pp. 24-27.

stantial as to make us dismiss Acts as unhistorical.'[701]

> 'The effect of our...comments is to show that there is a strong case for regarding Acts as an *essentially reliable account of what it reports.*'[702]

Acts is reliable. Can it be, then, that Church scholarship has misunderstood and misinterpreted Paul's letters concerning his thoughts on the Law of Moses in relation to a biblical lifestyle? Indeed, this is the case. What Luke writes about Paul's Torah observance is a biblical fact. It's also an extremely powerful refutation to anyone who claims that Paul did away with the Law, or that we 'cannot take theology' from the Book of Acts.

Did the Apostles ever stop worshiping at the Temple in Jerusalem because 'sacrifice was done away with by the one-time sacrifice of Yeshua'? Did Paul think that the Temple was no longer valid because believers 'are the Temple of God'?[703] The Book of Acts upholds God's Torah, His Temple *and sacrifices* in Jerusalem—with the Apostle Paul leading the way!

Some scholars and commentators, though, stuck in Church theology, say that the Lord's Apostles, many years *after* the resurrection, *still didn't realize* that Torah and Temple worship were no longer necessary or good! After stating that the Temple in Jerusalem would be superseded by the Body of believers, R. J. McKelvey writes,

> 'Some time elapsed, however, *before the full ramifications* of the work of Christ became apparent, and in Acts we find the apostles continuing to worship at the Temple of Jerusalem (Acts 2:46; 3:1ff.; 5:12, 20f., 42; cf. Lk. 24:52). It appears that the Hellenistic-Jewish party represented by Stephen was the first to discover that *belief in Jesus as Messiah meant the **abrogation** of the order* symbolized by the Jerusalem Temple (Acts 6:11ff.).'[704]

McKelvey seems to believe that Stephen was gifted with knowledge that neither Peter nor Paul ever had. Marcion would have been proud of Mr. McKelvey. Here is a Christian scholar interpreting the Book of Acts to suit his theology. There's no mention in Acts, or anywhere else for that matter, that it was wrong for the Apostles, including Paul, to worship at the Temple in Jerusalem, or that they would later come to some 'greater

---

[701] Ibid., p. 43.

[702] Ibid.

[703] There are three cites where Paul speaks of believers being the Temple of God (1st Cor. 3:16; 6:19; 2nd Cor. 6:16).

[704] Douglas, *The Illustrated Bible Dictionary*, part 3, pp. 1527-1528. The author of the article on the Temple is R. J. McKelvey.

understanding' that Temple sacrifice and Torah keeping weren't right. Could it be that the Holy Spirit forgot to have someone mention those monumental points in the New Testament?[705] According to many Church scholars like McKelvey the answer is 'Yes.'

As for McKelvey's alleged 'insight,' that Stephen and his 'Hellenistic-Jewish party' had, Witherington, after analyzing Acts seven, writes that Stephen is *not* coming against either the Law or the Temple. He was chastising the Jewish leadership *for failing to keep the Law and the Prophets!*

> 'Clearly enough Stephen *believes the Law* and indeed all of Scripture to be God's word, and so the ultimate indictment is that God's people have failed to keep it, including the prophetic portions which foretold the Righteous One. Stephen's speech *is not Law or temple critical*, it is people critical *on the basis of the Law* and the Prophets.'[706]

Witherington writes that Stephen didn't think that the Temple or sacrifice were abrogated by the sacrificial death of Yeshua. Stephen says nothing against the Temple, but against the Jewish leadership, a leadership that refused God's Messiah even though they said that they believed in God. McKelvey's grasp of the passage is not that of Stephen's, nor the Lord's.

Bruce and Marshall don't keep, or are even sympathetic to keeping, the Law of Moses. On the contrary, they both believe the Law to have been done away with,[707] but this only confirms Torah for all believers by two

---

[705] Yeshua speaks of the Father looking for those to worship Him in Spirit and Truth and of the time that was coming when it wouldn't be possible to worship at the Temple in Jerusalem (Jn. 4:21-23), but this *doesn't* negate Temple sacrifice. This is clear from Yeshua's words, the *Acts of the Apostles* (where it's written that believers met daily in the Temple), and Ezekiel's Millennial Temple (Ezk. 40–48) where sacrifice is a daily reality.

Some might point to the Book of Hebrews, but again proper interpretation of the letter is essential for understanding what the author is presenting. For instance, although Heb. 8:13 says that the Old Covenant is obsolete, it doesn't say that it *has* disappeared, but that it is *ready* to disappear. The writer, like many of the Apostles, believed that the End was near and that Yeshua was going to return in his lifetime. When the Body of Messiah is glorified, Mosaic Law will no longer be needed because then all believers will be glorified like Messiah Yeshua and truly have the Law 'on their hearts' (Jer. 31:31-34). Until then, Mosaic Law is valid for all believers (Mt. 5:17-19; Lk. 16:16; Rev. 12:17; 14:12).

[706] Witherington, *The Acts of the Apostles*, p. 275.

[707] Bruce, *The Book of the Acts*, p. 285, speaks of a 'law-free gospel.' He interprets Acts 10 as the '*abrogation* of ceremonial food laws' (p. 206) saying that it actually began when Jesus declared 'all foods clean' in Mark 7:14-19. Bruce has sorely misinterpreted the text, though. The KJV rightly translates

significant scholars who don't follow it. They have shown that even Paul, and of course all the other Apostles and believers, kept the Law throughout the time frame of Acts (30-64 AD).[708]

Luke does us a tremendous service in reporting Paul's Torah lifestyle. Most likely he wrote this in order to squelch the malicious rumor that Paul didn't keep the Law (Acts 21:21).

The Book of Acts is inspired, accurate and very reliable. There is nothing in it that speaks of the Law's demise or even remotely denigrates it. On the contrary, there are numerous places where the Law is strongly upheld, and that, by Paul, the very one whom the Church declares did away with it! Acts is a trustworthy historical-theological narrative from which we can base theology upon. Those who say that theology can't be taken from the Book of Acts, may not realize it, but they're part of Marcion's Church.

---

Mark 7:19, 'Because it entereth not into his heart, but into the belly, and goeth out into the draught, *purging* all meats?' Just from Peter's words in Acts (10:14, 28, 34-35; 11:8) we know that *Peter didn't think that Yeshua had declared all foods clean.*

Marshall, *Acts*, pp. 180-181, 198, also misinterprets Peter's vision and says that Peter would 'no longer distinguish between ritually clean and unclean foods.' For Acts 15:19-20 (p. 253) he states, 'the old rules of the Jewish religion no longer apply.' For why Bruce and Marshall's understanding of the dietary laws (and Law) is wrong, and why the KJV is accurate, see *Law 102* at http://SeedofAbraham.net/law102.html.

[708] Another major indication that the Law hadn't been abrogated is Luke's use of the Feasts of Israel as *time markers*. In Acts 20:6 Paul and his friends spend the days of Unleavened Bread (Passover week) at Philippi. In Acts 20:16 Paul is hurrying to be in Jerusalem for Pentecost (the Feast of Weeks; Leviticus 23:15-21; Dt. 16:16). In Acts 27:9 Luke speaks of inadvisable sailing weather because 'the Fast' (the Day of Atonement; Lev. 16:1-34; 23:26-32) had already passed. Why would Luke, a Gentile, use the Feasts as time markers for his *Gentile audience* unless the Law was still valid? Paul, too, uses the Feasts as time markers. The Apostle writes in 1st Cor. 16:8 of staying in Ephesus until Pentecost. First Corinthians was written about 53 AD, while the Book of Acts was written about 64 AD.

# REALITY RAMIFICATIONS

Many Christians love Jesus with all their heart, but in ignorance eat pig, assemble on Sunday (and not God's holy Sabbath) and keep Easter (not Passover), etc. The Apostle Paul pleaded with the Corinthians involved in cult harlotry and didn't immediately cast them out because they were only babes in understanding the Word. They did it in their pride and ignorance.

Today the Lord is calling to His people to stop all pagan practices and learn to walk in His Torah. The admonition in Revelation 'to come out of her My people' reveals Yeshua's desire for His people to stop practicing the ways of darkness, thinking that it's His Light:

> "And he cried out with a mighty voice saying, 'Fallen!, Fallen!, is Babylon the Great! She has become a dwelling place of demons and a prison of every unclean spirit and a prison of every unclean and hateful bird. For all the nations have drunk of the wine of the passion of her prostitution and the kings of the Earth have committed acts of harlotry with her and the merchants of the Earth have become rich by the wealth of her *sensuality*.'"

> "I heard another voice from the Heavens saying, 'Come out of her My people!, so that you will *not participate in her sins* and receive of her plagues, for her sins have piled up as high as the Heavens and God has remembered her iniquities.'" (Rev. 18:2-5)

Understanding God's Word, from His perspective, brings greater discernment of what is right and what is wrong according to His eyes. The Holy Spirit is getting the Bride ready for Messiah Yeshua. My wife Ruti said,

> 'God is not a polygamist. He wants one people, one Bride. That's why Torah and the Sabbath are also for the Gentile—the Gentile coming into, and becoming one with Israel, not Israel going out and becoming pagan. The wild olive branch is grafted into the natural olive tree[709] and not the other way around.'[710]

Many say they don't have to keep the Mosaic commandments, but they don't realize that the commandments are for our blessing and safety. They are God's wisdom for us. The Law is the verbal reflection of the One who gave it and its authority is established (Dt. 4:5-8; 2nd Tim. 3:14-17).

---

[709] Rom. 11:15-29.

[710] Quote from Ruti Yehoshua (Jerusalem, Israel, 16 December 1996).

Torah is for all followers of Yeshua, Jew and Gentile. For a biblical Gentile community to assemble together they would all have to come together on the Sabbath. For them to celebrate the time when the Passover Lamb was slain for their freedom they would want to celebrate Passover (1st Cor. 5:6-8). They would even come to the understanding that if they had a house with a flat roof (to walk on), they would want a parapet (a type of fence or railing so that people wouldn't accidentally fall over the edge).[711]

Many a Gentile finds himself as the 'only one' that sees the significance of Torah. Spouse, friends and church haven't been touched by this, yet. It's very lonely, but this is similar to how Father Abraham felt when God told him to leave the things he knew behind (Gen. 12:1-4). Follow Yeshua and trust Him. It will be a precious time of spiritual growth into His Image.

The Church needs to repent of its anti-Law theology and turn from its pagan ways to the Word of God. Sunday and Christmas, etc., are pagan, anti-God and anti-Semitic. They have no biblical basis. They should be thrown out and replaced with God's holy times and ways. This would also cause Jews to be astonished and take a second look at Messiah Yeshua.

Idolatry of any kind must not be practiced. Yeshua calls His people to be holy (1st Peter 1:13-19). The New Age movement dates all the way back to ancient Babylon. It's sorcery in modern clothes. As King Solomon once wrote, 'There's nothing new under the sun' (Eccl. 1:9c). Transcendental meditation is sweeping the Western world, with people ignorantly using mantras, and thereby, invoking demons.

On some continents ancestor worship still exists among Christians. Reading the daily horoscope (astrology), Tarot cards, Ouija boards, crystals, beads, pyramids and Eastern religions (Islam, Zen, Buddhism, etc.) are all part of the lure of the satanic Fisherman. Jewish mysticism (*Kabbalah*) is of Satan.[712] Harry Potter, magic, *Dungeons & Dragons* and all other so-called fantasy books and games are open doors into the Kingdom of Darkness (Lev. 19:26; Dt. 18:9-14; Acts 19:11-20). These sins need to be repented of and renounced 'by the blood of Yeshua.' Ask Messiah Yeshua to sever all connections with those people, spirits and practices and to fill you with His Holy Spirit and His ways.

---

[711] Dt. 22:8: 'When you build a new house, you shall make a parapet for your roof so that you will not bring blood guilt' (murder) 'on your house if anyone falls from it.'

[712] See *Kabbalah* at http://SeedofAbraham.net/kabbalah.html for why it's witchcraft in Jewish clothes.

# *A Word about Torah*

Some people might want to stone the blasphemer (Lev. 24:16) and perform other such acts of zealous righteousness, but there are a few considerations to take into account before the first stone is thrown. The Law was given to a *nation* that was a *theocracy*. Yahveh literally directed Israel through His Torah, His High Priest, His mediator-king (Moses) and His Shekinah Glory Cloud. There was no authority, but His. Under Joshua and King David it was similar, but not so in the days of Messiah Yeshua when the Jewish people were ruled by Rome. That's why the Sanhedrin needed *permission* from Rome (Pilate) to have Yeshua murdered. They didn't have authority to enact the death penalty themselves.

For the person to be stoned in King David's day the man would first have to be brought to the town's elders to be judged. It wasn't the responsibility of any one individual 'to take the law into his own hands.' For instance, if a believing Gentile in Corinth had *speared* the believing Gentile who had been involved in incestuous cult prostitution (1st Cor. 5:1f.), he would have been arrested, tried for murder in a Corinthian (Roman) court, found guilty and executed. They wouldn't have awarded him the Covenant of Peace, as Phineas received (Num. 25:11-12).[713]

Paul gave sinners time to repent (the ones accused of drinking the cup of demons; those involved in cult prostitution, etc.), but regarding the one who had had intercourse with his father's wife, Paul demanded that he be cast out of the congregation (1st Cor. 5:1-5; perhaps Paul only knew the specifics of this man, hence, why no similar action was taken against the others?). Not repenting of it would have meant eternity in Hell for him.

This is just one example of how Torah is affected or 'shifts' in a nation that is not Torah-observant, but we must be equally aware that we're not to spiritualize the commandants (i.e. just to look for the principles 'behind them' and do these *instead* of the commandments themselves).[714] This is not the primary reason why the commandments were given. The commandments are still in effect unless something overrides them, like circumcising a Jewish son on the Sabbath day (Jn. 7:21-24).

Yeshua came to reveal the deeper meaning or essence of Torah, but He didn't do away with any of it.[715] He unveiled the commandment not to

---

[713] In killing Zimri and Cozbi, Phineas followed the judgement of God, as given to Moses (Num. 25:4-5), and as a priest, Phineas was also a judge who had authority to act (Dt. 17:8-13).

[714] For instance, to try and keep Sunday as the Sabbath by not working on it, but resting, etc. The problem is that God never said one could change His holy day (Gen. 2:1-3; Ex. 20:8-11, etc.) by shifting its concept to another day.

murder by revealing that hate was its essence—but the commandment not to murder still stands. Yeshua revealed the divine essence of the commandments for us in His Kingdom. That's how Paul could say that the Law of Moses is spiritual.[716] The commandments are spiritual pillars of righteousness.

The Holy Spirit is preparing the Bride of Messiah by taking the veil away from her eyes so that she can see the beauty of God's holy Torah, which is a divine reflection of Yeshua. That's why Acts 15:20-21 needs to be seen for what it is—*the* passage that brings the Gentile into Torah that he might walk alongside his believing Jewish brethren who are walking the same way. This is truly what makes Acts 15 epoch-making in our day!

## *An Insight*

These next set of quotes are excerpts from a letter of my wife, Ruti. She speaks of what God desires for His people Israel:

> 'The Jewish man who comes to faith in Messiah Yeshua has a dilemma. Where can he go for fellowship and remain true to the God of Israel and Hebraic understanding? If he remains in the unbelieving Jewish community he is polluted and adulterated by the anti-Christ spirit that is throughout Rabbinic Judaism. This includes Jewish mysticism (*Kabbalah*) that is interwoven into the writings, and the manic-*mitzvah*[717] oriented belief system, which is a poor substitute for the Blood of Assurance and *Ruach haKodesh*' (the Holy Spirit).

> 'If on the other hand, he goes into the Gentile Church (and this includes many of the Messianic fellowships), he must enter a form of worship and practice that is scripturally unsound (anti-Torah) and anti-Semitic in attitude. Sunday, Easter, Thanksgiving[718] and Christmas are all pagan, as well as the symbols of the cross,[719] the fish,[720] the

---

[715] Mt. 5:17-19; 22:35-40; Lk. 16:16-17; John 10:35: 'and Scripture cannot be broken;' Rom. 3:31; 1st Cor. 7:17-19; Heb. 8:13; Rev. 12:17; 14:12, etc.

[716] Romans 7:14.

[717] *Mitzva* is the Hebrew word for 'commandment.' The word has also come to mean a 'good deed.' Jewish people do '*mitzvot*' (plural; good deeds) in their desire to be seen as righteous and to merit eternal life.

[718] See *Thanksgiving Day—Pagan?* at http://SeedofAbraham.net/thnksgiv.html.

[719] Hislop, *The Two Babylons*, pp. 197-205.

[720] The word for fish in Greek is ιχθυς (*ick'thoos*). It's an acronym: each Greek

Star of David,[721] and the so-called 'pictures of Jesus,' etc. Yeshua is leading the *called out* Jews and Gentiles to a Torah lifestyle rich in biblical Hebraic expression. God Himself is the Author of this Hebraic expression because it's His essence and His heart. As we surrender ourselves

---

letter has been made to represent a word meaning: Jesus Christ God's Son Savior. In Hebrew the word for the fish god was Dagon דָּגוֹן (*dah'goan*). Half fish and half man, it fell down and broke into pieces in front of the Ark of the Covenant of the God of Israel (1st Sam. 5:1f.).

Dagon is identified with Bacchus, who was known as *Ichthys* (the fish god) many centuries before Jesus was born. Hislop, *The Two Babylons*, p. 247 and note * states that it was, "From about AD 360, to the time of the Emperor Justinian, about 550...that our Lord Jesus Christ began to be popularly called *Ichthys*, that is, 'the Fish,' manifestly to identify him with Dagon."

Dagon was also known by other names. Hislop writes that, "Saturn and Lateinos are just synonymous, having precisely the same meaning, and belonging equally to the same god. The reader cannot have forgotten the lines of Virgil, which showed that Lateinos, to whom the Romans or Latin race traced back their lineage, was represented with a glory around his head, to show that he was a 'child of the Sun' (god). Thus, then, it is evident that, in popular opinion, the original Lateinos had occupied the very same position as Saturn did in the Mysteries, who was equally worshipped as the 'offspring of the Sun.' Moreover, it is evident that the Romans knew that the name 'Lateinos' signifies the 'Hidden One,' for their antiquarians invariably affirm that Latium received its name from Saturn 'lying hid' there. On etymological grounds then, even on the testimony of the Romans, Lateinos is equivalent to the 'Hidden One,' that is, to Saturn, the 'god of Mystery'" (ibid., p. 270).

"Latium Latinus (the Roman form of the Greek Lateinos), and Lateo, 'to lie hid,' all alike come from the Chaldee 'Lat,' which has the same meaning ...The name 'lat,' or the hidden one, had evidently been given, as well as Saturn, to the great Babylonian god. This is evident from the name of the fish Latus, which was worshipped along with the Egyptian Minerva, in the city of Latopolis in Egypt, now Esneh (Wilkinson, *Manners and Customs of the Ancient Egyptians,* vol. iv. p. 284, and vol. v. p. 253), that fish Latus evidently just being another name for the fish-god Dagon" (ibid., note ¶).

"*Ichthys,* or the Fish, was one of the names of Bacchus, and the Assyrian goddess Atergatis, with her son Ichthys, is said to have been cast into the lake of Ascalon (*Vossius de Idololatria,* lib. i. cap. xxiii. p. 89, also Athenaeus, lib. viii. cap. viii. p. 346, E). That the sun-god Apollo had been known under the name of Lat, may be inferred from the Greek name of his mother-wife Leto, or in Doric, Lato, which is just the feminine of Lat. The Roman name Latona confirms this, for it signifies 'The lamenter of Lat,' as Bellona signifies 'The lamenter of Bel."

"To identify Nimrod with Oannes, mentioned by Berosus, as appearing out of the sea, it will be remembered that Nimrod has been proved to be Bacchus. Then, for proof that Nimrod or Bacchus, on being overcome by his enemies, was fabled to have taken refuge in the sea, see Chapter IV, Section I, p. 129f. When, therefore, he was represented as reappearing, it was *natural* that he

261

to doing the will of the Father, which is Yeshua's heart, *Ruach haKodesh* will lead us to leave both perverted Camps. This doesn't mean that those Camps are devoid of helping us in our walk, but in these things we need to look to Him for His guidance, seeking only to please Him. We are no longer our own, but have been bought by His precious blood and delivered out of darkness to serve Him in the newness of His Spirit within us.'

"I believe the *Ruach'* (Spirit) 'is showing us today that the Gentile believer is also called to serve the Jewish people. How is this walked out? By coming out of Babylonian (Church) practices and moving into obedience of the Torah of the God of Israel, led by His Spirit. This way the Jewish unbeliever who is coming to faith in Yeshua is not made to stumble, but is rightly, truthfully restored to his or her God through His Son and Messiah, who does not

---

should reappear in the very character of Oannes, as a *Fish*-god. Now, Jerome calls Dagon, the well known Fish-god *Piscem moeroris* (Bryant, *Mythology*, vol. iii. p. 179) 'the fish of *sorrow*,' which goes far to identify that Fish-god with Bacchus, the 'Lamented one,' and the identification is complete when Hesychius tells us that some called Bacchus *Ichthys* or 'The fish' (*Lexicon, sub voce* 'Bacchos,' p. 179); Hislop, *The Two Babylons*, p. 114, note *.

There are some who say that the Philistine Dagon wasn't a fish god, but a god of grain, as the Hebrew word for grain דָּגָן (*dah'gahn*) and 'fish' דָּג (*dahg*) come from the same Hebrew verb, which means 'to multiply.' Davidson, *The Analytical Hebrew and Chaldee Lexicon*, p. 146, states that Dagon was a 'large fish,' properly the 'name of an idol of the Philistines worshipped at Ashdod.' He writes that the word can also mean 'grain.' There was also a *Dagon* in Mesopotamia, who was a god of grain, but it seems that the Philistines, who lived by the Mediterranean Sea, had Dagon as their fish god.

Brown, *NBDBG*, p. 186: In 1st Sam. 5:4, when Dagon had fallen down with hands and head cut off before the Ark of the Covenant, the trunk (body) of Dagon is literally called his 'fishy part' (as it was made in the form of a fish).

However one might understand this *Dagon*, the reality remains that *Ichthys* was the name of at least two pagan gods and worshiped as such. The name *Ichthys* only began to be identified with Jesus, late in the fourth century, and that, by the Roman Catholic Church...so why do Christians, who profess to follow the Word of God, have the fish symbol on their car bumpers and Bibles? Where in Scripture is Jesus ever symbolized as a fish or *Ichthys*?

Hislop's theme is that the Roman Catholic Church is a bastion of Babylonian paganism. His book is a 'must read' because it overwhelmingly proves this.

[721] See *The Star of David* at http://SeedofAbraham.net/stardavd.html for an understanding of why believers shouldn't wear it, and read *Jesus the Fish God?* at http://seedofabraham.net/fish.html for why believers shouldn't wear the fish symbol, either. (These two symbols negate the so-called 'Messianic Seal.')

look or act pagan. This, of course, holds true for the Gentiles coming to Messiah as well, that they are not led into pagan practices, either.'

'We are created to reflect God and His Truth. Let us walk hand in hand as one people with the One who is Truth.'[722]

There's a desensitizing to pagan things when pagan holy days and ways are 'Christianized.' How can one tell if something is pagan or not? What is the *standard* by which to judge things?

Pagans were worshiping their gods a certain way one day, and the next, the Roman Catholic Church took it and 'baptized' it for its people. When the Protestants came along they blindly followed many of her practices and theologies. This is the problem when one throws out the standard of Torah. It creates an ignorance and a vacuum for satanic things to come in.

The Roman Catholic Church filled the vacuum with satanic 'holy days' and concepts, and today, most Christians believe that these pagan days and ways are of God. When many find out otherwise, *tradition is so strong* that they can't, or won't, believe it. The veil is still over their eyes.

The Torah of Yahveh is the standard by which to judge religious concepts and practices. If people would read Torah they would know that God has given us His standard with His holy days and dietary laws, etc., and they would come to see the conflict between what the Church teaches and what God commands for those who believe in Yeshua. The Torah of Yahveh is not only the first five books of the Bible, but all the Bible, especially the words of Yeshua, and the rest of the New Covenant, as seen through the eyes of Yeshua, not the Church.

The God of Israel is not pleased with what the Church has done. This is clearly seen in the admonitions that He has given to Israel (Dt. 12:28-32; Acts 20:25-35; 2nd Tim. 3:16-17; 2nd Pet. 3:14-18; Rev. 18:2-5). With Torah observance each believer can have a fuller walk with Yeshua and be a greater *Light* unto both the Jew and the Gentile that need to come to Messiah Yeshua.

---

[722] Excerpt from a letter of Ruti Yehoshua (Jerusalem, Israel, 19 Dec. 1996).

# *Some Advice*

Our hearts continually wander from the attitude of serving and 'washing the feet' of our brethren, which is Yeshua's heart and attitude.[723] When we walk in this attitude the rest of Torah is easy to do. God doesn't expect us to walk in Torah overnight, but He does expect us to begin. He wants us to grasp the concept that all the Law that applies to us is for us.[724] In keeping His commandments, in being aware when we break them or sin, we are saying to *Abba El* (Papa God) that we recognize His Authority to govern our lives. He knows what is good for us, and what is sin and will destroy us. Walk in His Torah and let His Spirit lead you.

Torah is commanded, not suggested. If God demands it of us, we want to acknowledge this in our heart and not give way to the teaching of the Church or the 'wearing away' of our belief by 'well-meaning' friends who think otherwise. This isn't forcing someone to do His commandments; that's not His way. It's being honest about what is required or expected of us. This is the target or the goal—to do His will in all areas of our life.

Don't try to do all the commandments at once. Read the Word daily and include Torah in it.[725] The Lord will lead you into observing the commandments at a godly pace. Trying to do them all 'yesterday' will only bring confusion and disappointment. Trust Yeshua. He will guide you, strengthen your walk and deepen your understanding of His Word.

Don't let legalism stop you. Fear of legalism is a stumbling block for some. Under the guise of caution there's little movement toward the *doing* of the commandments. Legalism is the strict enforcing or perversion of a law. Legalism is *not* equal to the Law (except in the mind of the Church). If you're driving 61 miles per hour in a 60 mile per hour zone and a policeman gives you a ticket, that's legalism—but the law is good. The Law was given so there won't be chaos and accidents on the Highway of Life.

There were times that Yeshua had to correct me concerning a legalistic attitude. A heart that is open to Him will be led into His ways.

If you're afraid of making a mistake or of becoming legalistic, you've already sinned by being afraid. Don't be afraid (Mk. 5:35-36). Deal with the fear. Take it to your Father, who is gracious in forgiving and in granting

---

[723] John 13:14-17, 34-35.

[724] There are many commandments that apply to only certain individuals. The commandment of the parapet is only directed to those that have houses with a flat roof. If one doesn't have a house with a roof on which people can walk, one isn't expected to observe or to fulfill this commandment.

[725] For a Scripture reading plan see http://SeedofAbraham.net/scripture07.htm.

wisdom and strength to overcome the fear. He delights in setting us free!

Legalism is part of what we have to deal with in our lives. Legalism is part of our carnality. We are going to make mistakes. God allows this as part of our experiential training in righteousness. We must come to Him and His Torah as little children. No one has all the answers, but oh what joy there is in discovering (some of) them!

Keeping the Sabbath is not legalism. It's God's law for His chosen people Israel, both Jew and Gentile. Yeshua kept the Sabbath day holy all His life and never did it legalistically. He has given us His Spirit that we might follow His example.

Our understanding is faulty. That's why (His) love covers a multitude of sins. We should be excited with *joy* that He is teaching us His Torah (Genesis through Revelation). He will correct us as we walk with Him. He's a good *Abba* (Papa). Our learning Torah is like a child going with his *Abba* to the park on an adventure. He will take good care of us.

The teachings of the Rabbis can be insightful. They can flesh out understanding of a commandment or a passage of Scripture, but realize that the Rabbis can be very wrong, extremely shallow and diabolically perverse (Mt. 16:5-12; 23:1-36). Be careful.[726] Pray before swallowing. If you're not sure, or if you want another opinion, feel free to contact me.[727]

I've seen too many sincere Christians fall into the tar pits of Judaism, a Judaism that has been anti-Christ since the Gold Calf debacle. Also, without the infilling of His Spirit, we all too easily fall prey to the spiritual Magician who loves to seduce and lead astray to damnation. If you don't have the infilling of the Holy Spirit, seek it diligently! Study the Word. Learn Hebrew. It will open up hidden treasures for you. Yes, I know it's difficult, but the rewards are sweet.

To abstain from all unclean meat is Torah. To 'keep kosher' the Jewish way is both Torah and devastatingly rabbinic. There's a big difference. The Rabbis have added much of their nonsense to the Word and have perverted the laws. God wants us to eat only meat that is clean according to His Torah. 'Keeping kosher' means different things to God and Orthodox Judaism.[728] One of the differences is that the observant Jewish community does not allow the eating of dairy and meat together, but this is not scriptural. A faulty rabbinic interpretation of Ex. 23:19 is the reason for this.[729]

---

[726] For a brief outline of some of the idolatrous and perverted things of Judaism see *Jewish Idolatry* at http://SeedofAbraham.net/jewidol.html.

[727] See p. 293 for contact information.

[728] Why are the Rabbis wrong about the separation of meat and dairy foods? See *Kosher: Jewish vs. Biblical* at http://SeedofAbraham.net/kosher.html.

Judaism also requires different dishes for dairy and meat meals, even though neither the meat that they eat, nor the dairy, is unclean.[730]

If God leads, go to a synagogue service. Tell anyone at the synagogue, who asks you why you're there, that you've found the Messiah of Israel and He's leading you to keep Torah. Don't expect accolades, but perhaps you can learn Hebrew there.[731] Don't be afraid to be a living witness for Yeshua amongst the Jewish people.[732] They need to know.

Most Christians today don't fully understand how pervasive pagan wor-

---

[729] The Jewish view of Ex. 23:19 (of not boiling a kid in its mother's milk) is that one should not eat meat and dairy together, thus avoiding the possibility of eating the meat of the kid and the milk of the mother together. Of course, the possibility exists that one can eat the meat of the kid and the milk of the mother at different times. Extending the rabbinic interpretation to all meat and dairy, one finds the impossible situation of chickens, which don't give milk, but are nevertheless prohibited from being eaten with dairy products.

The Rabbis have misunderstood the verse. It has nothing to do with the separation of meat and dairy, but with an ancient pagan fertility rite. This prohibition comes immediately after the fall harvest, the Feast of Tabernacles (Ex. 23:16, 19; 34:22, 26), or just before it (Dt. 14:21-27). The prohibition was aimed at stopping Israel from copying the *magical* procedure of the pagans, in the hope that their future harvest would be bountiful.

Freeman, *Manners and Customs of the Bible*, p. 73, #133, states, this 'injunction is put in connection with sacrifices and festivals' (and not a dietary regulation). The seething of a kid in his mother's milk was an *idolatrous* practice done 'for the purpose of making trees and fields more fruitful the following year...on the authority of an ancient Karaite comment on the Pentateuch...it was an ancient heathen custom to boil a kid in the dam's milk, and then besprinkle with it all the trees, fields, gardens and orchards.'

Pfeiffer, *WBC*, p. 73, states, 'in the Ugarit literature discovered in 1930, it was learned that boiling a kid in its mother's milk was a Canaanite practice used in connection with fertility rites (*Birth of the Gods*, 1:14).'

Harris, *Theological Wordbook of the Old Testament*, vol. I, p. 285, writes, "Since a Ugaritic text (UT 16: Text no. 52:14) specifies, 'They cook a kid in milk...the biblical injunction' was 'directed against a Canaanite fertility rite.'"

[730] The eating of dairy with meat is strictly forbidden by the Rabbis, but this cannot be found anywhere in Scripture. This rabbinic prohibition is perverse because it sets up something as *sin*, which God doesn't call sin. The separation of meat and dairy dishes, pots and pans, etc., stems from the ruling to separate meat from dairy. This is part of 'kosher the Orthodox Jewish way,' but isn't found in God's Word. On the contrary, Father Abraham served the Lord and two angels meat and dairy at the same time and they ate it (Gen. 18:8).

[731] See http://seedofabraham.net/c&v.html for my Hebrew course and teachings.

[732] See *Jewish Newsletters* at http://SeedofAbraham.net/newsletr.html and *The Prophecy Card* at http://SeedofAbraham.net/theprophecycard.html for tools to use, and information to share, with Jewish people about their Messiah.

ship was in Yakov's day. *All the world* was deeply involved in it. From Chile to China and from India to Ireland, all the world was enslaved to pagan gods and their cruel practices. The names of the gods and goddesses would change in each country, but what tied them all together was their similar rites, practices, ceremonies and doctrines, which all stemmed from Babylon. For an excellent detailed account of this, read Alexander Hislop's classic, *The Two Babylons*.[733]

Rabbinically, the Law, symbolized in circumcision, was necessary for eternal life. This false teaching is mimicked by the Catholic Church with its (sprinkling) baptism. Circumcision, though, was given to Abraham as a *sign* of his covenant *relationship* with God. He was *already* walking with God (Genesis 12, 15, 17). Circumcision was the *sign* of his faith, not the guarantee of it. God expected Jewish infants to grow in their faith.

Water baptism is a picture or sign of being Born Again as a new creature, one that is destined to be like Yeshua is now, glorified (2nd Peter 1:4; 2nd Cor. 5:17). Believers, too, must grow in their faith. Yeshua, *coming up out of the waters* of His baptism pictured His *coming forth* or *being begotten* by His Father (Jn. 8:42; 16:27-28; 17:8) as the Word and the Light of Gen. 1:3. In Hebrew it speaks of the Spirit *fluttering,* like a bird, over the waters, whose waters pictured the Father.[734] He said, 'Let there be Light!' (Gen. 1:2-3), and Yeshua *came forth* from those Waters. This is reenacted when He *came up out of the waters* of His baptism, with the Spirit *alighting* upon Him as a dove and the voice of His Father proclaiming His Son.

We're called to walk in an intimate relationship with God, to keep His Torah and to teach our children to walk in it (Dt. 6:4-7f.). As we do this, we are their example and are preparing them to worship the King in the way that He desires when He comes to rule for 1,000 years upon this Earth in the city of Jerusalem (Rev 20:6). It's time for God's people Israel, both Jew and Gentile who love Yeshua with all their heart, to come out of Babylon and all her ways of darkness, as Rev. 18:4 states:

> "And I heard another voice from Heaven saying, 'Come out of her My people!, so that you may not participate in her sins and that you may not receive of her plagues'"

---

[733] Download *The Two Babylons*—complete with all illustrations and footnotes at http://SeedofAbraham.net/articles.html (under section Miscellaneous).

[734] For the Father, pictured as water, see Gen. 1:2-10; Psalm 104:3; 148:4; Is. 8:6; 55:1; Jer. 51:16; Ezk. 1:24; 2nd Peter 3:5; Rev. 22:1, 17.

# APPENDIX

## *Two Different Kingdoms?*

### The Stranger and the Native-Born

The following sections reinforce the two themes: that Yakov gave the four rules as a filter against sacrificial-sexual idolatry, and that Mosaic Law is for every believer in Yeshua. There are basically five different Hebrew words for Gentiles who resided within Israel. The Law applied to only two of them—the slave (by circumstance) and the stranger (by choice).

*Stranger* is an English translation for *ger* in the KJV, NKJV and NASB. The NIV uses *alien* and the NRSV uses *resident alien*.[735] The five Hebrew words are found in Ex. 12:43-48. It's the Passover chapter and the Lord is saying who can, and who cannot, take part in it:

1. foreigner       בֶּן-נֵכָר   (*ben nay'char*) ......No    Ex. 12:43

2. hired worker     שָׂכִיר   (*sah'chere*) ............No    Ex. 12:45

3. temporary resident   תּוֹשָׁב   (*toe'shav*) ..............No    Ex. 12:45

4. slave             עֶבֶד   (*eh'ved*) .................Yes    Ex. 12:44

5. stranger         גֵּר   (*ger*) ......................Yes    Ex. 12:48

Why one could or couldn't be a part of Israel (eat the Passover) revolves around his heart toward Israel. The meaning of the words brings this out:

1. The foreigner *could not eat* of the Passover (Ex. 12:43). The noun means 'what is strange, foreign;' the verb, 'to estrange, alienate...to seem strange...to reject.'[736] *TWOT* says it speaks of 'a foreign god,' 'Dt. 32:12,' and 'everything foreign (Neh. 13:30).'[737] This person worships other gods and *wants* to be alienated from Israel, her God and His Torah, all of which appear 'strange' to him.

2. The hired worker *could not eat* of the Passover (Ex. 12:45). The

---

[735] Some Bibles, like the KJV, NET and HCSB, don't make a distinction between the foreigner (#1) and the stranger (#5). This is unfortunate as it seems that God is contradicting Himself (e.g. the KJV for Ex. 12:43 has God saying that the *stranger* [#1] cannot keep the Passover, but in v. 48 the KJV has God saying that the *stranger* [#5] can keep it!).

[736] Davidson, *The Analytical Hebrew and Chaldee Lexicon*, p. 549. Another word that is associated with *ben nay'char* is *zar* (זָר) and is translated into English as 'stranger' or 'enemy,' but this word is also used of an Israeli who is not of Aaron (Lev. 18:4), or of Levi (Lev. 1:51). Koehler, *HALOT*, vol. 1, p. 279.

[737] Harris, *Theological Wordbook of the Old Testament*, vol. II, p. 580.

noun means a 'hired laborer, hireling.'[738] He's not interested in the God of Israel, but only in himself and finding work (Jn. 10:12-13).

3. The temporary resident *could not eat* of the Passover (Ex. 12:45). This is a person who is also called a 'sojourner.'[739] He's a migrant, a 'temporary, landless wage earner.' The word can also be 'a synonym for a hired servant (Lev. 22:10; 25:40).'[740]

4. The slave *could eat* of the Passover after he was circumcised (Ex. 12:44). The slave served his master, doing his will.[741] The slave seems to be 'one' with his Hebrew master (Gen. 17:9-13, 23-27).

5. The stranger *could eat* the Passover once he and all the males in his house were circumcised (Ex. 12:48). The verb means to 'dwell for a time.'[742] Once circumcised, the stranger kept the Sabbath laws (Ex. 20:10; 23:12) and expressed the same loyalty to God as the native-born (Lev. 20:2).[743]

  a. He was to hear the Law read (Dt. 31:12), and the Feasts applied to him (Ex. 12:19; Lev. 16:29; Num. 9:14; Dt. 16:14).

  b. Death was the punishment to the *ger* if he sacrificed to a foreign god (Lev. 17:8f.), and he was also forbidden to eat blood (Lev. 17:10-13). The special cleansing of the red heifer's ashes applied to him (Num. 19:10), as well as all the laws of forbidden sexual unions (Lev. 18:26).

  c. It's written that Yahveh *loves* this stranger, giving him his food and clothing (Dt. 10:18). He wasn't to be oppressed by the Israeli and he enjoyed the same rights as the native-born Hebrew (Ex. 22:21; Lev. 19:3; Jer. 7:6).[744] He was to be helped if he was poor (Lev. 19:10; Dt. 14:29; 16:11) and he could take of the gleanings of the olive trees and vineyards, which were only reserved for him, the widow and the orphan (Dt. 24:20-21).

The stranger (#5 *ger*) who was circumcised was just like the native-born

---

[738] Davidson, *The Analytical Hebrew and Chaldee Lexicon*, p. 715.

[739] Ibid., p. 352.

[740] Harris, *Theological Wordbook of the Old Testament*, vol. I, p. 412.

[741] Davidson, *The Analytical Hebrew and Chaldee Lexicon*, p. 583.

[742] Ibid., p. 134.

[743] Harris, *Theological Wordbook of the Old Testament*, vol. I, p. 156.

[744] Ibid. Although the stranger (#5 *ger*) is in a separate category from other non-Hebrews, there are times when the word seems to be used as a general designation for anyone not of Israel (e.g. Dt. 10:19; 28:43). It's possible that a #1 could become a #5 (Is. 56:3, 6-7).

Hebrew, but was still called a *stranger*, or more properly, a *ger*. Yahveh's Law extended to him. Basically, the Law was for both of them. If God's Law applied to the stranger in the midst of Israel under the Old Testament, *how much more* under the New Testament, where this stranger (Gentile) has been circumcised in the heart by God (Col. 2:11)?

The Gentiles come into Israel through the New Covenant, the covenant that God gave to the House of Israel and the House of Judah (Jer. 31:31-34; Eph. 2:13). They are to learn the laws of the God of Israel that they might gain *greater* spiritual knowledge of Yeshua and walk in His ways, with their Jewish believing brethren (Dt. 31:12-13; Acts 15:21).

The following is a partial list of cites which contain the *ger* (#5, stranger):

> Ex. 12:19: 'Seven days there shall be no leaven found in your houses, for whoever eats what is leavened, that person must be cut off from the Congregation of Israel, whether he is a *stranger* or a native of the Land.' (This pertains to Passover week.)

> Ex. 12:43-45, 48: "And Yahveh said to Moses and Aaron, 'This is the ordinance of the Passover: No foreigner (#1) shall eat it, but *every man's slave* (#4) who is bought for money, when you have circumcised him, then he may eat it. A temporary resident (#3) and a hired servant (#2) must not eat it.'"

> 'And when a *stranger* (#5) dwells with you and wants to keep the Passover to Yahveh, let all his males be circumcised and then let him come near and keep it. *And he shall be as a native of the land.*'

> Lev. 16:29: 'This shall be a permanent statute for you: in the seventh month on the tenth day of the month you must humble your souls and not do any work, whether the native or the *stranger* who sojourns among you.' (This is for the Day of Atonement.)

> Lev. 17:12: "Therefore, I said to the Sons of Israel, 'No person among you may eat blood, nor may any *stranger* who sojourns among you eat blood.'"

> Lev. 18:26: You 'are to keep My statutes and My judgments and must not do any of these abominations, neither the native, nor the *stranger* who sojourns among you.'

> Lev. 24:16: 'Moreover, the one who blasphemes the name of Yahveh must surely be put to death—all the Congrega-

tion must stone him. The *stranger* as well as the native, when he blasphemes the Name, shall be put to death.'

Num. 9:14: 'If a *stranger* sojourns among you and observes the Passover to Yahveh, according to the statute of the Passover and according to its ordinance, so he must do. *You shall have one statute both for the stranger* and for the native of the land.'

Num. 15:14-16: 'If a *stranger* sojourns with you, or one who may be among you throughout your generations, and he wishes to make a *sacrifice* by fire as a soothing aroma to Yahveh, *just as you do, so he shall do.* As for the Assembly, there shall be one statute for you and for the stranger who sojourns with you, a *perpetual statute throughout your generations.* As you are, so shall the *stranger* be before Yahveh. There is to be *one law and one ordinance* for you and for the *stranger* who sojourns with you.'

Num. 15:29: 'You shall have one law for him who does anything unintentionally, for him who is native among the Sons of Israel, and for the *stranger* who lives among them.'

Num. 15:30: 'But the person who does anything defiantly, whether he is native or a *stranger*, that one is blaspheming Yahveh, and that person must be cut off from among his people!'

Num. 19:10: 'The one who gathers the ashes of the heifer must wash his clothes, and be unclean until evening. And it shall be a perpetual statute to the Sons of Israel and to the *stranger* who lives among them.'

Num. 35:15: 'These six cities shall be for refuge for the Sons of Israel, and for the *stranger* (#5), and for the sojourner (#3, temporary resident) among them, that anyone who kills a person unintentionally may flee there.'

Dt. 31:12: 'Assemble the people, the men, the women, the children and the *stranger* who is in your town so that they may hear and learn and fear Yahveh your God, and *be careful to observe all the words of this Law.*'

Joshua 8:33-35: 'All Israel, with their Elders, officers and their judges, the *stranger* as well as the native-born, stood on both sides of the Ark, in front of the Levitical Priests who carried the Ark of the Covenant of Yahveh. Half of them in front of Mount Gerizim and half of them in front of Mount Ebal, as Moses the Servant of Yahveh had commanded, that they should bless the people of Israel. And afterward he read all the words of the Law, blessings and curses, according to all that is written in the book of the Law. There was not a word of all that Moses commanded that Joshua did not read before all the Assembly of Israel, and the women and the little ones and the *strangers* who resided among them.'

Ezk. 47:23: "'And *in the Tribe* with which the *stranger* stays, there you shall *give him his inheritance*,' declares the Lord Yahveh." (This speaks of the Millennial Kingdom of Yeshua: Ezk. 40–48; Rev. 20:1-6f.)

Isaiah 56:6-7: 'Also the *foreigners* who *join themselves* to Yahveh to minister to Him and to love the name of Yahveh, to be His servants; everyone who keeps from profaning the Sabbath and holds fast My Covenant, these I will bring to My holy Mountain and make them joyful in My House of Prayer.'

'Their burnt offerings and their *sacrifices* will be accepted on My Altar, for My House shall be called a House of Prayer for *all* peoples.'

This last cite in Isaiah doesn't speak of the stranger (*ger*), but of the *ben nay'char* (#1 the foreigner). It shows that Yahveh's compassion would extend to those who had been formerly excluded from the covenant. Now salvation is open to everyone who turns to Him through Messiah Yeshua.

Welcome to the Commonwealth of Israel (the Kingdom of God), where the wall of partition has been broken down:[745]

'So then, you are no longer *strangers and foreigners,* but you are fellow citizens with the holy ones and are of God's Household.' (Eph. 2:19)

"'And it shall be from New Moon to New Moon and from Sabbath to Sabbath, *all mankind* will come to bow down before Me' says Yahveh." (Isaiah 66:23)

---

[745]  Rom. 11:16-29; Eph. 2:1-22; 3:6.

# The Blood

Lev. 17:10-14: 'And any man from the House of Israel or from the *strangers* who sojourn among them who eats any *blood*, I will set My face against that person who eats *blood* and will cut him off from among his people.'

"For the life of the flesh is in the *blood* and I have given it to you on the Altar to make atonement for your souls. For it is the *blood*, by reason of the life, that makes atonement. Therefore, I said to the Sons of Israel, 'No person among you may eat *blood,* nor may any *stranger* who sojourns among you eat *blood.*'"

'So when any man from the Sons of Israel, or from the *strangers* who sojourn among them, in hunting, catches a beast or a bird, which may be eaten, he must pour out its blood and cover it with earth.'

"As for the life of all flesh, its *blood* is identified with its life. Therefore, I said to the Sons of Israel, 'You are not to eat the *blood* of any flesh, for the life of all flesh is its *blood*. Whoever eats it shall be cut off.'"

The animal was caught and slaughtered, and the blood drained upon the ground and covered. Hunters know that the blood needs to be drained immediately after the kill. This way the meat will not become contaminated with the blood in it. It is only with today's modern methods of mass slaughtering of cattle and chicken, etc., that most of the time the blood is not properly drained. Welcome to the 21st century.

'The *blood* however, you must not eat. You must pour it out on the ground like water.' (Dt. 12:16)

'Only be sure that you do not eat the *blood*. For the *blood* is the life and you must not eat the life with the meat.' (Dt. 12:23)

Eating the blood in roast beef is also wrong. It, too, is a sin (Lev. 7:26; 19:26; 2nd Sam. 14:32-34; Ezk. 33:25).

# The Harlot

Lev. 17:7: 'They must no longer sacrifice their sacrifices to the goat demons, with which they *play the cult harlot*. This shall be a permanent statute to them throughout their generations.'

Lev. 20:6: 'As for the person who turns to mediums and to spiritists, to *play the harlot* after them, I will also set My face against that person and will cut him off from among his people.'

Dt. 22:21: 'then they shall bring out the girl to the doorway of her father's house, and the men of her city shall stone her to death because she has done a disgraceful thing in Israel by *playing the harlot* in her father's house. Thus you shall purge the evil from among you.'

Dt. 23:18: 'You must not bring the hire of a *cult harlot*, or the wages of a dog (a *homosexual male cult harlot*), into the House of Yahveh your God for any votive offering, for both of these are an abomination to Yahveh your God!'

Dt. 31:16: "Yahveh said to Moses, 'Behold, you are about to lie down with your Fathers, and this people will arise and *play the cult harlot* with the strange gods of the land into the midst of which they are going, and will forsake Me and break My Covenant, which I have made with them.'"

Judges 2:17: 'Yet they did not listen to their judges, for they *played the cult harlot* after other gods and bowed themselves down to them. They turned aside quickly from the way in which their Fathers had walked, in obeying the commandments of Yahveh. They did not do as their Fathers.'

2nd Chron. 21:11: 'Moreover he made high places in the mountains of Judah and caused the inhabitants of Jerusalem to *play the cult harlot,* and led Judah astray.'

Psalm 106:35-40: 'But they *mingled with the nations and learned their practices* and served their idols which became a snare to them. They even *sacrificed their sons and their daughters to the demons* and shed innocent blood, *the blood of their sons and their daughters, whom they sacrificed to the idols of Canaan,* and the Land was polluted with the blood. Thus they became *unclean* in their practices and *played the cult harlot* in their deeds. Therefore, the anger of Yahveh was kindled against His people and He abhorred His Inheritance.'

Isaiah 1:21: 'How the faithful City has become a *harlot!* She, who was full of justice! Righteousness once lodged in her, but now murderers!'

Jer. 2:20: "For long ago I broke your yoke and tore off your bonds, but you said, 'I will not serve!' For on every high hill and under every green tree you have lain down as a *cult harlot.*"

Jer. 3:6-10: "Then Yahveh said to me in the days of King Josiah, 'Have you seen what faithless Israel did? She went up on every high hill and under every green tree and she was a *cult harlot* there.' I thought, 'After she has done all these things she will return to Me,' but she did not return, and her treacherous sister Judah saw it."

"'And I saw that for all the adulteries of faithless Israel, I had sent her away and given her a writ of divorce, yet her treacherous sister Judah did not fear, but she went and was a *cult harlot,* also! Because of the lightness of her *cult harlotry* she polluted the Land and committed adultery with stones and trees. Yet, in spite of all this, her treacherous sister Judah did not return to Me with all her heart, but rather in deception!,' declares Yahveh."

Ezk. 16:15-17, 26: 'But you trusted in your beauty and *played the cult harlot* because of your fame, and you poured out your *harlotries* on every passerby who might be willing. You took some of your clothes, made for yourself high places of various colors and *played the cult harlot* on them, which should never have come about, nor happened. You also took your beautiful jewels, made of My gold and of My silver, which I had given you, and made for yourself male images that you might *play the cult harlot* with them!...You also played the *cult harlot* with the Egyptians, your lustful neighbors, and multiplied your *cult harlotry* to make Me angry.'

Hosea 4:12-14: 'My people consult their wooden idol and their diviner's wand informs them. For a spirit of *cult harlotry* has led them astray and they have *played the cult harlot*, departing from their God. They offer sacrifices on the tops of the mountains and burn incense on the hills, under oak, poplar and terebinth because their shade is pleasant. Therefore, your daughters *play the harlot* and your brides commit adultery.'

'I will not punish your daughters when they *play the harlot,* or your brides when they commit adultery, for the men themselves go apart with *cult harlots* and offer sacrifices with *temple harlots*. So the people without understanding are ruined.'

Nahum 3:4: 'All because of the many *cult harlotries* of the Harlot, the Charming One, the Mistress of Sorceries, who sells nations by her *cult harlotries,* and families by her sorceries.'[746]

Rev. 17:1: "Then one of the seven angels who had the seven bowls came and spoke with me, saying, 'Come here! I will show you the judgment of the Great *Cult Harlot* who sits on many waters.'"

Rev. 17:15-16: "And he said to me, 'The waters which you saw where the *Cult Harlot* sits are peoples, multitudes, nations and tongues, and the ten horns which you saw, and the beast, these will hate the *Cult Harlot* and will make her desolate and naked, and will eat her flesh and will burn her up with fire.'"

---

[746] This is the Great Cult Harlot of Babylon. Hislop, *The Two Babylons*, p. 304: 'The first deified woman was no doubt Semiramis, as the first deified man was her husband' (Nimrod). Semiramis was known in Israel as Astarte and worshiped in other countries under many other names: Diana, Rhea, Venus, and Cybele (Madonna), etc. She was called 'an incarnation of the one spirit of God, the great Mother of all...the Holy Spirit of God.' Incredibly enough, these are designations that the Roman Catholic Church places upon its sinless and deified Mary. In other words, the attributes of the Mary of the Roman Catholic Church are not that of the Jewish mother of Jesus, but the great mother goddess of the pagans.

# The Fire of God

When Yahveh appears in Fire on Mt. Sinai (Ex. 3:1-6; 19:16-20), the identification of God with fire begins. The fire on the Altar of Sacrifice, of the Tabernacle of Moses, was never to go out.[747] It symbolized the eternal God. It's also a picture of the Fire of God on the heavenly Altar. This Fire is eternal, for it says that our God is a consuming Fire.[748]

The Altar fire was seen as a cleansing agent. The sacrifices were consumed by something that pictured the Fire of God (the Holy Spirit). Symbolically, the sinful person was transformed through this *living Fire* and ascended to God in smoke—totally dedicated and pleasing to Yahveh.

*Fire* is the closest thing, 'in the natural,' that we have for describing Yahveh's spiritual substance:

> Ex. 19:16-18: 'So it came about on the third day, when it was morning, that there were thunder and lightning flashes and a thick Cloud upon the Mountain, and a very loud *Shofar'* (Ram's horn) 'so that all the people who were in the Camp trembled. And Moses brought the people out of the Camp *to meet God* and they stood at the foot of the Mountain. Now Mount Sinai was all in Smoke because Yahveh descended upon it in *Fire,* and its Smoke ascended like the smoke of a furnace, and the whole Mountain quaked violently.'

> Ex. 24:17: 'And to the eyes of the Sons of Israel, the appearance of the Glory of Yahveh was like a *consuming Fire* on the mountain top.'

When the Tabernacle of Moses was first inaugurated, after Aaron and his sons were fully consecrated, Yahveh sent Fire from the Heavens to light the Altar of Sacrifice. It was a picture of the Holy Spirit in us:

> Lev. 9:23-24: 'Moses and Aaron went into the Tent of Meeting. When they came out and blessed the people the Glory of Yahveh appeared to all the people. Then *Fire* came out from before Yahveh and consumed the burnt sacrifice and the portions of fat on the Altar, and when all the people saw it, they shouted and fell on their faces.'

> 2nd Chron. 7:3 (Solomon's Temple): "All the Sons of Israel, seeing the *Fire* come down, and the Glory of Yahveh upon the Temple, bowed down on the pavement with

---

[747] Lev. 6:13: 'Fire shall burn continually on the Altar. It's not to go out.'

[748] Dt. 4:24; Heb. 12:29; also Ex. 19:16f.; Lev. 9:23-24; Lk. 12:49; Rev. 4:5.

> their faces to the ground and they worshiped and gave
> praise to Yahveh, saying, 'Truly He is good! Truly His
> faithful, forgiving loving-kindness is everlasting!'"

When the Holy Spirit was given to Israel in Acts 2, we see that same Fire
upon the Apostles:

> Acts 2:3: 'And there appeared to them tongues as of *Fire*
> distributing themselves, and they rested on each one of
> them.'

*This* Fire purges us on our journey to the New Jerusalem, tests our faith in
Yeshua, and transforms us into His Image:

> 1st Cor. 3:13: 'each man's work will become evident, for
> the Day will show it, because it is to be revealed with *Fire*
> and the *Fire* itself will test the quality of each man's
> work.'

> 2nd Cor. 3:17-18: '...where the Spirit of the Lord is, there
> is liberty, and all of us, with *unveiled* faces beholding, as
> in a mirror, the *Glory* of the Lord, are being transformed
> into the same Image, from Glory to Glory.'

> 1st Peter 1:7: 'so that the proof of your faith, *being more
> precious than gold*, which is perishable, even though test-
> ed by *Fire*, may be found to result in praise and glory and
> honor at the revelation of Yeshua the Messiah.'

The book of Revelation reveals that this Fire is seen in the Holy Spirit,
and on the heavenly Altar, and in the eyes of the Son of Man:

> Rev. 4:5: 'Out from the Throne come flashes of lightning
> and sounds and peals of thunder. And there were seven
> Lamps of *Fire* burning before the Throne, which are the
> seven Spirits of God.'

> Rev. 8:5: 'Then the angel took the censer and filled it with
> the *Fire* of the Altar and threw it to the Earth, and there
> followed peals of thunder and sounds and flashes of light-
> ning and an earthquake.'

> Rev. 19:12: 'His eyes are a flame of *Fire* and on His head
> are many crowns, and He has a Name written on Him,
> which no one knows except Himself.'

# The Fire of Paganism

Dt. 12:31: 'You must not behave thus, toward Yahveh your God, for every abominable act which Yahveh hates, they have done for their gods. *For they even burn their sons and daughters in the fire* to their gods.' (See also Dt. 18:9-10, where, to 'pass through the fire,' is prohibited.)

2nd Kings 16:3: 'But he' (Ahaz, King of Judah) 'walked in the way of the Kings of Israel and even made his son pass through the *fire,* according to the abominations of the nations, whom Yahveh had driven out from before the Sons of Israel.' (To 'pass through the fire' means that the infant died in the fire as a sacrifice, and was eaten by the pagan priest, and possibly, by his father and mother, also.)

2nd Kings 17:17: 'Then they' (the Sons of Israel in the northern kingdom) 'made their sons and their daughters pass through the *fire* and practiced divination and enchantments and sold themselves to do evil in the sight of Yahveh, provoking Him.'

2nd Chron. 33:6: 'He' (Manasseh, King of Judah) 'made his sons pass through the fire in the Valley of the Son of Hinnom, and he practiced witchcraft, used divination, practiced sorcery and dealt with mediums and spiritists. He did much evil in the sight of Yahveh, provoking Him to anger.' (See also Psalm 106:34-39)

Jer. 7:31: 'They' (the people of Judah) 'have built the high places of Topheth, which is in the Valley of the Son of Hinnom, to burn their sons and their daughters in the *fire* which I did not command. It never entered My mind.'

Jer. 19:5: 'and have built the high places of Baal, to burn their sons in the *fire* as burnt sacrifices to Baal, a thing which I never commanded, or spoke of, nor did it ever enter My mind.' (Also, Jer. 32:17-18, 25)

Jer. 32:35: 'They built the high places of Baal that are in the Valley of the Son of Hinnom, to cause their sons and their daughters to pass through the *fire* to Molech, which I had not commanded them nor had it entered My mind that they should do this abomination, to cause Judah to sin.'

Ezekiel 20:31: '"When you offer your gifts, when you cause your sons to pass through the *fire*, you are defiling

yourselves with all your idols to this day! Shall I be inquired of by you, Oh House of Israel?! As I live!' declares the Lord Yahveh, 'I will not be inquired of by
you!'"

Ezk. 23:37: 'For they have committed adultery, and blood
is on their hands. Thus they have committed adultery with
their idols and even caused their sons, whom they bore to
Me, to pass through the *fire* to them as food.'

# *Paganism*

Everything in God's Kingdom has its perverted counterfeit in paganism.
Sacrifice is the *outward expression* of surrender to God (or a god), with
heart-felt submission being the inner reality. Pagans offered to their gods
their best and their dearest as a sacrifice for sin, making even their infants
'pass through the fire.' The prophet Micah (742-687 BC) speaks of this
when he rhetorically asks,

> 'Shall I present *my firstborn* for my rebellious acts? The
> *fruit of my body* for the sin of my soul?' (Micah 6:7b)

Gentile (and Jewish) babies were burned alive, screaming, as their drunk-
en parents and other 'worshipers' shouted, sang and wildly danced, drums
and other instruments pounding away. They would eat the child as part of
their worship to gods like Molech, Baal and Dagon. Those gods *demanded* child sacrifice, a perversion of the Mosaic sacrificial system. In Lev.
20:1-8 it's written:

> "Then Yahveh spoke to Moses saying, 'You shall also say
> to the Sons of Israel, 'Any man from the Sons of Israel or
> from the strangers sojourning in Israel, who gives any of
> his sons to Molech, must surely be put to death! The peo-
> ple of the Land shall stone him with stones. I will also set
> My face against that man and will cut him off from
> among his people because he has given some of his chil-
> dren to Molech, so as to defile My Sanctuary and to pro-
> fane My Holy Name.'"

> 'If the people of the Land, however, should ever disregard
> that man, when he gives any of his sons to Molech, so as
> not to put him to death, then I Myself will set My face
> against that man and against his family and I will cut off
> from among their people, both him and all those who play
> the harlot after him, by playing the cult prostitute after
> Molech. As for the person who turns to mediums and to

spiritists, to play the harlot after them, I will also set My face against that person and will cut him off from among his people. You must consecrate yourselves and be holy!, for I am Yahveh your God! You must keep My statutes and practice them. I am Yahveh, *who makes you holy!*'

Not all pagan worship required human sacrifice, but collectively they form a perverse picture of Gentile worship. Pagans sought to reside in the 'safety and blessings' of their gods, to the destruction of their souls and their very own children.

Paganism and cult prostitution went hand in hand. There were also other satanic things that attached themselves to this 'worship,' like murder. *UBD* speaks of this and says of the goddess Asherah,

> "who is found in the Ras Shamra epic religious texts discovered at Ugarit in northern Syria (1927-37) as Asherat, 'Lady of the Sea' and consort of El. She was chief goddess of Tyre with the appellation Kudshu 'holiness' and she appears as a goddess by the side of Baal, whose consort she came to be, among the Canaanites of the south. Her worship was utterly detestable to faithful worshipers' of Yahveh '(1st Kg. 15:13)."[749]

> 'Asherah was only one manifestation of a chief goddess of western Asia regarded as both wife and sister of the principal Canaanite god *El*. Other names of the deity were Ashtoreth (Astarte) and Anath. Frequently' she was 'represented as a nude woman bestride a lion.'[750]

> Her "male prostitutes consecrated to the cult of the Kudshu and prostituting themselves to her honor were styled *Kedishim*, 'sodomites' (Dt. 23:8; 1st Kings 14:24)."[751]

> 'At Byblos (biblical Gebal), on the Mediterranean, north of Sidon, a center dedicated to this goddess has been excavated. She and her colleagues specialized in sex.'[752]

> It's also noted that 'lust and murder were glamorized in Canaanite religion[753]...On a fragment of the Baal Epic, Anath appears in an incredibly bloody orgy of destruc-

---

[749] Unger, *Unger's Bible Dictionary*, p. 412.

[750] Ibid.

[751] Ibid.

[752] Ibid.

[753] Ibid.

tion. For some unknown reason she fiendishly butchers mankind, young as well as old, in a most horrible and wholesale fashion, wading ecstatically in human gore up to her knees—yea, up to her throat, all the while exulting sadistically.'[754]

This is a glimpse not only into paganism, but also into the very essence of Satan and his plan for man: murder for the sheer glee of brutally extinguishing life, with sex aligned as 'worship' to entice the ignorant and unsuspecting:

Astarte was a Canaanite goddess 'of sensual love.'[755] 'Licentious worship was conducted in honor of her,'[756] and even 'Solomon succumbed to her voluptuous worship (1st Kings 11:5; 2nd Kings 23:13).'[757]

The Ras Shamra Tablets tell us that Baal 'was the son of El, the father of the gods and the head of the Canaanite pantheon.'[758] He is also 'the son of Dagon.'[759] The 'inhabitants of Canaan were addicted to Baal worship, which was conducted by priests in their temples.'[760]

'The cult included animal sacrifice, ritualistic meals and licentious dances'[761] that would end in sexual orgies. 'High places had chambers for sacred prostitution by male prostitutes (*kedishim*) and sacred harlots (*kedishoth*) (1st Kings 14:23-24; 2nd Kings 23:7).'[762]

*UBD* reports that the northern kingdom of Israel was infested with Baal worship:

'Ahab, who married' (Jezebel) 'a Zidonian priestess' (cult harlot), 'at her instigation, built a temple and altar to Baal, and revived all the abominations of the Amorites (1st Kings 21:25-26). Henceforth, Baal worship became so completely identified with the northern kingdom that it is

---

[754] Ibid.

[755] Ibid.

[756] Ibid.

[757] Ibid., p. 413.

[758] Ibid., p. 415.

[759] Ibid.

[760] Ibid.

[761] Ibid.

[762] Ibid.

described as walking in the way or statutes of the Kings of Israel (2nd Kings 16:3; 17:8).'[763]

Yahveh would put an end to these idolatrous practices by sending Assyria to destroy the northern kingdom in 721 BC. Idolatry and cult harlotry in Judah were just as detestable. Yahveh states in Jer. 17:1:

'The sin of Judah is written down with an iron stylus. With a diamond point it's engraved upon the tablet of their heart, and upon the horns of their altars.'

The Ras Shamra texts speak of cult harlotry being associated with the sun goddess Shaphash. This is unusual, as most deities of the sun were male. It reveals the high status and honor that this female goddess exerted over pagan men. Of course, in the worship of the various deities, 'prostitution was glorified.'[764] These women were 'professionals.' *UBD* states:

A '"*class of women* existed among the Phoenicians, Armenians, Lydians and Babylonians' (Epistle of Jer. v. 43). They are distinguished from the public prostitutes... and associated with the performances of sacred rites."[765]

This was the religious infrastructure in the ancient world. The names of the various gods and goddesses throughout the pagan world would change to suit each country and culture, but their rites and rituals were basically the same. What began at the Tower in Babylon spread all over the Earth. The gods and goddesses of Babylon are found throughout *all* ancient pagan peoples. The only major difference is their different names.

The god Vulcan is an example of how the gods and goddesses evolve from one country to the next. Interestingly enough, the name Vulcan was popularized on the TV show Star Trek, but the god was a murderer and devourer of infants sacrificed to him. Vulcan is also known as Hephaistos, which means, 'to break in pieces or *scatter* abroad.' Vulcan's other aliases included, but weren't limited to, Janus, Bel (the Confounder), Chaos, Baal and Merodach (the great rebel). They all stemmed from the human prototype, Nimrod. Because of his great apostasy, Nimrod caused the people of the Earth to be *scattered* after the destruction of the Tower of Babel.

The symbol of Vulcan was the hammer, which came from the club of Janus or Chaos, the god of confusion. The word *club* in Chaldee literally means 'to break in pieces or scatter abroad.'[766] In his identification with

---

[763] Ibid.

[764] Ibid.

[765] Ibid., p. 514.

[766] Hislop, *The Two Babylons*, pp. 27-28.

Nimrod, Vulcan possessed many of the titles and characteristics of Nimrod.[767] Hislop states that, 'Everything in the history of Vulcan exactly agrees with that of Nimrod.' Here are some parallels:

> "Vulcan was the head and chief of the Cyclops, that is, 'the kings of flame.'"[768] 'Nimrod was the head of the fire worshipers.'[769]
>
> 'Vulcan was the forger of the thunderbolts by which such havoc was made among the enemies of the gods. Ninus, or Nimrod, in his wars with the king of Bactria, seems to have carried on the conflict in a similar way.'[770]
>
> 'Vulcan (was) the god of fire of the Romans, and Nimrod, the fire god of Babylon.'[771]
>
> "Nimrod, as the representative of the devouring fire to which human victims, and especially children, were offered in sacrifice, was regarded as the great child devourer[772]...As the father of the gods, he was...called Kronos; and everyone knows that the classical story of Kronos was just this, that 'he devoured his sons as soon as they were born.'"[773] (see Rev. 12:4b) As "the representative of Moloch or Baal, infants were the most acceptable offerings at his altar[774]...Hence, the priests of Nimrod or Baal were necessarily required to eat of the human sacrifices; and thus it has come to pass that 'Cahna Bal...the Priest of Baal'[775] is the established word in our own tongue for a devourer of human flesh" (a cannibal).[776]

---

[767] Ibid., p. 229. Hislop's cite for this is *Heathen Mythology Illustrated*, p. 75.

[768] Ibid. "Kuclops, from Khuk, 'king,' and Lohb, 'flame.' The image of the great god was represented with three eyes—one in the forehead; hence the story of the Cyclops with the one eye in the forehead."

[769] Ibid.

[770] Ibid.

[771] Ibid., p. 230.

[772] Ibid., p. 231.

[773] Ibid. Hislop cites 'Lempriere, *Saturn*' as the source for his information.

[774] Ibid.

[775] Ibid., p. 232. The "word Cahna is the emphatic form of Cahn. Cahn is 'a priest,' Cahna is 'the priest.'"

[776] Ibid. "From the historian Castor (an Armenian translation of Eusebius, pars. i., p. 81) we learn that it was under Bel, or Belus, that is Baal, that the Cyclops lived, and the Scholiast of Æschylus...states that these Cyclops were the

Vulcan was a vicious god, but he was only a picture of Nimrod deified. Nimrod (Gen. 10:8-12) was the model for the chief gods of the world. Nimrod's deception was designed by Satan to lead the people of the Earth away from the one true God, in whose Son is our only hope.

Of course, the pagans had their 'holy days' and teachings, but how could the Church 'baptize' these things and call them Christian?! When the Torah was thrown out, and some words of Paul were falsely interpreted to justify it, the door was opened for Satan to enter (Dan. 7:25).

Christianity is the only religion in the world that doesn't emulate its founder. Jesus never ate pork or shrimp and always kept the Sabbath day holy. How is it that most Christians don't follow Him in these areas (Mt. 5:17-19; 1st Jn. 2:1-6)? Hopefully, *The Lifting of the Veil* will help many believers to see the deception, turn from it, and walk into God's Truth:

> 'Thus says Yahveh! Stand at the crossroads and look! Ask for the Ancient Paths' (Torah) 'where the Good Way lies and walk in it! And you will find rest for your souls.' (Jer. 6:16)

> 'Remember the Torah of My servant Moses! The statutes and ordinances that I commanded him at Horeb for all Israel. Behold! I will send you the prophet Elijah before the great and terrible day of Yahveh.' (Mal. 4:4-5)

As Yahveh God called Israel to be a separate and holy people from all the other peoples of the Earth, so too, He has called all believers in Messiah Yeshua to be separate and holy from all the pagan and perverse practices of the world, the Church, Judaism and Messianic Judaism.

---

brethren of Kronos, who was also Bel, or Bal...The eye in their forehead shows that originally this name was a name of the great god, for that eye, in India and Greece, is found the characteristic of the supreme divinity. The Cyclops then, had been representatives of that God, in other words, *priests* of Bel or Bal. Now, we find that the Cyclops were well known as cannibals, *Referre ritus Cyclopum*, 'to bring back the rites of the Cyclops,' meaning to revive the practice of eating human flesh (Ovid, *Metamorphoses*, xv. 93, vol. ii. p. 132)."

# BIBLIOGRAPHY

**Accordance Bible Software** (Altamonte Springs, FL: OakTree Software, 2010-2012).

Bacchiocchi, Samuele. **From Sabbath To Sunday** (Rome: The Pontifical Gregorian University Press, 1977).

> **The New Testament Sabbath** (Gillette, WY: *The Sabbath Sentinel*, 1987)

Bauer, Walter. Augmented by William F. Arndt, F. W. Gingrich and Frederick Danker. **A Greek–English Lexicon of the New Testament and Other Early Christian Literature** (London: The University of Chicago Press, 1979).

Berry, George Ricker, Editor and Translator. **Interlinear Greek–English New Testament** (Grand Rapids, MI: Baker Books, 2000).

Bivin, David and Roy Blizzard. **Understanding the Difficult Words of Jesus** (Shippensburg, PA: Destiny Image Publishers, 2001).

Botterweck, G. Johannes and Helmer Ringgren, Editors. John Willis, Translator. **Theological Dictionary of the Old Testament** (Grand Rapids, MI: William B. Eerdmans Publishing Company, 1997).

Bromiley, Geoffrey W., General Editor. Everett F. Harrison, Roland K. Harrison and William Sanford LaSor, Associate Editors. **The International Standard Bible Encyclopedia** (Grand Rapids, MI: William B. Eerdmans Publishing Company, 1979).

Brown, Dr. Francis, Dr. S. R. Driver and Dr. Charles A. Briggs, based on the lexicon of Professor Wilhelm Gesenius. Edward Robinson, Translator. E. Rodiger, Editor. **The New Brown, Driver, Briggs, Gesenius Hebrew and English Lexicon** (Lafayette, IN: Associated Publishers and Authors, 1978).

Brown, Robert and Philip W. Comfort, Translators. J. D. Douglas, Editor. **The New Greek–English Interlinear New Testament** (Wheaton, IL: Tyndale House Publishers, 1990).

Bruce, F. F., Author. Gordon D. Fee, General Editor. **The New International Commentary on the New Testament: The Book of the Acts** (Grand Rapids, MI: William B. Eerdmans Publishing Company, 1988).

**Companion Bible, The. The Authorized Version of 1611** (Grand Rapids, MI: Kregel Publications, 1990).

Davidson, Benjamin. **The Analytical Hebrew and Chaldee Lexicon** (Grand Rapids, MI: Zondervan Publishing House, 1979).

Douglas, J. D., M.A., B.D., S.T.M., Ph.D., Organizing Editor. **The Illus-trated Bible Dictionary** (Leicester, England: Inter-Varsity Press, 1998).

Edersheim, Alfred. **The Life and Times of Jesus The Messiah** (Peabody, MA: Hendrickson Publishers, 2000).

> **The Temple: Its Ministry and Services** (Peabody, MA: Hendrickson Publishers, 1994).

Findlay, G. G., B.A., Author. W. Robertson Nicoll, M.A., LL.D., Editor. **The Expositor's Greek Testament: St. Paul's First Epistle to the Corinthians** (Peabody, MA: Hendrickson Publishers, 2002).

France, R. T., M.A., B.D., Ph.D., Author. Leon Morris, M.Sc., M.Th., Ph.D., General Editor. **Tyndale New Testament Commentaries: Matthew** (Leicester, England: Inter-Varsity Press 2000).

Freeman, Rev. James M. **Manners and Customs of the Bible** (Plainfield, NJ: Logos International, 1972; originally written in 1874).

Friberg, Timothy and Barbara, and Neva Miller. **Analytical Lexicon of the Greek New Testament** (Grand Rapids, MI: Baker Books, 2000).

Gower, Ralph. **The New Manners and Customs of Bible Times** (Chicago: Moody Press, 1987).

Gray, Jonathan. **Ark of the Covenant** (Rundle Mall, South Australia, 2000).

Harris, R. L., Editor. Gleason Archer, Jr. and Bruce Waltke, Associate Editors. **Theological Wordbook of the Old Testament** (Chicago: Moody Press, 1980).

Hegg, Tim. **The Letter Writer: Paul's Background and Torah Perspective** (Littleton, CO: First Fruits of Zion, 2002).

Hislop, Alexander. **The Two Babylons** (Neptune, NJ: Loizeaux Brothers, 1959; originally published in 1858).

Jenni, Ernst and Claus Westermann, Authors. Mark E. Biddle, Translator. **Theological Lexicon of the Old Testament** (Peabody, MA: Hendrickson Publishers, 1997).

Keil, C. F. and F. Delitzsch. **Commentary on the Old Testament** (Peabody, MA: Hendrickson Publishers, 2001; originally published by T. & T. Clark, Edinburgh, Scotland, 1866-91).

Kittel, Gerhard and Gerhard Friedrich, Editors. Geoffrey W. Bromiley, Translator and Editor. **Theological Dictionary of the New Testament** (Grand Rapids, MI: Wm. B. Eerdmans Publishing Company, 1999).

Knowling, R. J., D.D., Author. W. Robertson Nicoll, M.A., LL.D., Editor.

**The Expositor's Greek Testament: The Acts of the Apostles** (Peabody, MA: Hendrickson Publishers, 2002).

Koehler, Ludwig, Walter Baumgartner, and J. J. Stamm, Authors; M. Richardson, Editor, Translator. **The Hebrew-Aramaic Lexicon of the Old Testament**, 2001 (Accordance Bible Software).

Kruse, Colin G., B.D., M.Phil., Ph.D., Author. Leon Morris, M.Sc., M.Th., Ph.D., General Editor. **Tyndale New Testament Commentaries: 2 Corinthians** (Leicester, England: Inter-Varsity Press, 2000).

Livingstone, E. A. **The Concise Oxford Dictionary of the Christian Church** (Oxford, England: Oxford University Press, 2000).

Louw, Johannes and Eugene A. Nida, Editors. **Greek–English Lexicon of the New Testament based on Semantic Domains** (New York: United Bible Societies, 1989).

Marshall, I. Howard, M.A., B.D., Ph.D., Author. Professor R.V.G. Tasker, M.A., B.D., General Editor. **Tyndale New Testament Commentaries: Acts** (Leicester, England: Inter-Varsity Press, 2000).

Montefiore, C. G. and H. Loewe. **A Rabbinic Anthology** (New York: Shocken Books, 1974).

Morris, Leon, The Rev. Canon, M.Sc., M.Th., Ph.D. **Tyndale New Testament Commentaries: 1 Corinthians** (Leicester, England: Inter-Varsity Press, 2000).

> **Tyndale New Testament Commentaries: Revelation** (Leicester, England: Inter-Varsity Press, 2000).

Mounce, Robert H., Author. W. Ward Gasque, New Testament Editor. **New International Biblical Commentary: Matthew** (Peabody, MA: Hendrickson Publishers, 1995).

Mounce, William D. **The Analytical Lexicon to the Greek New Testament** (Grand Rapids, MI: Zondervan Publishing House, 1993).

Perschbacher, Wesley J., Editor. **The New Analytical Greek Lexicon** (Peabody, MA: Hendrickson Publications, 1990).

Pfeiffer, Charles F., Old Testament. Everett F. Harrison, New Testament. **The Wycliffe Bible Commentary** (Chicago: Moody Press, 1977).

Pritchard, James B. **The Harper Atlas of the Bible** (New York: Harper & Row, Publishers, 1987).

Ryken, Leland; James Wilhoit and Tremper Longman III, General Editors. **Dictionary of Biblical Imagery** (Leicester, England: InterVarsity Press, 1998).

Scherman, Rabbi Nosson and Rabbi Meir Zlotowitz, General Editors. **The Chumash** (Brooklyn: Mesorah Publications, Ltd., 1994).

Sinclair, J. M., General Consultant. Diana Treffry, Editorial Director. **Collins English Dictionary** (Glasgow, Scotland: HarperCollins Publishers, 1998).

Stern, David. **Jewish New Testament Commentary** (Clarksville, MD: Jewish New Testament Publications, 1992).

Tessler, Gordon. **The Genesis Diet** (Raleigh, North Carolina: Be Well Publications, 1996).

Thayer, Joseph. **Thayer's Greek–English Lexicon of the New Testament** (Accordance Bible Software; Altamonte Springs, FL: OakTree Software, 2011).

תורה נביאים כתובים והברית החדשה (**Torah, Prophets, Writings and The New Covenant**), (Jerusalem: The Bible Society of Israel, 1991).

Unger, Merrill F. **Unger's Bible Dictionary** (Chicago: Moody Press, 1976).

Vos, Howard F. **Nelson's New Illustrated Bible Manners and Customs** (Nashville, TN: Thomas Nelson Publishers, 1999).

Williams, David J., Author. W. Ward Gasque, New Testament Editor. **New International Biblical Commentary: Acts** (Peabody, MA: Hendrickson Publishers, 1999).

Wilson, William. **Wilson's Old Testament Word Studies** (Peabody, MA: Hendrickson Publishers, no publishing date given).

Witherington III, Ben. **The Acts of the Apostles: A Socio–Rhetorical Commentary** (Grand Rapids, MI: William B. Eerdmans Publishing Company, 1998).

Woolf, Henry Bosley, Editor in Chief. **Webster's New Collegiate Dictionary** (Springfield, MA: G. & C. Merriam Co., 1980).

# *Internet Sites*

**Encyclopedia Mythical** at http://www.pantheon.org/articles/e/eros.html. Eros in mythology.

**JAHG–USA** (Jews and Hasidic Gentiles–United to Save America), **The Noahide Laws** at http://www.noahide.com/lawslist.htm.

McKnight, Scot at **Jesus Creed**:

- Aug. 6th, 2007. A summary of Sanders, Dunn and Wright at http://blog.beliefnet.com/jesuscreed/2007/08/new-perspective-1.html.

- Aug. 7th, 2007. Sociological markers at http://blog.beliefnet.com/jesuscreed/2007/08/new-perspective-2.html.

- Aug. 8th, 2007. The Law was given to the Jews to show them how to live (i.e. what was good and right in God's eyes). It wasn't legalism. This is found at http://blog.beliefnet.com/jesuscreed/2007/08/new-perspective-3.html.

- Aug. 9th, 2007. Israel's election, covenant and Law, found at http://blog.beliefnet.com/jesuscreed/2007/08/new-perspective-4.html.

**Wikipedia: The Free Encyclopedia**

http://en.wikipedia.org/wiki/E._P._Sanders. A summary of Sanders.

http://en.wikipedia.org/wiki/Fornication. The Latin definition of fornication.

Wright, Nicholas T. **New Perspectives on Paul** at http://www.ntwrightpage.com/Wright_New_Perspectives.htm. August 25-28, 2003. Wright's view on the works of the Spirit, as defining those who are in the Kingdom.

**The Paul Page** at http://www.thepaulpage.com/Conversation.html. Oct. 25th, 2004. Dunn's view on Judaism's New Perspective.

**Paul in Different Perspectives** at http://www.ntwrightpage.com/Wright_Auburn_Paul.htm. January 3rd, 2005. Wright's view on the Greek word *gar*.

Yehoshua, Avram. **The Seed of Abraham** at http://SeedofAbraham.net/ and http://the-Seed-of-Abraham.com.

- Articles (partial listing)
  - \* Biblical:
    - *Do as the Pharisees Say?! Mt. 23:2-3*
    - *Kingdom Violence: Mt. 11:12*
    - *Micah 5:2 and Messiah's Deity*
    - *No Longer Under the Law? Two Important Phrases*

- • *Yahshua, Jesus or Yeshua?*
  - • *Yeshua—God the Son*
  - \* Christian:
    - • *Jesus the Fish God?*
    - • *Thanksgiving Day: Pagan?*
  - \* Jewish:
    - • *Kabbalah*
    - • *Kosher: Jewish vs. Biblical*
    - • *The Kipa*
    - • *The Star of David*
  - \* Miscellaneous:
    - • Scripture Reading Schedule
    - • The Ordination Process
    - • The Two Babylons—Complete with Illustrations (PDF)
- • Books & CDs:
  - \* *Hebrew: The Lord's Way!* A basic biblical Hebrew course
  - \* *Shark Bait! The Serpent in Israel* (four CDs on the holiness of Messiah Yeshua from *The Hebraic Perspective*)
  - \* *The Tabernacle of Moses: A Picture of Heaven*
- • Feasts of Israel
- • *Gentile Circumcision?*
- • *Goodbye Messianic Judaism!*
- • Jewish Newsletters (a partial listing)
  - \* *Lion Hands*
  - \* *The Angel of the Lord*
- • *Law 102*
- • Mosaic Sacrifice and Messiah
  - \* *The Mosaic Sacrifices and the Blood of Jesus*
  - \* *Sacrifice in the New Testament*

**Contact Information**

**Avram Yehoshua**

AvramYeh@Gmail.com

http://SeedofAbraham.net

http://the-Seed-of-Abraham.com

Printed in the United States
By Bookmasters